THE BATTLE FOR GEORGE SQUARE

Dr Gordon Barclay FSA, FSA Scot, FRHistS worked as Principal Inspector and Head of Policy at government heritage agency Historic Scotland. He has published extensively on the history and surviving remains of the defence of Scotland, including *'If Hitler comes': Preparing for Invasion: Scotland 1940* and (with Ron Morris) *The Fortification of the Firth of Forth, 1880–1977*. His main research interests lie in the misuse of the past for political ends by British, English and Scottish nationalism.

Dr Louise Heren FSA Scot, FRHistS has a doctorate in Scottish male violence from the University of St Andrews and is published in Scottish violent crime history. Her most recent work *Sex and Violence in 1920s Scotland* examines masculinities, gender, judicial attitudes and juridical responses to violence in the aftermath of the First World War War; all topics that help explore what really happened in Glasgow in 1919.

Dedicated with thanks to
Bailie Malcom Cunning
1957-2022

THE BATTLE FOR GEORGE SQUARE, 1919

Myth, Memory and the Military in Red Clydeside

Gordon J. Barclay and Louise Heren

First published in 2025 by
John Donald, an imprint of
Birlinn Limited
West Newington House
10 Newington Road
Edinburgh
EH9 1QS

www.birlinn.co.uk

ISBN: 978-0-85976-741-5

British Library Cataloguing-in-Publication Data
A catalogue record for this book is available from the British Library

Set in Sabon by Tom Johnstone Editorial Services

Printed and bound by TJ Books, Padstow, Cornwall

MIX
Paper | Supporting responsible forestry
FSC® C013056

Contents

PART IV: INTERLUDE

PART V: AFTERMATH

Illustrations

Maps

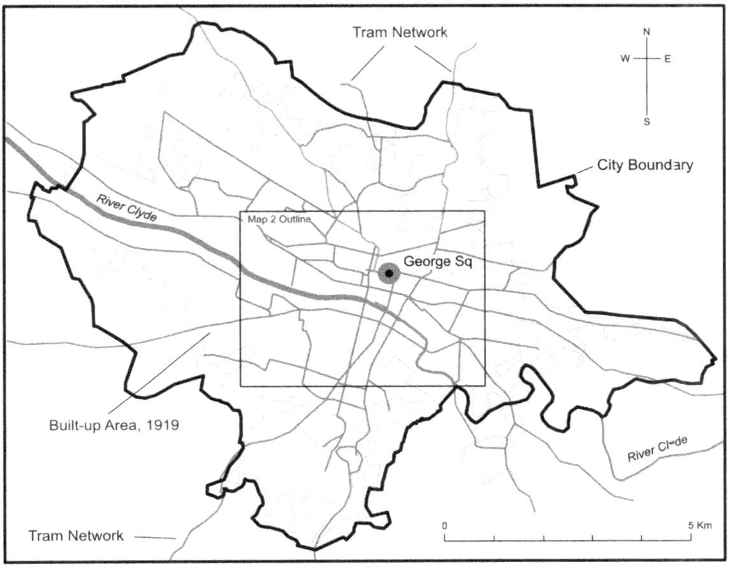

Map 1.

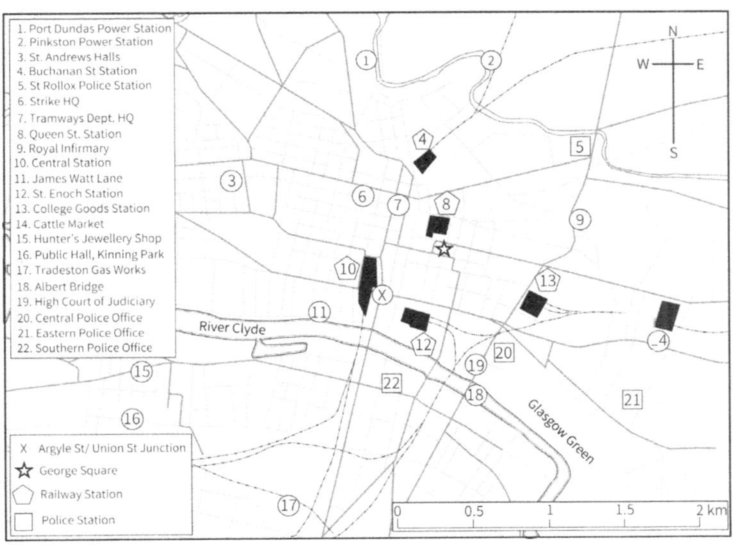

Map 2.

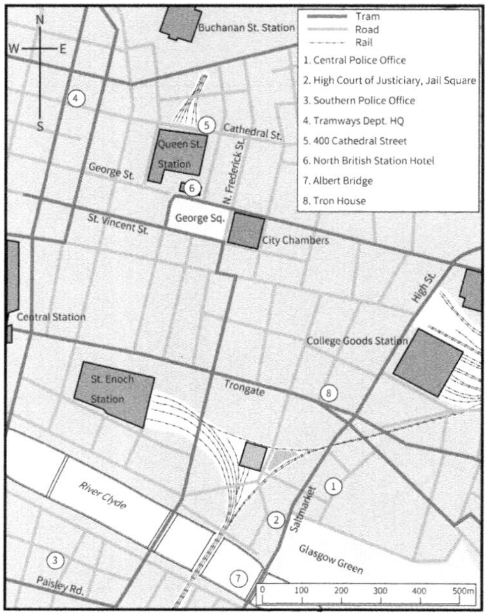
Tram
Road
Rail
1. Central Police Office
2. High Court of Justiciary, Jail Square
3. Southern Police Office
4. Tramways Dept. HQ
5. 400 Cathedral Street
6. North British Station Hotel
7. Albert Bridge
8. Tron House
N
W
E
S
Buchanan St. Station
Cathedral St.
Queen St. Station
George St.
N. Frederick St.
George Sq.
St. Vincent St.
City Chambers
High St.
Central Station
College Goods Station
St. Enoch Station
Trongate
River Clyde
Saltmarket
Glasgow Green
Paisley Rd.
0 100 200 300 400 500m

Map 3.

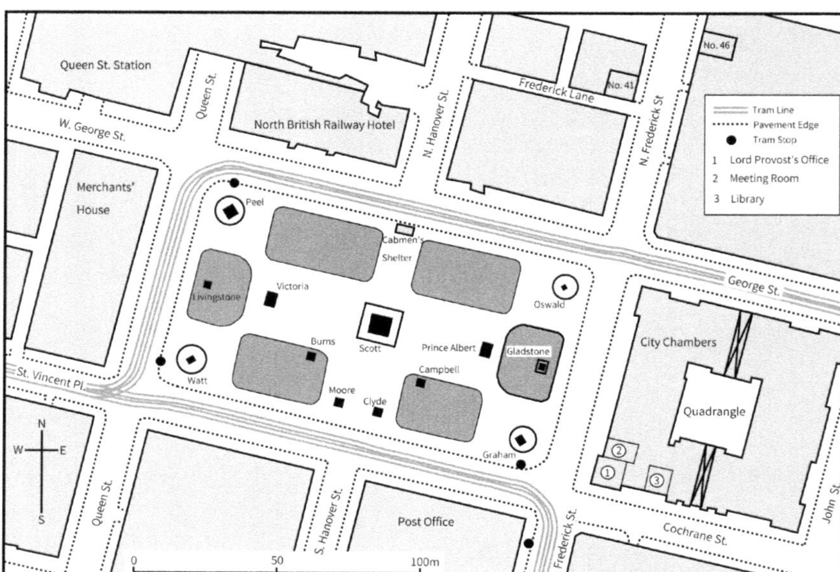
Queen St. Station
Queen St.
North British Railway Hotel
N. Hanover St.
Frederick Lane
No. 46
No. 41
N. Frederick St.
W. George St.
Tram Line
Pavement Edge
Tram Stop
1 Lord Provost's Office
2 Meeting Room
3 Library
Merchants' House
Peel
Cabmen's Shelter
Livingstone
Victoria
Oswald
George St.
Scott
Burns
Prince Albert
Gladstone
City Chambers
Watt
Campbell
Moore
Clyde
Quadrangle
St. Vincent Pl.
Graham
N
W
E
S
Queen St.
S. Hanover St.
Post Office
S. Frederick St.
Cochrane St.
John St.
0 50 100m

Map 4.

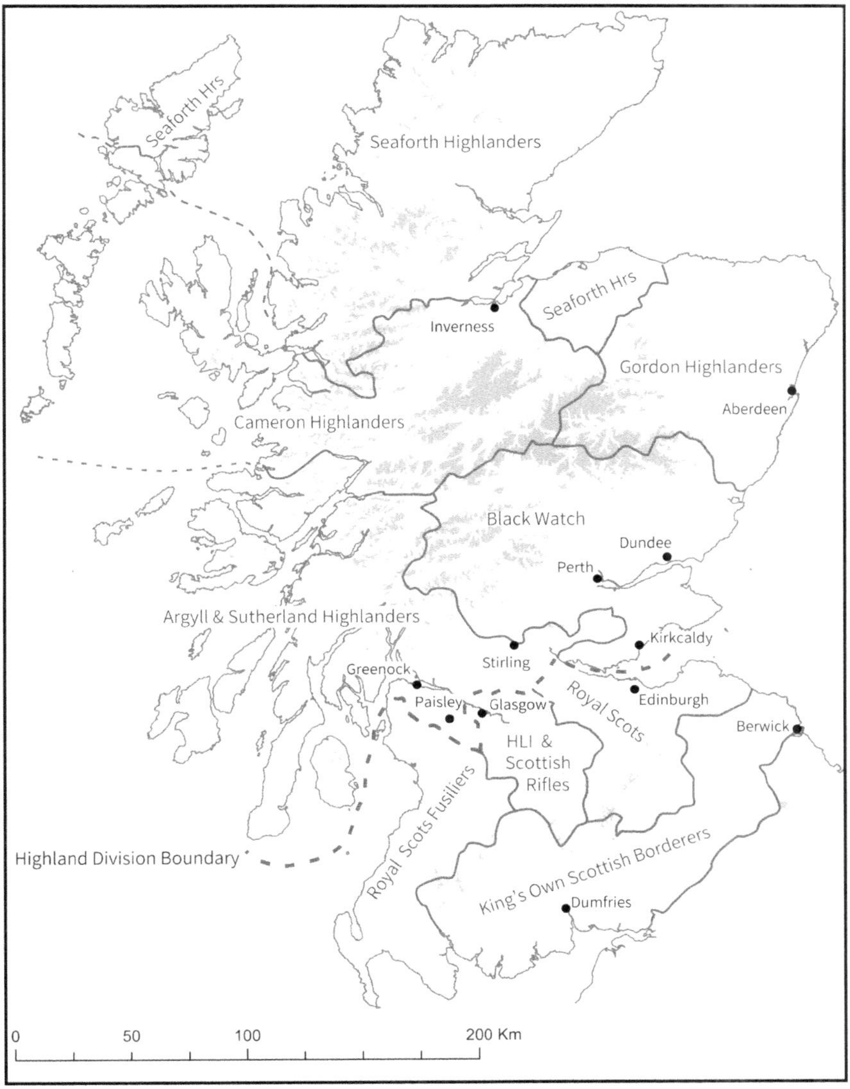

Map 5.
Recruiting areas for the ten Scottish regiments in 1919.

Foreword

The Historians

Lawrence Stone paraphrased E. H. Carr: 'before we read the history, examine the background of the historian'.[1] Published accounts of the Battle of George Square, which took place on 31 January 1919, demonstrate how difficult it has been for single authors to approach the events completely dispassionately. The Battle is an iconic but surprisingly little-studied event in twentieth-century Scottish history, and perhaps the most mythologised.

As collaborators, we come from different backgrounds and inevitably bring different perspectives, but we believe our combined approach enables either of us to examine critically the other's preconceptions and prejudices. Gordon is a lowland Scot from Aberdeen and had never heard of the Battle until 2017. He came to it through a research interest in the use of mythologised history in contemporary politics. He has applied methods from earlier projects in the marshalling of large amounts of evidence to create a soundly-based, coherent narrative. Unlike many writers about these events, he has no particular research interest in, or commitment to, labour history. The son of a policeman, he was himself a public servant and union member for over 30 years, and finds distasteful the glorification of the extreme violence, especially against the police, so common in accounts of the Battle. He is a member of the successor party (Liberal/Liberal Democrat) to which many of the 'establishment' protagonists belonged.

Louise is a social historian whose work is always grounded in primary research and dataset analysis. She analyses first, exploring trends in the data before attempting to explain their meaning. Her approach is not: What do I think, now where do I find archive sources to support my ideas? She is the daughter of a marine fitter and grand-daughter of a ship's boilermaker, both of whom worked in the Port of London and who experienced long periods of unemployment at the hands of the shipyard management. Louise has never carried a political party's card, but she considers herself to be a small 's' socialist.

We literally bumped into each other on 16 November 2018 in the National Records of Scotland locker room. Initial apologies led to enquiries about what each was working on; he was copying parts of the transcript of the trial of the leaders of the Forty Hours Strike, for allegedly fomenting the riot, the 'Battle of George Square', on 31 January 1919. She remarked that she had for some years been trying to promote the idea of a television documentary on the events of that day. Within five minutes we had agreed in principle to write this book. By Christmas, we had made an informal approach to a publisher. Our first book has since been published – *Tanks on the Streets? The Battle of George Square, Glasgow 1919* – an avowedly popular rather than scholarly work, aimed at informing a general audience, providing a wider background to events but consistently grounded in the archival evidence to prove our points.[2] This volume complements it, as a definitive presentation of our evidence and of our discussion of the problematic historiography of the Battle.

Our shared approach explicitly tries to avoid the problems caused by framing the story of the Battle of George Square solely as an iconic symbol of working-class struggle, centring on the strike leaders and the idea of 'Red Clydeside' as established in those leaders' unreliable memoirs. Instead, we analyse events in Glasgow in 1919 as they unfolded, as a particular event growing out of local circumstances, although viewed through a prism of wider domestic and international events. We have avoided allowing later events and people's later careers to cast a retrospective shadow. For example, one anonymous referee chided us for not introducing Emanuel Shinwell earlier since he was 'perhaps the most important figure in the narrative'. Shinwell's importance in the context of the Battle is perhaps as the least reliable of narrators. An approach so centred upon the point of view of the strike leadership and their followers has shown itself to be unproductive of good history, so far as the Battle is concerned.

---

1. L. Stone, 'History and Post-Modernism', *Past and Present*, no.135 (1992), p.189.
2. L. Heren and G. J. Barclay, *Tanks on the Streets? The Battle of George Square, Glasgow 1919* (Pen and Sword, 2023).

Part I
INTRODUCTION

1 A Warning to the Curious

The events of George Square were incredibly symbolic, and an important landmark in working class history.

(Neil Davidson, quoted in the *Daily Record*, 29 January 2014.)

This is not a history of Glasgow in the twentieth century. Nor is it a history of Red Clydeside, nor an account of labour relations in west Scotland; not even a history of the Forty Hours Strike. This book provides sufficient context in the labour and political history of Britain after the First World War, but the reader looking for the continuation of the debate between Iain McLean and John Foster and their adherents as to the nature of the 'Legend of Red Clydeside' will be disappointed. To date, that debate has failed to explore in detail the key archival sources in order to present an evidence-based account of what happened on Friday 31 January 1919, in the days before and after, and at the subsequent trial in April; instead, that debate has curated a mythology that began to develop at lunchtime on that very day.

On 31 January 1919 there was a riot in George Square, Glasgow, now most often recalled as 'the Battle of George Square'. It occurred on the fifth day of the Forty Hours Strike (27 January to 12 February 1919), which was held with the aim of reducing the number of weekly hours worked without any reduction in pay, in order to absorb the vast numbers of working men returning from the Great War.[1]

The Forty Hours Strike had limited support beyond greater Glasgow, and the city is the scene for most of the action (Maps 1, 2 and 3). The great civic space, George Square, at the heart of the city, is the focus for the most memorable events (Fig. 1.1). The monumental City Chambers, also referred to as the Municipal Buildings both at the time and in this text, dominate the whole of the eastern end of the Square (Map 4, Fig 1.2). Immediately in front of the Chambers, the

1.1. *Postcard showing George Square, looking from the south-east corner towards the Merchants' House. First decades of the twentieth century (out of copyright).*

plinth of the statue of William Gladstone (moved in 1924 to accommodate the Glasgow War Memorial) was used as a speaking platform by some of the main movers of events, who were overlooked from the balconies of the City Chambers by other significant actors.

Around noon on Friday 31 January, some 20-25,000 strikers arrived in George Square by prior arrangement in a series of processions from different parts of Glasgow, along with an unknown number of onlookers, to hear the outcome of an approach made by the strike leaders via the Lord Provost to the government, seeking intervention in the strike. They were faced initially by around 100 policemen, growing to about 180-200 as policemen accompanying the processions joined their colleagues, and reserves were brought forward from the open quadrangle of the City Chambers (Map 4). The approach to government had emerged from a meeting on Wednesday 29 January between six strikers (a possibly imagined 'seventh man' may have been invented to take the blame for some of the more inflammatory contributions), three prominent figures in the strike leadership, the Lord Provost and the Town Clerk. Whatever was said, and this is dealt with in Chapter 7 below, the Provost

1.2. *Postcard showing George Square, looking from the west side towards the City Chambers, showing the south-east corner (right). First decades of the twentieth century (out of copyright).*

and Town Clerk left the meeting believing they had heard credible threats of violence, particularly against the tram system and the non-striking tram workers. The strikers' anger with the tram staff had been expressed throughout the week by a growing level of barracking of working drivers and conductors, low-level violence and the obstruction of trams by the strikers' marches. Attempts to block the tram traffic in the south-east corner of George Square on Friday 31 January led to police intervention, a number of baton charges, and violence in the Square directed towards the police and the trams, which spread across the city centre. The Riot Act was read and, fearing the under-strength Glasgow Police might be overwhelmed, the Sheriff called for military aid. Mainly Scottish troops began to arrive late on Friday evening, after most of the trouble had died down. Key members of the strike leadership were tried in April 1919 for incitement to riot and for mobbing and rioting.

When we have spoken publicly about our research, the description of the Battle of George Square as the most mythologised event in twentieth-century Scottish history has not been challenged. Almost everything widely believed about 'Bloody Friday' – its cause and its aftermath – is untrue. In the case of the Battle, history was not 'written by the victors' and the narrative established at the time by the authors of the *Strike Bulletin*, at the trial of the key protagonists and subsequently in the strike leaders' memoirs has become the dominant one. John Foster has suggested the Crown's case against the strike leaders has largely 'entered the history books'; but in reality, it is, if mentioned at all, dismissed.[2]

The mythology is widespread in popular and academic history, school textbooks, and in political discourse, from Parliament to social media. The myths can be summarised in one sentence:

> The police, acting on instructions, attacked a peaceful demonstration of 100,000 people in George Square and Churchill sent the tanks, a howitzer and 12,000 young, inexperienced English troops against them to occupy the city, while Scottish troops were locked up in case they joined the strikers. The crowd routed the police.

Every version of the accepted narrative includes one or more elements of this mythology, but none are supported by the contemporary evidence, or are even directly contradicted by it. Challenging the cherished myths and common beliefs and assumptions – typified by the quotation at the head of this chapter – meets with incomprehension, scorn or even hostility.[3] As a consequence, our account of what happened is detailed, as we wish to provide firm foundations in the archival evidence for the narrative we present.

This book sets out to describe what happened over a century ago, and to analyse how the actual events, as evidenced in contemporary sources, have been replaced by an almost wholly mythologised 'usable history', in some ways as a reflection of the way people remember, through accidental or deliberate falsification, and through problematic engagement with the story by popular and, more worryingly, by academic history.

Surprisingly, no-one has looked in any detail at these aspects of the Battle of George Square during the past 100 years. The Battle is seen as an iconic moment in the political history of Red Clydeside and Glasgow, but it has never itself been the sole focus of a historical study.

Academic historians have discussed it as a coda, crisis or interruption in the wider historical and political narrative of Red Clydeside; as a catalyst for subsequent developments; or, perhaps most often, as a symbol for something important to an individual author – notably, as reflecting the oppressive intent of the government. Sometimes the events of the days on either side of the Battle are dealt with in a few sentences or paragraphs, at most a few pages, before the author hurries on to other parts of the story.

We also look at how the largest single provision of 'military aid to the civil power' on the British mainland has been dealt with in writings on the use of the military in the maintenance of order. The deployment has generally been treated as a dramatic interruption to the history of labour relations, requiring no more than a mention.[4] The troops simply 'arrive', 'sent by government', to deal with 'a Bolshevist rising', or to 'crush the strike', as an agent of oppression. Even historians specialising in the role of the army in supporting the civil power have shown little interest in exploring the detail of the post-Battle deployment, a key example of its use.[5] This is explored in Chapter 17.

The history of labour relations in the west of Scotland and the creation of the 'legend' of Red Clydeside, Iain McLean's challenge to it, and the defence mounted by Tony Dickson, John Foster and others, is documented in a rich academic literature. The 'legend' has also formed a significant part of a popular historical literature of varied accuracy, in which the 'legend' in its most heroic and romantic forms has continued to flourish, relatively undisturbed by reality. In both academic and popular literature, however, the subsidiary 'legend' of the Battle of George Square has been transmitted almost wholly unchanged from the narrative published during the strike, in the run-up to and at the trial, and in the writings of Emanuel Shinwell, William Gallacher and others.

When Iain McLean's *The Legend of Red Clydeside* (1983) was reprinted in 1999, he added a long introductory chapter, part of which responded to the criticisms of the first edition. McLean summarised the 'legend' as established by 1969 as 'a heroic struggle against both capital and government'.[6] He suggested 'this picture was set out in the many memoirs of participants', mentioning William Gallacher's *Revolt on the Clyde* (1936) whom he considered 'an untrustworthy witness', and David Kirkwood's *My Life of Revolt* (1935). In considering the criticisms levelled against his work, McLean agreed, *inter alia*, that he had underestimated 'the repressive intentions of government', apparently referring to the government's ways of dealing with wartime unrest and disruption on the Clyde.[7]

McLean's 'most formidable' critic, John Foster, has also based his consideration of the Forty Hours Strike on the premise that the government was actively oppressive, and that the deployment of the military in 1919, supposedly by the UK government, was the main symbol of this.[8] Foster notes but does not altogether agree with McLean's view that too much credence has been given to the 'self-serving accounts of wartime shop stewards', and suggests that by the late 1970s 'Clydeside's revolutionary potential had become sufficiently recognised to be integrated into a larger rewriting of British history'.[9] But the main arguments between McLean and Foster are not directly about the Forty Hours Strike, except insofar as its aims and impacts were deliberately or incidentally 'political'.

Foster has generally written on the premise that the military deployment from 31 January to 17 February was not only instigated by government but represented a deliberate attempt at repression, thus taking issue with the revisionists' view of it as 'simply [a] laughable and ill-informed over-reaction'.[10] No-one in this debate appears to have taken on board the fact that the army was called for by the Sheriff to assist the city police, not 'sent by government'.[11] Foster has introduced the role of the powerful Engineers' and Shipbuilders' Association. The Chief Constable had told the Association that his under-strength force might need military aid for policing the strike. The Association, however, on 30 January, 'did not view with favour – at least up till now – the bringing in of the Military'. Foster suggests that circumstances then 'induced the employers to revise their tactics and call for military intervention'.[12] But at neither of the employers' meetings on 31 January or 4 February 1919 was any military intervention requested. Their discussion on 31 January was limited to suggesting that a 'Civic Guard' of loyal employees be formed. On 4 February they discussed billeting.[13]

Many writers have touched on the Battle, and few have resisted the temptation to (over)dramatise their narrative. Some have relished their role as creators of usable pasts for Glasgow's working class, have ignored or downplayed evidence, or have even changed it or in a few cases invented it, to suit their narrative.[14] Richard Evans describes the particular problem of the rise of explicitly committed forms of history written from the point of view of the industrial working class, to recover workers' history as a means of strengthening their class-consciousness and political commitment – a story of resistance to oppression and the forward march of the organised working class. He believes 'politically committed history only damages itself if it distorts, manipulates or obscures historical fact in the interests of the cause it claims to represent'.[15] This is, unfortunately, evident in much writing about events in Glasgow in January and February 1919. Which, it is argued below, deserve a dispassionate, critical analysis of *all* the available evidence, and paying attention to *all* the available voices.

The structure of the book is intended, first, to provide the reader with a basic foundation in the circumstances of 1919. Part I provides some introduction to the aims of the book, and although it has been suggested that this section should focus on individuals (Shinwell, Gallacher *et al*) whose later careers in British politics cast a retrospective shadow on events, there are other ways to frame the narrative, for example by taking more notice of three institutions than is usual: the War Cabinet, the Glasgow Police and the Tramways Department, which we explore in Chapter 2. Chapter 3 considers the sources available and explores the problems of memory and of reminiscences recorded decades after the event.

The second part of the book sets the scene and takes us to the evening of Thursday 30 January. Chapter 4 provides a brief summary of the situation in Glasgow in its wider context in 1919, compares the Forty Hours Strike in Glasgow with the contemporaneous 44-Hours Strike in Belfast and closes with a summary of events in the week before the strike. In Chapters 5 to 9 the evidence for events in the days leading up to the Battle is set out, highlighting events in George Square and the City Chambers on Monday 27 and Wednesday 29 January, and on the strikers' growing frustration with the non-striking tram staff. Particular attention is paid to the meeting between the Lord Provost and the strikers on Wednesday, as what happened there – what was said or understood to have been said – led directly to the violence on Friday 31 January, and was subsequently used to try to deflect blame for events. The rioting over Thursday night and Friday morning in Lanarkshire is briefly described. The deliberations of the War Cabinet on Thursday 30 January are also considered.

The third part of the text describes in detail the events of 'Bloody Friday'.[16] Chapters 10 to 15 cover in detail the events in and around the Square: the arrival of the processions; the origins of the violence; the intervention of the police and the first baton charge; the supposed threat to the City Chambers and the second and third charges; the spread of the violence north into Cathedral Street and south to Glasgow Green and over the Clyde. Chapter 15 also deals with the War Cabinet's deliberations on Friday afternoon. Chapter 16 considers the Sheriff's decision to call for military aid, how he reached his decision, and how the decision was then and has since been interpreted.

At this point the fourth part of the text leaves the Square to consider, in Chapter 17, the way in which this example of 'military aid to the civil power' in the United Kingdom has been dealt with in academic studies.[17] This is followed in Chapter 18 by an exploration of the rich mythology that has arisen, expanded and been curated in the last century, which leads on, in Chapter 19, to a consideration of the historiography of the Battle, exploring what has often been a problematic engagement with primary evidence.

The fifth and final part of the text returns, in Chapter 20, to the aftermath of the riot, including the arrest of some of the strike leadership, before dealing with the preparations for the trial in April. Chapters 21 and 22 deal respectively with the trial and the charge to the jury by the judge, summarising the proceedings, and finally the verdicts. Chapter 23 concludes the text.

---

1. I. McLean, *The Legend of Red Clydeside* (John Donald, 1999), chapters 10 and 11.
2. J. Foster, 'Strike Action and Working-Class Politics on Clydeside 1914–1919', *International Review of Social History*, 35 (1990), p.30; K. MacAskill, *Glasgow 1919: The Rise of Red Clydeside* (Biteback, 2019), p.205.
3. For example, S. Damer, 'In the Rapids of Revolution?', *Scottish Affairs*, 28 (2019), pp.339-48.

4. For example, M. Pittock, *Scottish Nationality* (Red Globe Press, 2001), p.103; T. Devine, *The Scottish Nation: A Modern History* (Penguin, 2012), pp.314-5.
5. For example, K. Jeffery and P. Hennessy, *States of Emergency: British Governments and Strikebreaking since 1919* (Routledge and Kegan Paul, 1983), p.10; B. Weinberger, *Keeping the Peace: Policing Strikes in Britain, 1906-1926* (Berg, 1991), pp.152-62.
6. McLean, *Legend*, p.xiv.
7. McLean, *Legend*, p.xx.
8. J. Foster, 'The 1919 Forty Hours Strike', *Theory and Struggle*, 120 (2019), 30-40.
9. Foster, *Strike Action*, p.35; Foster, 'Red Clyde, Red Scotland', in *The Manufacture of Scottish History*, eds. I. L. Donnachie and C A. Whatley (Polygon, 1992), p.121.
10. Foster, *Strike Action*, p.56.
11. Some have, however, presented any local authority involvement as a mere cloak for government action, although without providing supporting evidence.
12. Foster, *Strike Action*, pp.54, 56.
13. TD241, 'Clyde Shipbuilders' Association, Minute Book', 1918-19, minutes of 30 and 31 January, 4 February, Glasgow Archives.
14. To be discussed in Chapters 18 and 19.
15. R. Evans, *In Defence of History* (Granta, 1997), p.252.
16. 31 January 1919 has at various times been termed 'the Battle of George Square', 'Black Friday' and 'Bloody Friday'. 'Black Friday' is now an online shopping opportunity. 'Bloody Friday' is now more often used, with more justification perhaps, to describe the brutal murder of nine people and the serious injury of 130 by the detonation of 20 bombs by the Provisional IRA on 21 July 1972.
17. In 1919 the 'United Kingdom of Great Britain and Ireland' (1801-1922).

2 To Begin

The events in Glasgow and Clydeside of January to April 1919 are usually framed through the personalities, memoirs, later careers and supposed intentions of the strike leaders, within the context of the Clyde Workers' Committee (CWC) and a wider 'Red Clydeside'.[1] Rather than focus on the generally better-known personalities in the strike leadership, Emanuel Shinwell, David Kirkwood, William Gallacher, Neil Maclean MP, and others are introduced briefly as they appear.[2] The role of three other key institutions is often underplayed in accounts of the Battle: the War Cabinet, Glasgow Police and the Glasgow tram system.

The War Cabinet

The War Cabinet's role has, in many accounts, been reduced to its alleged role in 'sending the tanks to Glasgow' in a panic, or the actions of Winston Churchill, who attended the War Cabinet but was not in fact a member. The War Cabinet and its papers, however, play an important part in this story. Its minutes are available on the website of the National Archives.[3] In the period under review, the minutes of some sensitive discussions were typed up and distributed individually, rather than being sent to the unionised printers as was normal practice. No relevant 'secret minutes' for January 1919 have been found.[4]

The War Cabinet was a small executive group of five members, most of whom had no departmental responsibility, formed in December 1916 to streamline decision-making, replacing the full Cabinet of 23 members. The Prime Minister, David Lloyd George, Andrew Bonar Law and Earl Curzon served until the War Cabinet was discontinued in December 1919.[5] In January 1919, the additional members were Austen Chamberlain (served 18 April 1918 to 31 October 1919) and Sir Eric Geddes (10 January to 31 October 1919).[6] War Cabinet meetings were attended by relevant members of the full Cabinet, senior military figures and civil servants, who were present to contribute on specific agenda items. Thus Winston Churchill, Secretary of State for War and Air, although not a member of the War Cabinet, was present on 28, 30 and 31 January, as the War Cabinet was considering his proposals for a fairer demobilisation system. The War Cabinet, in the days before the strike, was dealing with a wide range of topics apart from Churchill's proposals: the increased supply of beer; the pay of the armed forces; the threatened police strike; sugar beet cultivation; as well as the agitation for a shorter working week.

The Glasgow Police

The role of the Glasgow police has, in many accounts, been reduced to a cartoonish violent incompetence, the policemen supposedly overawed by the 'heroic crowd' in George Square, after 'running amok' and making a 'savage and unprovoked attack' at the behest of its establishment masters. Since 1857, the City of Glasgow Police Regulations had identified the object of policing as: 'the prevention of crime, the protection of life and property, and the security, peace and comfort of all citizens'.[7] The papers relating to the riot trial in April 1919 contain a list of all the police on duty during the week commencing 27 January 1919.[8] It includes the names of 160 men on duty in George Square on Friday 31 January 1919, more than the 140 often quoted, but does not include the names of individual policemen drawn into the violence in Cathedral Street, Trongate or south of the Clyde, who came from other divisions, which would bring the total to between 200 and 220 men.

To understand the decision to call for military aid on 31 January 1919, it is important to understand the particular circumstances obtaining in this city of a million inhabitants just after the end of the war (Map 1). On 31 December 1918, the formal establishment of the Glasgow Police was 1,996 men and one woman.[9] The main burden of day-to-day policing on the streets was borne by a nominal 1,638 uniformed constables, 123 sergeants and 72 inspectors – 1,833 men in total. There were 99 men and one woman in the detective staff and fifteen clerical staff. In December 1918 the force was 705 below establishment, with many men still in military service, leaving a total of 1,291 men and one woman in the force.[10] The Chief Constable made reference to his force being 600 under strength.[11] And at the War Cabinet on 30 January, it was mentioned that approximately 500 of the force were still in the armed forces.[12] Some 748 Glasgow police joined the armed forces during the war (145 being killed or missing).[13] The disbanding of wartime temporary constables, the semi-mothballing of the Special Constabulary, and a shortage of experienced men meant the Glasgow force frequently had to cancel rest days and to impose compulsory overtime.[14] The police worked an eight-hour shift, meaning only about a third of the force was available at any time. In December 1918 there were only 1,138 uniformed men available on the streets, 380 men for each of the three shifts. In time of need the men could move onto a twelve-hour shift pattern and this was implemented on the morning of 31 January.[15] Thus, the Glasgow police force that day might have been able to field only about 569 uniformed constables, sergeants and inspectors. The pressure on the force was so great that on one occasion during the rioting on 31 January, a 50-year-old uniformed superintendent – a divisional commander, third in the hierarchy of the force – was with his men in the front line wielding a baton.[16]

The hyper-masculinity present in Glasgow society was also reflected in 'a hyper-masculinity that emphasised toughness' in the police.[17] However, Jackson *et al*'s study of policing in Scotland in the twentieth century relies to a great extent on interviews with living retired officers, who recalled the force and its ethos in and after the period of 'Sillitoe's Cossacks' from 1931, when the force was tackling high levels of street-gang violence. They described a 'specifically "Glasgow" identity and style of policing' and a police group identity which was 'robust', 'tough' and 'no-nonsense'. It is unclear to what extent the later attitudes already formed part of the force's character, but constables of the 1930s had learned their profession from an earlier generation. It is therefore not so hard to imagine the description of 'being firm and holding your own' with 'physical restraint or force' never far from the surface, was also relevant in 1919.[18] The average height of the Glasgow policeman in 1920 was approximately 180cm, significantly taller than the average Glaswegian male factory-worker (162cm) or labourer (157cm). The average age of policemen was 34 years.[19]

Jackson *et al* note that men were still drilled and marched out from the muster hall to their beats as late as 1960. Reading accounts of police reinforcements being sent to George Square and its environs on 31 January before and during the riot, one should envisage a body of men led by their officers and sergeants moving at a quick march in single file towards the trouble. In the 1930s in Aberdeen, Gordon's father recalled being one of a dozen constables quick-marched towards two riots (one between fascists and communists, the other outside a brothel) in this way from police headquarters under the command of an inspector.

Jackson reports that 'some officers sometimes lied in court in the 1960s to provide corroboration' for events they had not seen, to get a 'genuine conviction'; and further, lawyers and magistrates knew this happened.[20] Analysis of the evidence provided to the trial in 1919 reveals this was nothing new. What has seemingly hitherto not been much explored is that the evidence presented by the defence was just as problematic.

A particular event may have influenced the mood of the Glasgow Police in the first week of the Forty Hours Strike. On Thursday 23 January, four days before the strike began, the funeral of PC James Campbell took place. Campbell had been shot on 20 January by burglars he had disturbed. Over 150 policemen attended his funeral, including the Chief Constable, two Assistant Chief Constables (including Alexander Mennie* who had himself survived being shot on duty in 1888), and the Superintendents of Eastern, Central and St Rollox Districts. Sixty men from Campbell's Eastern division under the command of Superintendent Samuel and accompanied by the Police Pipe Band marched from the police office to Campbell's home in Dennistoun and thence to Alexandra Park, whence the small funeral party proceeded by car to Bannockburn for the burial.[21] Such significant attendance at Campbell's funeral demonstrates

* Assistant Chief Constable Alexander Ferguson Mennie (1863-1927). Born East Lothian. Son of a police constable from Aberdeenshire. Joined Glasgow police 1882. By 1886 Mennie was a police detective. Shot and seriously wounded in 1888; he carried the bullet for luck for the rest of his career. Promoted superintendent 1900. In 1913 awarded King's Police Medal for Distinguished Service. Assistant Chief Constable in charge of the detective department in 1916. Retired 1922 after a period of ill-health.

the cohesion within Glasgow's police force on the eve of the strike.

The Corporation Trams

The Glasgow tram system, its management and its crews, played a pivotal role in the events of 1919, because the tram staff did not join the strike. James Dalrymple was the general manager of the city's Tramways Department for over two decades.[22] He was the second man in the post, serving from 1904 to 1926. He was a man described as intolerant of 'slackness or disobedience' and 'aloof'.[23]

After taking over the tram system in 1894, the Glasgow Corporation expanded it by new building and by taking over the systems of burghs well beyond the city's boundaries, eventually operating over 800 tramcars on 320km of track (Map 1).[24] The Corporation built its own power station at Pinkston, separate from the city's electricity department. By 1914, the tram network was carrying over 900,000 passengers a day.[25] It was a model of a large municipal tram system 'the finest and greatest of its kind' which managers of other systems came to observe. And it was hugely profitable.[26] Its six-storey headquarters building lay at the junction of Bath Street and Renfield Street, a short distance west of George Square (Map 3, no. 4).

The importance of the tram system to the city's functioning explains why the strike leaders wanted so much to 'get the cars off the streets' during the week of 27 January 1919. The city, in the days when few people had their own private transport, relied on the tram system for journeys to work, to visit friends and relatives, to seek entertainment. Stopping the trams would stop the city.[27] The service ran 20 hours a day, a 'two- to three-minute service . . . even on outlying routes'.[28] Consequently, certain places in the city could become very congested: the junction of Jamaica Street and Renfrew Street was allegedly the busiest in the world, with 466 cars an hour on weekdays and 516 on Saturdays.[29]

Municipal tram systems provided many recruits for the armed services, with a national recruitment rate of around 50 per cent of male tram staff compared to a recruitment rate of 25 per cent in engineering.[30] Dalrymple opened a recruiting office in the tram headquarters and encouraged his men to enlist. Nearly 1,000 men came forward on one day in September 1914. Of a uniformed tram staff of

3,249 in 1914, 1,902 enlisted. To backfill the gap created by these enlisted men, Glasgow was the first tram system in the United Kingdom to employ women as conductors and later as drivers ('motresses'), on the same rates of pay as the men (27 shillings for a 51-hour week). A female workforce of over 800 conductors included single women, married women whose husbands were in the forces, and widows.[31] By May 1916, 68 women were driving or training to drive.[32] In April 1919 the women drivers were stood down, either becoming conductors or facing dismissal. Female drivers were re-engaged in the Second World War, let go at its end, and engaged again in 1950 in the face of labour shortages. In July 1919 the Bridgeton Branch of the

2.1. *Glasgow women tram driver and conductress around the end of the First World War. The photograph shows how unprotected the driver was from anyone in the street (Trustees of the Imperial War Museum Q 28389; LIC-02166-Y5J9K4).*

Federation of Discharged Soldiers protested against *any* women being retained and demanded their dismissal.[33]

Excepting the earliest-built cars, the driver stood on a platform behind a glass windscreen. Cars could be driven in either direction and, in the double-decker cars, there were access stairs at both ends with whatever was currently serving as the rear of the tram open for passengers. The driver stood by the forward stairs, with a closed door to separate them from the passengers. They were not, however, protected from the street. Many of the standard cars had an open balcony at both ends of the upper floor, until the last of them were enclosed between the wars. One such balcony played a part in the events of Wednesday 29 January.

These three key institutions play a vital part in what would happen in the week commencing 27 January 1919. Their low profile in so many accounts, in which only the strike leaders seem to have a voice, has helped to mask the complexity of the train of events that led to the violence on Friday 31 January 1919.

---

1. See K. MacAskill, *Glasgow 1919: The Rise of Red Clydeside* (Biteback, 2019), Appendix C, for an example.
2. Brief pen-portraits are provided as footnotes for a range of men and women who played their part in events, normally, but not always, on their first appearance in the narrative. The names of key protagonists have been spelled in a variety of ways in contemporary and later documents. The variants preferred by the people themselves and their families have been used, and the spelling of names, even in quotations, has been silently corrected to avoid confusion. Except where there might be misunderstanding, individuals are usually referred to by surname after their first appearance. Protagonists' jobs or other titles are occasionally included and the ranks of policemen are noted. The pen portraits are drawn from the *Dictionary of National Biography*, W. W. Knox (ed), *Scottish Labour Leaders 1918-1939: A Biographical Dictionary* (Mainstream, 1984) and a range of online resources.
3. https://www.nationalarchives.gov.uk/education/resources/cabinet-papers-1915-1984/
4. There is an apparently complete set in Bonar Law's papers in the Parliamentary Archives, which were consulted by us.
5. J. P. Mackintosh, *The British Cabinet* (Stevens, 1977), p.371.

6. https://www.nationalarchives.gov.uk/cabinetpapers/cabinet-gov/david-lloyd-george-1916.htm
7. L. A. Jackson *et al*, *Police and Community in Twentieth-Century Scotland* (Edinburgh University Press, 2020), p.71.
8. AD15/19/11, 'Precognitions against Joseph Brennan, Harry Hopkins, David Kirkwood, William Gallacher, Robert Loudon, Daniel Stewert Oliver, George Ebury, Neil Alexander, James Murray, Emanuel Shinwell, David McKenzie, William McCartney for the Crime of Mobbing and Rioting at George Square, Glasgow and Other Locations' (1919); Document 47, List of defence witnesses – Police. (See p.27, note 24 below.)
9. Glasgow Police Department, *Report of the Chief Constable of the City of Glasgow* (1918); A. L. Goldsmith, *The Development of the City of Glasgow Police c. 1800-1939,* unpublished PhD thesis (University of Strathclyde, 2002), p.88.
10. Glasgow Police Department 1918, Table 14.
11. TD241, 'Clyde Shipbuilders' Association, Minute Book', 1918-19, minutes of 30 and 31 January, Glasgow Archives.
12. CAB23/9/9, War Cabinet Minutes, meeting 522, 30 January 1919.
13. Goldsmith, *Glasgow Police*, p.88.
14. Goldsmith, *Glasgow Police*, pp.86-87.
15. Alastair Dinsmor, personal communication, October 2020; AD15/19/11 [A05], J. V. Stevenson, Chief Constable.
16. AD15/19/11 [A82], W. McGowan, Police Lieutenant.
17. L. Heren, *Sex and Violence in 1920s Scotland: Incest, Rape, Lewd and Libidinous Practices, 1918-1930* (Bloomsbury, 2024).
18. Jackson *et al*, *Police and Community*, pp.55, 60, 64.
19. Goldsmith, *Glasgow Police*, p.407; Jackson *et al*, *Police and Community*, p.57; J. M. Winter, 'Military Fitness and Civilian Health in Britain During the First World War', *Journal of Contemporary History,* 15 (1980), p.237.
20. Jackson *et al*, *Police and Community*, p.86.
21. *Glasgow Herald,* 24 January 1919.
22. D. L. Thomson, *A Handbook of Glasgow Tramways* (Scottish Tramway Museum Society, 1962), p.7.
23. R. Brash, *Glasgow in the Tramway Age* (Longman, 1971), p.50.
24. In Glasgow at the time the tramcars were often simply called 'cars'; we have followed this usage, although we also refer to 'trams' or 'tramcars', where the system as a whole is implied, or to avoid confusion. We refer to 'motor cars/motor vehicles' when such things are mentioned.

25. B. Aspinwall, 'Glasgow Trams and American Politics 1894-1914', *Scottish Historical Review,* 56 (1977), p.65.

26. D. Thomson, *Glasgow Tram Services* (Venture Publications, 2009), p.5.

27. Thomson, *Glasgow Tram Services*, p.5.

28. Aspinwall, 'Glasgow Trams', p.65.

29. Aspinwall, 'Glasgow Trams', p.65.

30. P. E. Dewey, 'Military Recruiting and the British Labour Force During the First World War', *The Historical Journal,* 27 (1984), Table 6.

31. Brash, *Glasgow Tramway Age*, p.59. J. Dalrymple, 'Tramway labour Problems Affected by the War', *Tramway and Railway World,* 14 October 1915, pp.281-2.

32. *Tramway and Railway World*, 11 May 1916. p.356.

33. *Glasgow Herald*, 15 April 1919. C. A. Oakley, *The Last Tram* (Glasgow Corporation, 1962), pp.68, 98, 100, 104-5. Glasgow Corporation Minutes, 2 July 1919.

3 Memory and Sources

Investigators must treat any information gathered from people who have talked to others as not being separate, independent reports.[1]

This chapter introduces another aspect often overlooked in telling and re-telling the story of the Battle: the nature of remembering, the frailty and vulnerability of memory to subsequent manipulation and distortion especially if recorded long after. These factors have a significant impact on the way the events of 31 January 1919 were reported at the trial in April 1919, and have been 'remembered' since, particularly as some authors rely on reminiscences recorded decades later.[2]

A key element in considering the reliability of witnesses is the way in which people 'remember' and retell their memories. If anything has been learned about memory after a century of psychological research, it is that it is fragile and error prone, not an objective record of the past but a reconstructive process replete with distortions and, at times, gross inaccuracies.[3] Eyewitness memory is malleable and vulnerable to external influences, including the effects of post-event information or misinformation.[4]

There are many ways in which a witness to an event can end up having a clear, vivid memory of something they did not see, something different from what they saw, something someone else saw, or something someone else wanted them to remember. This can arise from the individual, from group interactions, and from the processes of gathering evidence. Eyewitnesses are often asked to remember things they saw in extremely stressful circumstances, sometimes long afterwards. People who experience the same event talk to one another, overhear each other talk, or gain access to new information from the print media, interviewers, speeches or statements about the events, film or, nowadays, television or online sources.[5] Witnesses may be asked leading questions or face conflicting pressures to be both accurate and helpful to the interviewer. They may be presented with a version of an event by a 'dominant narrator' or be offered suggestions about what they saw. They may face social pressures to make their narrative conform to that of a group or feel they need to impress an interviewer with their knowledge.[6]

Through the contamination of memory, witnesses can develop vividly detailed, emotionally-laden memories of entirely false events or false details of events – what are known as 'rich false memories'.[7] Witnesses can even 'remember' seeing things that were merely suggested to them. They may start with very little memory, but after several suggestive interviews filled with misinformation they may 'recall' the false events, including details that were only suggested to them, and can express these false memories with confidence and in detail.[8]

Eyewitnesses tend to talk to other co-witnesses after an incident. Through such acts of social remembering individuals may incorporate details about the past they did not actually experience – the process known as 'social contagion'. Inaccurate post-event information or misinformation is particularly problematic when introduced to a group of witnesses, because a consensus of witness evidence may be taken by the justice system to be a sign of accuracy and to be corroborative. But an inaccurate consensus may arise because all the witnesses have been misinformed by a single source. What one person says about an event can affect what others will say and hearing about someone else's report can alter a person's confidence in their own version. Thus, reports from multiple witnesses who have discussed their memories are not truly independent or corroborative.[9]

Evidence may be affected by other social dynamics: a witness may decide that the social cost of disagreeing with other witnesses is too high, and so they adjust their reports accordingly. Or through discussing what happened, a witness may come to endorse a version of events different from what they remember, because they believe it to be more accurate than their own memory. Individuals who have authority within a group, or who have a trusted position, who are considered knowledgeable, to have 'expertise', may have a particularly powerful role, leading to the listener adopting a shared reality.[10] These 'dominant narrators' may have a greater impact on shaping the collective memory; they may be better able to craft the storyline than other conversational participants and thus may draw greater attention to what they say.[11] 'Dominant narrators' may introduce new information into the conversation in the form of unshared memories; these introduced memories may then reshape the memories of other conversational participants.[12]

Through 'social contagion' and with the influence of a 'dominant narrator', autobiographical memories will converge; collective memory may be developed. This may help to define and bind together a group, to establish a collective identity.[13] With so many participants on both sides precognosced and exposed to newspaper and other reportage, it is certain that testimony about the events of 31 January 1919 was susceptible to these processes.

Being questioned about an event puts considerable pressure on witnesses to recall as much as possible.[14] People are particularly prone to having their memories affected by misinformation when it is introduced after the passage of some time and there is less likelihood of a discrepancy being noticed.[15] Buckley *et al* list procedures routinely used in interviewing witnesses, which might be used to, or result in, changing witnesses' memories of an event or details of an event. Interviewees may be asked to agree or disagree with an item of information they may not have previously known, but which is introduced by the interviewer. Witnesses may face 'non-coercive challenges', where once questions have been asked and answered, the answers are rejected, and interviewees are asked to consider whether other answers are correct. This may develop into 'enforced disagreement', where, once questions have been asked and answered, the answers are rejected, and interviewees are told their answers are false, possibly on the basis of someone else's testimony, or through appeal to logic, external authority, common sense, or the assertion that a contrary fact is true. This approach may be backed up by negative or positive social acceptance of the answer – how the witness's peer group would respond to the witness's version of events. These processes are certain to have been in play in 1919. Finally, individuals may fill in gaps in their memories of events by guessing what happened in the missing elements because these inventions explain or somehow make sense of what happened.[16]

Conforming groups within which events and memories may be compared and discussed included: the police, division by division; the strike leadership; strike activists and strikers; tram staff; town councillors, both pro- and anti-strike. The policemen within each division would have discussed the events while on duty, in the muster hall, on meal-breaks and off-duty in the days after 31 January.[17] 'Dominant narrators' in the form of sergeants, inspectors or more senior figures in the force may have provided information which may have helped guide individuals to 'make sense' of what they saw, in particular ways. For example, the police seem to have expected an attack on the City Chambers, and the unintended movement of the crowd after the first baton charge on 31 January may have confirmed their assumption (Chapter 11). The precognoscing process may have steered the evidence further. Finally, as the defence claimed in the closing statements at the trial, the police created versions of events, no doubt partly because of communal memory manipulation, but also, regrettably, as the result of deliberate falsification, to which men swore in court, either to exculpate individuals, for example Sergeant Steele for his assault on David Kirkwood, or to support the prosecution's line. Police forces in the UK were, in general, hostile to left-wing politics.[18]

The taking of precognitions for the prosecution adhered to the rules set out in the Procurator Fiscal's *Book of Regulations*. Precognitions were to be conducted as soon after the events as possible to avoid the corruption of evidence from other sources. The process is set out precisely, and it is instructed to be unbiased. In her research into sexual offences in the immediate post-war period, Louise gained the impression that Glasgow's Procurator Fiscal, John Drummond Strathern, who himself took many of the precognitions for the riot trial, not only adhered strictly to the regulations, taking precognitions often with 48 hours of a crime being reported, but he was very much his own man, on occasion prosecuting against the guidance of the Crown. Would he have organised the taking of intentionally biased precognitions under pressure from the Lord Advocate? This is unlikely. No evidence has been found for John Foster's belief, apparently based solely on the day-by-day newspaper accounts of the trial, not on the precognitions themselves, that 'we can be fairly sure that the precognition statements represented the narrative which the government wished to project'.[19]

No defence precognitions survive. Defence witnesses' testimony is visible in the trial transcript where they fall into a number of subgroups: those close to the central organisation of the strike; those involved in local union or labour organisation; other labour or socialist activists; ordinary strikers; and finally, passers-by.[20] The meeting structure of the strike and the holding of many meetings of protest after the Battle provided opportunities for 'dominant narrators' to steer the memories of those present in the Square; the strike organisers' versions had already been presented in the *Strike Bulletin* editions after the Battle, on 1, 2 and 3 February 1919. As evidenced by the argument in the *Strike Bulletin*, it is certain the version of events repeated was that of outrage that a peaceful demonstration had been deliberately attacked. In the files of the Glasgow Trades Council there are many motions of censure from labour organisations across Britain, which repeat without question the version of events presented to them. The creation of any defence precognitions, by which time 'memories' of the event will have become shared widely and fixed, may have involved some of Buckley *et al*'s list of procedures described above.

The processes described here are seen in the evidence given at trial, including the deliberate manipulation of memory, and indeed of fabrication. The intervening 100 years of 'remembering' the Battle have created a different issue regarding how the events in January 1919 are recalled, retold and explained. For example, there are four recordings made in the 1970s in the William Gallacher Memorial Library, of interviews with Communist Party members, over 50 years after the events. While identifiable events are recalled, albeit in a confused way, other events for which no evidence can be found are described: for example, two Royal Navy destroyers moored in the Clyde at Jamaica Bridge, machine guns from which were mounted on the tops of buildings; many double-decker buses or trams pushed over onto their sides along the streets; a regiment of Gordon or Argyll and Sutherland Highlanders under orders to India refusing to fire on the crowd *during the riot* and refusing to leave Maryhill Barracks; half a million strikers on the streets.[21]

3.1. *'Julian's Baby' in a fund-raising parade in January 1919, almost two weeks before the Battle. The image has been passed off, for example in the 'Age of Tanks' documentary (Chapter 18), as a tank in Glasgow after the Battle (out of copyright).*

One of the abiding myths of the Battle, that there were 'tanks in the streets' or even 'tanks in George Square' provides a useful example. The tanks that arrived on 3 February 1919 may indeed have driven through the streets, but only a matter of 1,500m from College Goods Station to the Cattle Market (Map 2, nos. 13 and 14). The city, however, had seen 'tanks in the streets' only two weeks before the Battle. The *Glasgow Herald* reported the arrival on 13 January of three tanks: two heavies, known as 'Haig' and 'Beatty', and a light Whippet type – 'Julian's Baby'. Minus the Whippet, which broke down, the tanks drove from College Goods Station to Glasgow Green, where they put on an obstacle-crossing display. Various dignitaries took rides in 'Haig' in processions along Queen Street and Argyle Street. Most of the time the tanks were parked outside the City Chambers in George Square to promote the sale of Victory Bonds.[22] How many false memories of 'tanks in George Square' or 'tanks in the streets' stem from these events?

If many accounts of the Battle gathered decades after the events are discounted, what can be relied upon? The sources for a study of the events in Glasgow in 1919 are rich. The War Cabinet minutes have been accessible at the National Archives, Kew since 1969 and are now available online. The pages of the *Glasgow Herald* and other key newspapers have always been available at the Mitchell Library and other repositories; the *Glasgow Herald* is now accessible free of charge on Google. Other newspaper archives are accessible online by subscription. One of the most useful illustrated newspapers, however, *The Bulletin* (not to be confused with the strikers' *Strike Bulletin*) is accessible only in hard copy at the Mitchell and the National Library of Scotland and is rarely referenced in other studies. The fourteen-issue run of the *Strike Bulletin* is accessible in part in three archives.[23]

The transcript of the trial in April 1919, held in the National Records of Scotland, was available at least as early as the 1990s; Gordon consulted it in 2018. Attempts to revisit it a few months later to conduct further research were prevented by a GDPR sensitivity review, which had extended the closure of all trial papers to 100 years. Under a Freedom of Information request, these and the file of prosecution precognitions were opened a year early for our research. Louise had consulted the precognition papers (AD15 series) in 2012 without restriction; it is understood they had been released in the 1970s. Only later was it discovered that the Glasgow City Archive holds a beautifully bound – and more consistently paginated – copy of the trial transcript. None of this material – the GDPR blip aside – has been sequestered in hard-to-access archives.

For this book all of the available primary source material has been carefully read and much of it transcribed – High Court of Justiciary trial papers, contemporary printed sources, newspapers and other commentaries – before turning to secondary sources – books and articles written by historians and politicians in the intervening century.[24] The intensive analysis of the archival material has looked actively not only for corroboration but also for contradiction or greater-than-expected complexity. And no 'fact' on which any significant part of the narrative relies has been left unchecked no alleged quotation; no statement; no assumption; no event; no supposed cause or effect. The more significant the event, the more central the 'fact' to the interpretation being presented, the more carefully these have been checked and corroborated or dismissed. There is further consideration of 'hypothesis testing' in Chapter 21.

This approach has been criticised for getting the balance wrong between, on the one hand, reporting what happened and, on the other, analysis, interpretation and the assigning of meaning and significance. Has there not in the historiography of the Battle been rather too much analysis and interpretation, based on an inadequate exploration and exposition of the evidence?

---

1. D. Wright *et al*, 'Memory Conformity: Exploring Misinformation Effects When Presented by Another Person', in *British Journal of Psychology* (2000), pp.189, 200.
2. For example, S. Damer, 'Review of McLean's "Legend of the Red Clyde"', *History Workshop*, 18 (1984), pp.199-203; J. Foster, 'Working Class mobilisation on the Clyde 1917-20', in C.W. Wrigley (ed), *Challenges of Labour: Central and Western Europe 1917-1920* (Routledge, 1993), pp.149-75; p.70 and p.174 note 32.
3. E. F. Loftus, 'Planting Misinformation in the Human Mind: A 30-Year Investigation of the Malleability of Memory', *Learning and Memory,* 12 (4) (2005).
4. J. Buckley *et al*, *The Science of False Memory* (Oxford University Press USA, 2005), p.37; S. J. Frenda *et al*, 'Current Issues and Advances in Misinformation Research', *Current Directions in Psychological Science*, 20 (2011), p.20; A. Brown *et al*, 'Memory's Malleability: Its Role in Shaping Collective Memory and Social Identity', *Frontiers in Psychology,* 3 (2012), p.1.
5. E. F. Loftus and H. G. Hoffman, 'Misinformation and Memory: The Creation of New Memories', *Journal of Experimental Psychology: General,* 118 (1989), p.103.
6. Wright *et al*, 'Memory Conformity', pp. 189-90; Loftus, 'Planting Misinformation', p.365; Frenda *et al*, 'Current Issues', p.20.
7. S. J. Frenda *et al*, 'False Memories of Fabricated Political Events', *Journal of Experimental Social Psychology,* 49 (2013), p.280. Loftus, 'Planting Misinformation', pp.363, 364-65.
8. Loftus, 'Planting Misinformation,' p.364.
9. Brown *et al*, 'Memory's Malleability', p.2; Wright *et al*, 'Memory Conformity', pp.190-1, 200-1.
10. Frenda *et al*, 'Current Issues', p.20; Brown *et al*, 'Memory's Malleabil-

ity', p.2.

11. Brown *et al*, 'Memory's Malleability', p.2; A. Brown *et al*, 'The Role of Narratorship and Expertise in Social Remembering', *Social Psychology*, 40 (2009), p.120.
12. Brown *et al*, 'Role of Narratorship', pp.120, 126; Brown *et al*, 'Memory's Malleability', p.2.
13. Brown *et al*, 'Memory's Malleability', p.1.
14. Buckley *et al*, *Science of False Memory*, p.34.
15. Loftus and Hoffman, 'Misinformation and Memory', p.103; Loftus, 'Planting Misinformation', p.361.
16. Loftus and Hoffman, 'Misinformation and Memory', p.103.
17. L. A. Jackson *et al*, *Police and Community in Twentieth-Century Scotland* (Edinburgh University Press, 2020), pp.62ff.
18. Jackson *et al*, *Police and Community*, pp.56-7.
19. J. Foster, 'Mobilising Working Class Action on Clydeside, 1919 and 1971: How the Arguments Were Won', *Colloque Internationale Discours et Dispositivs Anti-syndicaux* (Lyon, 2010), p.30.
20. AD15/19/11, List of possible defence witnesses. (See note 24 below.)
21. Tapes held in National Library of Scotland, Special Collections, Acc.14114, William Gallacher Memorial Library: William Ferguson (24 July1974) 3/13/2 WFA; Thomas Graham (19 July 1977) 3/13/2 TGA; Finlay Hart (13 June 1970) 3/13/2 FHA and FHB; Bob Saunders (February 1976) 3/13/2 BSA.
22. *Glasgow Herald,* 14 January 1919; 15 January 1919; 18 January 1919.
23. For our study, sourced as follows: Glasgow University Archives (nos. 1-4, 10, 11); National Library of Scotland (nos. 5-8, 12, 13); London School of Economics Shinwell Archive (no. 9).
24. Notes prefixed AD15 are precognitions; JC26 are miscellaneous court process papers; JC36 are trial transcript. The [...] notation added to all JC36 files follows the folio divisions within the legal case papers which has also been used in our internal file numbering system. All can be found in the High Court of Justiciary (HCJ) collection kept at the National Records of Scotland (NRS). Hereafter their attribution will be cited in its shorter form with NRS catalogue reference followed by the individual's name and position. Because of the difficulties experienced with pagination across different documents, no page numbers are given.

Part II
GLASGOW, JANUARY 1919

4 The Simmering Pot: Glasgow, 1914 to 1919

> *. . . in this 40 hours movement all semblance of democracy had been thrown to the winds, and those in the trades union movement had not had a chance of expressing their opinion . . . the way in which [the strike] had been started was a disgrace to trades unionism.*[1]

Retelling, yet again, the story of 'Red Clydeside' is not the purpose of this book, but some background to the period in which the events in Glasgow in January to April 1919 are set is required.

The events of January 1919 grew from syndicalist ideas in trade unionism before the First World War. Only by combining in strikes – direct action – and especially a general strike, could workers overthrow the capitalist system and seize power in the state. Revolutionary syndicalism gained relatively little support among official trade union leaders, but stimulated rank-and-file militancy.[2] It is from this activism that some of the main movers of events in 1919 emerged.

During the war, activists such as James Maxton and John Maclean[*] opposed the war and the effort required of Clydeside's heavy industries to supply it.[3] Clydeside's industrial workers found a new voice which recognised their pivotal position in shipbuilding and munitions. The skilled workforce resisted the erosion of their craft and their prestige when dilution of their working practices by unskilled men and women in the shipyards and machine shops was introduced.

The wartime partnership between workers, employers and government enhanced the status of the trade unions and membership rose across the United Kingdom from 3,416,000 in 1913 to 6,533,000 in 1919.[4] As Jeffery and Hennessy argue, 'the compact between unions

* John Maclean (1879-1923). Born Glasgow. Active and influential in left-wing politics for most of his life, latterly as a Communist. Outspoken opponent of World War One. Imprisoned for sedition under the Defence of the Realm Act (DORA), from which his health never recovered. The most iconic figure to emerge from the leadership of Red Clydeside.

and government muted the full expression of labour grievances and stimulated the emergence of unofficial union leaders', who initially organised themselves as the Withdrawal of Labour Committee. A widespread movement led by the shop-stewards, they demonstrated their power in February 1915, when there was a major stoppage of engineers on Red Clydeside.[5]

In 1921, Scotland's population was 4.8 million, of whom approximately one million lived in and around Glasgow.[6] The city had been a magnet for Scots and Irish immigrants for over a century. Clydeside was arguably the centre of Britain's global industrial empire with its unique combination of workforce, wealth, raw materials and maritime transport links. Clydeside's shipbuilding industry accounted for 757,000 tons of new shipping in 1913 and over a million horsepower of marine engines – 49 per cent of the United Kingdom's total output.[7] The sobriquet 'Clyde-built' recognised the precision skills of the men, but these heavy industries suffered cyclical depression.

Economic success was not accompanied by better standards of living for all. Glasgow possessed some of the worst working-class housing in Europe.[8] In the UK, only Dundee's infant mortality rate exceeded that in Glasgow's working-class wards.[9] Glaswegian men endured an arduous working life, often with poor nutrition and the constant risk of industrial injuries and disease. Male average life-expectancy was 50 years, with women living only slightly longer at 53 years.[10] Some of Glasgow's working-class districts were described as 'earth's nearest suburb to hell'.[11]

The war created two particular crises in civilian working-class life in Clydeside. In 1915-16 the opportunistic increasing of rents by private landlords prompted a successful campaign of rent strikes led by Mrs Mary Barbour, wife of an engineer living in Govan.[12] When individual tenants were taken to court, shop-floor leaders prominent in the events of 1919, William Gallacher* and

* William Gallacher (1881-1965) was a leader of the Forty Hours Strike and was found guilty and imprisoned after the riot. He was born and lived in Paisley. Brass-finisher by trade. Prominent socialist leader and speaker. Convicted 1916 for a contravention of the DORA Regulations for printing and publishing a seditious article in a newspaper and sentenced to 12 months imprisonment. Founding member of the Communist Party of Great Britain, to which he belonged until his death. His reputation has suffered,

David Kirkwood* helped to orchestrate workshop delegations to the court and an unofficial and, at that time, illegal strike was threatened across Clydeside and the government acted to reduce rents.[13]

The second crisis arose in March 1915, when the government legislated for an expanded workforce through the Munitions Act. The Clyde workers' response to the Act concentrated on two key provisions: first, the Act prohibited men from moving employers, and despite the reluctance of many skilled men to move job, an important principle was at stake.[14] Second, the introduction of unskilled men and women into the workforce to increase production – 'dilution' – created fear that these unskilled workers would replace skilled men at lower rates of pay. To protect the skilled workers' status and higher wages, the Clyde Workers' Committee (CWC), under Gallacher's leadership, sought to control the implementation of dilution.[15]

The Prime Minister, David Lloyd George, accepted an invitation by official trade unions to visit Glasgow in December 1915, but he refused to acknowledge or meet the CWC. Before a gathering of 3,000 men on 22 December at St Andrew's Halls, instead of addressing their concerns on dilution, Lloyd George had attempted to rouse their patriotism. According to Kirkwood, the meeting had been an embarrassing fiasco for Lloyd George. Official news reports were restricted to a government-supplied text, and on New Year's Day, the workers' newspaper *Forward,* which contained its own account of the meeting, was suppressed.[16]

By 3 March 1916, Kirkwood's position at Parkhead Forge had become untenable and he resigned. Among those who risked striking (illegally) to have him re-instated was Gallacher. Kirkwood was

outside Communist circles, for his uncritical support for the Stalinist dictatorship and the Soviet suppression of the Hungarian Uprising.

* (Lord) David Kirkwood (1872-1955) was a leader of the Forty Hours Strike and was acquitted at the trial after the Battle. Born in Shettleston, Glasgow. Engineer to trade and Convenor of Shop Stewards in Beardmore's, Parkhead, until February 1916. Arrested March 1916 and deported to Edinburgh. Remained in Edinburgh to January 1917. Returned to Glasgow without leave. Re-arrested at Crieff Hydropathic January 1917. Released from Edinburgh Castle February 1917. Member of Independent Labour Party and a prominent socialist speaker. After 1919 went on to have a distinguished parliamentary career.

arrested under the terms of the Defence of the Realm Act (DORA), court-martialled in his absence and transported into internal exile in Edinburgh, forbidden to travel within the Clyde Munitions Area.[17] Soon joining him was democratic socialist and pacifist, James Maxton. Gallacher followed within days, along with the editors, John Muir and Tom Bell, of the recently established *The Worker*, and John Maclean for writing an article which the authorities interpreted as an incitement to use force. By the end of March 1916, most of Clydeside's leaders were incarcerated in Edinburgh or restricted to the city's limits. As resolve waned, some accepted positions working at munitions factories in England in return for their freedom. Kirkwood refused, and after a trip to speak at the Labour Party Conference in Manchester in January 1917, he was re-arrested and unceremoniously re-deported to Edinburgh Castle. Fourteen months later, Kirkwood was released.[18]

After the Armistice in November 1918, an economic slump was inevitable as naval and munitions orders ceased and demobilising soldiers required re-employment. One solution proposed was a reduction in working hours for no reduction in wages and eventually a forty-hour week was the demand adopted by the CWC, supported by the Glasgow Trades Council. Individual unions balloted their members and received mixed responses: the Amalgamated Society of Engineers was in favour of a stoppage; the National Union of Scottish Mine Workers advised its members to remain at the coal face. Negotiation with the employers was a non-starter, and so a proposal for a forty-hour week became the Forty Hours Strike. It commenced on Monday 27 January and ended on 12 February.

January 1919 was a troubled and troubling month. Abroad, the Armistice of November 1918 had not stopped the fighting along the new borders of countries formed from Europe's collapsing empires. Germany's revolutionary chaos was a frightening example of what any country might face if its government lost control. Britain was one of a number of countries intervening in the Russian Civil War.

At home and in military camps abroad, British troops verged on mutiny or actually disobeyed their officers. The main driver of discontent was the unfair process of demobilisation, which released 'pivotal' men first, even if they had served for much shorter periods than others.

The first mutiny was only two days after the Armistice, on 13 November 1918, at Shoreham. The unrest culminated in a march on Downing Street on 6 January 1919. One of Winston Churchill's first acts as the newly appointed Secretary of State for War and Air that month was to introduce a fairer demobilisation system based on age, length of service and whether a man had been injured, which defused the situation. His proposals were discussed at the War Cabinet on 28 January.[19] In Ireland, the country had never settled after the Rising in 1916, and in December 1918's general election, Sinn Fein won 91 per cent of seats outside Ulster. On 21 January 1919, ten days before the Battle, Sinn Fein formed a breakaway government and declared Irish independence, marking the effective beginning of the War of Irish Independence, which culminated in the Anglo-Irish Treaty of December 1921.[20]

In the face of all these foreign and domestic concerns, alarmist reports from Special Branch and other intelligence sources about industrial and political unrest fuelled the government's anxieties.[21]

A Tale of Two Cities: Glasgow and the 44-Hours Strike in Belfast

In January 1919 a strike began in Belfast in parallel with the Forty Hours Strike in Glasgow, for a 44-hour working week. The strike in Glasgow and the strike in Belfast, which began before Glasgow and ended after it, were not co-ordinated, despite contemporary news reports' attempts to link the two through a supposed network of activists intent on emulating recent events in Russia and Germany.[22] The Belfast strike took place in a different political and labour landscape, where nationalist and unionist politics closely defined the boundaries of the General Strike Committee's (GSC) activities in the city.[23] During the First World War, Belfast had not developed the industrial militancy seen on Clydeside, and no shop stewards' movement grew. No 'legend of Red Laganside' evolved, no prominent radical leadership developed, no-one was imprisoned or sent into internal exile for militant opposition to government policies, and no cohort of left-leaning politicians subsequently went to Westminster. The Belfast strike differed from Glasgow in one key feature, in that it operated under a system of mutual support from affiliated unions, thus the city's municipal workers came out 'despite their absence of grievances . . . against the Belfast Corporation'.[24]

Emanuel Shinwell* was the chair of the Forty Hours Strike Committee in Glasgow, and one of its prime movers. Although by the time of the George Square riot trial and by April at the latest, he was anxious to promote a view of the Glasgow strike as non-political, the strike movement was nevertheless viewed as political by the hostile broadsheet press and seems to have been considered political by some of those prominent in the strike leadership.[25] For example, English socialist George Ebury† related the strike to the freeing of the working class from oppression. By contrast, in Belfast the organisers repeatedly stressed that the 44-hours strike was solely a local labour dispute unconnected with 'foreign' agitation in Dublin and Glasgow, and they would 'oppose any attempt to introduce socialist politics into the strike'.[26]

The mainstream press's attempt to paint the Belfast strike organisers as 'Red Flaggers' presented a 'very inflated notion of the strike-leaders' radicalism'; only a small minority of the organisers were influenced by Marxism or militant socialism.[27] Indeed, 'from the beginning, the strike committee's marches and demonstrations were avowedly British and maintained . . . a determinedly insular course'.[28] It is these differences between the recent histories of the two cities that, most likely, explained the different outcomes in terms of the use of the military.

* (Lord) Emanuel Shinwell (1884–1986). Leader of the Forty Hours Strike and convicted at the trial in April 1919. Born in London. His family moved to Glasgow where Shinwell was apprenticed at age 11 to the tailoring trade. Joined first trade union at age 17. Elected Glasgow Trades Council 1906 and was Chair in 1919. Early member of ILP. Active socialist crusader. Glasgow Town Councillor 1916. Continued militant union activities during the war. Elected to Parliament 1922. Long and prominent career in Labour politics, serving as a junior minister in Ramsay MacDonald's government and as minister for war and power in the post-war Attlee government. Ennobled 1970.

† George Ebury (1867-1939) became interested in socialist politics in Glasgow in 1884. Worked as a carpet designer in Heckmondwike until 1908, when he was sacked following his election as a socialist councillor. Proposed in 1914 as British Socialist Party parliamentary candidate for North Islington. He joined the Communist Party on its foundation but subsequently left it.

Simon Webb suggests both the Glasgow and Belfast strikes sought changes against their own interests, claiming the strikers were prepared 'if necessary, to be paid less themselves' to make room for discharged men through a shorter working week. This supposed altruism, he suggests, alarmed the government because it implied a political motive. However, Glasgow's Forty Hours Strike explicitly called for a reduction in working hours *with no reduction in pay*.[29]

The Belfast strike began on Saturday 25 January 1919 and spread beyond the shipyards and engineering plants, to include workers in the city's gas and electricity stations. Within a few hours of the strike's starting, all the trams were off the streets and the city's gas supply had been cut off. Initially, supply to hospitals was maintained only by clerical workers and managers, although later, the strike committee maintained a skeleton crew to provide services to the hospitals. They established a 'Permits Committee' to consider applications by businesspeople for permission to use the reduced supplies, thus effectively taking control of the city's ability to function.[30]

By the end of the Belfast strike's first week, some 60,000 workers were directly or indirectly affected, and the cutting of fuel supplies had led to a serious bread shortage.[31] There were no trams and the streets were unlit; there was the threat of coal shortages; most houses were without light and gas.[32] The strike committee 'viewed these disruptive repercussions on the city's social and commercial life as a central bargaining weapon'. They hoped the 'widespread inconvenience' would pressure the public to force the employers into negotiating.[33] By early February, Belfast's Strike Committee's control of the city had forced the employers into negotiations; the strikers would return to work on a 57-hour week, while a national conference would begin negotiations for a 47-hour week.[34] In Glasgow, the strike committee failed to achieve this level of disruption and inconvenience to the wider population – the trams still ran, the streets remained lit, and the gas and bread supplies continued uninterrupted.

In Belfast the organisers' determination to keep the strike local and apolitical was only strengthened by the military intervention in Glasgow. Contrasting the peaceful conduct of the Belfast strike with Glasgow, one of its organisers said in a speech over the weekend of 1 and 2 February, 'They seem to have made a mess of things over there'.[35]

John Thom was deputed to Belfast by the Glasgow strike subcommittee on Friday 24 January 'with the explicit purpose of asking the Belfast Committee to fall in line with us on the forty hours demand', rather than 44 hours. Thom remained in Belfast until the night of Monday 27 January. He reported what had happened in a speech to a strike meeting at Kinniston Park on 30 January, and that he had been 'assisting in the strike organisation' there.[36]

Because Deputy Prime Minister Andrew Bonar Law MP* believed there was a good possibility of the Belfast strike ending amicably, the War Cabinet, on 4 February, had not considered it wise to use troops. But by 10 February, with no sign of a solution, the War Cabinet sanctioned a joint committee of local and national government officers to discuss how to restart municipal services. It was decided to take over the municipal gas and electricity supply, and at 6am on Saturday 15 February, troops began to move into the works; on the same day volunteers were sought to run them. Power supplies were restored by the afternoon and the tram service resumed on Sunday.[37] Belfast's strike committee seems to have seen the military intervention as the end of the strike: the possibility of a repetition of events in Glasgow weighed heavily. By the following weekend, the city's industries had returned to normal.[38] The strike organisers had eschewed revolutionary rhetoric and consequently distanced themselves successfully from any accusations of Bolshevism in a way Glasgow's strike committee failed to do. But the Belfast strike 'failed to establish lasting solidarity among the workers of Belfast, a solidarity that would have overcome any further incitement to sectarian hate'.[39]

Preparing to Strike, Glasgow 20-26 January 1919

For Gallacher, leader of the CWC, the formal structure of the trade unions had lost their allure; he was a socialist and a syndicalist, spreading his doctrine workshop by workshop. As president of the

* Andrew Bonar Law MP (1858-1923). Born in Canada to Scottish parents. Moved to Scotland in 1870. Industrialist. Entered Parliament in 1900 as Conservative MP. Leader of Conservative party from 1911 to 1921 (and again in 1922). Served in wartime coalition cabinet. In 1919 he was Lloyd George's deputy Prime Minister and MP for Glasgow Central, in which George Square lay. Prime Minister 1922-23.

Glasgow Trades Council, city councillor and recently involved in a Clydeside sailors' dispute that resulted in a violent race riot, Emanuel Shinwell chaired the Strike Committee.

Support for the Forty Hours Strike was increased by the men's disgruntlement about the 47-hour working week then being trialled: the loss of breaks meant they worked from 7.30am until noon without stopping. However, the Forty Hours movement on Clydeside was launched without the strike leadership having obtained adequate support from workers other than the engineers and electricians. Iain McLean has argued the strike was 'foredoomed' as 'another craftsmen's strike' not involving the unskilled or women. The three largest unions representing the unskilled – the dockers, carters and municipal employees – either agreed shorter working hours separately or did not strike at all, reflecting what McLean called the 'familiar vendettas' between skilled and unskilled men. It may be that McLean's sharp differentiation between the two camps is overstated – driving a tram, after all, requires 'skills' – but in the hierarchy of working-class Glasgow, craftsmen were a notch or two above the 'unskilled'. Political educator John Maclean tried, ineffectively, to link the Clydeside engineers with other bodies of workers, to realise the claim that this was a 'general strike'.[40] A national conference held on 27 January aimed to garner support further afield.

And so, the scene was set for the eventful week commencing on Monday 27 January 1919. The story is told here in detail and in chronological order, as it developed from the first day of the strike. This degree of detail is necessary because it documents thoroughly the challenge to the established narrative. The narrative follows the key protagonists as they organise meetings, marches and, most controversially, mass picketing of works. Problematic aspects of the strike are explored, such as the intimidation of individuals and of works that had voted *not* to strike. The growing resentment of the strikers against the non-striking tram-workers, and how this provided the catalyst for the violence on Friday in George Square and across the city centre, is investigated. The strike leadership's meeting with the Lord Provost and Town Clerk on Wednesday 29 January is analysed; what the attendees said and were understood to have said and how those words sowed the seeds of Friday's violence. The growing concerns of the Chief Constable and the Sheriff that violence was planned, especially towards the tram-drivers, and the precautions they took, are noted. Finally, the crowd's movements and the reactions of public officials as the protestors gather on Friday morning are dissected in detail.

---

1. Chairman, Edinburgh Trades Council, *Glasgow Herald*, 29 January 1919.
2. K. Jeffery and P. Hennessy, *States of Emergency: British Governments and Strikebreaking since 1919* (Routledge and Kegan Paul, 1983), p.2; T. Johnston, *The History of the Working Classes in Scotland* (Forward Publishing, 1922), pp.340-4.
3. I. McLean, *The Legend of Red Clydeside* (John Donald, 1999).
4. Jeffery and Hennessy, *States of Emergency*, p.4.
5. Jeffery and Hennessy, *States of Emergency*, p.4.
6. National Records of Scotland, https://www.nrscotland.gov.uk/research/research-guides/research-guides-a-z/census-records/1921-census; Gazetteer for Scotland, https://www.scottish-places.info/towns/townfirst338.html
7. C. Harvie, *'No Gods and Precious Few Heroes' Scotland 1914-1980* (Arnold, 1st edn 1981), p.4.
8. Almost 11 per cent of Glasgow's houses contained over four persons per room with almost 56 per cent housing over two people per room; comparable figures for England were under one per cent and ten per cent respectively. Scotland Royal Commission on Housing, *Report of the Royal Commission on the Housing of the Industrial Population of Scotland, Rural and Urban* (HMSO, 1917), pp.4-54, 40-2.
9. T. C. Smout, *A Century of the Scottish People 1830-1950* (Collins, 1986), p.50.
10. W.H. Fraser and R.J. Morris, *People and Society in Scotland: 1830-1914* (Tanner Ritchie, 2022), p.30, table 1.
11. W.W. Knox, *James Maxton* (Manchester University Press, 1987), p.9.
12. McLean, *Legend*, pp.21-2.
13. J. Foster, 'Strike Action and Working-Class Politics on Clydeside 1914–1919', *International Review of Social History,* 35 (1990), pp.33-70; T. Bell, *John Maclean, a Fighter for Freedom* (Communist Party, 1944), pp.50-2.
14. D. Kirkwood, *My Life of Revolt* (London, 1935), pp.100-2.

15. J. Smith, 'Labour Tradition in Glasgow and Liverpool', *History Workshop,* 17 (1984), p.38.

16. W. Gallacher, *Revolt on the Clyde*, fifth edition (Lawrence and Wishart, 2017 [1936]), pp.82-3; *Glasgow Herald*, 28 December 1915. Gallacher, in 1935, published a first draft of his version of events from 1914 to 1919, in a booklet titled *The Clyde in Wartime*. There are no substantive differences between it and the version he published in *Revolt* in 1936 and we have not separately referenced the booklet here or subsequently.

17. The Defence of the Realm Act (1914) was passed in order to control communications, the nation's ports, requisition property and subject civilians to the rule of military courts. Key provisions were to prevent causing 'disaffection' in the armed forces.

18. Kirkwood, *My Life of Revolt*, pp.140-62; L. Heren and G. J. Barclay, *Tanks on the Streets? The Battle of George Square, Glasgow 1919* (Pen and Sword, 2023), p.40.

19. CAB 23/9/8, War Cabinet Minutes, meeting 521, 28 January 1919.

20. J. C. Beckett, *The Making of Modern Ireland 1603-1923* (Faber and Faber, 2008), Chapter 13.

21. CAB 24/74/13, pp.1-2; 'Report No.31' *Fortnightly Report on Revolutionary Organisations in the United Kingdom and Abroad.*

22. *The Times*, 1 February 1919, p.9.

23. P. Stewart et al, 'The Independent Workers Union: Class, Nation and Oppositional Labour Movements in Ireland from 1900 to the Celtic Tiger', *Labour History,* 55 (2014), p.7.

24. O. Coquelin, 'A Strikers' "Soviet" in Belfast'? The Great Belfast Strike of 1919', *Labour History Review*, vol.87, no.3 (December 2022), p.259.

25. H. Patterson, *Class Conflict and Sectarianism: the Protestant Working Class and the Belfast Labour Movement 1868-1920* (Blackstaff, 1980), p.105.

26. Stewart *et al*, 'Independent Workers Union', p.7; Patterson, *Class* Conflict, pp.104-105.

27. Patterson, *Class Conflict,* p.105.

28. Stewart *et al*, 'Independent Workers Union', pp.6-7.

29. S. Webb, *1919: Britain's year of Revolution* (Pen and Sword, 2016), pp.51-53.

30. Patterson, *Class Conflict*, p.102.

31. *Daily News,* 28 January 1919.

32. *Glasgow Herald*, 19 February 1919.

33. Patterson, *Class Conflict*, p.103.
34. Coquelin, '"Soviet" in Belfast?', p.261.
35. Patterson, *Class Conflict*, p.107.
36. JC36/31/08 [08/B]; John Thom, Strike Committee Member.
37. Patterson, *Class Conflict*, p.109.
38. Patterson, *Class Conflict*, p.109.
39. M. Farrell, 'Lessons of the Great Belfast Strike of 1919', (Workers' Liberty website, 2008), https://www.workersliberty.org/story/2018-12-14/lessons-great-belfast-strike-1919
40. McLean, *Legend*, pp.117-120.

5 Monday 27 January 1919

[The Red Flag] was brought into the procession by people who had no connection with the strike . . . an intervention by people who had nothing to do with us.[1]

The *Glasgow Herald*, quoting the Strike Committee, reported that 40,000 men were out on this, the first day of the strike. The *Bulletin* estimated between 50,000 and 60,000, and the *Manchester Guardian* offered the improbably precise 56,000.[2]

The first formal event of the strike was a large meeting in St Andrew's Halls, a large complex of rooms and halls which stood behind the Mitchell Library at Charing Cross, on Monday morning; 'hundreds of men were unable to gain admission'.[3] The *Glasgow Herald* provided the most complete account, which must be read with caution given its political stance. It reported that the meeting passed a series of resolutions: no work would resume 'until the demand for a 40-hour week, with no reduction of pay, had been conceded'; and 'no rent or Income-tax would be paid until a satisfactory settlement of the demand for a 40-hours week had been come to'.[4]

Despite strong feeling among the strikers that the press should be excluded as it was felt they had misrepresented the strike, the press was allowed to stay.[5]

Although it was an otherwise relatively quiet day, evidence from Monday's events was employed at the trial to try to prove incitement to riot, a number of witnesses giving evidence concerning words allegedly spoken by William Gallacher, and, to a lesser extent, by Emanuel Shinwell. Almost every defence witness at trial was asked a series of questions to confirm that no explicit incitement to violence or unrest had been made by the two men, and to confirm that Shinwell had in fact stressed that all proceedings should be orderly.[6] In the end, the Lord Justice-Clerk excluded events from Monday from consideration at trial.[7]

The prosecution emphasised that at various points during the week it had been recognised there might be a 'disorderly element' amongst the strikers, who might cause trouble of different kinds. As Herbert Highton,* iron-turner and member of the Associated Society of Engineers (ASE), admitted:

> There is in all strikes a small element who feel that things are not going as strongly as they might, and in order to prevent that . . . it was emphasised at the meetings . . . that the thing was a purely industrial strike, and must be kept within the limits of an industrial strike.[8]

At the trial, Highton explained: 'The press made out that [the strike] was being fomented by extremists' and the strike was being represented as 'a Bolshevik political movement'; he repeated his determination that the strike would remain purely industrial.[9]

The press coverage provides a salutary example of how far the *Glasgow Herald* could pursue its own editorial agenda, by selectively quoting Shinwell's speech:

> He was all for constitutional action. He was prepared to try any method at all. But if the wheels of constitutional activity would not revolve as they should revolve then it was up to them to adopt other and more expeditious measures to achieve their object.[10]

Shinwell, as quoted, seems to promote unconstitutional action, perhaps violence. The *Herald* report, however, omitted three key sentences quoted in the *Scotsman* which show Shinwell spoke *solely* about the difference between strike action led by the official trade

* Herbert Edward Rayner Highton (1880- 1971) was born in Govanhill. Iron-turner. In 1919 he was a shop steward with the Amalgamated Society of Engineers, describing himself as a constitutional trades unionist opposed to unofficial strike action, despite his involvement in the Clyde Workers' Committee. Later president of the Glasgow Trades Council. He gave lectures to the economics section of the Royal Philosophical Society. Organiser for the Workers' Educational Association. By 1939 he was an extra-mural university lecturer in economics in Yorkshire, where he died.

union structure which he considered had failed the workers and the 'unofficial' body which now replaced them.[11] Shinwell concluded with clear instructions about maintaining order, although the speech included potentially troubling remarks (audience reactions omitted):

> Their instructions were to preserve order . . . to indulge in no unseemly disturbance . . . to act in a perfectly constitutional and legitimate manner . . . to carry on this fight in a clean manner right until the happy end, to indulge in their picketing, but to adopt merely moral suasion . . . and to adopt those methods *until the Joint Committee instructed them to act otherwise . . . If, however, there were breaches of discipline and interference with picketing, the Joint Committee would accept no responsibility.*[12] [our emphasis]

The italicised words might be understood not only as an implied threat of tactics not 'constitutional and legitimate', but as the refusal to accept any responsibility for trouble. Might some of the men have taken this as suggesting they could employ violence if they chose? The evidence suggests that throughout the week most speakers did not deliberately try to incite the crowd. Rather, this sort of radical rhetoric, frequently used until Thursday evening, was merely performative. The strike leaders had to appeal to varied groups of men, and it seems this led them at times to express themselves in very strong or even violent language to meet the expectations of part of their constituency. However, some of their audience may have been what one defence witness termed, 'disorderly elements'. After Shinwell's speech, the audience formed up and, headed by a band, marched through the city to George Square.[13] Harry Hopkins* reportedly instructed the strikers 'not to allow their ranks to be broken on the way'.[14]

The prosecution and defence accounts of events on Monday begin to diverge at this point.[15] Iron-turner and convener of the ASE,

* Harry Hopkins (1875-1943) born in Exeter but moved to Dumbarton when very young. Served his apprenticeship as an engineer in Dumbarton. According to *Forward* (12 April 1919) 'one of the most prominent men in the Labour and Socialist movement in Scotland'. Tried and acquitted.

5.1. *The procession from St Andrew's Halls to George Square, Monday 27 January 1919 (*Bulletin*, 28 January 1919).*

John Forman was not alone among the defence witnesses in claiming the procession was 'very orderly', although 'at various points the tramcars were held up, and as the strikers passed the cars they raised cries of "Blackleg" against the drivers'. The *Bulletin* published a photograph of the procession, which held up tram traffic at crossings and corners.[16]

Tram Inspector Andrew Imrie described the procession deliberately spreading itself to prevent the trams passing for the full length of Sauchiehall Street, Renfield Street and Union Street, and Tram Inspector James Erskine met a large body of strikers with tramcars having to follow slowly behind.[17] Constables Robert Davidson and Thomas Turner and Chief Detective Inspector Duncan Weir confirmed these reports.[18] Police Lieutenant Lawrence Gray* reported strikers refusing to allow a motor containing wreaths for a funeral

* Police Lieutenant Lawrence/Laurence Gray (1868-1934) was born on North Yell, Shetland. By 1891 he was a 22-year-old police constable in Glasgow. In October 1911 at the age of 42 he was promoted to Lieutenant and by then he and his wife had three sons. He was promoted to Superintendent in the Western Division of the Glasgow Police in December 1921.

5.2. *Crowds in George Square, Monday 27 January 1919 (*Bulletin, *28 January 1919).*

to proceed; also, a private motorcar was pushed back with threats to its driver.[19] Chief Detective Inspector Andrew Keith saw the procession being led by someone carrying a red flag, blocking all the traffic in the street as they passed along.[20] The only reported violence was when a number of strikers climbed on to a tramcar and one (seventeen-year-old apprentice riveter, Alexander Wallace) assaulted the female tram-driver, Janet Reid, when she refused to bring her car to a halt.[21] On Wednesday, Wallace was fined £8 8s or 21 days imprisonment.[22]

The Town Clerk was with the Lord Provost, James Stewart,[*] in his room overlooking the Square when he saw a crowd holding a meeting, packing the space in front of the City Chambers, and he saw a red flag run up the city's flagpole opposite the entrance to the Chambers.[23] Six witnesses estimated the size of the crowd as between 5,000 and 8,000 people. *The Scotsman* estimated about 10,000 had set off from St Andrew's Halls and Police Constable Davidson

* (Sir) James Watson Stewart, Lord Provost (born Rome 1852-1922), Dumbarton County Councillor. Head of firm Messrs J. W. Stewart & Co, Chartered Accountants. Lord Provost 1917-1920. Created Baronet in 1920.

5.3. *Emanuel Shinwell and Harry Hopkins speaking to the crowd from the plinth of the City Chambers, Monday 27 January 1919 (*Bulletin, *28 January 1919).*

suggested an unlikely 20,000.[24] Shinwell and others addressed the crowd from the front of the City Chambers.

The appearance of a red flag during the procession and in the Square became part of the prosecution case alleging there was a wider political agenda and even a whiff of revolution to the strike. This assumption has been shared, or at least not critically assessed, by many writers, some of whom celebrate the appearance of the socialist emblem, often claiming erroneously it was raised on 31 January.[25] The most coherent account of events in the Square and which is corroborated by other sources, is provided in the *Glasgow Herald*:

> During the speechmaking [from the front of the City Chambers] a red flag was carried from the rear of the crowd to the 'platform' and there it was held aloft by Mr Hopkins and Mr Gallacher in turn. Later the banner was run up to the top of the flag post opposite the City Chambers. As it spread to the

breeze the crowd cheered enthusiastically and sang 'The Red Flag'.[26]

The London *Daily News* carried a report from their correspondent in Glasgow which suggested the red flag had been prominent inside 'the meeting of strikers in St Andrew's Hall'.[27] Two witnesses reported the flag had first appeared in the street behind the Halls, where a woman had handed it down from a window.[28] The Chief Constable saw the red flag and, seeing the speakers addressing the crowd, which was jostling against the building, 'gave instructions that the crowd was not to be allowed close up against the Buildings on future occasions'.[29] This would affect events on Friday, when a line of police was positioned to prevent this.

Frank Chappell reported that some resented that the red flag was put on the flagpole.[30] Secretary of the Trades Council, William Shaw, said Shinwell and he were crossing the Square when they heard cheering and laughing; he looked round when Shinwell said, 'That is them with the Red Flag'. Shaw said, 'I think that is nonsense',

5.4. *The red flag flying from the corporation flag pole, George Square, Monday 27 January 1919 (*Bulletin*, 28 January 1919).*

*5.5. The most frequently used image to represent the events of 31 January. In reality, the red flag was in George Square five days earlier, on Monday 27 January 1919 (*Daily Record*).*

and Shinwell replied, emphatically, 'This damned nonsense has got to stop; this is the 40 hours movement'.[31] Alfred Moloney reported subsequent discussions at the strike committee on Tuesday 28 January: 'the Strike Committee resented . . . the hoisting of the red flag, as it was altogether contrary to the arrangements made by the Strike Committee . . . [and] the red flag being hoisted was likely to . . . associate the idea of the red flag with some revolutionary movement outside the strike'.[32] Highton quotes Shinwell's description of the flag as 'an intervention by people who had nothing to do with us . . . who were not to be allowed to butt in'.[33] At trial the defence wished to affirm the non-political nature of the strike and presented the red flag as 'a joke'; the judge also described it as 'a trivial incident'.[34] So much for the radical symbol.

Police Lieutenant Lawrence Gray claimed Gallacher had said that if they took possession of the City Chambers it might also be necessary to take possession of the North British Station Hotel [on the north side of the Square] and that he observed, 'Of course we do not mean to do that to-day'. Gray said he took Gallacher's words 'to mean that they had designs on the City Chambers on a later date'.[35] He explicitly said he saw Shinwell and Gallacher waving the red flag. However, no-one else claimed Shinwell did this.[36]

Analysis of the evidence for events on 27, 29 and 31 January suggests that groups of police witnesses may have conferred in advance of being precognosced, evidenced by the recurrence of specific words and phrases in their statements. It may, however, merely reflect the taker of the precognition taking linguistic shortcuts in dealing with the same story over and over again. In this case, Sergeant Steele and Constables Ritchie and Andrew Gallagher used almost identical wording to claim Shinwell, 'said, pointing to the Municipal Buildings "We do not want to take possession today but we will come back again"'.[37] Notably, the newspaper *Forward*, which was sympathetic to the strike, did confirm: 'Willie Gallacher announced "we are not taking over the Municipal Buildings today"'.[38]

According to Chief Detective Inspector Duncan Weir, Gallacher said if the employers failed to negotiate, the strikers might be advised to take 'certain definite and drastic action'.[39] But at trial, Weir testified that nothing he heard at either of the meetings on 27 (or 29) January led him to 'apprehend any disturbance'.[40]

Although at the trial Neil Maclean MP* insisted he became involved in the march only by accident, he claimed 'there was a desire expressed' that he should 'say something' during Monday's meetings.[41] Maclean had returned from Edinburgh by train, when he 'encountered a procession on its way from the St Andrew's Halls to George Square' which he accompanied.[42] For someone who was so closely involved with events to claim he had no 'official connection with the strike', and that his involvement on this and two other occasions where he

* Neil Maclean MP (1873-1953), son of a Mull mariner. Worked to support his family from an early age. Apprentice at Singer Sewing Machine Co. Became full-time organiser for Scottish Wholesale Co-operative Society in 1912. Joined Scottish Labour Party at 15 but was later expelled. Active in wartime Clydeside labour struggles. Elected to Parliament in 1918. Established a reputation as an 'extreme left-wing Socialist'. Held no position of importance in Parliament. He remained in Parliament as a radical Labour member until after the Second World War.

made public speeches to vast crowds, was 'entirely accidental', appears disingenuous. At trial, the Lord Advocate came as close as etiquette allowed to calling him a liar in describing this 'series of coincidences' in his cross-examination.[43] The *Bulletin* report included this description of Maclean's involvement in the Square:

> Mr Neil Maclean . . . said he was informed that one of the main electrical power stations in the Clyde was guarded by soldiers, armed with fixed bayonets, in case the workers would attempt to interfere with the supply.[44]

There is no corroboration for Maclean's claim, although it became true within a week.

Gallacher returned to the plinth and read out a message he said he had received from the staff of the North British Station Hotel, to the effect that they were 'serving the best of food to their customers while they themselves were starving'.[45] His words were used at the trial to support the claim that he had incited Friday's riot.

The police witnesses slanted their evidence to suggest strongly that Gallacher had seriously incited the crowd to take over both the City Chambers and the hotel at a future date. Police Sergeant Robert Thomson claimed Gallacher had said, 'When we take possession of the Chambers it may also be necessary to take possession of the Hotel'.[46] Defence witness Frank Chappell said that Gallacher's words were 'in quite a jocular manner and [were] received as such by the people' and 'the crowd were all laughing at the time. It was treated as a joke'.[47] It does indeed seem likely that Gallacher was joking, as he was on Wednesday 29 January about the drink available to Councillors in the City Chambers.

Monday's Other Events

Tuesday's *Glasgow Herald* reported that although the 'flour mill workers . . . are all idle, and the mills are closed down' the bread supply had by 27 January not yet been affected. The same edition reported that the Parliamentary Committee of the Scottish Trades Union Congress had approached the Minister of Labour in London,

Sir Robert Horne, who had rejected their request for intervention because 'the reduction of working hours was a matter which should form the subject of negotiations between the unions and employers' associations'. The Committee decided to communicate further with the Ministry, because, in their view, 'the Scottish movement for a 40 hours week is general and cannot be dealt with by individual employers' associations'.[48] That night, the Strike Committee issued a rather optimistic statement claiming the 'carters, flour millers, electricians, shore labour at Glasgow Harbour, and miners in Lanarkshire' had ceased work and 'the whole of the Forth area is out on strike'.[49]

The Municipal Employees' Association (MEA) members, notably the tram staff, did not join the strike on Monday or subsequently. This was a source of growing tension between strikers and tram staff that played out on the streets during the week. The *Glasgow Herald* reported only engineers at Coplawhill tram works, who were not members of the MEA, had come out. The tram staff were already working fewer than 50 hours per week, and as of 27 January, Tram Manager Dalrymple had received no application for a reduction to 40 hours.[50]

The War Cabinet did not meet on Monday 27 January and the forthcoming strike had not been discussed during the preceding week.

On the first day of the strike, there were developments which would lead to the violence on Friday: the first speeches that might have put violence into the minds of the more inflamed strikers; the beginnings of the tension between the strikers and the non-striking tram-workers. Threats, taken seriously by some, had been made about taking over the City Chambers. Already, George Square had become the focus of events that would culminate on Friday.

---

1. JC36/31/07 [07/B] Herbet Highton, shop steward. The second phrase reports Shinwell's words.
2. *Glasgow Herald,* 28 January 1919; *Manchester Guardian,* 28 January 1919.
3. *Glasgow Herald,* 28 January 1919.
4. *Glasgow Herald,* 28 January 1919.
5. *Glasgow Herald,* 28 January 1919. Events on the day were reported in the following day's press and described in more detail in precognitions

given in mid February by a number of police witnesses. The *Strike Bulletin*, published from Thursday 30 January, provided the contemporary counterweight to the mainstream media, along with D. S. Morton's and John Maclean's pamphlets and the defence evidence led at the trial.

6. For example, JC36/31/08 [08/F], Frank Chappell.
7. Chapter 22.
8. JC36/31/07 [07/B], Herbert Highton.
9. JC36/31/07 [07/B], Highton.
10. *Glasgow Herald,* 28 January 1919.
11. *The Scotsman,* 28 January 1919; *Glasgow Herald*, 28 January 1919.
12. *The Scotsman,* 28 January 1919.
13. *Glasgow Herald,* 28 January 1919.
14. AD15/19/11 [A17], Andrew Gallagher, Police Constable.
15. AD15/19/11 [A08], John Steele, Police Sergeant.
16. JC36/31/08 [08/C], John Forman; *The Scotsman,* 28 January 1919; *The Bulletin*, 28 January 1919.
17. AD15/19/11 [A07], Andrew Imrie, Tram Inspector; AD15/19/11 [A27], James Erskine, Tram Inspector.
18. AD15/19/11 [A14], Robert Davidson, Police Constable; AD15/19/11 [A19], Thomas Turner, Police Constable; AD15/19/11 [A28], Duncan Weir, Chief Detective Inspector.
19. AD15/19/11 [A20], Lawrence Gray, Police Lieutenant.
20. AD15/19/11 [A25], Andrew Keith, Chief Detective Inspector.
21. AD15/19/11 [A25], Andrew Keith, Chief Detective Inspector.
22. *Glasgow Herald,* 30 January 1919.
23. AD15/19/11 [A04], Sir John Lindsay, Town Clerk.
24. AD15/19/11 [A04], Lindsay, Town Clerk; JC36/31/02 [02/R; 03/B], Sir John Lindsay; AD15/19/11 [A20], Gray, Police Lieutenant; AD15/19/11 [A26], R. Thomson, Police Sergeant; AD15/19/11 [A08], Steele, Police Sergeant; AD15/19/11 [A09], James Ritchie, Police Constable; AD15/19/11 [A21], adopted by Sergeant David Murdoch from that of the late Inspector Simon Fraser; AD15/19/11 [A17], Gallagher, Police Constable; AD15/19/11 [A14], Robert Davidson, Police Constable; *The Scotsman,* 28 January 1919.
25. H. Bell, *John Maclean: Hero of Red Clydeside* (Pluto Press, 2018), eBook ref 306.0; S. Webb, *1919: Britain's Year of Revolution* (Pen and Sword, 2016), p.56; R. Finlay, 'The Turbulent Century: Scotland since 1900' in J. Wormald (ed), *Scotland: A History* (Oxford University Press, 2005) p.206.

26. *Glasgow Herald,* 28 January 1919. We have deliberately ended the quotation here to exclude a significant misrepresentation of what Gallacher said. JC36/31/07 [07/B], Highton.
27. *Daily News*, 28 January 1919.
28. JC36/31/07 [07/N], Alexander Duncan; JC36/31/08 [08/G], James Kerlie.
29. AD15/19/11 [A05], James Verdier Stevenson, Chief Constable.
30. JC36/31/08 [08/F], Frank Chappell.
31. JC36/31/07 [07/V], William Shaw, Secretary of the Trades Council.
32. JC36/31/08 [08/L], Alfred Moloney, Amalgamated Society of Toolmakers.
33. JC36/31/07 [07/B], Highton.
34. JC36/31/10, Lord Justice-Clerk's charge to the jury.
35. AD15/19/11 [A20], Gray, Police Lieutenant.
36. AD15/19/11 [A20], Gray, Police Lieutenant.
37. AD15/19/11 [A08], Steele, Police Sergeant; AD15/19/11 [A09], Ritchie, Police Constable; AD15/19/11 [A17], Gallagher, Police Constable.
38. *Forward*, 1 February 1919.
39. AD15/19/11 [A28], Weir, Chief Detective Inspector.
40. JC36/31/03 [03/D], Weir, Chief Detective Inspector.
41. JC36/31/09 [09/V], Maclean, MP.
42. JC36/31/09 [09/V], Maclean, MP.
43. JC36/31/09 [09/V], Maclean, MP.
44. *The Bulletin* [Glasgow], 28 January 1919.
45. JC36/31/07 [07/K], Neill.
46. AD15/19/11 [A26], R. Thomson, Police Sergeant; AD15/19/11 [A08], Steele, Police Sergeant; AD15/19/11 [A09], Ritchie, Police Constable; AD15/19/11 [A17], Gallagher, Police Constable.
47. JC36/31/08 [08/F], Chappell; JC36/31/09 [09/V], Maclean, MP.
48. *Glasgow Herald,* 28 January 1919.
49. *Glasgow Herald*, 28 January 1919, but, *Scotsman*, 28 January 1919; 29 January 1919.
50. Corporation of Glasgow, *Minutes of the Corporation of Glasgow*, 30 January 1919, Glasgow City Archives, p.569.

6 Tuesday and Wednesday Morning, 28 and 29 January 1919

Tuesday, the second day of the strike, was a relatively quiet day. There were no marches to George Square and consequently no large-scale focus for events. On the international scene, the newspaper reports of the dire events in Germany, 'Spartacus Outbreak: Martial Law Declared Wilhelmshaven', can hardly have reduced any concerns about events on the Clyde, but in London the War Cabinet did not discuss the strike. A national conference held in St Andrew's Halls, Glasgow, attended by delegates from other parts of the country, including Edinburgh, Dundee, Arbroath, Bathgate, Bo'ness, Dumbarton and Greenock, as well as Grimsby, Rugby and the London shipbuilders, pledged its support to the strike.[1] But in the light of events on Wednesday, it should be noted 'the conference definitely and emphatically declined to approach the Government or the employers directly'.[2]

The *Glasgow Herald* reported the surprising news that the Glasgow Carters, originally part of the Forty Hours Strike, were likely to settle their dispute after separate discussions on the offer of a 48-hour working week; currently they worked 60 to 62½ hours. The settlement was confirmed on 30 January by Hugh Lyon,* leader of the carters and Clyde Workers Committee (CWC) member, who had been initially deeply involved in planning the Forty Hours Strike and even remained on the strike committee.[3]

In the strike's first week, the *Glasgow Herald* reported on mass picketing during Monday and Tuesday at a number of major works at Dalmuir, Clydebank and Linthouse.[4] The Trades Disputes Act 1906, provided, *inter alia*, for peaceful picketing, but a key issue that emerged in 1919 was the scale of mass picketing.[5] Eyewitness

* Hugh Lyon (1872-1940) was a prominent trades unionist and ILP functionary. General Secretary of the Carters' Association and its successor, the Scottish Horse and Motorman's Association from 1902. Chair of STUC 1918 and prominent in the agitation for a forty-hours week. The Carters' withdrawal from the Forty Hours Strike when they settled separately saw the beginning of the decline of his reputation.

6.1. *A strike picket at Weir's of Cathcart's works, Thursday 30 January 1919 (*Illustrated London News*, 8 February 1919).*

evidence reveals that crowds hundreds or even thousands strong picketed, intimidating men and whole workplaces to bring them out on strike where employees had either not asked for shorter hours, had already been granted them, or had voted not to strike. As Ernest Board, a fitter at Yarrows engineering works, put it: 'Very many of the workers had no desire to leave work. It was the threatening attitude of the pickets that kept them out'. Board himself, walking along the narrow passage left by a mass picket, 'received two severe blows on the head' and was unable to return to work in the afternoon.[6] Andrew Edgar, a joiner at Yarrows, reported his union had not held a ballot and 'the workers . . . would not have struck but for the outside interference'.[7] At Mechan's works, the men had 'unanimously decided to remain at work', but men were afraid to continue to come in.[8] Likewise, at the North British Locomotive Co. Ltd., a majority of men decided not to strike, but on Monday 27 January at about 12.30pm a crowd of 800 to 1,000 men gathered outside and jostled and shouted at workers, and called them scabs and other names. In the afternoon a second ballot also decided against striking. Finally, at a third meeting after working hours, by which time many of the workers had gone home, 'The men then agreed to stop work rather than stand the abuse they had received. There was no apparent desire on their part to strike. No request for a 40-hour week had been made to the management'.[9]

George Lingard, a blacksmith at the North British Railway Company Cowlairs works, and a member of the Amalgamated Society of Engineers (ASE), reported an almost unanimous vote against strike action was overturned by individual meetings in departments on Monday morning. Lingard claimed not all the men in his department were summoned to it, and several did not know it was being held. As he put it, 'There are some of the people now in these Societies who go on holding meetings till one ultimately gives them the result they wish'.[10] Lingard remained at work until 29 January, using different ways in and out of the works to avoid the pickets. The head foreman reported that Lingard had had a deputation of seven men at his home on the evening of 29 January and was now in such fear he had stopped work.[11] Even the usually sympathetic *Manchester Guardian* thought many of those absent from work were unwilling participants and the strike was consequently unsustainable, and as the Chairman of Edinburgh Trades Council had put it, 'in this 40 hours movement all semblance of democracy had been thrown to the winds'.[12]

Strike pamphleteer D. S. Morton described the mass picket during the Forty Hours Strike of up to 10,000 workers as 'entirely legal', echoing a claim in the *Strike Bulletin* of 9 February 1919 which in turn quoted the Sheriff of Dumbarton, that picketing was legal whether by one man or 10,000.[13] John Foster suggests the intimidation of workers by mass picketing was largely a baseless accusation made by the employers.[14] However, the contemporary news reports, precognitions and trial evidence strongly suggest otherwise.

To keep order at these pickets, the police used a range of actions, up to and including baton charges. On 28 January, the Chief Constable issued orders to his force about keeping order while not preventing legal picketing:

> It is reported that men have been deterred by intimidation from going to their work.

Strong patrols should be kept adjacent to the entrances to works . . . during hours of entering and leaving to afford the fullest possible protection to men who desire to continue work. Strikers should not be permitted to assemble in force at the entrances or on the adjacent roadway. If found obstructing the roadway near a work they should be dispersed and free access kept.

While peaceful picketing – that is, peacefully persuading any person to abstain from working – is not to be interfered with while it is carried out by individuals, it cannot be considered peaceful picketing when a number of strikers acting together obstruct or accost a man entering or leaving. Such action would be clearly intimidation.

In his precognition, the Chief Constable described the precautions he had taken since before the strike commenced, making explicit reference to the threat to the tram system:

I had repeated intimations of attempts to arrange a general strike for Monday 27th January. Intimation also reached me that attacks on the tram cars were intended. Following thereon I made special arrangements to have men in reserve at the different Divisions over the City.[15]

His order of 26 January set out the reserve arrangements:

A strike of Clyde Workers is called for Monday, 27th instant, and it is rumoured that the Strike will be accompanied by disorder. An attack on the tramway cars passing through Govan is threatened . . .

A peaceable meeting or an orderly procession which does not unduly disturb the traffic should not be interfered with, but if a meeting or a procession should become disorderly either by organised obstruction of the traffic, or injury to the persons or property of the lieges, it should be broken up and the ringleaders arrested if possible.[16]

His order included instructions that men from each of eleven police divisions – a total of 171 men – were to be held in reserve, as well as ten mounted men. The trams were already considered to be at risk and a potential flashpoint.

The Chief Constable told the trial he believed 'the processions were interfering more with the traffic as the week went on' and that this was reported to him as deliberate. Dealing with a question concerning the management of processions, he said, 'It is endeavoured to keep the procession in the left side so that they won't interfere with the traffic in the centre of the street, and that is done more or less successfully'.[17] Discussing the issue of trams and processions the following day, the Lord Provost described how, after the meeting with the strikers' delegation on Wednesday 29 January, he had consulted the Sheriff and the Chief Constable, as part of the 'active preparations against the violent obstruction of the pavement', but he denied there had been any subsequent discussion about details. He said only that the 'whole intention was to secure that the public services of the city should not be interrupted'.[18]

The War Cabinet met twice on 28 January, at noon and again at 3pm. The second meeting's main subject was the demobilisation of parts of the army, considering Winston Churchill's scheme for a fairer system.[19] The only other item, 'Industrial Unrest', occupied the last part of the meeting. Sir Robert Horne, the Minister of Labour, outlined the aims of the strikes in Glasgow and Belfast, expressing his belief that both strikes had been 'disavowed by the Union leaders'. Horne was concerned that he and the government could not be seen to 'actively interfere in the settlement of these strikes over the heads of the Union Executives'. Significantly, Horne felt the newspapers had been 'unduly alarmist about the situation'. Austen Chamberlain, MP, one of the three War Cabinet members present, regretted the 'increased reliance placed on the Government as the ultimate arbiter in labour disputes'. Robert Munro,* the Scottish Secretary, stated that

* (Lord) Robert Munro (1868-1955). Born Ross-shire. Advocate at the Scottish Bar 1893. King's Counsel 1910. Liberal MP for Wick Burghs 1910 until abolition of the seat in 1918. MP for Roxburgh and Selkirk to 1922. Lord Advocate 1913-1916. Scottish Secretary 1916-1922. Lord Justice-Clerk 1922-1933. Peerage 1934. Government whip in wartime coalition government 1940.

'certain leading Glasgow citizens' suggested the need for 'unofficial propaganda'. Bonar Law agreed:

> The War Cabinet requested the Minister for Labour to give to the Press, at latest on the following day the full facts regarding the present unrest, laying stress on the unauthorised character of the strikes.[20]

On 28 January 1919, Bonar Law wrote to Lloyd George to tell him the King was in a 'funk' about the prospect of revolution. Bonar Law decided to quell these fears by supporting the proposal made by the War Cabinet to Horne.[21]

Wednesday Morning, 29 January 1919

By comparison with Tuesday, Wednesday was a much more eventful day. What happened had a direct causative effect on Friday's events. Fifty-two witnesses for the prosecution and thirteen for the defence gave pre-trial statements and/or evidence at the trial concerning events on 29 January. Some were present only at specific times and places, while some provided no information of any great significance, or only corroborated the evidence of others. The prosecution precognitions were taken within a fortnight of the events.

The most immediate reports covering events on 29 January were published in the establishment, anti-union and anti-strike *Glasgow Herald* and the strikers' own *Strike Bulletin*. By the time they were published on 30 January, words spoken on 29 January had not yet become key elements in a criminal prosecution, and consequently lack the obvious bias detectable in some trial evidence on both sides. The *Glasgow Herald*'s leading article, probably written or at least approved by the editor, Sir Robert Bruce,* was sneering in tone; the motives of the strike leaders and a 'terrorist' minority were cast in the darkest terms, with hints of origins in psychological damage

* Sir Robert Bruce (1871-1955) was the son of an Alloa shoemaker. Working as a journalist by 1891. London correspondent for the *Aberdeen Journal* from 1895. Joined *Glasgow Herald* in 1898. Assistant editor 1914. Editor 1917 to 1936. Conservative in outlook, but with a reputation for taking his own line. Married with four children.

caused by the war.[22] There was also considerable coverage of the 'rough handling' of non-strikers by pickets, ballot 'fixing' and violence.[23] However, much of what the newspaper published on that subject can be corroborated.

The *Glasgow Herald*'s reporting of Wednesday's events was extensive, covering another meeting at St Andrew's Halls, marches to the power stations at Pinkston and Port Dundas, a key meeting with the Lord Provost, and various speeches in the Square, as well as the government's refusal up to that point to intervene.[24] The *Herald* also confirmed the shocking news that the Carters' Union, led by Hugh Lyon, had accepted the offer of a 48-hour week and were, therefore, out of the strike.[25]

The *Glasgow Herald*'s leading article, reporting carefully selected quotes from the strike leaders during Monday's and Tuesday's events, greatly contributed to the 'unduly alarmist' tone of mainstream media coverage thereafter:

> Obviously this is the language of revolutionaries. People who have any real respect for 'constitutional' methods do not angrily demand that the life of a busy community shall be suspended either for the purpose of allowing a large number of voluntarily idle persons to demonstrate the already conspicuous fact that they are idle, or in order that they may violently achieve by the exercise of force, an object which they could not accomplish by reasoned arguments.[26]

William Gallacher spoke to a meeting at 10am, in a cinema in Partick. According to Detective Sergeant Ross, he urged the men present to form up in procession to St Andrew's Halls, from where they would proceed to Port Dundas and Pinkston Power Stations 'to bring out the men who were working there. He said if they were successful in taking out these men it would stop all the tram cars and inconvenience the businessmen of the City'.[27] The *Glasgow Herald* described 'an enormous crowd' in St Andrew's Halls, overflowing into the street and also described the procession (singular) that formed after further speeches as being almost a mile in length. Shinwell was reported to have said:

> When we leave this hall we are going to take a walk in an orderly way with bands heading the procession to the power stations for the purpose of holding a meeting. (Laughter.) On the road we will not permit our ranks to be broken.[28]

At trial, Herbert Highton reported Shinwell had referred to the need for 'being orderly' and:

> referred generally to the desire for conducting the meeting as a purely industrial meeting, and pointed out what endeavours had been made to represent it as a revolutionary meeting, and that we must not allow anything to intervene, and he referred to the red flag [on 27 January] as an intervention by people who had nothing to do with us.[29]

Defence witness John Angus mentioned Shinwell's reference to 'the importance of getting the Municipal Employees out' because if the electrical and municipal workers joined them the strike would only last a few days.[30] The failure of the strike committee to persuade the Municipal Employees' Association (MEA) to come out fuelled a resentment in some strikers, which was played out on the streets. The continued running of the trams was the most visible manifestation of the failure of the Clyde Workers' Committee to promote their cause to a wider body of workers.

According to Sergeant John Steele, outside the St Andrew's Halls, speaker Andrew Smith told the crowd to march to Pinkston Power Station and en route 'they were not to allow their ranks to be broken by any traffic' nor were they 'to be afraid of the Soldiers'. In context, this latter seems to have been a general rather than a specific remark expressing a fear of the military being used against the strike. Steele and Constable Turner described the procession holding up the tramway traffic deliberately, 'in accordance with the advice which Smith had given them. Hopkins held up his hands frequently en route and told the crowd to stop the tram cars'.[31] The *Strike Bulletin* confirmed the 'strikers afterwards marched in processional order to Pinkston Power Station and to George Square, the trams being held up en route'.[32] Two processions set off from St Andrew's Halls to the two power stations. One, accompanied by Hopkins, to Pinkston Power Station, never reached George Square. The other, which Highton accompanied, reached the Square via Port Dundas.[33]

The Power Stations

Port Dundas Power Station was run by the city's Electricity Department and provided power for the streetlighting, major public buildings and for sale to large industrial concerns. These industrial sites included the large engineering works most severely hit by the strike. Closing Port Dundas would affect the industrial concerns' capacity to operate, even if men wanted to work. Employees of the Electricity Department were already on a 48-hour week, an hour longer than the offer of 47 hours made to the engineering workers before the Forty Hours Strike commenced.[34]

The processions going to and from Port Dundas also 'deliberately held up' the trams by walking in the middle of the thoroughfare. 'They shouted to the drivers of the [tram] cars to stop which, of course, the drivers had to do' and 'deliberately zigg zagged across the track.

6.2. *A strikers' procession, Tuesday 28 January 1919 (*Bulletin, *29 January 1919).*

6.3. *A placard in a procession on Tuesday 28 January 1919, showing a blackleg being hanged (*Bulletin*, 29 January 1919).*

They would not allow the cars to pass'.[35] A photograph published in Glasgow's *The Bulletin* captured the procession on its way to Port Dundas. It shows there was room, at least from the angle of the photograph, for the procession to march without obstructing the trams.

At Port Dundas, Constable Davidson described a solid mass of 5,000-6,000 'congregated outside the works gates. No passage was left to allow any person who wished to enter or leave the works'.[36] Shinwell gave a speech reported by the *Glasgow Herald* in which he castigated the 'miserable attitude of the Municipal Employees' Association' and said, 'The workers on strike . . . were not going to allow friend or foe to stand in their way in enforcing the demand for the 40 hours week'.[37] Constable Gallagher added that Shinwell also asked the workers and the power station to come out and he threatened to 'keep them out of the Power Station' if they attempted to re-enter after their break.[38]

Inspector John Florence, who was corroborated by three colleagues, but not by any independent witness, gave a detailed account of Shinwell's speech:

> If I ask you to burst these gates and take the men out by the back of the neck there is nothing here to prevent you. There is a body of Police behind the gate but in spite of any force put up against us and we mean to attain our object and bring the capitalists to their knees . . . were it not for the despicable attitude taken by the Municipal Employees Association this fight would have been won before now. The time for bursting gates has not yet come and if those men are not out by to-morrow we will burst the gates and drag them out. We are out here to see this matter to a finish and I am of opinion that before it's finished there will be blood spilt.[39]

Florence also reported, again uncorroborated, that Kirkwood said:

> The Municipal Employees Association is not represented in this demonstration but if they do not join us we will not allow them to work as scabs. We mean to attain our object no matter what obstacles may be placed on our way we will sweep them aside, even although the street should run with human blood. You must stand together and trust your leaders who will see you through at whatever cost.[40]

According to Constable Gallagher, 'Kirkwood then asked the strikers to form into processional order and to march to George Square' and he instructed them 'not to allow their ranks to be broken on the way'. Constable Gallagher 'followed the strikers to Sauchiehall Street . . . Traffic was deliberately held up the whole way'.[41]

The picket was successful: the staff of Port Dundas joined the strike. At first, three men were to be left on duty to provide essential power to hospitals and the streetlights, but Shinwell reportedly demanded on 30 January that this be reduced to two men, to maintain power to 'infirmaries and Hospitals only'.[42] The opportunities for public disorder and criminality in the absence of streetlighting were a matter of great concern, as was demonstrated by the emphasis given to the maintenance of the streetlighting in the War Cabinet's discussion on 30 January 1919.[43] The Chief Engineer, Mr Lackie, and three men were, however, able to maintain all the streetlighting, although supplies to all factories were cut off. Thursday's *Glasgow-Herald* interpreted the Strike Committee's actions as a breach of their 'undertaking' to stay their hand until Friday, which would be given to the Lord Provost at the meeting about to take place on Wednesday afternoon.[44]

Pinkston Power Station, on the banks of the Forth and Clyde Canal, was a short distance east of Port Dundas and 2km as the crow flies from St Andrew's Halls (Map 2). Pinkston was run by the Tramways Department, and supplied power solely for the tram system. Shutting down Pinkston would only stop the trams. Tram Inspectors Ramsay and McCaskill followed the march from St Andrew's Halls to Pinkston, noting the procession 'persistently refused to allow cars to pass them', which the *Strike Bulletin* also confirmed.[45]

The crowd of strikers, about 7,000-8,000 strong, arrived at Pinkston around 12.30pm. The station's manager, David Baillie, called his men together to ask who would 'remain faithful', promising they would be 'well paid, have ample food, bedding, tobacco and comfort'. Pinkston storeman, Charles Lynn, called and chaired a meeting to decide if the men would 'stand by the management'. A representative later informed Baillie that the men would remain until 5pm. Some who had left for a break at 1pm and 3pm did not, or could not, return. Others departed during the day or simply did not arrive for their shift.[46]

The crowd was addressed at Pinkston by Harry Hopkins and a man named Ogilvie in the police evidence. Both police witnesses claimed Hopkins compared what the people in Dublin had done with what the crowd in Glasgow could do, if they were 'properly united'; it was assumed referring to the 1916 rising.[47] Ogilvie was reported as saying a rope on the building opposite would be 'fine for hanging men like . . . Tzar Dalrymple', the manager of the Tramways Department. He encouraged the crowd to hamper the shift change at 3pm.[48] Detective Sergeant James Wilson reported Hopkins said:

> I call upon you men to see that no workmen get into the Power Station at the change of shift . . . If the men in Pinkston do not come out we will go in and drag them out . . .[49]

Thursday's *Glasgow Herald* reported only that an 'appeal to the workers' had been made outside the gates, while Wednesday's *Evening Times* confirmed the men in Pinkston had not come out on strike.[50]

At 12.55pm at the busy junction of Argyle Street, Jamaica Street and Union Street, south-west of George Square, Constable Donald McDonald witnessed the procession commandeer a tramcar to provide an impromptu speaking platform for Kirkwood who, in the company of Shinwell and Gallacher, addressed the crowd for ten minutes from the open upstairs balcony. Kirkwood reportedly shouted, 'Never mind holding up the traffic boys. We are the workers and the cars belong to us'. The female conductor of the halted tram tried repeatedly to replace the trolley, while the strikers kept removing it.[51] Tram Inspectors Ramsay and McCaskill corroborated these accounts, noting, 'A block at this point practically paralyses the whole tramway system in the City'.[52] The *Glasgow Herald* reported the seizure of the tram while the *Manchester Guardian* and *Scotsman* recounted a brief episode of bottle-throwing by the marchers.[53] The *Strike Bulletin*'s version stated 'At the junction of Argyle and Union Streets the strikers stopped the tram traffic entirely until the procession past [sic]'.[54]

At 1pm, the Town Clerk Sir John Lindsay* reported the procession arriving at George Square, estimating its size between 7,000 and 10,000 people.[55] Police Lieutenant Lawrence Gray, having been advised of the meeting, was positioned in front of the Municipal Buildings in charge of a considerable body of police 'with instructions to prevent the strike leaders addressing the crowd from the ornamental stone-work of the Buildings', which had been ordered by the Chief Constable after Monday's meeting. Gray estimated the crowd between 4,000 and 5,000.[56]

A number of sources recorded another attempt to raise the red flag: 'on the flag staff at the front of the Municipal Buildings but a

* Sir John Lindsay, KBE, DL, JP (1860-1927). Started working for Glasgow Council in 1891. Appointed Town Clerk 1912. Author of publications on the law and history of Glasgow. Described as '. . . a leading authority on municipal law and procedure . . . a man of great ability [with] a genial personality which enabled him to guide successive Town Councils in Glasgow through difficult times with great success'. Knighted in 1915. Retired 1927.

constable cut the rope with his knife and pulled it down: some of the crowd made to rush him.[57] What followed – the strikers' meeting with the Lord Provost – became the catalyst for the violence on Friday. The marches across the city during Wednesday morning and early afternoon gave strikers the opportunity to display their anger with the non-striking tram staff, as they took every opportunity to block the tram traffic. Strike leaders had spoken in heated terms about the how the strike would be over quickly if the tram-workers would only come out. The growing resentment towards the non-striking MEA and the tram system was the proximate cause of the riot on Friday, and the failure of the strike leadership to shut down the tram system by means other than persuading the tram crews to strike – the closure of Pinkston Power Station – further raised the stakes.

---

1. D. S. Morton, *The Forty Hours Strike: An Historic Survey of the First General Strike in Scotland* (Clydebank Branch SLP, 1919), p.7.
2. *Glasgow Herald*, 29 January 1919.
3. W. W. Knox (ed), *Scottish Labour Leaders 1918-1939: A Biographical Dictionary* (Mainstream, 1984), p.167.
4. *Glasgow Herald*, 29 January 1919.
5. B. Weinberger, *Keeping the Peace: Policing Strikes in Britain, 1906-1926* (Berg, 1991), pp.9, 15.
6. AD15/19/11 [B63], Andrew Edgar; AD15/19/11 [B64], Ernest Board; AD15/19/11 [B57], George Lingard, Blacksmith.
7. AD15/19/11 [B63], Edgar.
8. AD15/19/11 [B29], Michael Mckeown, Timekeeper, Mechans; [B30], William Harrison, Manager, Mechans.
9. AD15/19/11 [B52], Thomas Johnston, Works Manager.
10. AD15/19/11 [B57], George Lingard, Blacksmith.
11. AD15/19/11 [B55], William Henderson, Head Foreman.
12. *Manchester Guardian*, 30 January 1919. Chairman, Edinburgh Trades Council, *Glasgow Herald*, 29 January 1919. See also Edinburgh Trades Council *Annual Report 1919*, p.9, for further criticism
13. Morton, *Forty Hours Strike*, p.12; Weinberger, *Keeping the Peace*, pp.152, 154.
14. J. Foster, 'Mobilising Working Class Action on Clydeside, 1919 and 1971: How the Arguments Were Won', *Colloque Internationale Discours et Dispositivs Anti-syndicaux* (Lyon, 2010), p.30.

15. AD15/19/11 [A05], James Verdier Stevenson, Chief Constable.
16. AD15/19/11 [A05], Stevenson.
17. AD15/19/11 [A05], Stevenson.
18. JC36/31/03 [03/C], James W. Stewart, Lord Provost.
19. CAB23/9/8, War Cabinet Minutes, meeting 521, 28 January 1919.
20. CAB23/9/8, War Cabinet Minutes, meeting 521, 28 January 1919.
21. Lloyd George Papers, F/30/3/9, Bonar Law to Lloyd George, 28 January 1919, quoted in N. H. Morrison, *Official Responses to Industrial Unrest in Post-War Britain, 1919-1921* (PhD thesis, University of Swansea, 1986), p.71.
22. *Glasgow Herald*, 30 January 1919.
23. *Glasgow Herald*, 30 January 1919.
24. *Glasgow Herald*, 30 January 1919.
25. *Glasgow Herald*, 30 January 1919.
26. *Glasgow Herald*, 30 January 1919.
27. AD15/19/11 [A50], George Ross, Detective Sergeant.
28. *Glasgow Herald,* 30 January 1919.
29. JC36/31/07 [07/B], Herbert Highton.
30. JC36/31/08 [08/K], John Angus.
31. AD15/19/11 [A08], John Steele, Police Sergeant; JC36/31/03 [03/G], John Steele, Police Sergeant; AD15/19/11 [A09], James Ritchie, Police Constable.
32. JC36/31/08 [A19], Thomas Turner, Police Constable. *The Strike Bulletin*, no.1, 30 January 1919, p.4.
33. JC36/31/07 [07/B], Highton.
34. Minutes of the Corporation of Glasgow, 30 January 1919.
35. AD15/19/11 [A14], Robert Davidson, Police Constable; AD15/19/11 [A17], Andrew Gallacher, Police Constable; AD15/19/11 [A07] and JC36/31/02 [02/E], Andrew Imrie, Tram Inspector; AD15/19/11 [B22], Florence, Inspector.
36. AD15/19/11 [A14], Robert Davidson, Police Constable.
37. *Glasgow Herald,* 30 January 1919.
38. AD15/19/11 [A17], Gallacher, Police Constable.
39. AD15/19/11 [B18], John Florence, Police Inspector; AD15/19/11 [A17], Gallacher, Police Constable.
40. AD15/19/11 [B18], Florence, Police Inspector.
41. AD15/19/11 [A17], Gallacher, Police Constable.

42. *Glasgow Herald*, 30 January 1919; AD15/19/11 [B16], William Roxburgh, Clerk.
43. CAB23/9/9, War Cabinet Minutes, meeting 522, 30 January 1919.
44. *Glasgow Herald,* 30 January 1919.
45. AD15/19/11 [B14], Ramsay, Tram Inspector; [B15], Allan McCaskill, Tram Inspector; *Strike Bulletin*, 30 January 1919, p.4.
46. AD15/19/11 [B58], David Baillie, Manager, Pinkston; [B59], John Wilson, Foreman Engineer, Pinkston; [B60], Charles Lynn, Storeman, Pinkston.
47. AD15/19/11 [A08], Steele, Police Sergeant; [A09], Ritchie, Police Constable.
48. AD15/19/11 [A08], Steele, Police Sergeant; [A19], Thomas Turner, Police Constable.
49. AD15/19/11 [A33], James Wilson, Detective Sergeant.
50. *Glasgow Herald*, 30 January 1919; [Glasgow] *Evening Times,* 29 January 1919; AD15/19/11 [B58], Baillie, Manager, Pinkston.
51. AD15/19/11 [B10], Donald Mcdonald, Police Constable; AD15/19/11 [B12], Arthur Clark, Police Constable.
52. AD15/19/11 [B15], Allan McCaskill, Tram Inspector; AD15/19/11 [B14], Ramsay, Tram Inspector.
53. *Manchester Guardian*, 30 January 1919; *The Scotsman*, 30 January 1919.
54. *Strike Bulletin*, 30 January 1919.
55. AD15/19/11 [A04], Sir John Lindsay, Town Clerk.
56. AD15/19/11 [A20], Lawrence Gray, Police Lieutenant.
57. AD15/19/11 [A29], Louis Noble, Detective Inspector.

7 Afternoon, Wednesday 29 January 1919: the Meeting with the Provost

> I went to see the Lord Provost of Glasgow asking him to [make] . . . a request that the Government should intervene in order to settle the strike . . .[1]

> . . . a huge crowd gathered and a delegation of strike leaders led by Shinwell went in to ask the Lord Provost to communicate with the government on their behalf. He agreed . . .[2]

These quotations, one by a protagonist, the other by a popular historian, are typical of the way the meeting between the strikers' delegation and the Lord Provost has been described.[3] If the defence evidence led at the trial was correct, however, neither version is true. Six defence witnesses swore Shinwell, although present, was not even part of the delegation, let alone its leader; and almost as many witnesses testified that the delegation had no set purpose at all. The prosecution used its understanding of the meeting to prove threats of violence had been made, by what the *Glasgow Herald* described as 'a blustering, threatening delegation of lawless men'.[4]

What was said at this meeting, and what was understood to have been said, became a direct cause of the violence on Friday. The efforts made by those present and by others since to control the narrative (in Neil Maclean's case to the extent of risking perjuring himself at trial and in Shinwell's to invent things) confirms its significance. The trial evidence indicates the delegation, although presented as an off-the-cuff initiative arising from the crowd in the Square, was in reality pre-planned by Shinwell, to evade the instructions of Tuesday's national conference not to involve government,[5] but that he lost control of the meeting, with dire results. Beyond the importance of this meeting and the telegram sent to Westminster afterwards, it is pivotal to understanding Friday's events to unravel the detail of the meeting: how it happened, who was there, who planned it and how the narrative has been steered. No evidence-based account of the meeting, the formation of the delegation or the outcomes and consequences of the meeting has ever been published. It is unsustainable to continue to ignore what happened and to allow the simplistic paraphrase 'there was a delegation, and a telegram was sent' to underpin an inaccurate grand narrative.[6] Both sides at the trial used what was said, and what was understood to have been said, at the meeting to try to attribute blame for Friday. The conflict of interpretation of often untruthful evidence became pivotal to counsel's arguments for both sides in the subsequent trial.

There were eleven or twelve participants. No minute was taken. At the trial, four defence witnesses gave evidence: Harvey, Sim, Kennedy and Neil Maclean MP, who put the defence case most coherently and in greatest detail. Not called to give evidence at their trial, David Kirkwood and Emanuel Shinwell later briefly described events in their memoirs.[7] Five defence witnesses gave evidence only concerning events in the Square, the selection of the delegates and the role of Shinwell, Kirkwood and Maclean.[8] The people at the meeting, or who entered the City Chambers, or who were reported erroneously as being present, were:

Present

Isaac Sim	Engineer. Discharged soldier
William Harvey	Member, Amalgamated Society of Engineers
Donald Kennedy	Miner
Delegates 4, 5 and 6	Unidentified
The 'seventh man'	Not identified. 'Erratic'. Blamed for many of the problematic contributions. Did he exist?
Emanuel Shinwell	Claimed not to be part of the deputation. Introduced the delegation.
David Kirkwood	Claimed not to be part of the delegation.
Neil Maclean MP	Claimed not to be part of the delegation.
James W. Stewart	Lord Provost
Sir John Lindsay	Town Clerk

Not Present

'The woman'	Did not get beyond the stairs; also failed to gain entry on Friday.
Harry Hopkins	Initially named in the Town Clerk's precognition in error.
Chief Constable and the Sheriff of Lanarkshire	Erroneously named as present by the *Glasgow Herald*.

For the prosecution, the Town Clerk provided a precognition and detailed testimony.[9] The Lord Provost gave his implausible and self-exculpatory version in a statement to fellow councillors on 6 February and provided only a brief precognition; at trial he was led through the events by the Lord Advocate.[10]

There is a clear tendency in the evidence of both the Lord Provost and Neil Maclean MP to remove themselves as far as possible from involvement in or responsibility for events. The Lord Provost dramatised the narrative to play up the perceived threat and his own prescience, and Maclean's evidence is, in places, as the Lord Advocate tactfully put it, 'thin'. Maclean was the final defence witness. His evidence was led by Mr Constable who tried to disassociate the MP from the organisers of the strike. Maclean's 'accidental' involvement in the key events in George Square on the 27, 29 and 31 January was treated with some sarcasm by the Lord Advocate in cross-examination, who suggested his involvement was 'more like design'.[11]

Neil Maclean was speaking to friends in George Square when he turned round to find, 'a suggestion had been made from the crowd [during Shinwell's speech] to send a deputation to the Lord Provost, and Councillor Shinwell was putting that request to the crowd to find out if they were favourable to it'. The delegates were called forward and 'Councillor Shinwell intimated that being a rank and file deputation they had to go in themselves . . . and they could arrange the order of the speakers themselves'.[12] John Angus and Archibald Gillies reported, however, neither Shinwell nor Kirkwood seemed very anxious the deputation should go in.[13] Isaac Sim, in contrast, claimed

Shinwell 'thought it was a good idea . . . and asked that a deputation of six be appointed from the ranks of the strikers *to visit the Lord Provost and ask him to use his influence with the Government*' (our emphasis).[14] Sim was the *only* defence witness to claim this purpose was already explicit at this stage, although Chief Detective Inspector Weir also reported, and was corroborated by Detective Inspector Noble, that Shinwell asked the crowd 'to form a deputation to represent the strikers to urge the Lord Provost to send a message to the authorities to have the strike settled'.[15] Sim volunteered, feeling he went 'representing the discharged and demobilised soldiers'.[16] According to Herbert Highton, Shinwell suggested the deputation should be composed of people from the crowd, and should include none of the Strike Committee officials.[17] Donald Kennedy, a miner from Ayr, had been on his way to St Enoch Station when he met the procession in Argyle Street, and turned into George Square with them. Unknown people put Kennedy's name forward as a delegate. His object in accompanying the delegation was 'as a Trade Unionist and as a follower of Christ for the benefit of all mankind'. He said he had 'not been appointed at all' and, when asked how he was allowed to come along, answered 'I cannot say'.[18]

How much time elapsed between the suggestion of the delegation, its selection, and their negotiating entry to the Chambers has been impossible to ascertain, nor how long it took the men to get to the library, nor exactly how long the Lord Provost kept them waiting. It is therefore impossible to know if the men had sufficient time to discuss and agree any sort of agenda.

Six witnesses (Mitchell, Gillies, Harvey, Sim, Kennedy and Maclean MP) stated under oath that Shinwell, Maclean and Kirkwood were not actually members of the delegation but were present only because the actual delegation could not otherwise gain access to the City Chambers.[19] Maclean described the circumstances at the Chambers' door:

> They were . . . not allowed to enter and they called over to the Chairman of the meeting, Councillor Shinwell, that they could not get in. He went over and Mr Kirkwood went along with him. They evidently were held back also and as I thought

> I might be of some service I went across too. They were for keeping me out until Councillor Shinwell intimated who I was.[20]

It is not clear in this account why Maclean and Kirkwood went beyond the entrance. Maclean, in response to a question as to whether Shinwell, Kirkwood or himself had been intended to form part of the deputation, replied:

> No, there was no one but those who had volunteered or had been nominated from the crowd, and I would not have been there but for the holding up of the deputation at the doorway.[21]

Whatever the evidence from the defence witnesses, it was clear that Shinwell, Kirkwood and Maclean were seen by the Town Clerk and Lord Provost not merely as members of the delegation, but the only delegates of any substance, because they recalled they did most of the talking.[22] Isaac Sim was the only witness to deny Shinwell's and Kirkwood's greater contribution.[23] In a speech Shinwell made to seamen on 30 January, he reportedly described himself as 'one of a deputation to the Lord Provost on the previous day'.[24]

D. S. Morton's account, published before the April trial, adds to the confusion: 'Mr David Kirkwood and Mr Neil Maclean, M.P. for Govan, together with a few discharged soldiers, made up a deputation' and Shinwell 'agreed to accompany them' as 'they had been unable to gain admission' to the Chambers.[25] The *Strike Bulletin*'s version of events, written for Thursday 30 January's issue, names *only* Shinwell, Kirkwood and Maclean as delegates, the three who at the trial were sworn not to be delegates at all! Presumably this represented the 'official' line that the delegation had been intended to comprise Shinwell, Maclean and Kirkwood; the other individuals merely giving the deputation a veneer of spontaneity.

Of the two other people who are claimed to have accompanied this group, the 'seventh man' was supposedly allowed into the meeting, but an eighth delegate, a woman, was turned away.[26] William Harvey reported that the woman, when asked why she was there, said she was 'on some mission for the Lord' to which Kirkwood had responded 'it was no place for a subject like that'.[27] Harvey reported that the woman also appeared in the library at Friday's second visit to the Lord Provost, 'but we told her to go away'.[28] She has remained impossible to identify.

Thus, the composition and purpose of the delegates who mounted the stairs to the City Chambers' library was unclear from the outset and remained confused at April's trial. Neil Maclean told the court that the men had determined no programme for the meeting, and he had 'no idea what they were intending to say . . . or what was their purpose'.[29]

Although Kirkwood and Maclean appear to have had no locus even in getting the deputation into the Buildings, and Shinwell had no locus once he had facilitated entry, it is not clear what the delegation might have said or done had Shinwell, Kirkwood and Maclean not been present. It is likely that Shinwell, Maclean and probably Kirkwood were always intended to be the real delegation, and they alone knew what the meeting was intended to achieve. The Lord Provost claimed to have been left in no doubt as to the delegation's aims when he enquired of Shinwell, who he recalled had responded 'they had come to ask me to remove the tramway cars from the streets . . . the next morning'.[30]

Although Isaac Sim suggested the meeting had intended from the first 'to visit the Lord Provost and ask him to use his influence with the Government', Sim himself contradicted this retrospective and problematically tidy narrative in the witness box:

> Q. . . . had you any prior consultation as to what your line of policy should be or what proposal you should combine to make to the Lord Provost?
>
> A: Not one word, with the exception that some of the strikers said to me to bring up the car incident of driving into the processionists.
>
> Q. So that you were a random lot, each with his own ideas?
>
> A. Yes.[31]

In their memoirs 36 and 16 years later, both Shinwell and Kirkwood also retrospectively imposed meaning and order on events:

> On Wednesday, January 29, 1919, a committee approached the Lord Provost James Stewart to intervene with the Government in favour of a forty-hour week. He agreed, and asked us to come back on Friday, the 31st.[32]

The *Glasgow Herald* mentioned the meeting twice in its 30 January edition: 'Six strikers were appointed as a deputation to see the Lord Provost', and, in an article about the power-station workers, 'the deputation was accompanied by Mr Shinwell, Mr David Kirkwood, and Mr Neil Maclean, MP'. It also claimed, inaccurately, that Sheriff MacKenzie and the Chief Constable were present; they were not.[33]

In his *apologia* to the Council on 6 February, the Lord Provost stated that when informed of the delegation just after 2pm, he had had to make a decision on the spur of the moment whether to meet them, because he claimed to fear the consequences of refusal: disorder directed towards the trams by a crowd 'already beginning to show signs of rowdyism'.[34] Two months later at trial, he said only that he looked out the window and saw a considerable crowd had gathered before the delegation arrived; no other prosecution witness mentioned any 'rowdyism'.[35] He left the meeting he was in and went into the library with Sir John Lindsay to meet the delegation.[36] Everyone agreed Shinwell was the first to speak and that he introduced only Maclean and Kirkwood by name, before everyone shook hands. The Lord Provost recorded he was given 'a fraternal grip of the hand' – a masonic handshake – by one delegate.[37] According to Neil Maclean the delegation was seated:

> in a rather hap-hazard manner that the member sitting next to the Lord Provost should be the first speaker, and so on . . . I think I was in the middle of what was practically a half circle. Mr Kirkwood was on my right and Councillor Shinwell was at the far away end. He would have been the last in order of the speakers if we had kept to the order, but it never got

beyond the first speaker, because the other members of the deputation began chipping in with odd remarks.[38]

Sim, however, claimed he was the first man to speak, at length, about the aims of the strike, asking the Lord Provost to persuade

39 J.W. Stewart (Cross.)

A no one would be so silly as to give such instructions. The
other had some grievance which I did not understand.
But they seemed to have a grievance that the
cars had been driven through the procession? - Yes, and
another had a grievance that women were employed on cars
B at all, and Mr Shinwell pulled him up and said. "We did not
"come here to discuss questions of that sort", and another
~~discharged~~ discharged soldier seemed to have a grievance that
not sufficient was being done for them.
So that there was a general conversation or
C discussion going on the whole time? - Yes.
It was a perfectly pleasant interview? - Yes.
I got a fraternal grip of the hand by some member, and he
said he was very pleased to meet me.
After further discussion you shook hands with
D the deputation as it was going out, and then you went and saw
Sheriff Mackenzie and the Chief Constable to make preparations
for the deputation coming back again? - I did not know whether
they were going to return or not.
Do you mean to say when the deputation left
E you on Wednesday you did not know they were coming back on
Friday? - I did not know.
Did you have a talk with Sir John Lindsay when
they had gone? - I had many meetings with Sir John Lindsay
that week, also with the Chief Constable and the Sheriff of
F Lanarkshire, and others associated with me in preserving
order in the city.
But/

7.1. *Lord Provost James Stewart denies knowledge of Friday's deputation having arranged to meet him. (Reproduced by kind permission; Crown copyright. National Records of Scotland, JC36/31/03.)*

the government to intervene. Sim claimed the subject of the trams was not mentioned until well into the discussion, and then by neither Shinwell nor Kirkwood.[39] William Harvey confirmed Sim was the first speaker after Shinwell's introductions, and he spoke about the purpose of the strike and government intervention.[40] Sim's and Harvey's evidence was, however, contradicted by Neil Maclean, who said the first speaker (whom he did not identify) was the one who introduced the subject of the tramway traffic, and this speaker and the others who interrupted 'rendered the deputation really a hopeless thing altogether'.[41] Donald Kennedy contradicted Sim and Harvey, stating that the matter of the tramcars had been mentioned by Shinwell, Kirkwood and Maclean, of whom Shinwell was the first to refer to it. Although given a hint by defence advocate Watt that the matter had been opened by the discharged soldier, Sim, Kennedy blithely told the court that Shinwell had mentioned:

> In connection with the 40 hours and to try if they could not get the procession led quietly in the streets and to keep the cars from doing any harm and hurting any person.[42]

Sim admitted that there had been 'quite a lengthy discussion about the car services' and claimed during this discussion the 'very erratic' 'seventh man' had said 'if the Lord Provost did not use his influence in getting the cars put off the streets altogether they would damned well take them off'.[43] Defence witness Kennedy also blamed the seventh man for saying the time for constitutional methods was past, and the best thing was 'to remove the cars and to put down the cars'.[44] It should be noted that contemporary reports speak of a six-man delegation (for example, this is the number mentioned by Shinwell in his speech to the crowd immediately after). Was the 'seventh man' an invention to allow the blame for the more violent statements to be placed on someone other than a delegate?

However, defence witness Harvey claimed it had been Shinwell, in his introduction, who had initiated the notion of 'constitutional action', reportedly saying: 'so far we had adopted constitutional action but as time would go on naturally the temper of the crowd might rise' and 'if no efforts were made to meet us, we could not hold responsibility for whatever way the crowd would take action'.[45]

The order of speakers and what they said will never be definitively established. However, what can be ascertained is that Shinwell and later Kirkwood emerged as the speakers of greatest importance and, whatever was claimed at the trial, the discussion of the trams took up a good bit of the meeting. It was as important for the strike leaders to 'get the cars off the street' as it was for the Town Council to maintain this vital service. The importance of preventing organised disruption to the system had been reflected in the Chief Constable's orders of 26 January.[46] The Lord Provost and Town Clerk understood the strikers wanted the tram system to be completely closed down to put pressure on the government, supported by the threat of 'drastic action'. The defence, stressing the trams were only a secondary matter, suggested the delegation had only intended the system to be partly closed, or to be closed completely by persuading the tram staff to strike.

At trial, the defence downplayed the apparent emphasis put on the trams by the delegation. Evidence was led that any suggestion of the trams being removed by any sort of force or 'direct action' or 'unconstitutional action' was a misunderstanding of those terms. Further, the defence advocates and witnesses emphasised the removal of the trams related solely to the safety of marchers, rather than as a weapon to force the government to intervene. But Shinwell had already referred that morning to 'the importance of getting the Municipal Employees out' to hasten the success of the strike.[47]

The terms 'constitutional action' – and its implied opposite 'unconstitutional action' – and 'drastic action' were used both during and after the meeting. The joint defence approach suggested that these phrases referred only to a narrow trade-union meaning, 'unconstitutional methods' being to go out on strike without the official support and approval of the trade-union hierarchy, while 'drastic action' meant the voting out of office of elected trade-union officials. It was a vain attempt to diminish the threats implied by the common meaning of these words, which is how the Lord Provost and Town Clerk understood them, and it was agreed by Sim in cross-examination by the Lord Advocate that this meant they were 'free to use any method, legal or illegal'.[48]

Harvey admitted that no-one had informed the Lord Provost

and Town Clerk that these terms were being used with any narrow meanings and Neil Maclean's explanation of these arcane matters in his testimony was confused.[49] The Lord Advocate, clearly losing patience, suggested Maclean 'knew perfectly well that that did not refer to constitutional means in the strict Trade Union sense . . . it is perfectly plain that you were not thinking about the strict Trade Union meaning at all'.[50] It is difficult to believe otherwise than that the words used were intended in their commonly understood sense, especially in the light of Shinwell's use of the terms in his speech in the Square after the meeting.

The Lord Provost, Sir John and Shinwell all testified that Kirkwood was one of the main contributors on the subject of the trams, and according to Shinwell's authorised biographer Peter Slowe, Kirkwood was also the first to speak at the meeting. Sir John reported Shinwell and Kirkwood both saying 'the object of this deputation representing the crowd outside was to ask His Lordship to order that the tramway cars *throughout the City* should be taken off the streets the next morning' [our emphasis]. He rejected any suggestion that the matter of the trams had been secondary to the delegation's main object: 'In one sense it may have been subsidiary, and in another it was not, for this reason, that the very first request that was made to the Lord Provost was to stop the next morning the tramway cars'.[51] Recounted 74 years later, Slowe's version of events presumably represents how Shinwell wanted the meeting to be remembered. After Shinwell introduced Kirkwood, he:

> . . . took over while Shinwell seethed . . . Kirkwood, now and again backed up by an excitable miner, would talk only about the trams, suggesting how the Lord Provost should call a special meeting of the Tramcars Committee to get them stopped . . . Kirkwood droned on and on . . . [52]

Other evidence suggested Kirkwood spoke no earlier than fifth, after Shinwell's introduction, Sim, Harvey and the alleged 'seventh man'.

What did the Lord Provost and Town Clerk take away from this discussion? The Lord Provost testified, 'Mr Kirkwood shouted to me "We want you to tell the Government we will take the cars off the streets unless they compel the employers to give the forty hours' week"'.[53] Sir John recalled being told the trams being stopped 'was with a view to compelling the Government to intervene in the dispute', and if they did not, 'whilst hitherto they had adopted constitutional methods they would adopt other methods as best suited their purpose' which would completely paralyse 'the business of the City'.[54] The Lord Provost believed 'it was quite plainly stated that if the cars were not taken off in accordance with their request that they would take them off themselves'. On advising 'rather to hesitate to proceed to extremes, that the effect would be to alienate sympathy. Mr Shinwell replied [to the Provost] they did not want sympathy, they wanted a 40 hours week, and that they were going to take any method they required to get it'.[55] Sim alone claimed that Shinwell had said the trams were to be stopped or restricted only where they might clash with processions.[56]

On 29 January, how realistic was it to hope that the tram-workers might strike? Monday's *Glasgow Herald* had reported that mass meetings of Municipal Employees Association (MEA) members had shown little enthusiasm for, or even opposition to, strike action, and the MEA in London had requested members to remain at work, declining to pay strike benefit.[57] Peter Campbell, Joint Secretary of the MEA in Glasgow, was a member of both the Joint Strike Committee and the executive Strike Sub-Committee. Despite the apparent hostility of union HQ and his members, he remained strongly in favour. On 30 January an 'exceedingly lively' mass meeting of about 2,000 tram staff defeated a proposal to stop work immediately on a show of hands, in favour of another to hold a ballot on the matter.[58] Eventually the union reported on 6 February that, 'by a substantial majority the municipal employees have decided against the strike'.[59] Campbell was active in trying to persuade his members to strike, but his claim in evidence at trial that on 29, 30 or even 31 January, it was still an 'open question' as to whether the tramway staff would decide to strike was surely disingenuous.

Iain McLean has attributed the refusal of the employees of the tramways department to join the 1919 Forty Hours Strike to the 'familiar vendettas between skilled and unskilled in engineering', with the Forty Hours Strike being regarded as 'another craftsmen's strike'.[60] However, the bitter memory of the 1911 tram strike may have contributed. The 1911 strike had aimed to force the management to resolve more speedily a long-running dispute about working hours and conditions, fuelled by resentment over 'unnecessary "espionage" by inspectors, fines for petty offences and the system of summary dismissals'.[61] Using non-striking crew, inspectors and timekeepers, the tram management had kept services running. The strikers' frustration had led to violent scenes: attacking vehicles bringing non-strikers into the depots; damaging and derailing trams; causing dangerous collisions. Violent confrontations between large bodies of police and pickets had seen non-strikers surrounded by strikers and freed by baton-wielding policemen.[62] Many tram-workers had been sacked and not reinstated.

In 1919, the tram staff seemed unprepared to risk a similar outcome. In the aftermath of the Forty Hours Strike, John Maclean wrote, 'The failure of the tramwaymen to respond to the strike call embittered the strikers, who on occasions became very nasty to them'. His description of the crowd on Friday 31 January in George Square being 'provoked by the treachery of the tramway men and women' tends to support the role the blocking of trams played in the outbreak of violence. Maclean blamed the failure to strike on the women, who comprised almost half of the staff, who 'had neither interest in the union as a rule nor in any fight for a shorter working week'.[63] Therefore, there was little realistic chance of the tram staff joining the strike on Wednesday 29 January 1919. Whether the delegation fully comprehended this at the time of the meeting remains moot.

As the meeting drew to a close, the Lord Provost and Town Clerk reported the trams were the first matter raised; the removal of the trams was discussed at length, some speakers had become heated on the matter, and the Lord Provost had been asked to convene a meeting of the Tramways Committee for the next day to shut down the whole system, explicitly to put pressure on the government. The Lord Provost claimed Shinwell had said that the men's blood was on the boil.[64] They had listened to threats of 'unconstitutional' or 'drastic' action without explanation of their supposed alternative meanings.[65] Ominous but vague references to Belfast left the Lord Provost not knowing 'what steps they intended to take [in stopping the trams] but the impression they left on my mind was quite distinct . . . and serious'.[66]

At this point in the meeting the idea arose that a telegram should be sent to the government. Several different people have been credited with or claimed for themselves responsibility for this idea: the Lord Provost, who later denied it firmly in cross-examination, Harvey, Sim, Shinwell and Neil Maclean MP, who said:

> It is very difficult to form an idea [of the object of the deputation], and that is why I made the suggestion that the Prime Minister should be asked to intervene. The way matters were being spoken to by the various members, there seemed to be no object at all. The deputation seemed to have been arranged in such a scratch fashion that no objective had been decided upon, and it was to focus the discussion round a particular point that I made the suggestion that the message should be sent. *I did not know at that time that the Strike Committee had at a previous meeting decided not to ask for intervention.*[67] [Our emphasis; actually, the national conference held on Tuesday.]

Sir John Lindsay said the Lord Provost had asked the deputation what they wanted him to do and they said 'to communicate with the Government that unless their request for intervention was at once entertained they would take the matter into their own hands'. They agreed 'to stay their hand' until Friday morning and the Lord Provost agreed to communicate with both the Minister for Labour and the Prime Minister and 'hoped to have their replies for the deputation on Friday at Noon'.[68]

The Lord Provost had taken 'some pencilled jottings', which he re-read to the delegation. He started by referring to the threat of the removal of the trams if the government intervention was not conceded. Neil Maclean said he thought no reference should be made to that particular point in the telegram and he suggested, and the others agreed with him, that the telegrams should be worded that the strikers 'would dislocate by such methods as they thought fit all the business and all the industries of the City if the request was not immediately granted'.[69] Neil Maclean was the only defence witness to claim the wording of the whole telegram from its beginning to the words 'to communicate your reply' had *not* been read out for approval.[70] The telegram eventually sent to Westminster reads:

> I have been waited upon by a deputation appointed by a largely attended meeting of those who are dissatisfied with the present working conditions, and which was held in front of the City Chambers. The deputation consisted of eleven members [odd, as even with the 'seventh man' there were no more than ten] including Messrs Shinwell, Kirkwood and Maclean, M.P. for Govan, and they requested me to represent to the Prime Minister and also to the Minister of Labour that they wished the Government to intervene with the employers in order to secure a reduction of the working hours to forty per week with no reduction in wages so as to provide those who had been demobilised and are without employment. It was further stated that they had hitherto adopted constitutional methods in urging their demand, but that, failing consideration being given to their request by the Government, they would adopt any other methods which they might consider would be likely to advance their cause. They have, however, agreed to delay taking any such action until Friday in order that I may be able to communicate your reply.

The next sentence was added after the delegation had left, and therefore without their consultation:

> I have just learned from the manager of the electricity department that all the men in the generating stations have been compelled to-day to join the strike, and that only sufficient men will be allowed to run the plant necessary to provide lighting and power for hospitals and infirmaries and possibly lighting of private dwelling-houses.[71]

Iain McLean suggests the Lord Provost's additional statement

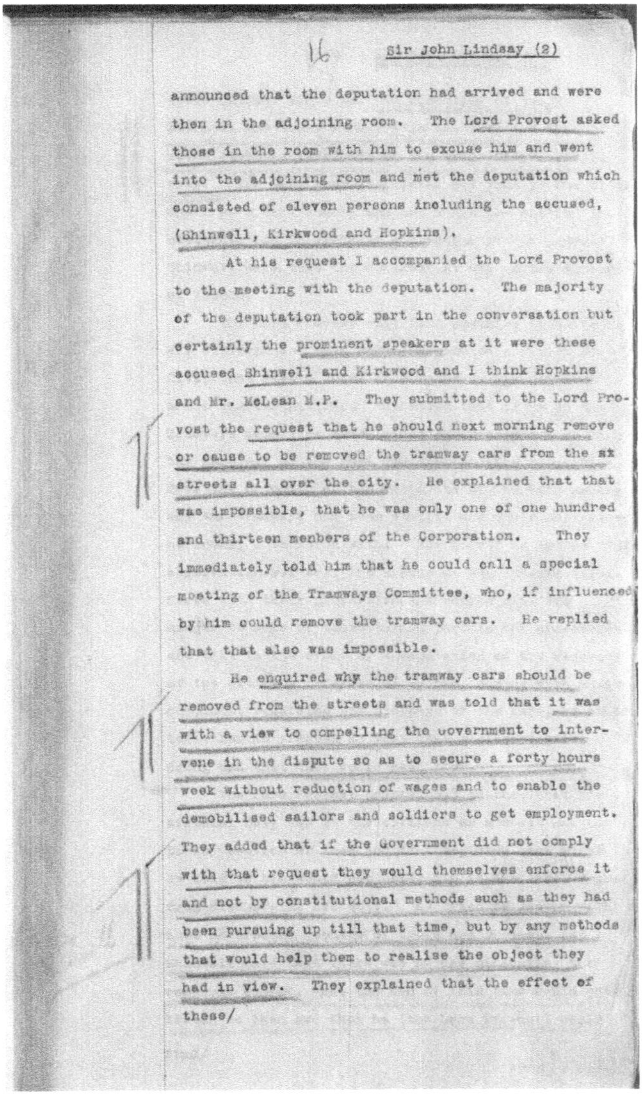

16 Sir John Lindsay (2)

announced that the deputation had arrived and were then in the adjoining room. The Lord Provost asked those in the room with him to excuse him and went into the adjoining room and met the deputation which consisted of eleven persons including the accused, (Shinwell, Kirkwood and Hopkins).

At his request I accompanied the Lord Provost to the meeting with the deputation. The majority of the deputation took part in the conversation but certainly the prominent speakers at it were these accused Shinwell and Kirkwood and I think Hopkins and Mr. McLean M.P. They submitted to the Lord Provost the request that he should next morning remove or cause to be removed the tramway cars from the st streets all over the city. He explained that that was impossible, that he was only one of one hundred and thirteen members of the Corporation. They immediately told him that he could call a special meeting of the Tramways Committee, who, if influenced by him could remove the tramway cars. He replied that that also was impossible.

He enquired why the tramway cars should be removed from the streets and was told that it was with a view to compelling the Government to intervene in the dispute so as to secure a forty hours week without reduction of wages and to enable the demobilised sailors and soldiers to get employment. They added that if the Government did not comply with that request they would themselves enforce it and not by constitutional methods such as they had been pursuing up till that time, but by any methods that would help them to realise the object they had in view. They explained that the effect of these/

7.2. *Town Clerk Sir John Lindsay's precognition describing the start of Wednesday's meeting. (Reproduced by kind permission; Crown copyright. National Records of Scotland, AD15/19/11.)*

about the power stations was untrue which 'misinformed' the War Cabinet, consequently making 'the strike seem more serious than it was'.[72] However, despite the ambiguity in not naming which power station had come out, the Lord Provost had clearly stated, accurately, that the power station run by the Electricity Department (i.e. at Port Dundas), providing electricity to streetlighting and hospitals, was on strike; he did not mention the power station run by the Tramways Department at Pinkston.

Sir John reported that after the delegation left, he and the Lord Provost had together 'made sure that it [the telegram] accurately represented the request definitely made by the deputation'. The text was then typed up and delivered to the Post Office by a member of Sir John's staff.[73] There is no evidence that either the Town Clerk or the Lord Provost tampered with the wording, other than to add the sentence about the power stations. However, both confirmed the meeting had been 'perfectly agreeable'.[74]

At the trial of the strike leaders in the aftermath of the riot on 31 January, some witnesses risked perjuring themselves to fend off responsibility for the violence. Decades later, Shinwell, in particular, reinvented the events to suit his own personal narrative. What is certain, however, is despite what was claimed at the trial, the meeting spent a considerable amount of time discussing the trams, and the Lord Provost and Town Clerk came away from the meeting having heard what they believed to be real threats to close the tram system, perhaps by violent means, to force the hand of government to intervene, with a deadline of Friday for action. Had the delegation been, as some claimed, without purpose, aimless, pointless, until the idea of government intervention was introduced? Or was there another agenda – Shinwell's – in play?

Whatever the intention, the meeting put a real fear of violent unrest in the minds of the Lord Provost and Town Clerk, and thus established the expectations of the local authority and police of violence on Friday, when the deputation was to return to hear the government's response. The trams, as had been the case all week, continued to be the single most obvious sign of the strike's failure and became the lightning-rod for the frustrations of the strikers and their leaders.

1. E. Shinwell, *Conflict without Malice* (Odhams, 1955), p.62.
2. K. MacAskill, *Glasgow 1919: The Rise of Red Clydeside* (Biteback, 2019), p.194.
3. The terms 'delegation' and 'deputation' were used interchangeably in the trial evidence and in other accounts.
4. *Glasgow Herald*, 1 February 1919.
5. See Chapter 6.
6. An anonymous peer-reviewer considered it was 'self-indulgent' to bother with the details of the meeting, because the fact of the meeting itself and the telegram are the only significant outcomes. That reviewer is wrong.
7. JC36/31/08 [08/Q], William Harvey; JC36/31/09 [09/B], Isaac Sim; JC36/31/09 [09/C], Donald Kennedy; JC36/31/09 [09/V], Neil Maclean, MP.
8. JC36/31/05 [05/MM], E. Rosslyn Mitchell; JC36/31/07 [07/B], Herbert Highton; JC36/31/08 [08/J], Archibald Gillies; JC36/31/08 [08/K], John Angus; JC36/31/08 [08/L], Alfred Moloney.
9. AD15/19/11, JC36/31/02 [02/R] and [03/B], Sir John Lindsay, Town Clerk.
10. AD15/19/11 [A03] and JC36/31/03 [03/C], James Stewart, Lord Provost. He had communicated an earlier version to the Engineers' and Shipbuilders' Association on the morning of 31 January, TD241/1/18, *Clyde Shipbuilders Association Minute Book* (Glasgow City Archives).
11. JC36/31/09 [09/V], Maclean, MP.
12. JC36/31/09 [09/V], Maclean, MP.
13. JC36/31/08 [08/K], Angus; JC36/31/08 [08/J], Gillies.
14. JC36/31/09 [09/B], Sim. Isaac Sim's evidence diverges frequently from other defence witnesses' statements; he tends to impose a tidy retrospective narrative.
15. AD15/19/11 [A28], Duncan Weir, Chief Detective Inspector; AD15/19/11 [A29], Louis Noble, Detective Inspector.
16. JC36/31/09 [09/B], Sim.
17. JC36/31/07 [07/B], Highton.
18. JC36/31/09 [09/C], Kennedy.
19. JC36/31/09 [09/V], Maclean, MP; JC36/31/05 [05/MM], Mitchell; JC36/31/08 [08/J], Gillies; JC36/31/09 [09/B], Sim; JC36/31/08 [08/Q], Harvey.
20. JC36/31/09 [09/V], Maclean MP.

21. JC36/31/09 [09/V], Maclean MP.
22. JC36/31/02 [02/R] and [03/B], Lindsay, Town Clerk.
23. JC36/31/09 [09/B], Sim.
24. AD15/19/11 [A17], Andrew Gallacher, Police Constable.
25. D. S. Morton, *The 40 Hours Strike: An Historic Survey of the First General Strike in Scotland* (Clydebank Branch SLP, 1919), p.8.
26. JC36/31/09 [09/B], Sim; JC36/31/09 [09/C], Kennedy.
27. JC36/31/08 [08/Q], Harvey.
28. JC36/31/08 [08/Q], Harvey.
29. JC36/31/09 [09/V], Maclean, MP.
30. JC36/31/03 [03/C], Stewart, Lord Provost.
31. JC36/31/09 [09/B], Sim.
32. D. Kirkwood, *My Life of Revolt* (Harrap, 1935), p.171. Shinwell wrote similarly in E. Shinwell, *Conflict without Malice* (Odhams, 1955), p.62.
33. *Glasgow Herald*, 30 January 1919.
34. *Glasgow Herald*, 7 February 1919.
35. JC36/31/03 [03/C], Stewart, Lord Provost; JC36/31/02 [02/R; 03/B], Lindsay, Town Clerk.
36. AD15/19/11 [A04], Lindsay, Town Clerk.
37. JC36/31/09 [09/B], Sim; JC36/31/03 [03/C], Stewart, Lord Provost.
38. JC36/31/09 [09/V], Maclean, MP.
39. JC36/31/09 [09/B], Sim.
40. JC36/31/08 [08/Q], Harvey.
41. JC36/31/09 [09/V], Maclean, MP.
42. JC36/31/09 [09/C], Kennedy.
43. JC36/31/09 [09/B], Sim.
44. JC36/31/09 [09/C], Kennedy.
45. JC36/31/08 [08/Q], Harvey.
46. AD15/19/11 [A05], Stevenson, Chief Constable.
47. JC36/31/08 [08/K], Angus.
48. JC36/31/09 [09/B], Sim.
49. JC36/31/08 [08/Q], Harvey.
50. JC36/31/09 [09/V], Maclean, MP.
51. JC36/31/02 [02/R; 03/B], Lindsay, Town Clerk.
52. P. M. Slowe, *Manny Shinwell: An Authorised Biography* (Pluto Press, 1993), p.82.

53. JC36/31/03 [03/C], Stewart, Lord Provost. Stewart did not give a detailed precognition in early February and it is arguable that his recall by mid-April had been informed by discussion with his Town Clerk.

54. AD15/19/11 [A04] and JC36/31/02 [02/R] and [03/B], Lindsay, Town Clerk.

55. JC36/31/03 [03/C], Stewart, Lord Provost.

56. JC36/31/09 [09/B], Sim.

57. *Glasgow Herald*, 24 and 27 January 1919.

58. *The Scotsman*, 31 January 1919.

59. *Glasgow Herald,* 7 February 1919.

60. I. McLean, *The Legend of Red Clydeside* (John Donald, 1999), p.119.

61. *Glasgow Herald,* 14 August 1911; W. A. C. Smith, 'The 1911 Tramway Strike', *Scottish Transport,* 25 (1974), p.12.

62. *Glasgow Herald,* 14 August 1911.

63. J. Maclean, *Sack Dalrymple; Sack Stevenson. Let Labour Revenge Bloody Friday* (J. Maclean, 1919), pp.2-4.

64. JC36/31/03 [03/C], Stewart, Lord Provost; AD15/19/11 [A04] Lindsay, Town Clerk; JC36/31/09 [09/B], Sim.

65. JC36/31/08 [08/Q], Harvey.

66. JC36/31/03 [03/C], Stewart, Lord Provost.

67. JC36/31/08 [08/Q], Harvey; JC36/31/09 [09/B], Sim; Shinwell, *Conflict,* p.62; JC36/31/09 [09/V], Maclean, MP.

68. AD15/19/11 [A04], Lindsay, Town Clerk.

69. AD15/19/11 [A04], Lindsay, Town Clerk; JC36/31/03 [03/C], Stewart, Lord Provost.

70. JC36/31/09 [09/V], Maclean, MP.

71. CAB23/9/9, War Cabinet Minutes, meeting 522, 30 January 1919.

72. I. McLean, *The Labour Movement in Clydeside Politics, 1914-1922* (Dphil, University of Oxford, 1972), p.211.

73. AD15/19/11 [A04], Lindsay, Town Clerk.

74. JC36/31/03 [03/C], Stewart, Lord Provost; JC36/31/02 [03/B], Lindsay, Town Clerk.

8 Wednesday 29 January: after the Meeting, in the Square

While the delegation was meeting the Lord Provost, William Gallacher spoke to the crowd outside in the Square, emphasising the importance of stopping the trams: 'If the strike was not settled by the end of the week they would not hesitate to stop every tramcar, shut off every light and generally paralyse the business of the city'. There was nothing mentioned here about only closing the routes affecting processions.[1] After the delegation emerged, Shinwell reported to the waiting crowd that the delegation:

> had represented to the Lord Provost that the tramcars on the street were impeding their orderly progress and that if the tramcars were not stopped 'You will stop them yourselves'. . . They accordingly arranged that the Lord Provost should send an urgent message to the authorities to have the strike settled. Mr Shinwell added that the strike had been conducted in a constitutional fashion but that the Lord Provost was reminded that unconstitutional tactics might develop if the workers' demands were ignored. There were two of the deputation of six, he said, who were discharged soldiers, and it was significant that these two men were the speakers who warned the Lord Provost that drastic action would have to be resorted to if the reply to the Lord Provost's message was unsatisfactory.[2]

Shinwell's use of the term 'unconstitutional means' in the Square cannot be construed in any narrow technical sense as he later claimed had been his intention inside the Chambers. He also explicitly suggested to his hearers that they should stop the trams before quite crudely shifting the blame for any 'drastic action' to the two discharged ex-servicemen. Defence witnesses confirmed Shinwell had indeed said these things.[3]

At the trial, the Lord Advocate suggested to Neil Maclean that Shinwell's subsequent repetition of 'drastic action' to the crowd outside after the meeting was 'unwise, and eminently calculated to suggest disorderly ideas to the minds of the crowd'. He concluded ominously that it was more than coincidence the 'disorder' on Friday was 'unconstitutional', employing 'drastic action' to stop the trams.[4] While there is no evidence to suggest there was a conspiracy to cause a riot on Friday, for an accomplished speaker like Shinwell it was surely foolhardy to sow any such seed among the strikers.

The crowd in the Square departed peacefully. Contrary to the Lord Provost's suggestion in his statement on 6 February, there had been no rowdyism or disturbance among them.

The picket had remained at Pinkston Power Station all afternoon and evening. The station manager, David Baillie, arranged for the shift due to arrive at 11pm to congregate at the tramways head office. Four cars filled with supplies and men were driven into the power station after midnight. A crowd of 350 pickets rushed them and 'would have driven the cars into the canal' if the police, having failed to persuade the men to stand back, had not forced them back to Pinkston Road with their batons. Having sent home his nine female staff, Baillie was left with two-thirds of his normal complement of 96. The mass picket was sustained on 30 and 31 January and the station operated under siege conditions until 6 February.[5]

On Wednesday evening, the *Manchester Guardian*'s correspondent summed up the strike leaders' position, who:

> have behind them and ready to back up any kind of extreme measure only a moderately large section, perhaps a minority, of Clyde workers. With such a section and with an effective method of picketing they see they can bring out, though against their will, a good many more. But to this there comes a limit . . . The only way to force intervention [by government] is to upset the public, and that is why measures which are very near the border-line of intimidation are being adopted.[6]

Hardly a ringing endorsement from a sympathetic newspaper.

The *Glasgow Herald* was much displeased with the Lord Provost's despatch of the telegram to the Prime Minister when, in its view, the only response should have been a refusal to become involved. In its leading article on Friday, the editor wrote that the Forty Hours Strike was not a matter 'for municipal interference'.[7]

On 6 February 1919 the Lord Provost defended his actions on 29 January in front of his colleagues on the Town Council, clearly attempting self-exculpation. He claimed he had temporised and agreed to send the telegram in part to gain time for military aid to be mobilised. This is palpably untrue. Further, there is no evidence of any disorder in the Square on 27 or 29 January, which he also claimed. He was not aware until Wednesday afternoon's meeting concluded that a further mass demonstration would take place on Friday, bringing with it a possible risk of disorder. The Sheriff of Lanarkshire made his preliminary enquiry about military aid only *after* the meeting, on Wednesday afternoon or evening.[8] The Provost lied to his fellow councillors.

Shinwell's and MacAskill's quotations at the beginning of Chapter 7 summarise the accepted narrative: the delegation, led by Shinwell, had intended to persuade the Lord Provost to intervene in the strike by contacting the government. Close reading of all the defence evidence indicates that, in all probability, Shinwell had intended to achieve this by forcing the trams off the streets. The deputation had intended to shut the whole system, not just the procession routes, to paralyse the city: by persuading the Lord Provost to close the system; getting the tram staff out on strike; closing the Pinkston Power Station or perhaps by 'unconstitutional' or 'drastic' action, before or on Friday if the government had not intervened by then. Later, evidence of plans to sabotage the power station came to light.[9] On Wednesday evening the Strike Committee issued a statement that, *inter alia*, the deputation had 'agreed not to put into operation their threat to stop the cars' until Friday.[10] That some action was intended and that there was a real threat is incontrovertible. It is understandable that the Lord Provost and Town Clerk, and through them the Sheriff and Chief Constable, were worried.

The defence at the trial, especially for Neil Maclean, made great efforts to prove the delegation had no particular purpose, except perhaps to make some limited representations about the interaction of the trams with the strikers' marches; that Shinwell, Kirkwood and Maclean were not part of the delegation and did not do most of the talking. Defence counsel aimed to distance these leaders from responsibility, from the delegation, its aims, what was said, and its outcome, at least until the trial was over. A different story emerged later in their memoirs, when they placed themselves at the centre of events.

One contemporary and two later accounts show the delegation was in reality pre-planned by Shinwell, in that there had been, at least since the previous day, an intention to send a delegation to the Lord Provost comprising Shinwell, Maclean and probably Kirkwood, and that Shinwell always intended to seek government intervention. In Slowe's authorised biography based on interviews with Shinwell, he appears as the deputation's leader and prime mover:

> Shinwell collected a delegation to see the Lord Provost . . . in the City Chambers. It was not, as it happens, *the delegation agreed on the night before*. Several Clyde Workers Committee men were left out and representatives from other groups, such as the miners and railwaymen who were playing lesser roles in the strike itself, pushed in. Even if he had wanted to, on the spur of the moment there was little Shinwell could do; a dozen men, about half of them quite unknown to their supposed leader, entered the Chambers.[11] [our emphasis]

Gallacher's account states:

> To my surprise, I discovered Shinwell was taking names for additional members to a delegation, *the official representatives of which he had already announced*. The deputation was going in to see the Lord Provost, for what purpose wasn't clear . . .[12] [our emphasis]

Shinwell's account was published 74 years after the events; Gallacher's seventeen years. Neil Maclean, corroborated by two other defence witnesses, suggested why plans for a delegation had been concealed. At the trial Maclean said: 'I did not know at that time that the Strike Committee had at a previous meeting decided not to ask for intervention'.[13] To what decision was he referring? Had he confused it with the national conference's earlier direction that no approach should be made to the government? On Thursday 30 January, the Strike Committee expressed strong disapproval of the previous day's request for government intervention, because it was 'likely to create a wrong impression in the minds of the men who were on strike'. Shinwell's reported response to this censure was 'it might serve the purpose of formally drawing the attention of the civic authorities to the fact that there was a strike in progress'.[14] Presumably it had been his intention in leading the delegation into the City Chambers to follow his own agenda, which he knew was contrary to the feelings of his committee. Maclean denied being aware of any such decision. Kirkwood's position is unknown.

At face value, the evidence describes a haphazardly selected collection of half-a-dozen individuals sent to meet the Lord Provost with no very clear purpose. However, most of the talking was conducted by three men who at the trial claimed to have been included by accident. Yet in Thursday's edition of the *Strike Bulletin*, these three men were depicted as the whole of the delegation, with no mention of others, and the tram system was the main topic discussed.

Two alternative explanations are possible. First, that Shinwell, many years after, desired to place himself at the centre of events and mis-remembered the off-the-cuff and apparently purposeless nature of the delegation and that Kirkwood also mis-remembered it. Alternatively, Shinwell had disagreed with the National Conference's decision and unilaterally decided to approach the Lord Provost, and through him the government. In this scenario, the suggestion from the crowd to form a deputation was merely a device to disguise the fact that Shinwell, Maclean and probably Kirkwood *were* the delegation. However, his plans were disrupted in the chaos of selecting further delegates. Both Shinwell and Kirkwood subsequently expressed the purpose of the meeting as being to get the Lord Provost to intervene. The first version imposes retrospective order and meaning on an otherwise chaotic event while the second implicates at least Shinwell, and possibly Maclean and/or Kirkwood in a plan to circumvent the National Conference's decision.

Neither explanation places Shinwell in a particularly good light. Either he was running his own agenda against any agreement not to involve the government or he was partly responsible for leading a group of ill-prepared men into what was an almost pointless meeting, which, if it achieved nothing else, placed firmly in the minds of the city's officials that there was a threat of violence focused on the tram system. And the subsequent rhetoric to the crowd in the Square may have prepared the ground for Friday's events among those who chose to take his words at face value. This becomes pivotal when apportioning responsibility for Friday's violence and the trial verdict.

George Square had again become the focus for events. One of the processions, from Port Dundas Power Station, had walked to the Square after its success in closing down the station. No such success was reported from the men who had gone to, and stayed outside, Pinkston Power Station. The trams continued to run. The meeting between the delegation and the Lord Provost reveals a deliberate attempt by some of the strike leadership to impose their own agenda – to get government involved. Was this, with the failure to close the tram system down and the defection of the Carters' Union, their last resort? The meeting had certainly left the Lord Provost and Town Clerk rattled. The Lord Provost, in reply to the question, '. . . had you any apprehension as to what might happen on the 31st?' answered 'Yes, in the event of a reply such as did come [from the government], I was a little afraid there might be trouble'. Sir John, responding to the question 'Did you anticipate any trouble at this meeting on Friday?', answered 'It looked like trouble from the start'.[15] At the trial, the Lord Provost said he took 'a very serious view of the violence to the tramway system which was being threatened' and consequently 'had been in very close conference with the Chief Constable' and had consulted with the Sheriff, and he had given no specific instructions to the Chief Constable, other than to 'ensure there was sufficient force to prevent any disorder'.[16]

At the trial, Gallacher, who would defend himself, led the Sheriff through his preparations for Friday: 'We took certain precautionary measures in case disturbances arose . . . I ascertained whether it would be possible to get the assistance of the Military if the Civil Authorities could not cope with the disturbance' when the strikers returned on Friday.[17] However, the Chief Constable had already made his own contingency plans issuing orders earlier in the week. His order dated 29 January 1919 had cancelled all police leave.[18] The meeting on Wednesday and the rhetoric of Shinwell, Gallacher and others since Monday had prepared the explosion. Who would light the fuse?

The War Cabinet did not meet on Wednesday 29 January.

---

1. *Glasgow Herald,* 30 January 1919.
2. *Glasgow Herald,* 30 January 1919.
3. JC36/31/08 [08/K], Angus; JC36/31/09 [09/V], Maclean, MP.
4. JC36/31/09 [09/V], Maclean, MP.
5. AD15/19/11 [B58], David Baillie, Manager, Pinkston; AD15/19/11 [B60], Charles Lynn, Storeman, Pinkston.
6. *Manchester Guardian*, 30 January 1919.
7. *Glasgow Herald*, 30 and 31 January 1919.
8. *Glasgow Herald*, 7 February 1919; AD15/19/11, Meeting of the Town Council of the City of Glasgow held within the City Chambers on Thursday, 6 February 1919.
9. R. K. Middlemas, *The Clydesiders: A Left-wing Struggle for Parliamentary Power* (Harvard University Press, 1965), p.92; P. M. Slowe, *Manny Shinwell: An Authorised Biography* (Pluto Press, 1993), p.85.
10. *Evening Times,* 29 January 1919.
11. Slowe, *Shinwell*, p.81.
12. W. Gallacher, *Revolt on the Clyde* (Lawrence and Wishart, 2007 [1936]), p.157.
13. JC36/31/08 [08/Q], Harvey; JC36/31/08 [08/L], Moloney; JC36/31/09 [09/V], Maclean, MP.
14. JC36/31/08 [08/L], Moloney.
15. JC36/31/03 [03/C], Stewart, Lord Provost; JC36/31/02 [03/B], Lindsay, Town Clerk.
16. JC36/31/03 [03/C], Stewart, Lord Provost.
17. JC36/31/04 [04/S], Alastair Oswald MacKenzie, Sheriff of Lanarkshire.
18. AD15/19/11 [A05], Stevenson, Chief Constable.

9 Thursday 30 January 1919

There was no gathering in George Square on 30 January to provide a focus for events, but strike meetings and pickets were organised elsewhere. The *Glasgow Herald* reported the Ministry of Labour's official response to a telegram from the Scottish Trades Union Congress sent on 27 January, asking the Minister of Labour to visit Glasgow: 'that as the strikes throughout the country are entirely unofficial and not backed by responsible trade union leaders, it is not possible to intervene'.[1] The government's response to Wednesday's telegram from the Lord Provost had yet to arrive, but the first edition of the *Strike Bulletin* was published on Thursday. This four-page newsletter:

> reached a daily circulation of 20,000 copies. Every day of the week saw an issue, Sunday included . . . Thursday, 30th January, saw the first issue, and following the news items, reports, etc., was an intimation, 'To All Strikers', asking them to attend to George Square on Friday, 31st January, for the purpose of hearing replies from the Prime Minister and Sir Robert Horne to the Lord Provost's request to them to give their views on the 40 hours demand.[2]

Also on 30 January, the executive joint committee of the Engineers' and Shipbuilders Associations held a routine meeting at which the 'Irregular Strike' was discussed. The meeting heard only 25 per cent of the workforce had struck, and a collapse of the strike was 'only a matter of time'. The Association's Mr Biggart had called upon the Chief Constable, who 'was quite alive to the position' regarding mass picketing but he faced the problem of 600 of his men still being in the armed forces. Biggart had told the Chief Constable that the employers' position was, 'at least up till now' not in favour of the military being called in. The meeting resolved that a deputation of the president and three other members would be sent on Friday to see the Lord Provost.[3]

Just before noon on 30 January there was a meeting of some 200-300 seamen in James Watt Lane, Broomielaw. The seamen were not part of the Forty Hours Strike. Sergeant Steele was again the senior policeman of seven present; he had also observed the riot involving white, black and Chinese seamen a few days before.[4] The earlier Broomielaw riot had been a dispute about white workers' entitlement to employment in a shrinking labour market. Shinwell had addressed white sailors the morning before the riot, emphasising their need to exclude Chinese sailors and to take action.[5] A week later, Steele reported that Shinwell said he had:

> no quarrel with the black men as they received the same wages as our own men but that the yellow men were cheap labour and if the Government did not take them off the boats he would go down at the head of a body of men and chase the Chinamen for their lives.

Two defence witnesses confirmed Shinwell spoke about 'yellow labour' at this second meeting.[6] Shinwell claimed he had 100,000 men at his back and 'neither the employers nor the Chinamen could stand up against him'. The police witnesses claimed Shinwell said, about the Forty Hours Strike, that 'It was now the time for action, drastic action, and he strongly invited all those present to be in George Square tomorrow'.[7] The events were described very briefly in Thursday's *Evening Times* and Friday's *Glasgow Herald*, in rather less dramatic terms.[8]

Detective Sergeant Ross and Constable MacCaskill reported on a meeting in the Star Picture House, Partick. The chair of the meeting, Allan Ireland, a member of the Amalgamated Society of Carpenters and Joiners, after speaking about the progress of the strike, asked his audience to go in their thousands to George Square the next day, remarking, as reported by the police, that if the Square was not big enough 'they would hold an overflow meeting in the Municipal Buildings'. Joseph Brennan then asked the audience to form up for a march to Scotstoun and Whiteinch 'where it was their intention to bring out the scabs who were still working'. The crowd then marched to Mechan's works under Brennan's* leadership.[9]

Events at Mechan's were initially used by the prosecution to prove incitement to riot against Brennan, and what happened provides an example of how mass picketing worked in practice. The firm employed about 1,200 men, of whom 200 had gone on strike, and 80 women. Timekeeper Michael McKeown, William Harrison the works manager and Henry Mechan himself all claimed the workforce was being intimidated into strike action.[10] On 30 January, 380 men were working and stopped for lunch between 12 and 1pm. Inspector McLellan was on duty at the works with 23 men, when a large but orderly crowd, some 2,000-3,000 strong, marched up. When he telephoned Partick Police Station, the Inspector was told, 'to do the best I could with the men at my disposal'.[11]

Sergeant Gordon reported that Brennan told the crowd, 'If there's not room in the Square we will have to have an overflow meeting. It might be in the Municipal Buildings' and 'all [tram]cars would be off by 12 o'clock next day as all the men in the Power Stations would be out'.[12] Brennan was reported as saying, 'The apprentices inside [Mechan's] want to get out' and if they had not been let out by management within fifteen minutes 'you are to burst in the doors and take them out'. McLellan, recognising that he had insufficient men to deal with any violence, decided to speak to Mechan's management.[13] Although the workforce was apparently reluctant to go out on strike, the hostility of the crowd made the men feel it was safer to leave, and Mechan also wished to avoid damage to his works. It was agreed that men would remain behind to close down the plant and the crowd left in the direction of the Albion Motor Works.[14] At the trial, Allan Ireland took responsibility for the 'joke' about the Municipal Buildings in his speech (ascribed to Brennan by police witnesses) which witness James Ross corroborated.[15]

Sergeant William Ferguson of Southern Division was on duty at about 5pm at Scotland Street, in the company of Inspector Innes,

*Joseph Brennan (1889-1940) was a blacksmith. Secretary of the Partick Branch of the Blacksmith's Society, an active socialist and active in the rent strike of 1915. Emigrated with his wife to America in 1923. He worked as a blacksmith until he became the licensee of a tavern. Tried and acquitted.

Sergeant Lauder and some constables.[16] A quiet crowd of men marched along Scotland Street and turned into West Street towards Tradeston Gas Works. Innes followed with two sergeants and twelve constables, passing the crowd before they reached the Gas Works and took up position in front of the gates. Innes telephoned for reinforcements, which arrived in the form of two inspectors, two sergeants and three or four constables picked up en route.[17]

The crowd pushed up against the police and refused to go back, shouting and jeering. When the workmen came out of the Gas Works at 5.30pm, they were drawn into the centre of the crowd and 'Comrade Ebury' spoke to them 'in a forcible fiery tone', setting out the aims of the strike. George Ebury also spoke of the oppression of the working class by the Conspiracy Act and Defence of the Realm Act and 'advised all present to take part' in the strike. The police witnesses reported that he concluded:

> If we don't get all the workers out by the present method of massed picketing we shall by the living God above us get them out by force and by this time tomorrow there will not be a car running in Glasgow and damn the consequences.[18]

The foreman at Tradeston, Thomas Moffat, corroborated these words.[19] Again, if as violently worded as reported, Ebury's speech may be included in the category of 'performative radicalism', unwise words to men whose 'blood was on the boil'.

On the evening of 30 January, a 'Victory at Home' was held in Govan to celebrate Neil Maclean's return to Parliament in December's general election. A number of witnesses reported Shinwell as stressing, 'in walking along they were to take care of the car lines and get into the Square in the most orderly fashion . . .'. He said that Shinwell had hoped 'that everything would pass off orderly and successfully the following day'.[20] Defence witnesses Peter Neill and Thomas Henderson corroborated Shinwell's keenness to avoid bringing discredit to the strike movement. However, when asked whether 'there is sometimes a disorderly element that requires control', Henderson conceded that there was.[21]

District Nurse Allison Moir claimed Shinwell, at the 'At Home' 'stated he had it on good authority that the military had arrived in Glasgow, and he wished the demonstrators to go very peaceably and come away peaceably'. Shinwell, she thought, 'referred to the military being brought out in other Countries against the Labour movement, and he said it might be expected it would be done also here'. Maclean, however, 'did not catch' any such reference to the military.[22]

Elsewhere on Thursday evening about 500 people attended a meeting in a public hall at Kinning Park, south of the river. Four police witnesses entered the meeting in two pairs. Two uniformed constables entered the hall at about 9pm and stood at the rear as the speaker, striker James MacDougall, was introduced. They left having heard MacDougall's speech. Constable McGlashan explicitly referred to notes he made after leaving the meeting.[23] Two other policemen from Govan Division, Detective Sergeant James Mulherrin and Acting Detective Constable William MacFarlane had entered the hall earlier, in plain clothes.[24] In contrast to the avowedly non-political character of the strike, this meeting verged on the revolutionary. John Thom, a member of the executive strike subcommittee, who spoke, was roughly handled in cross-examination at the trial by the Lord Advocate, who clearly had access to the police notes of the speech. From Friday 24 until Monday 27 January, Thom had been in Belfast liaising with the 44-hour strike committee, and in his speech reported that in Belfast if strikers collided with police, 'they placed their hand on their hip pocket and pretended to produce something' – a revolver. Thom did not deny it but said it was done 'in a jocular fashion' as 'Irishmen are humorous'. The Lord Advocate also suggested Thom had said, 'We are united in our demands; the soldiers are with us; why should we let a handful of policemen stand in our way'.[25] The Lord Advocate pressed Thom about threats he had been recorded as making against the tram system: 'The cars in Glasgow are still running, but we will take damned good care they will not run this week-end; we can do the same here as they did in Belfast'. In reply to Thom's claim that his speech had not suggested any violence, the Lord Advocate said, 'I should have thought that a revolver was pretty plain hinting'.[26]

James MacDougall's speech was reported in detail. A follower of John Maclean, MacDougall was later described by Harry McShane as 'the best informed man I ever met'. He was active in the Clyde

Workers Committee (CWC) during the war and a prominent opponent of the war, for which he was imprisoned in 1916-17. He was so radical that the CWC banned him from their meetings and William Gallacher moved for his expulsion.[27] He was introduced at Kinning Park as 'a young man who might still be first president of the British Republic'.[28] The police reported that MacDougall claimed, 'The soldiers in Hamilton Barracks were asked to come out and preserve order in the streets but they refused' telling 'their Officers to go to Hell'. He was also reported to have said 'Revolution was coming and the British Republic was coming' and that there had been 'a mutiny on the largest battleship in the British Navy lying in the Forth and 20 men were killed'.[29] There had indeed been a mutiny by 150 seamen serving on destroyers at Port Edgar during the month, objecting to being sent to intervene in the Russian Civil War, but the other claims were nonsense.[30] MacDougall claimed there were 600 policemen (more than all the police on duty in the whole city) waiting at the Gas Works for the men, and 'If blood is to be spilled don't have it all on the one side . . . You need not fear the Soldiers. The Soldiers are with us'.[31]

Across the city in the afternoon and evening, preparations were being made for the demonstration on Friday. In the authorised biography, Slowe recorded that Shinwell and 'Gallacher, Hopkins, Kirkwood and Edith Hughes were left to plan the next day's events'.[32] The authorities were also making preparations. The Chief Constable issued further orders, doubling the size of the reserve to be held at the Divisional offices from 31 January onwards and putting the force onto a twelve-hour shift, meaning around 569 men would be available for duty in the city. They were to 'be especially directed to the protection of the public services of tramways, gas, electricity and water'. All police leave had been cancelled the previous day.[33]

As one of fifteen Sheriffs in Scotland, Alastair MacKenzie* was the chief official of the county of Lanarkshire and on formal occasions took precedence over all except members of the royal fami-

* Alistair Oswald Morrison MacKenzie, KC (1858-1949). An Edinburgh man, son of a senior Scottish judge. Loretto School and Brasenose College, Oxford. Called to the Bar in 1885. By 1911 Sheriff Substitute in Glasgow. Sheriff Principal of Inverness, Elgin and Nairn from 1912 and Sheriff of Lanarkshire from 1917 to 1933. He died in Kent at the age of 91.

ly.[34] Sheriff MacKenzie had understood 'unconstitutional methods' spoken of by the strikers' delegation to mean illegal actions and, in cross-examination, confirmed it was his duty to be prepared should there be any disturbance. It is not recorded whether his inquiry about the availability of military aid was made on Wednesday afternoon or early on Thursday. He had certainly made it before the War Cabinet met at 3pm, when his inquiry to ascertain 'whether it would be possible to get the assistance of the Military if the Civil Authorities could not cope with the disturbance' was mentioned by the Scottish Secretary.[35]

Bonar Law chaired Thursday's War Cabinet meeting with two further members present, Austin Chamberlain MP and Eric Geddes MP. Also present were politicians Winston Churchill MP, Minister for War and Air; Auckland Geddes MP, Minister for Reconstruction; Robert Munro MP, Secretary for Scotland; James Clyde MP,* the Lord Advocate and Sir Robert Horne, Minister for Labour. Five senior military officers were also present: General Sir Henry Wilson, Chief of the Imperial General Staff; General Sir William Robertson,† Commander-in-Chief of all forces in the UK; Major General Sir George Macdonogh, the Adjutant General; Major General Childs,‡

* James Avon Clyde, MP, KC (1863-1944). Called to Scots Bar in 1889. King's Counsel 1903. Dean of the Faculty of Advocates 1915-1918. Solicitor General 1905. Liberal Unionist MP 1909-1918. Coalition Unionist MP for Edinburgh North 1918-1920. Privy Councillor 1916. Lord Advocate 1916–1920. President of the Court of Session 1920-1935.

† Sir William Robertson (1860- 1933). Son of a Lincolnshire tailor. Started working life as garden boy in 1873. Footman in the Countess of Cardigan's household. Enlisted as private soldier 1877. Commissioned in 1888. Promoted Major General in 1910. Wide-ranging military career including Commandant of the Staff College, Quartermaster General, Chief of Staff of the British Expeditionary Force in France, and Chief of the Imperial General Staff from 1915 until forced from office in 1918 and succeeded by Sir Henry Wilson. Officer Commanding-in-Chief Home Forces, June 1918. The only man who joined the army as a private soldier and ended his career as Field-Marshal.

‡ General (Sir) B. E. W. Childs KCMG KBE CB (1876-1946). British Army officer who also served as Assistant Commissioner, Metropolitan Police, 1921-28. A protégé of General Macready who had, in 1910 in Wales, appointed him to liaise (apparently successfully) with the strike committee.

Director of Personal Services, and Major General Romer,* with internal security duties. The military men present included representatives of two camps in the army: Wilson and Childs, prominent in the hawkish 'reds under the bed' party, and Macdonogh, a more moderate figure. This sort of turnout was not unusual: on 28 January Churchill and several senior military men had been present to discuss the main agenda item – demobilisation.[36]

The minutes of the War Cabinet meeting have been accessible since 1969, and the 'Conclusions' and 'Memoranda' for the period are now available online.[37] Because some writers have selected what was said to support a particular narrative, it is necessary to present a fairly full account of what was said and what was decided.[38]

The first item on the agenda was the 'Strike Situation in Glasgow'. Bonar Law opened by reading the Lord Provost's telegram and the draft response from the government, which had been read to and approved by Lloyd George, who was in Paris. The main aim of the response was, Bonar Law explained, to 'show the public the Government did not mean to intervene' and 'to reinforce the authority of the Trades Unions'. There followed a discussion of the maintenance of the electricity and municipal services, preferably by Special Constables rather than soldiers, and the 'separate problem of guarding those who carried out this work'. Bonar Law said:

> He thought it vital for the War Cabinet to be satisfied that there was a sufficient force in Glasgow to prevent disorder, and to protect those volunteers or others who could be made available to take over the operation of the generating stations and municipal services. It was certain that if the movement in Glasgow grew, it would spread all over the country.

The discussion moved on to the possibility of using the Glasgow police to guard these workers, and a question about whether the

* General (Sir) C. F. Romer GCB KBE CMG ADC (1869-1962). Protégé of Sir Henry Wilson, CIGS, and was present at the War Cabinet meetings on 30 and 31 January. Wilson's nominee for failed proposal to appoint a commander of all troops in Britain in the event of revolutionary unrest. In 1919 he was actively involved in General Head Quarters Great Britain's work on industrial unrest and military aid. Adjutant General in 1933.

demobilisation of the 500 or so Glasgow policemen still in the armed forces could be speeded up. Churchill explained it was impossible to single out these men amongst the thousands being demobilised. Munro referred to the Sheriff's enquiry about military aid, feeling 'bound to lay this request made to him by the Sheriff before the Cabinet'. Munro also said, 'there was the question as to who should take the initiative [to call the military]. The Lord Provost and Sheriff were jointly responsible for law and order in the city'. Later in the discussion Munro responded positively to an enquiry as to whether the Glasgow police were trustworthy. General Robertson said:

> The military part of the question was quite simple. The civil authorities were responsible for law and order, and the military could not step in except at their requisition in accordance with King's Regulations. This did not apply, however, if martial law were declared.[39]

He described the resources available in Scotland:

> 19 infantry battalions, which were all Scottish but one. One of these battalions was in Glasgow, one at Greenock, and about 12 in the vicinity of Edinburgh. They were all reserve-finding units, and consisted of all sorts of men, old, young, convalescent, and men with wounds. As regards their officers, these were not very efficient. He drew the Cabinet's attention to this in view of the purposes for which the troops might be used. It would not be legal to use soldiers for taking over and running the generating stations.

Responding to an observation that a few soldiers had been used to replace railwaymen in pre-war strikes, General Childs explained:

> but at that time we had a well-disciplined and ignorant army, whereas now we had an army educated and ill-disciplined.

Sir William Robertson said, 'there were certain disadvantages in employing Scottish troops, but on the whole he thought it would be safer to use them than to import English battalions'. Churchill intervened at this point, saying 'we should not exaggerate the seriousness of the disturbances. In times of peace we had had to go through strikes just as dangerous as this one', and noted the:

> present situation in Glasgow had been building for a long time. The disaffected were in a minority, and, in his opinion, there would have to be a conflict in order to clear the air. We should be careful to have plenty of provocation before taking strong measures. By going gently at first we should get the support we wanted from the nation, and then troops could be used more effectively. The moment for their use had not yet arrived. In the meantime the Defence of the Realm Act was still in force, and some of the leaders of the revolt should be seized.

This is one of two occasions during this meeting when Churchill used the surely inappropriate word 'revolt'. Bonar Law agreed and was, he said, only:

> anxious that there should be some responsible person in Glasgow ready to call in the military when necessary, and this person should be told that the military had received orders to hold themselves in readiness. Steps should be taken to get the Special Constabulary ready.

There was some discussion about representatives of the Ministry of Labour being sent north, but it was decided this would contradict the message about government non-intervention. Munro offered instead to send the Assistant Under-Secretary of his department, John Lamb,* whom Bonar Law said 'should get in touch with the Lord

* (Sir) John Lamb (1871-1952). Educated Brechin High School and Merchiston Castle, Edinburgh. Studied law at the University of Edinburgh. In 1919 Assistant Under-Secretary of Scottish Office. Permanent under-secretary of the Scottish Office 1921 to 1933. Companion of Honour in 1915 and KCB in 1926. In a tribute at his death, it was written that his watchword was 'Duty'; 'he left all credit to others and shouldered all responsibility and blame'. Served under nine Scottish Secretaries. A Liberal in politics.

Provost of Glasgow and the Sheriff' to present the government's view, which was:

> that the situation should be dealt with patiently but firmly, and the military only called in when asked for in order to prevent serious disorder and intimidation, and to preserve the lighting arrangements of the city.

At this stage, Horne suggested that any opportunity should be taken to arrest the strike leaders, as they were not trade union leaders 'and most of them were well known extremists'. The Lord Advocate 'undertook to consider this suggestion' but it seems that nothing further was done. Churchill suggested they should wait until some 'glaring excess had been committed' by the strikers, because 'the moment the revolt advanced over the line of a pure wage dispute, and the strikers were guilty of serious breach of the law, then was the moment to act'. Once again, Churchill used the word 'revolt', this time to describe a strike that had not yet exceeded its status as 'a pure wage dispute' and was thus not a 'revolt' in any sense. Munro, whose voice throughout had been the sole one showing any panic, suggested that stage was near and 'threats had been made to wreck the newspaper offices in Glasgow'.

Sir Eric Geddes raised the final matter, the possible disruption of rail traffic over the weekend, which might affect troop movements. Churchill said, 'the War Office would take all the necessary steps to meet such eventuality and would consider arrangements for placing troops in the vicinity of Glasgow'. To date, no evidence that any particular preparations were made has been discovered. The War Cabinet decided:

> (a) To approve the telegram . . .
>
> (b) That the Secretary for Scotland should inform the Lord Provost and the Sheriff of Lanarkshire that, in the view of the Government, the lighting of the city must be kept up if there is any possibility of doing it; that the military will be in readiness to give their services when requested by the civil authorities; and that firm, but not provocative action should

be taken to put down disorder and prevent intimidation.

(c) That Mr John Lamb should proceed to Glasgow that evening in order to acquaint the Lord Provost and the Sheriff of the Government's policy, and to keep the Government informed of any development in the situation.

(d) That the following Committee should be set up for purposes of consultation during the continuance of the disorder: –

The Secretary for Scotland (*Chairman*)
The Lord Advocate
The Minister of Labour
The Director of Personal Services (War Office) [General Childs]

(e) That the Lord Advocate should examine the legal grounds for the arrest of the ringleaders of the strike, should it be found desirable to do so.[40]

Lamb's dispatch to Glasgow suggests the War Cabinet needed a man on the ground to provide them with reliable information.

Scottish Command would have worked late to prepare the orders ready to be sent out to the units, should they be needed: to select suitable men for deployment; to prepare for movement; and to issue arms and rations. It is likely the decision to include tanks in any force despatched was made at this time, rather than in the short period between the Sheriff calling for military aid on Friday at about 1.30pm and Friday's War Cabinet meeting at 3pm, when their dispatch was reported. The booklet *Duties in Aid of the Civil Power* provided advice to officers organising deployments: to ensure the men had three days' rations; necessary camp, telegraphic and telephonic equipment; twenty rounds of ammunition per man; waggons and so on. The responsible officer had to make an immediate report to the War Office by telegram on arrival, stating the size of the force, and telephone communication was to be kept open to the War Office night and day. Arrangements for rail transport and for ensuring there was sufficient rolling stock were to be made locally.[41] But it must be emphasised that the decision to call for military aid to the civil power had to be made by the civil power itself: no one among the War Cabinet had authority to make that decision, only the Sheriff of Lanarkshire was empowered to do so, and he remained in Glasgow.

Overnight, there was a precursor to the George Square riot, when there was a violent disturbance in the early hours in Lanarkshire, south of Glasgow. Ten men from Burnbank, Hamilton and Blantyre were later charged with having formed part of a mob of 50 men. On their way to picket collieries that had decided to remain at work, the mob had entered lamp cabins at two collieries and removed and smashed safety lamps and terrorised men preparing for the day's work. At the second colliery they attacked, Hamilton Palace Colliery, the mob also ransacked and smashed up the office, tried to break open a safe containing £5,000 in wages, and attacked a police constable who was holding an accused rioter in his custody.[42]

Nine men later appeared at the High Court in Glasgow, where the same judge who would also preside at Shinwell *et al*'s trial – Lord Justice-Clerk, Charles Scott Dickson* – presided over this one. That a mob had caused damage was not denied and the defence had little to work with. One man was acquitted, another found guilty on four counts and all except one other were found guilty of mobbing and rioting.[43] The eight convicted men were sentenced on 30 April, the one charged on four counts receiving the longest sentence, six months, of all those convicted at this and the strike leaders' trial earlier in the month.[44]

Thursday saw a heightening of tensions and mass-picketing some perceived as intimidating. There was more 'performative radicalism' in the speeches of some of the strike leaders, and the most violent event to date, the Lanarkshire colliery riot. The Lord Provost, Town Clerk, Sheriff and the Chief Constable were fearful of violence on Friday. The Sheriff had asked whether military aid would be available to him if he needed it. Friday's events might force his hand.

* Charles Scott Dickson (1850-1922). One of eight children of a well-known physician. Glasgow High School and Glasgow and Edinburgh Universities. Married with two sons. Advocate 1877, Queen's Counsel in 1896. Solicitor General May 1896 to 1903; Lord Advocate 1903-1905. 1908-1915 Dean of the Faculty of Advocates. Unionist MP for Bridgeton 1900-1906, Glasgow Central 1909-1915, when he became a judge.

1. *Glasgow Herald*, 30 January 1919.
2. D. S. Morton, *The 40 Hours Strike: An Historic Survey of the First General Strike in Scotland* (Clydebank Branch SLP, 1919), p.8.
3. TD241/1/18, *Clyde Shipbuilders Association Minute Book* (Glasgow City Archives), pp.141-43. The Chief Constable's figure is clearly a rough one.
4. J. Jenkinson, *Black 1919*; J. Jenkinson, 'Black Sailors on Red Clydeside: Rioting, Reactionary Trade Unionism and Conflicting Notions of "Britishness" following the First World War', *Twentieth Century British History*, 19, no 1 (2008), pp.29-60; B. Weinberger, *Keeping the Peace?: Policing Strikes in Britain, 1906-1926* (Berg, 1991), p.83; I. McLean, *The Legend of Red Clydeside* (John Donald, 1999), *passim*.
5. AD15/19/11 [A08], John Steele, Police Sergeant.
6. JC36/31/09 [09D] William Blamires; [09E] James Kennedy.
7. AD15/19/11 [A08], John Steele, Police Sergeant; AD15/19/11 [A09], James Ritchie, Police Constable; AD15/19/11 [A17], Andrew Gallagher, Police Constable; JC36/31/03 [03/F], Charles Smith, Police Constable.
8. *Evening Times*, 30 January 1919; Glasgow *Herald*, 31 January 1919.
9. AD15/19/11 [A50], George Ross, Detective Sergeant.
10. AD15/19/11 [B29], Michael McKeown, Timekeeper; AD15/19/11 [B30], William Harrison, Works Manager.
11. AD15/19/11 [A48], Kenneth Mclennan, Police Inspector.
12. AD15/19/11 [A50], Ross, Detective Sergeant; AD15/19/11 [A51], Robert Gordon, Police Sergeant.
13. AD15/19/11 [A48], Mclennan, Police Inspector.
14. AD15/19/11 [A48], Mclennan, Police Inspector.
15. JC36/31/09 [09/G], James Ross.
16. Inspector Innes had died by the time of the trial.
17. AD15/19/11 [A42], John Fordyce, Police Inspector.
18. AD15/19/11 [A41], William Ferguson, Police Sergeant; JC36/31/05 [05/T], John Wishart, Police Sergeant.
19. AD15/19/11 [A45] and JC36/31/05 [05/R], Thomas Moffat, Tradeston Gas Works.
20. JC36/31/09 [09/V], Neil Maclean, MP; [07K], Peter Neill, member Amalgamated Society of Carpenters and Joiners; [08/D], Thomas Henderson.
21. JC36/31/07 [07K], Peter Neill, member Amalgamated Society of Carpenters and Joiners; JC36/31/08 [08/D], Thomas Henderson.

22. JC36/31/08 [08/P], Allison Moir, District Nurse; JC36/31/09 [09/V], Maclean, MP.
23. AD15/19/11 [B05], Archibald McGlashan, Police Constable; AD15/19/11 [B06], Douglas Rattray, Police Constable.
24. AD15/19/11 [B03], James Mulherrin, Detective Sergeant; AD15/19/11 [B04], 'Precognition against Joseph Brennan Etc [B04] Acting Detective Constable William Macfarlane'. Mulherrin provided a precognition which MacFarlane corroborated. The two pairs of policemen gave their precognitions two weeks apart. One set of precognitions is initialled, the other is not, which suggests they were not precognosced by the same official.
25. JC36/31/08 [08/B], John Thom, Strike Committee.
26. JC36/31/08 [08/B], Thom, Strike Committee.
27. He later joined Mosely's 'New Party', and in later life was a Conservative Party supporter known for his anti-Catholicism. W. W. Knox, *Labour Leaders 1918-1939: A Biographical Dictionary* (Mainstream, 1984), pp.170-75.
28. AD15/19/11 [B05], McGlashan, Police Constable; AD15/19/11 [B03], Mulherrin, Detective Sergeant.
29. AD15/19/11 [B03], Mulherrin, Detective Sergeant.
30. *Scotsman*, 30 January 1919; *Motherwell Times*, 31 January 1919; AD15/19/11 [B03], Mulherrin, Detective Sergeant; AD15/19/11 [B05], Mcglashan, Police Constable.
31. AD15/19/11 [B05], McGlashan, Police Constable.
32. P. Slowe, *Manny Shinwell: An Authorised Biography* (Pluto Press, 1993), p.83; JC36/31/08 [08/C], John Forman.
33. AD15/19/11 [A05], James Verdier Stevenson, Chief Constable.
34. E. R. Keedy, 'Criminal Procedure in Scotland', *Journal of the American Institute of Criminal Law and Criminology*, 3 (1912), p.734.
35. AD15/19/11 [A01] and JC36/31/04 [04/S], Alastair Oswald Morison MacKenzie, Sheriff of Lanarkshire.
36. CAB23/9/8, War Cabinet Minutes, meeting 521, 28 January 1919.
37. https://www.nationalarchives.gov.uk/education/resources/cabinet-papers-1915-1984/
38. Weinberger, *Keeping the Peace*, pp.157-8; Jenkinson, *Black* 1919, p.42; J. Burrowes, *Great Glasgow Stories* (Mainstream, 1998), ebook ref 629.5/640; CAB23/9/9, War Cabinet Minutes, 30 January 1919 provides a verbatim report.
39. Martial law was not declared. See Chapter 17.

40. CAB23/9/9, War Cabinet Minutes, meeting 522, 30 January 1919.
41. Army Great Britain, *Duties in Aid of the Civil Power* (War Office, 1912), p.4.
42. AD15/19/54, Precognition against Joseph Comerford [and others] for the Crime of Mobbing and Rioting at Glasgow Road; Whistleberry Road at Craighead Colliery [and other places], 1919.
43. *Glasgow Herald*, 30 April 1919.
44. *Glasgow Herald*, 1 May 1919.

Part III
'BLOODY FRIDAY'/'BLACK FRIDAY'

10 Before the Violence: Mid-Morning in George Square, Friday 31 January 1919

Friday morning was, according to Meteorological Office records, dry but overcast with a temperature just above freezing. The *Glasgow Herald* noted that the gathering which formed in George Square had taken place in 'bright new sunshine', also confirmed by the Meteorological Office records. Writing in the 1930s, William Gallacher recalled it had rained 'during the night and the square was wet and muddy'; yet no rain was recorded by the Meteorological Office.[1]

Unless a witness's job necessitated checking the time regularly, notably the tram crews and their inspectors, the time at which an event started or finished, or the length of time an event lasted cannot be relied upon. Although accounts should not be given more or less credence because they differ one from another in this way, the defence version of what occurred in the south-east corner of George Square, where the violence that symbolises 'Bloody Friday' began, relied to some extent on the timeframe being compressed, to give the impression it all happened more quickly than a detailed analysis of the various witness statements suggests.

The Lord Provost's telegram and the government's reply were published in the newspapers on Friday morning to the Lord Provost's 'greatest surprise', as neither he nor the Town Clerk had authorised their release. The Lord Provost 'thought as a matter of courtesy it would be sent to me and not disclosed to anyone until I had an opportunity of seeing the deputation'.[2] The government offered no explanation or apology to the Lord Provost, and it has been impossible to discover if there was any purpose to the release, or whether it had been simple discourtesy. Friday morning's *Scotsman* noted the government's telegram, in reply to the Lord Provost's, had been sent from London at 4.20pm on 30 January.[3]

It is unclear when people other than the Lord Provost became aware of the government's stance on non-intervention in the strike.

Many years later, Shinwell alone claimed the strike committee received news of the government's refusal to intervene on the evening of 30 January.[4] However, William Shaw, Secretary of the Trades Council, told the court that the strike committee had not received the news on Thursday evening and he was amazed to read it in the *Glasgow Herald* on Friday morning. There was a discussion in the strike office that morning whether to proceed with the demonstration, but it was too late to countermand the previous day's instructions clearly printed in the *Strike Bulletin* to 'Be in Time and Be There'.[5] Further, some processions had set off earlier that morning.[6] John Thom also suggested in any case 'the Lord Provost might have something to add to the reply'.[7] Thus, the processions from across Glasgow began walking towards the Square, intending to arrive around mid-day.

The Lord Provost felt, because of what had been said to him at the meeting on Wednesday, that the publication of the response made him 'a little afraid there might be trouble'.[8] The editor of the *Glasgow Herald* published a leading article in Friday's paper:

> The telegrams which have been exchanged between the Lord Provost of Glasgow and Mr Bonar Law in regard to the strike position in Glasgow are not pleasant reading for loyal citizens. The Lord Provost was waited upon on Wednesday by a deputation which demanded under threats that he should communicate with the Government, and – to put it bluntly – invite intervention . . . The answer which Mr Bonar Law has made is what was expected . . . the matter was not one for municipal interference.[9]

The planned deputation from the joint committee of the Engineers' and Shipbuilders' Association to the Lord Provost arrived during Friday forenoon, but the meeting was not minuted. The outcome, and the subsequent outbreak of violence, was reported at the joint committee meeting held later on Friday. The Lord Provost had explained to them his reasons for seeing the strikers' delegation on 29 January, claiming his prime concern had been to alert the government to the situation.[10]

During Friday morning, the Lord Provost and the Town Clerk worked in the Lord Provost's room, observing from time to time what was happening in the Square.[11] At about 11am the Sheriff arrived 'by previous arrangement' in consequence of 'the threats . . . made by [the] strikers' deputation'. He had also heard the previous evening that the government had refused to intervene. While waiting for the Lord Provost to emerge from his meeting with the deputation from the Engineers' and Shipbuilders' Association, he was joined in the Lord Provost's room by the Town Clerk, Sir John Lindsay, and Mr John Lamb, the Scottish Office official sent by the War Cabinet.[12] The Lord Provost joined them and together they watched the growing crowd. Then the Lord Provost left for the magistrates' meeting in an adjoining room, probably the meeting room just north of the Lord Provost's room, with a view over the Square (Map 4, 2). The meeting had been called for 11.45am.[13]

The Lord Provost claimed there had been no specific arrangement made for the strikers' delegation to be supplied with the government's answer, although at trial, he explained 'on the Friday morning . . . a letter had come . . . from the Trades Council advising me that the deputation would call at twelve o'clock'. The Lord Provost believed he would be 'down in plenty time to meet the deputation' but the Council Officer came to the Lord Provost while he was still in the magistrates' meeting to let him know the delegation had arrived. The Lord Provost asked the Council Officer 'to make an explanation to the deputation and ask them to wait say a few minutes until we finished the special business that I had called the meeting for'.[14]

The Processions Arrive

As the crowds massed, the Chief Constable walked across George Square to the City Chambers, arriving at about midday, to satisfy himself that the police were properly disposed.[15] Superintendent Auchterlonie Williamson* of Central Division was in operational

* Superintendent Auchterlonie Williamson (1868-1934). Born Fife, youngest child of a ploughman. Joined the West Lothian Constabulary in 1887; transferred to Glasgow three or four years later. Inspector by 1901. By 1911, Lieutenant. Promoted to Superintendent of the Central Division in 1914. In 1926 promoted to Assistant Chief Constable of Glasgow Police. King's Police Medal, 1927. Retired in 1933 after 46 years' service.

command with his deputy, Lieutenant Gray.[16] The Chief Constable 'had issued instructions to the Superintendent as to taking a force of police into the Square to keep order', making 'such provision there as I thought would meet any circumstance that might arise' and he considered 140 men were sufficient to maintain order in front of the Municipal Chambers, occupying the whole eastern side of the Square (Map 4).[17] Three lieutenants, six inspectors, eight sergeants and 54 constables also accompanied the different processions to the Square. There were also six mounted police as part of the small reserve of 26 men in the quadrangle of the City Chambers, who were included in the overall total of 140.[18]

The list of police officers and constables on duty on 27, 29, 30 and 31 January includes for 31 January 160 names, but does not, for example, include the St Rollox Division men sent later in the afternoon to the relief of the police in Cathedral Street, nor men on ordinary beat duty, such as Sergeant Caskie and Inspector McDonald, who had been in the area around the Square and were attacked.[19] The total number of police who became involved in the violence around the Square was probably nearer 170-180, and a further 30 constables and four sergeants, under Inspectors Innes and Fordyce, were drawn up from south of the river to Jail Square or became involved in the violence south of the river.[20] The overall total of about 200-220 men constituted well over one third of the 569 men available to police the whole city on the twelve-hour shift pattern instituted on Friday morning. There seems to have been no particular preparation of the men. One of the strands of the defence was to suggest to Lieutenant Gray, the first prosecution witness, in four separate questions, 'when you police apprehend trouble there is always a course of baton drill', clearly implying the police had been specially prepared for violence on Friday. Gray responded, 'I never heard of the police getting baton drill before any trouble'.[21]

William Shaw explained the arrangements made for each procession's location in the Square: simply put, the marches from the north took up positions on the north side, and so on.[22] The Dennistoun procession, accompanied by police Inspector Gillies, arrived in the Square about noon, at which time he reckoned there were 8,000 people present.[23] John Forman, a member of the Joint Strike

Committee and the Springburn District Strike Committee, accompanied the Springburn procession to George Square, headed by a brass band and a pipe band, arriving two or three minutes before noon. The Springburn procession took up a position at North Hanover Street.[24] However, Lieutenant Gray observed no order in the way the crowd arrived or were placed in the Square, 'because they trampled all over the flower plots and seemed to take up their positions promiscuously'.[25] A feature of much of the defence evidence from men who came in procession to the Square is that many moved from their allocated positions towards the east side of the Square. It is clear from the evidence of those arriving around 12.30pm that the violence had already begun. Sergeant Steele was in charge of a group of constables accompanying a procession some 8-9,000 strong from Partick. Steele claimed the procession 'filled the whole breadth of the street' as it proceeded along Sauchiehall Street and other main streets and 'deliberately held up the traffic . . . if a tramcar attempted to pass them, even although there was room for it to do so, it was immediately boarded by the strikers and the trolley removed from the overhead wire'.[26]

The policemen who had accompanied the processions to the Square moved towards the City Chambers, where they joined the line of men in front of the building. Inspector Gillies and his eight men, for example, left a Dennistoun procession and took up a position to the south of the entrance to the City Chambers. He thought there were about 40 policemen in front of the Buildings at that time.[27] The Western Division detachment under Sergeants Steele and Blackhall also joined their colleagues. Plain-clothes policemen were also on duty in the Square, for example Detective Inspector McKay and Detectives Wilson and Graham.[28]

Some of the district processions arrived after the trouble had started. Herbert Highton accompanied a Springburn procession on a circuitous route, via premises where they hoped to get men to join the strike, consequently arriving at 12.30pm. Highton met Harry Hopkins in South Hanover Street, who said there was trouble in the Square and told him 'For God's sake get them out of here'.[29] Peter Neill was one of the marshals of a Govan procession, which also arrived around 12.30pm.[30] Several men told witness Alexander

Maclean, leading the Govan band, 'For Christ's sake don't take your band there; people are being knocked down like ninepins'. He kept the band marshalled and went away to Glasgow Green.[31]

The delegation's meeting with the Lord Provost was intended to be central to the demonstration in the Square; the deputation comprised the same men who had been involved on Wednesday. Delegate Isaac Sim reported that Shinwell called the deputation together, saying a few words, appealing, before they approached the Buildings, to the crowd to 'be on their best behaviour'. Slowe puts an interesting interpretation on Shinwell's supposed intentions, claiming Shinwell had anticipated the anger of the crowd at the government's sharp rebuff which had provided the opportunity 'for Shinwell to use the full powers of his oratory. He would let rip. He would rouse the assembled masses . . .' [ellipsis in the original].[32]

Assistant Chief Constable Mennie confirmed Shinwell, Gallacher, Hopkins and Kirkwood arrived around noon and addressed the crowd from the Gladstone Statue in front of the City Chambers before moving off, leaving Gallacher behind.[33] The Keeper of the Municipal Buildings met the delegation before they entered the building and took them first into his room, before leading them upstairs where they were shown into the library by the Council Officer (Map 4, 3).[34] Once again, the woman who had been turned away from the meeting on Wednesday tried to take part, but was told to go away.[35] The possibly invented 'seventh man' is not mentioned. The Town Clerk thought the delegation had waited 'five or ten minutes' because the Lord Provost was still at his meeting with the magistrates' committee.[36] Bailie John Stewart, the second defence witness to be examined, thought the delegation had waited 'from 12 to 15 minutes'.[37] Their presence was not, according to the Lord Provost, announced to him until after noon.[38] In the meantime, the delegates had received a message via the Council Officer that 'we would not be long, and if they would give us a little time to complete our business, we would come to them'.[39] The Lord Provost thought the Sheriff appeared at the magistrates' meeting around 12.20pm and Isaac Sim confirmed it was about 12.20pm when the delegates knocked on the door to try to speak to the Lord Provost on their way out, which was after the trouble had begun.[40]

After the deputation had gone into the Chambers, Gallacher remained on the plinth of the Gladstone statue addressing the crowd, and described how the crowd in front of the City Chambers turned towards him with their backs to the police. This positioning was given retrospective importance in Gallacher's version of events at April's trial and in his memoir, in which he claimed the police attacked the rear of the crowd as a whole.[41] At this time the police line extended right along the front of the City Chambers.[42] Detective Inspector Louis Noble reported the passage of a motor van in front of the Municipal Buildings. Andrew Smith, who was 'chairing' the meeting in the Square, said he called for the police to stop the traffic, as two people had been injured by the van.[43] The *Strike Bulletin* published on 1 February claimed this event alone triggered the ensuing violence, and that when the strikers 'appealed to the police to turn the vehicular traffic by another street', they responded with an 'attack on the strikers'. D. S. Morton also ascribed the van and the police's reaction as the sole trigger for the violence.[44] Sergeant Robert Thomson described the crowd around Gallacher as 'noisy and threatening and paid little attention' to him.[45] Thereafter, the events unfolded for which Friday 31 January 1919 has become legendary or infamous, according to taste.

---

1. *Glasgow Herald*, 1 February 1919; Meteorological Office, *Daily Weather Report 1st January to 31st March 1919* (Meteorological Office, 1919); W. Gallacher, *Revolt on the Clyde* (Lawrence and Wishart, 2017 [1936]), p.160.
2. JC36/31/02 [02/R] and [03/B], Lindsay, Town Clerk; JC36/31/03 [03/C], Stewart, Lord Provost.
3. *Scotsman*. 31 January 1919, p.4.
4. P. M. Slowe, *Manny Shinwell: An Authorised Biography* (Pluto Press, 1993), p.83; I. McLean, *The Legend of Red Clydeside* (John Donald 1999), p.119.
5. *Strike Bulletin*, 30 January 1919.
6. JC36/31/07 [07/V], William Shaw, Secretary, Trades Council.
7. JC36/31/08 [08/B], John Thom, Strike Committee Member.
8. JC36/31/03 [03/C], James W Stewart, Lord Provost.
9. *Glasgow Herald*, 30 January 1919.

10. TD241/1/18, *Clyde Shipbuilders Association Minute Book* (Glasgow City Archives), p.147.
11. JC36/31/02 [02/R; 03/B], Sir John Lindsay, Town Clerk.
12. AD15/19/11 [A01], Alastair Oswald MacKenzie, Sheriff of Lanarkshire.
13. AD15/19/11 [A04], Sir John Lindsay, Town Clerk.
14. JC36/31/03 [03/C] and AD15/19/11, Stewart, Lord Provost.
15. JC36/31/04 [04/H], James Verdier Stevenson, Chief Constable; AD15/19/11 [A06], Alexander Mennie, Asst Chief Constable.
16. 'Lieutenant' was a police rank then being phased out; already, the equivalent rank in the detective branch was 'Chief Inspector'.
17. JC36/31/04 [04/H], Stevenson, Chief Constable.
18. JC36/31/04 [04/H], Stevenson, Chief Constable; JC36/31/02 [02/J], Thomas Mcclure, Police Sergeant.
19. AD15/19/11 Doc 47, Return of Names of Officers and Constables Who Were on Duty.
20. AD15/19/11 [A41], William Ferguson, Police Sergeant.
21. JC36/31/01 [01/C], Lawrence Gray, Lieutenant.
22. JC36/31/07 [07/V], William Shaw, Secretary of the Trades Council.
23. AD15/19/11 [A36], Neil Gillies, Police Inspector.
24. JC36/31/08 [08/C], John Forman.
25. JC36/31/01 [01/C], Lawrence Gray, Police Lieutenant; AD15/19/11 [A22], Duncan Mcdonald, Police Sergeant.
26. AD15/19/11 [A08], John Steele, Police Sergeant; AD15/19/11 [A17], Andrew Gallacher, Police Constable; AD15/19/11 [A11], Francis McCormick, Police Constable.
27. AD15/19/11 [A36] and JC36/31/02 [02/C], Neil Gillies, Police Inspector.
28. AD15/19/11 [A33], James Wilson, Detective Sergeant.
29. JC36/31/07 [07/B], Herbert Highton.
30. JC36/31/07 [07/K], Neill.
31. JC36/31/07 [07/D], Alexander Maclean, Member of Boiler Makers' Union.
32. Slowe, *Shinwell*, p.83.
33. AD15/19/11 [A06], Mennie, Asst Chief Constable; AD15/19/11 [A14], Robert Davidson, Police Constable; AD15/19/11 [A15], Thomas Gargan, Police Constable; JC36/31/09 [09/B], Isaac Sim.
34. JC36/31/02 [02/P], Charles Robertson, City Chambers Keeper.
35. JC36/31/08 [08/Q], William Harvey.

36. JC36/31/03 [03/B], Lindsay, Town Clerk.
37. JC36/31/06 [06/B], Bailie John Stewart.
38. JC36/31/03 [03/C], Stewart, Lord Provost.
39. JC36/31/03 [03/C], Stewart, Lord Provost.
40. JC36/31/09 [09/B], Sim.
41. W. Gallacher, *Revolt on the Clyde* (Lawrence and Wishart, 2017 [1936]), p. 227; JC36/31/09 [09/D], John Mackenzie.
42. JC36/31/07 [07/L], Frederick Sievwright, Sheriff Court shorthand writer.
43. AD15/19/11 [A29], Louis Noble, Detective Inspector.
44. *Strike Bulletin*, 1 February 1919, p.1; D. S. Morton, *The 40 Hours Strike: An Historic Survey of the First General Strike in Scotland* (Clydebank Branch SLP, 1919), p.9. This obviously contrived explanation has not, unsurprisingly, found its way into the catechism of the Battle.
45. AD15/19/11 [A26], Robert Thomson, Police Sergeant.

11 The Riot: 31 January 1919: the Prosecution Evidence

> *Depend upon it, he who pretends to give an account of a great battle from his own observation deceives you – believe him not. He can see no farther (that is, if he be personally engaged in it) than the length of his nose . . .*[1]

With the delegates inside the building, a large crowd in the Square and more arriving, significant numbers moved towards the City Chambers and into the south-east corner of the Square. The version of events told by William Gallacher in his 1936 memoir is the one that frequently frames the narrative:

> Suddenly, without warning of any kind, a signal was given and the police made a savage and totally unexpected assault on the rear of the meeting . . .[2]

What happened in the Square has often been presented in this way, as a pre-planned and unprovoked assault on a peaceful meeting, the deliberate plan of an oppressive establishment using 'the disruption of the trams as a pretext to dispel the protesters'.[3] Iain McLean describes the police as making 'unprovoked attacks . . . designed to intimidate or scatter the crowd', essentially a 'police riot'.[4] In a recent biography of Sylvia Pankhurst, the crowd is described as 'savagely attacked by the police'.[5]

In describing the origins of the violence in the Square, Kenny MacAskill repeats Gallacher's memoir. He writes that months later at the trial 'two quite separate versions were given of the same events, when witnesses from both sides testified'. He contrasted the police version that 'they were required to intercede with batons drawn to allow tramcars to move as the crowd surrounded them' with the defence version 'that they were charged indiscriminately by baton-wielding officers who responded to an order to attack'. Without providing any supporting evidence, MacAskill prefers the strikers' version.[6]

These and other writers seem not to have considered the evidence of the twenty Tramways Department employees who described events during the week of 27 to 31 January in precognitions and, some, at trial. Six witnesses – two giving evidence at the trial – were tram inspectors; ten, including two women, were drivers – two of whom, including one woman, testified at trial; four were female conductors who gave precognitions only. Eleven of the tramway staff provided precognitions describing what they saw in the south-east corner, where the trouble started. Three further employees of the tramway department also described events in the north-east corner of the Square, although only one gave evidence at the trial.

There had been constant harassment of and even violence towards the tram staff during the week. As Shinwell's biographer, Peter Slowe put it, 'The working tram-drivers were indeed a potent symbol of what the strike had not yet achieved'.[7] This tension provides the context for what occurred in the south-east corner of the Square and the violence against the trams and their staff throughout the city for the rest of Friday.

It is important to understand the layout of the tramlines in the Square (Map 4). A pair of lines entered the Square at the south-west corner from St Vincent Place. The east-going line was the northern of the two, the west-going line was the southern. As soon as the lines entered the Square there was a set of points where the lines diverged. One pair of lines ran northwards along the west side of the Square before turning east along the north side of the Square, in front of the North British Station Hotel and exiting the Square at the north-east corner along George Street. From the set of points at the south-west corner, the other pair of lines ran along the south side of the Square, in front of the Post Office. The lines left the Square at the south-east corner, where they immediately turned into South Frederick Street. There were four tram stops within or just outside the Square on these lines.

No trams ran on the fourth side of the Square in front of the Municipal Buildings. Iain McLean describes the second of the police baton charges moving 'up the east side of the square, past the City Chambers' rather than the reality, which was westward away from the Chambers. He suggests that this was odd, as 'no tramlines ran along the east side of the square'.[8] However, McLean's view is based on the premise that *all* the baton charges within the Square (of which there were three) were 'supposedly to clear a way for the tramcars', but this was the purpose only of the first charge, from the south-east corner, according to police, tramways and defence witnesses. McLean's confusion is explained by a map in his doctoral thesis, which erroneously placed the beginnings of the riot in the *south-west* corner of the Square, thus mistakenly directing the first baton charge west-east along the south side of the Square, in front of the Post Office, the second baton charge, as noted above, running south-north in front of the City Chambers, and the third up North Frederick Street.[9]

The Trams

Witnesses who were neither police nor involved in the strike and who might be considered to provide less biased testimony include tram inspectors, conductors and drivers. However, the extent to which tram witnesses at inspector/management level or rank-and-file workers reacted to being vilified and harassed by the strikers as blacklegs and scabs all week, is unrecorded. The circumstantial details and corroboration between tram employees – not in the obviously scripted way seen in some police and defence evidence – suggest their eyewitness testimony and personal experiences are credible.

William Gallacher, in cross-examining Lieutenant Gray, suggested longer-term hostility between the tram-workers and organised labour, asserting 'whenever there is a Labour procession in Glasgow there is always . . . an attempt to drive a car into the procession' or even 'there has always been a tendency for the cars in Glasgow to run into a Labour procession'.[10] Gray dismissed Gallacher's suggestion that other processions in Glasgow, such as the large Meat Trades procession, had disrupted the trams, because 'these processions always keep to the side of the street to allow the cars to pass when they come'.[11]

The first tram to run into trouble in the Square at 12.08pm was eastbound along the south side of the Square, driven by Margaret Buchanan with Frances Simeone as conductor. The two women were accompanied by Tram Inspector David Cree, who stood beside Buchanan. Eastbound trams ran on the northern of the two sets of rails closer to the centre of the Square. Cree reported:

> I warned the driver to be very careful. At the Post Office a number of men got in front of the car and ordered it to stop . . . They shouted that the car was being driven on to them and used horrible language. Two of the strikers got hold of me. They tried to pull me off the car. A soldier [a 'colonial'] came to my assistance and released their hold. He told the men to get out and allow the car to proceed. Some of the crowd then tried to take the driving handle from the driver.[12]

Cree was asked whether there 'was anything to prevent these people from clearing off the line?'; he answered, 'No'.[13] Driver Buchanan told a similar story:

> Just as I reached the corner of the Square at Cochrane Street, several hundred people got on to the car rails and I was unable to proceed. Several of the persons in the crowd shouted to me that they had gone out to fight and I was now keeping them from getting their job back. They were using filthy and abusive language towards myself and Inspector Cree who was with me. One young man was trying to take the power handles from the front of the car but he did not succeed as the Inspector and I held on to the handles.[14]

Conductor Frances Simeone, on the rear platform, recalled the crowd 'shouting and using very bad language' and 'several of the crowd told me to come off and if I did not do so they would make short work of me'. 'Four Soldiers, three of whom were Australians, got on to the platform beside me to protect me', after which they 'went upstairs to keep the trolley on the wire'.[15] Neil Lawson, driving the tram immediately behind Buchanan's, saw the soldiers on Buchanan's rear platform and heard them shout to the crowd 'to go and work'.[16] Having been held up for a few minutes he saw police coming from the Municipal Buildings in single file. The police told the crowd to clear the way, but they paid no heed and shouted abusive remarks to the police. The police pressed the crowd back with their hands.[17] Defence witness Walter Stewart confirmed the police at first 'forced the crowd back with their hands prior to the batons coming out at all'.[18] Buchanan noted they 'had no batons in their hands while I was there'.[19]

Cree recalled people shouting 'Stop your ____cars. We are going to put you off the street', and they 'began to get hostile towards the police', calling them 'Dirty ______' and shouting 'Go for the swine'.[20] Cree testified he was told repeatedly by the crowd 'they were out to stop us' – that is, the trams.[21] A soldier 'got on to the front of [Lawson's] car and waved his hand as if to get the crowd to keep back'; the angry crowd shouted 'Pull him down'. At that point the police cleared the way sufficiently for Lawson to get his tram round the corner into South Frederick Street, with the crowd 'jeering and shouting'.[22] Lawson's conductor, Janet Drummond, said 'One of the crowd came to the rear of my car and pointing to a discharge badge he was wearing said "Do you see that lassie, that's what you're doing keeping me out of a job and I have a wife and children"'. Drummond heard someone in the crowd say 'Pull her off the car' but nobody interfered with her.[23]

By this stage, the police had assisted two tramcars round the corner into South Frederick Street by pushing the crowd back only with their hands. After Margaret Buchanan's tram had escaped, Cree dismounted and joined a tram heading in the opposite direction into the Square from South Frederick Street:

> A shout then got up, 'Go for the Police'. The Police were then being pushed right back . . . I then heard a smash of glass . . . The Police then drew their batons and charged the mob. The crowd was driven on to the north pavement of the south side of the Square . . . Their language was very menacing. It was directed against the Police. The Police were being overpowered. I know of no other method the Police could have adopted to keep an upper hand . . . Several Sailors and Soldiers came to our assistance at the Post Office. Had it not been for this we would have had a bad time.[24]

Produce merchant James Cummings was a passenger on Buchanan's tram and corroborated accounts of men blocking the rails who refused to move even though there was plenty of room. When

Buchanan rang the bell, 'they folded their arms' and demanded the car to stop. He said that Buchanan edged the car slowly forward 'in easy jerks' but the men refused to move, then clung to the splash-boards and complained 'they were being run over', which, according to Cummings, was untrue. He said members of the crowd had tried to pull him off the tram and 'one man threatened what he would do to me if I stepped off'. He reported, 'the crowd then surged forward and drove the Police up against the cars. The Police were very badly treated. I saw at least one Policeman being kicked and another man I saw kicked at me'.[25]

Cecil Naismith was one of the soldiers who went to protect Buchanan on her tram: 'The lady driver repeatedly rang her bell to clear the way. They paid no heed . . . I heard the crowd threaten her with sticks and stones. I saw the sticks they were carrying'. When the car stopped, a Colonial Flying Corps Officer standing beside Naismith told him to step on to the front of the car with him to protect the driver: 'They cursed and swore at the two soldiers and called them shirkers'. Naismith moved to the rear platform, while the officer stayed at the front. Naismith saw seven or eight policemen stand in front of the car who tried to clear a passage for it with their hands. He heard shouts, 'Go for the Police'. The crowd then attacked the police using sticks and he recalled that stones and clods of grass were thrown. He said a stone had gone through one of the car windows and immediately after that the police had drawn their batons and charged the crowd. There is a manuscript addition to Naismith's precognition, which might affect consideration of his evidence: 'Witness an applicant for appointment to the Glasgow Police'.[26]

The first tramcar into the Square from South Frederick Street was driven by John McGibbon, a few minutes after noon: 'The Police came forward and endeavoured to push the crowd back so as to allow my car to proceed'. McGibbon managed to move his tram forward 'about 12 yards when the crowd again rushed on to the track and prevented me proceeding'. They were 'very disorderly and [were] crying to us to stop work'. One of his tram's windows was smashed and as the crowd 'continued to get more disorderly and violent . . . I saw the Police charge them with their batons. They cleared a track and my car was then allowed to proceed'.[27] The driver of the third car to try to get into the Square from the south, at about 12.15pm, saw 'The crowd was shouting and swaying at the time . . . I then saw the Police charge the crowd with drawn batons and drive them into the Square and down South Frederick Street'. He was then able to proceed.[28]

Driver John McKelvie arrived from the south at 12.16pm and saw Margaret Buchanan's tram moving off after the police had cleared the crowd. He recalled hearing the glass of McGibbon's tram being broken: 'the crowd was getting hostile and roughly handled the Police. The Police were acting with great caution and did nothing in my view to create a feeling of hostility'. He noticed the crowd 'continued to sway and became very unmanageable. I saw the Police charge the crowd with their batons and drive them back'.[29]

Police and Other Public Servants

Just as the testimony of many of the defence witnesses must be seen through the prism of their loyalties, the evidence of police witnesses, and others in public service, must be considered in terms of theirs. Some clearly lied under oath to promote a particular narrative or to protect colleagues.

The most senior policeman present, Chief Constable Stevenson, could describe only in general what happened. His testimony suggests he was probably standing at the front of the City Chambers:

> My attention was then directed to a number of [tram]cars being held up on the south-east corner of the Square. I saw a number of Police at that stage endeavour to clear a way for the cars. The demeanour of the crowd at this time became menacing. There was some commotion at that part of the Square. I took that to be caused by the endeavour of the Police to clear a way for the cars. The cars then began to move. The commotion rapidly grew greater. The crowd in the centre of the square then surged towards the south-east corner and I next saw the crowd fly before the Police who had drawn their batons. Missiles then were thrown from the crowd and the Police then advanced against the crowd with drawn batons.[30]

He had not ordered any police to deal with the trams but 'My instructions generally were . . . that organised obstruction of traffic should not be permitted', and that the officers in charge had carried out his instruction. He was pressed several times in cross-examination whether the tram traffic should have been suspended for the day but responded consistently that he had not seen any reason for this.[31] He personally gave no order for batons to be used, contrary to the subsequent claims that the police were obeying his order to make an unprovoked attack.[32]

Inspector Sutherland, Sergeant McClure and ten constables went to the south-east corner 'to regulate the crowd and to allow the cars to proceed'.[33] McClure believed the obstruction of the trams had been deliberate, as 'they were hanging on to the front of the car, and also hanging on to the canopy rail'. McClure saw 'a number of soldiers intervene in the interests of the drivers' and saw a window smashed and had heard someone shout 'Rush the f—g police'. McClure confirmed that batons had been drawn only when missiles were thrown and when the police had been 'hustled' up against the cars. The crowd had swept forward again, and the police had been pressed back. A chisel had been thrown. McClure recalled shouting 'Keep together boys' to his men. He reported missiles at first from the direction of the Graham Statue and later from near the Post Office.[34] He was corroborated by Assistant Chief Constable Mennie.[35]

The Town Clerk, Sir John Lindsay, the Sheriff and John Lamb observed events from the second floor of the City Chambers in the Lord Provost's office (Map 4, 1).[36] The Sheriff noted two bodies of strikers, the first being about 100 men, step onto the tram rails and stay there as the main body assembled in the Square:

> partly on the pavement in front of the Post Office, facing north, and partly on the pavement on the other side . . . This part of the Square was not, so far as I knew or had previously observed, a place where speeches were delivered, and the aggregation of people on each side of the tramway lines at this part of the Square attracted my attention and induced in my mind the suspicion that an attempt was going to be made to stop the tramway cars at this point. I remarked at the time to

Sir John Lindsay or Mr. Lamb, or both, that that was not a usual place for the crowd to gather.[37]

Sir John Lindsay recalled their suspicions had been confirmed when tramcars came along and were stopped: 'They interfered with the woman driver and practically took possession of the tramway

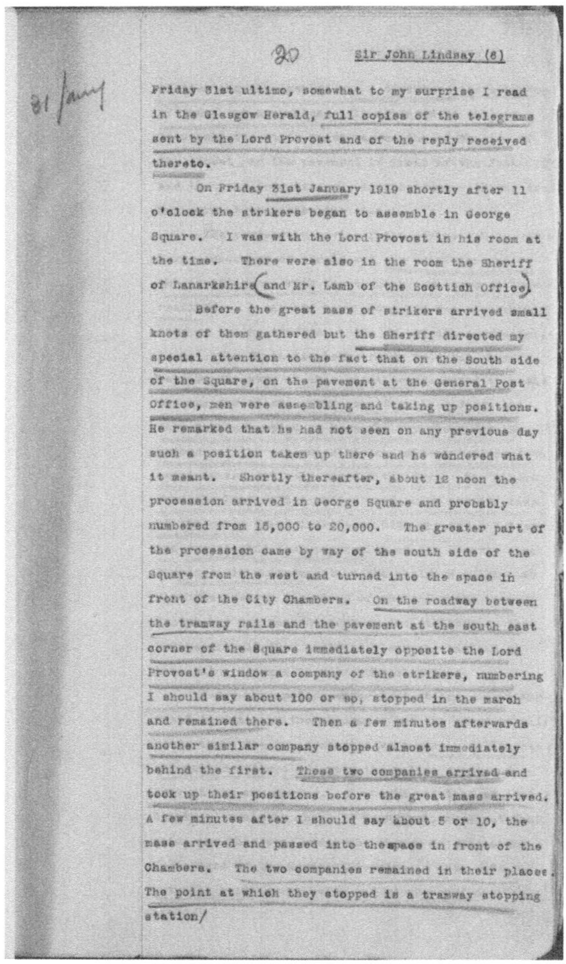

20 Sir John Lindsay (6)

Friday 31st ultimo, somewhat to my surprise I read in the Glasgow Herald, full copies of the telegrams sent by the Lord Provost and of the reply received thereto.

On Friday 31st January 1919 shortly after 11 o'clock the strikers began to assemble in George Square. I was with the Lord Provost in his room at the time. There were also in the room the Sheriff of Lanarkshire (and Mr. Lamb of the Scottish Office)

Before the great mass of strikers arrived small knots of them gathered but the Sheriff directed my special attention to the fact that on the South side of the Square, on the pavement at the General Post Office, men were assembling and taking up positions. He remarked that he had not seen on any previous day such a position taken up there and he wondered what it meant. Shortly thereafter, about 12 noon the procession arrived in George Square and probably numbered from 15,000 to 20,000. The greater part of the procession came by way of the south side of the Square from the west and turned into the space in front of the City Chambers. On the roadway between the tramway rails and the pavement at the south east corner of the Square immediately opposite the Lord Provost's window a company of the strikers, numbering I should say about 100 or so, stopped in the march and remained there. Then a few minutes afterwards another similar company stopped almost immediately behind the first. These two companies arrived and took up their positions before the great mass arrived. A few minutes after I should say about 5 or 10, the mass arrived and passed into the space in front of the Chambers. The two companies remained in their places. The point at which they stopped is a tramway stopping station/

11.1. *Town Clerk Sir John Lindsay's precognition describing his view from the City Chambers' window onto the south-east corner of George Square. (Reproduced by kind permission; Crown copyright. National Records of Scotland, AD15/19/11.)*

car. A soldier in uniform got on the platform of the car with the obvious intention of assisting the woman driver but was shoved about by the strikers'.[38]

There is no evidence that the strike leadership had had any definite plans to block the tram traffic, but it is clear from the evidence quoted above that some members of the crowd acted in concert to do

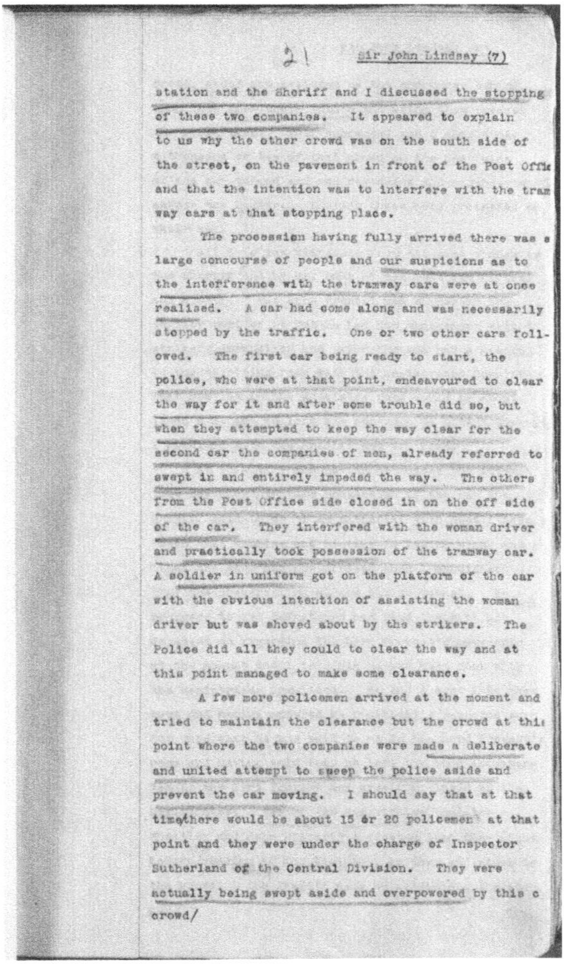

21 Sir John Lindsay (7)

station and the Sheriff and I discussed the stopping of these two companies. It appeared to explain to us why the other crowd was on the south side of the street, on the pavement in front of the Post Offic and that the intention was to interfere with the tram way cars at that stopping place.

The procession having fully arrived there was a large concourse of people and our suspicions as to the interference with the tramway cars were at once realised. A car had come along and was necessarily stopped by the traffic. One or two other cars foll-owed. The first car being ready to start, the police, who were at that point, endeavoured to clear the way for it and after some trouble did so, but when they attempted to keep the way clear for the second car the companies of men, already referred to swept in and entirely impeded the way. The others from the Post Office side closed in on the off side of the car. They interfered with the woman driver and practically took possession of the tramway car. A soldier in uniform got on the platform of the car with the obvious intention of assisting the woman driver but was shoved about by the strikers. The Police did all they could to clear the way and at this point managed to make some clearance.

A few more policemen arrived at the moment and tried to maintain the clearance but the crowd at this point where the two companies were made a deliberate and united attempt to sweep the police aside and prevent the car moving. I should say that at that time there would be about 15 or 20 policemen at that point and they were under the charge of Inspector Sutherland of the Central Division. They were actually being swept aside and overpowered by this c crowd/

11.2. *Town Clerk Sir John Lindsay's precognition describing his observations of the tram stoppage and the soldier assisting Margaret Buchanan, tram driver. (Reproduced by kind permission; Crown copyright. National Records of Scotland, AD15/19/11.)*

so, reflecting the considerable hostility evinced against the 'blackleg' tram staff throughout the week and putting into effect the leaders' often violently-expressed statements about the trams being taken off the streets on Friday.

The Sheriff's account corroborated the testimony of the tram staff and he believed the crowd had had room to run away 'very freely in the Square behind them' and noted they had not been forced back into the corner by weight of numbers and that the trams had run unhindered for the rest of the day.[39]

At about 12.15pm, Inspector Fraser, accompanied by Inspector William Murray and Sergeant David Murdoch with eight to a dozen constables, was sent from the front entrance of the City Chambers to reinforce Inspector Sutherland in the south-east corner. Murray described the crowd as 'violent and threatening' and using 'horrid language'.[40] Sergeant Murdoch had experienced difficulty getting to the south-east corner and had been 'rushed against the Buildings' and kicked, even before batons were drawn.[41] Fraser and his men had approached the west-going car; Sutherland's men had already reached the east-going car.[42]

No-one denied the hail of bottles from North Frederick Street which came later, but the police witnesses all recalled missiles being thrown in the south-east corner. Whether this commenced prior to the police drawing their batons has been disputed. A tram window was certainly smashed. Defence advocate Constable suggested in cross-examination that missiles 'did not come until you [police] had drawn your batons and used them'; McClure maintained that was not the case.[43] The *Daily Record* reported stones picked from the macadamised road surface being thrown.[44]

As matters got out of hand in the south-east corner of the Square, Superintendent McCulloch of the Lanarkshire Police was standing in Cochrane Street from where he claimed to have observed five men at two windows on the second floor of the City Chambers. He claimed they had gesticulated and shouted to the crowd below and he was 'satisfied from their gesticulations that they were hostile to the police'. He identified one of them as David Kirkwood, and at trial it became clear he meant the two windows of the library where the delegates were waiting to see the Lord Provost (Map 4, 3). His description of Kirkwood 'urging the crowd forward with wild gesticulations' and shouts of 'Go for them . . . into them' above the noise of the crowd, is unconvincing.[45] All the defence witnesses actually present beside Kirkwood contradicted McCulloch's claim and Inspector Sutherland confirmed he had not heard anyone shouting 'rush the police' from one of the windows.[46] McCulloch's evidence was corroborated only by his subordinate Detective Sergeant Mutch in precognition, who proved too ill to appear at trial as a witness.[47] Analysis of the evidence suggests strongly that neither Kirkwood nor the other delegates shouted the alleged words from the library window.

Inspector Sutherland stated that the half-dozen mounted police on duty in the quadrangle came out in two groups of three after the baton charges were over, and only three of them were in place before the North Frederick Street affair started. At least five of the mounted men are visible, standing in front of the City Chambers, in the short newsreel film of events.[48]

Lieutenant Gray believed events in the south-east corner had been deliberately planned 'to divert the attention of the Police from the front of the Municipal Buildings and that thereupon the bulk of the mob would rush the front entrance'.[49] Many defence witnesses were asked at some stage if they had heard any of the accused incite the crowd to attack the police or seize the Municipal Buildings or the North British Station Hotel. All answered in the negative. Analysis of all the court evidence suggests that no such incitement was made and the prosecution had to work hard to present jocular or off-the-cuff remarks as serious incitement. However, other witnesses confirmed there were individuals – not the strike leaders – who *were* inciting the crowd once the violence had started, one of whom was the accused James Murray.[*] According to Murdoch, when the police in the south-east corner charged, the crowd had moved towards the Municipal Buildings, and this prompted the drawing of batons right

* James Davidson Murray. Born Aberdeenshire. Joined Glasgow Police 1906. Dismissed December 1910 for insolence and insubordination. Emigrated to Canada 1911 to 1915. Returned to Glasgow to work at munitions at Beardmore's until December 1918. Employed Caledonia Engineering workshop, Springburn, until he came out on strike on 28 January 1919. Member of the Blacksmiths Society. Tried and convicted.

along the police line in front of the Buildings. At the Buildings, Inspector Sutherland said, the crowd got to within eight to nine yards of the door.[50] This had prompted the second baton charge of the day.[51] Although there is no sign of a preconcerted plan by the protestors to attack the Chambers, the police may have believed such a plan existed and their reaction to the movement of the crowd may have reflected this.

---

1. C. Mercer and C. A. Mercer, *Journal of the Waterloo Campaign, Kept throughout the Campaign of 1815* (Blackwood, 1870), p.314.
2. W. Gallacher, *Revolt on the Clyde* (Lawrence and Wishart, 2017 [1936]), p.160. It is clear that this relates only to that part of the crowd surrounding and listening to Gallacher (p.123 above).
3. G. Mooney, 'Why Glasgow's "Bolshevist Uprising" in 1919 wasn't quite the red threat to UK many believed', *The Conversation*, 8 February 2019, https://theconversation.com/why-glasgows-bolshevist-uprising-in-1919-wasnt-quite-the-red-threat-to-uk-many-believed-110474?utm_source=twitter&utm_medium=twitterbutton .
4. I. McLean, *The Legend of Red Clydeside* (John Donald, 1999), p.134.
5. R. Holmes, *Sylvia Pankhurst: Natural Born Rebel* (Bloomsbury, 2020), p.521. As we describe in more detail below (Chapter 19), one of the features of the historiography is the extent to which Gallacher's and the other strike leaders' versions have been accepted uncritically, as though they were dispassionate and omnipresent observers. We look in more detail at the coverage of events in the mainstream and socialist press, and in the memoirs of the strike leaders in Chapter 12.
6. K. MacAskill, *Glasgow 1919: The Rise of Red Clydeside* (Biteback, 2019), p.205.
7. P. Slowe, *Manny Shinwell: An Authorised Biography* (Pluto Press, 1993), p.81.
8. McLean, *Legend*, p.133.
9. I. McLean, *The Labour Movement in Clydeside Politics, 1914-1922* (Dphil thesis, University of Oxford, 1972), p.213. The description of the event in the *Glasgow Herald* of 1 February 1919 in which the police were descibed as 'making a straight charge along the front of the Chambers' may have misled McLean to interpret the baton charge being *across* the front of the Chambers, south to north, rather than a charge into the Square (east to west) by the line of police who were standing right *along* the frontage of the building. McLean did not have access to the trial papers (pers. comm.).

10. JC36/31/01 [01/C], Lawrence Gray, Police Lieutenant.
11. JC36/31/01 [01/C], Gray, Police Lieutenant; *Glasgow Herald*, 2 May 1918, p.8.
12. AD15/19/11 [A24], David Cree, Tram Inspector.
13. JC36/31/02 [02/H], Cree, Tram Inspector.
14. AD15/19/11 [A70], Margaret Buchanan, Tram Driver.
15. AD15/19/11 [B36], Frances Simeone, Tram Conductor.
16. AD15/19/11 [A71], Neil Lawson, Tram Driver.
17. AD15/19/11 [A24], Cree, Tram Inspector.
18. JC36/31/06 [06/C], Walter Stewart, Amalgamated Society of Engineers.
19. AD15/19/11 [A70], Buchanan, Tram Driver.
20. JC36/31/02 [02/H], Cree, Tram Inspector.
21. JC36/31/02 [02/H], Cree, Tram Inspector.
22. AD15/19/11 [A71], Lawson, Tram Driver.
23. AD15/19/11 [B37], Janet Drummond, Tram Conductor.
24. JC36/31/02 [02/H], Cree, Tram Inspector.
25. AD15/19/11 [A67] and JC36/31/02 [02/F], James Cummings, Produce Merchant.
26. AD15/19/11 [A111], Cecil Naismith, Private, Royal Scots.
27. AD15/19/11 [B33], John McGibbon, Tram Motorman.
28. AD15/19/11 [B38], James Lawrie, Tram Motorman.
29. AD15/19/11 [B39], John Baird McKelvie, Tram Motorman.
30. AD15/19/11 [A05], James Verdier Stevenson, Chief Constable.
31. JC36/31/04 [04/H], Stevenson, Chief Constable.
32. JC36/31/04 [04/H], Stevenson, Chief Constable; J. Cameron, *Red Flag over the Clyde: The Story of John Maclean and Red Clydeside* (Scottish Militant Labour, 1993), p.21. MacAskill, *Glasgow 1919*, p.205.
33. AD15/19/11 [A68], Sutherland, Police Inspector.
34. AD15/19/11 [A62], adopted by Thomas McClure, originally given by David Murdoch, Police Sergeant; JC36/31/02 [02/J], Thomas McClure, Police Sergeant.
35. AD15/19/11 [A06], Alexander Mennie, Asst Chief Constable.
36. AD15/19/11 [A02], John Lamb, Scottish Office.
37. AD15/19/11 [A01], Alastair Oswald MacKenzie, Sheriff of Lanarkshire.
38. AD15/19/11 [A04], JC36/31/02 [02/R] and [03/B], Sir John Lindsay, Town Clerk.

39. Corroborated by JC36/31/02 [02/Q], Sutherland, Police Inspector; JC36/31/02 [02/G], William Murray, Police Inspector; JC36/31/04 [04/D], McArthur, Police Sergeant.

40. AD15/19/11 [A21], adopted by Police Sergeant David Murdoch, originally given by the late Inspector Simon Fraser.

41. JC36/31/02 [02/B], David Murdoch, Police Sergeant.

42. AD15/19/11 [A21], adopted by Police Sergeant David Murdoch, originally given by the late Inspector Simon Fraser; AD15/19/11 [A61], Murray, Police Inspector.

43. AD15/19/11 [A62], adopted by Thomas McClure, originally given by David Murdoch, Police Sergeant; JC36/31/02 [02/J], McClure, Police Sergeant.

44. *Daily News*, 3 February 1919.

45. AD15/19/11 [A65], Matthew McCulloch, Lanarkshire Police Superintendent; JC36/31/02 [02/N], McCulloch, Lanarkshire Police Superintendent.

46. JC36/31/09 [09/B], Isaac Sim; JC36/31/08 [08/Q], William Harvey, ASE; JC36/31/09 [09/C], Donald Kennedy; JC36/31/09 [09/V], Neil Maclean, MP; JC36/31/02 [02/Q], Sutherland, Police Inspector.

47. AD15/19/11 [A66], Alexander Mutch, Detective Sergeant.

48. JC36/31/02 [02/Q], Sutherland, Police Inspector. Pathé Films, 'Striking workers in Glasgow, 1919'. https://www.britishpathe.com/asset/170243/ Some subsequent accounts claim the mounted police were part of the group sent to clear the way for the trams in the south-east corner; there is no evidence to support this (e.g. R.K. Middlemas, *The Clydesiders: A Left-wing Struggle for the Parliamentary Power* (Harvard University Press, 1965), p.94.

49. AD15/19/11 [A20] and JC36/31/01 [01/C], Gray, Police Lieutenant.

50. JC36/31/02 [02/Q], Sutherland, Police Inspector.

51. JC36/31/02 [02/B], Murdoch, Police Sergeant.

12 The Riot: 31 January 1919: the Defence Evidence and the Press

The defence promoted four strands of argument, that:

- there had been no deliberate attempt to stop the trams and the presence of people on the tram tracks was entirely due to numbers and pressure in the crowd;
- the crowd was peaceful, there was no trouble and there was no justification for the police intervention; some witnesses went so far as to claim the police attack was premeditated;
- 'all the offence . . . came from the police' and that the police had behaved 'like savages';[1]
- finally, had anyone wanted to stop the tram traffic, George Square was not the best place to do it.

Of 58 witnesses called by the defence, only three of those who were in the Square were not involved with the strike or active in the Labour movement and might therefore be expected to be disinterested. They were Rennie Ferrie, a clerkess on business at the Municipal Buildings; Frederick Sievwright, a court shorthand writer 'without sympathy' for the strike, and Robert Johnston, a traveller from Larbert. He had been batoned by a policeman on the shoulder and the tone of his responses suggests he may have continued to hold a grudge.

Rennie Ferrie was in the Square around noon and she stood for a moment between the Graham Statue and the Gladstone Statue (Map 4), over 30m from the tramcars with a crowd intervening, from where she said she saw 'some holding up of the tramway cars' and a soldier replacing a trolley on the wire; she saw the police arriving, but did not see what they did, only that there 'was a great cry and a great rush of people'.[2]

Frederick Sievwright, while passing through the Square, stood listening to Gallacher speaking from the plinth of the Gladstone Statue for five or six minutes, from where he heard some disturbance and undistinguishable shouts from the south-east corner. He thought he heard someone say, 'The Police are drawing their batons' and, turning round, saw a policeman about six feet away drawing his baton. Sievwright 'jumped in among the crowd rather than run the risk of being struck by this policeman'. Counsel asked him whether any action by the crowd had warranted the baton charge, to which he answered, 'Not in my vicinity. What happened at the south-east corner I cannot say. There may have been justification for a bayonet charge for all I know'.[3]

Robert Johnston was passing up South Frederick Street into George Square around noon. He reported a dense but 'perfectly orderly' crowd but had observed tram cars standing at the corner and the body of policemen coming from George Square. Twice he described a 'feeble' or a 'faint' effort by the police to clear the rails. He had seen no justification for the drawing of the police batons. When the Lord Advocate asked him 'what purpose' the police had when they rounded the south-east corner, Johnston admitted he did not know but then said, 'there was a determination on their faces' and they had come 'with an order or orders to strike'. The Lord Advocate asked if he thought 'the police came on the scene for the purpose of making an attack on the crowd' and Johnston replied, 'that was my impression'.[4]

A number of the defence witnesses who were more closely associated with the strike testified under oath to have seen clearly and certainly events of which, from their stated position, they could have had only a very restricted view, or which had happened before they arrived in the Square. Several denied what other corroborated defence witnesses reported seeing. For example, John Forman asserted that he had not seen any behaviour to justify the baton charges; not in George Square, North Frederick Street during the bottle-throwing, Trongate or Saltmarket, Jail Square or Great Clyde Street, where there had indeed been extreme violence by elements of the crowd.[5]

This is absurd. Edith Hughes* claimed to have seen, from 30m away and *behind* Margaret Buchanan's tram, that the 'man' [sic] was driving it 'to the danger of the crowd'.[6] William Inglis claimed to have seen no disturbance until the police made a charge, but he had been in North Frederick Street, the whole width of the Square – 100m – away.[7] District Nurse Allison Moir, by her own admission, 'did not see what happened in the south-east corner of the Square', but nevertheless declared firmly 'the disorder and confusion and violence which ultimately resulted [was] due entirely to the action of the police in making the unprovoked attack on the crowd'. She was also convinced the police had either taken 'it into their head' to charge from the City Chambers or 'somebody told them to do it'.[8]

The first defence witness, Councillor Edward Rosslyn Mitchell,† arrived at the City Chambers at about 11.40am. He witnessed processions arriving and described a 'good crowd' but had no difficulty crossing the Square.[9] He, and the second witness, John Stewart, were both Glasgow city councillors and members of the Independent Labour Party (ILP) and presented the key strands of the defence case. Both had observed events from the Council Officer's second-floor windows in the City Chambers, just north of the Lord Provost's office. Mitchell observed large crowds standing at the south-east corner by the Post Office, and at the north-east corner, describing both as 'congested' with more people arriving, and in front of the Chambers

* Edith Hughes (1889-1978) born in Edinburgh. Living in Glasgow by 1914. Prominent figure in Labour circles in Glasgow. Organising Clerk and a member of the National Executive of the National Union of Clerks; Honorary Treasurer of Glasgow Trades and Labour Council; a member of the Administrative Council of the Scottish Labour Party; a director of the Scottish Blind Asylum; a member of the Women's Standing Committee of the Local Advisory Committee of the Glasgow Labour Exchange. By 1932 widowed and resident in London. In Edinburgh again by the 1950s.

† Councillor Edward Rosslyn Mitchell (1879-1965) was born in Wiltshire. By 1891 the family had moved to Glasgow. He studied law at Glasgow University starting practice in 1904. In 1909 he entered the Town Council of Glasgow as an independent radical. In 1910 he contested Buteshire as a Liberal. In 1919 he joined the ILP and contested Glasgow Central for Labour, coming second to Bonar Law. Chairman of the council's Parks Committee and the Art Galleries and Museums Committee. Labour MP for Paisley from 1924–29, beating Asquith.

around the Gladstone Statue (Map 4, no. 1).[10] He saw nothing of note apart from the delegation entering the Municipal Buildings and a motor van driving in front of them, passing from north to south Frederick Street.[11]

Mitchell described the stopping of the trams very generally and then was allowed to make an uninterrupted statement 695 words long, condensing the ten to twenty minutes of struggle, with accompanying threats, violence and missile-throwing, to no more than a few moments during which nothing of note happened, before the sudden and unaccountable action of the police.[12] Several defence witnesses similarly reduced events in the south-east corner into a brief and comparatively uneventful period, in contrast to the tramworkers' and police evidence. Mitchell said the driver of the foremost east-going tramcar had 'sounded his [sic] gong very loudly', started his car, the west-going car starting at the same time, and someone standing at his side shouted,'Oh, they will be killed', which had also crossed Mitchell's own mind at the time. He had witnessed the police, with their hands, clear away the people for the foremost car to continue into South Frederick Street and reported that the crowd near the Graham Statue and the Gladstone Statue had begun to press towards the south-east. People had been crushed against each other and the police had been pressed up against the car. They had then drawn their batons, holding them in front of them to move the crowd back; they had not used them to strike. He said the front twelve or fifteen ranks of the crowd had appeared willing to move and had done so, but the crowd behind had not and they surged forward. He also said that no missiles had been thrown by the crowd at this stage, nor had any violence been offered to the police. He had not considered the first police 'charge' as a charge at all. Instead, he suggested, they had moved forward with their batons over their shoulders, without the momentum of 'big men running . . . without any great intent to injure in the body at that stage'. Mitchell thought the 'whole business in the south-east corner lasted [no] more than five, or, at the most, ten minutes, and after that the cars passed without interruption'.[13]

Bailie John Stewart reported the crowd had appeared densest in the south-east corner. Having left the window when the Lord Provost called the magistrates' meeting to order, he immediately after heard a very considerable commotion outside and returned to the window. He saw the crowd 'rapidly dispersing with the police chasing them with their batons'. Stewart confirmed he had not actually witnessed the beginning of the trouble, but nevertheless felt able to state, 'I could almost try to visualise in my own mind that there had been an attack made and that created the commotion'.[14]

The Lord Advocate, as he did with a number of witnesses (e.g. John Mackenzie), asked Bailie Stewart why the crowd was so dense in the south-east corner. Stewart only noted there had also been a dense crowd in the north-east corner, which in retrospect might rather have reinforced the idea that other efforts were being made to stop the cars there, supporting the Town Clerk's observations. Stewart reported the crowd in the south-east corner as being 'absolutely quiet' while he was observing the police trying to clear a way, which again contradicts evidence given by the tram crews, who were in the middle of it.[15] As noted above, the defence claim was that the crowd was quiet and that people were on the tracks solely because of pressure from the Square.

Much effort was put into establishing the second and third strands of the defence case, that the police started the violence and were undisciplined 'savages'. As Walter Stewart put it, 'all the offence . . . came from the police'. Stewart described a fifteen-year-old boy 'clubbed by a policeman' who 'fell like an ox' and whom he had carried out of the way.[16] This incident appears again in Slowe's account of the trial, where he claimed the Lord Justice-Clerk referred to 'a fifteen-year-old boy whose head had been cracked open'. But the judge made no such reference in his charge to the jury nor in any interventions he made during the trial.[17] This boy's alleged ordeal was also described in the *Strike Bulletin* and by two other defence witnesses. No such child appears in the casualty list.[18] Defence witness John Mackenzie described a 'wounded soldier' who had been struck on the head and knocked down by a young policeman 'three times very brutally about the body and legs', including after he had fallen. He had also seen 'a woman crying very bitterly' who claimed she had been 'struck by the police'.[19] Mackenzie was the first trial witness to suggest that the police had deliberately fomented the violence. The

Lord Advocate put it to him, 'You mean the police had made a plan the night before to attack the crowd, and they were then doing it?' Mackenzie answered: 'That was my idea'. This notion had already been published in the *Strike Bulletin* and had been repeated by John Maclean before the trial. To the Lord Advocate's question, 'And you really tell the Jury that your evidence is that your notion was that these 20 policemen were the authors of a made up plan the night before to attack a crowd of 20,000?' Mackenzie answered 'Yes'.[20]

Archibald Wallace, a member of the General Strike Committee, repeated the defence line that the obstruction of the trams was not deliberate but only the result of the density of the crowd.[21] Archibald Stewart arrived in the west part of the Square with the Partick procession about 11.50am and, like many others, went to the south-east corner, apparently without difficulty. He again claimed the pressure of the crowd around the trams had been caused by people pushing from the centre of the Square and that no policemen had been mishandled and no missiles had been thrown. He said the police 'just sort of pressed forward to shove the crowd back' and blamed the violence on the police drawing their batons.[22] John Mann had arrived with a procession from Govan, but once again moved to the south-east corner of the Square. Mann admitted there were indeed 'a few young chaps . . . fooling about' in front of the stalled east-going tramcar, young men 'hanging on to the front of the car as if they wanted to be carried through the crowd'. He confirmed the police twice cleared them away using their hands.[23] John Thom was on the plinth of the Gladstone Statue. The motor lorry driven in front of the Chambers, injuring two men, had, in his opinion, changed the mood of the crowd in that part of the Square. In common with other defence witnesses, he compressed the timescale of events in the south-east corner so that only moments had passed from the delegation entering the Chambers to the drawing of batons. At first, he claimed 100 policemen charged into the south-east corner, who, he said:

> batoned the crowd then indiscriminately without regard to either age or sex. Wherever a head appeared they struck it. By this time the police seemed to me to have lost all control of themselves. They went into the crowd with the abandon of

street urchins, and their faces were flamed with passion, and they were using curses at every blow . . .[24]

Archibald McPhie arrived in George Square with the Flour Millers' Union procession around noon. He said although the Square had not filled up at this time, 'they were wedged in at the south-east corner'; he offered no explanation for this but adhered to the defence line that the sheer density of the crowd had prevented the cars moving. The Lord Advocate elicited the admission that, after the baton charge had cleared the way for the trams in the south-east corner, the traffic had run uninterrupted for the rest of the afternoon. McPhie described police brutality, using the same cast of characters: the 'small boy' who had blood running down his face; helping two 'nearly hysterical' elderly women onto the steps of the Post Office; helping a man who had been struck repeatedly, even when sitting to recover from the first blow. McPhie, however, admitted he had seen power trolleys taken off cars by the crowd and that people had hung off the splash-boards of the cars.[25]

The final defence witness was Neil Maclean, MP for Govan, who had been in the library with the delegation when the trouble broke out. As with other defence witnesses, although he did not see the beginning of the unrest in the south-east corner, it was nevertheless his firm view in cross-examination that 'the police had made some blunder', and 'in some way a slight disturbance had been by some one of the police magnified into an exaggerated attempt to start a riot and they had immediately drawn their batons on the crowd'.[26] The Lord Advocate asked Maclean, 'what leads you to entertain those suspicions with regard to events in the south-east corner which you did not see?' Maclean responded that because in the past a procession had been baton-charged unjustifiably, it 'was quite natural for me to assume that a blunder had been committed again by some over-zealous police constable'. His statement that any 'body of men may have several in their ranks who may be guilty of over zealousness', received the Lord Advocate's irony-laden response: 'I agree with you'.[27]

The final strand of the defence was to suggest that no attempt had been made to stop the trams in the Square, because such a blockage could have been made more effectively elsewhere in the city.

Defence counsel asked Peter Campbell, the pro-strike Joint Secretary of the Municipal Employees' Association in Glasgow, to suppose where the strikers could more effectively have brought the tram service to a stop. Campbell named Jamaica and Union Streets. Defence advocate Constable asked John Thom, an iron-moulder, eight questions to elicit from him his opinion on tram routes, possible diversions out of the Square, even details about the location of loop lines which could have been used to turn trams away from the Square.[28] Constable's aim seems to have been to prove that George Square was far from ideal if one was intent on stopping the tram network, but it is unclear why he thought an iron-moulder was the person to ask. His line of questioning seems in any case to miss the point; the demonstration had occurred in George Square and it was there where some strikers had decided to make their gesture, where they had the cover and support of the rest of the crowd, not elsewhere in the city.[29]

At this stage in the evidence (including that provided by some defence witnesses) it is clear this was not a peaceful crowd subjected to an unprovoked attack, whether or not planned. Rather, the apparently deliberate movement of people onto the tram tracks was an attempt, evidenced by both prosecution and defence witnesses, to block the trams in the south-east corner, to express frustration at the non-striking drivers and conductors. These efforts were accompanied by verbal and physical abuse, shouts about blacklegs and scabs and attempts to drag tram staff and other people off the platforms. It is clear from the eyewitness testimony that the police tried at first to push the crowds back with their hands, before missiles were thrown and batons were drawn.

The Press

Having considered the eyewitness testimony, how did the mainstream and socialist press cover the beginnings of the riot? The *Glasgow Herald* described events in a series of articles:

> The car traffic was being held up at the corner of Cochrane Street owing to the crowd overflowing from the Square, and although now and again a car moved slowly ahead it was evident that traffic was almost at a standstill. It was stated

> that frequently deliberate attempts were made to hold up the service by young fellows thrusting their legs before the cars. The position became at last so serious that an extra force of police was hurried from the Council Chambers to cope with it. Then the storm broke. It had its origins at this corner, but what was the immediate cause is not quite clear. But the effect was instantaneous. The police now proceeded to draw batons and clear the Square, or at least a portion of it, and they proceeded to that task with vigour and determination that was a prelude to the extraordinary scenes which the Square was afterwards to witness, and to which the city, with all its acquaintance with labour troubles can happily offer no parallel. A strong body converged from the south-east corner of the Square, and, advancing in extended order, swept the crowd in front of them, raining a hurricane of blows which fell indiscriminately on those actually participating in the strike and on those who had been drawn to the scene merely through curiosity.[30]

While the *Glasgow Herald* had been no friend of the strike during the preceding week, at least three major national titles had special correspondents in the city who corroborated its accounts.[31] The *Manchester Guardian* reported the riot 'began when the police used their truncheons to keep clear passage for the tramcars through the densely packed sides of George Square'.[32] The *Times*' correspondent reported:

> some foolish enthusiasts are said to have tried to stop the running of the tramway cars by laying themselves full length across the rails or pulling down the trolleys of the cars. Two soldiers took the part of a conductress who was being troubled by a rowdy group, and brought on themselves the attention of the malcontents. The police intervened and cleared the crowd away from the car by a truncheon charge.[33]

The *Daily Record* confirmed 'the interference of a band of young fellows' had held up the trams.[34] The account of the special correspondent of the *Daily News* published three days later, on Monday 3 February, was quoted by Iain McLean in support of a 'police riot':

> . . . it cannot be said that the authorities managed their business very happily on Friday. In the first place, if it was intended to maintain a service of tramcars through George Square during the demonstration, it was inexcusable to leave the square virtually unguarded by police until the whole of the roadway was blocked by a dense crowd and to endeavour to force the tramcars through it.
>
> I was within a few yards of the tramcars during the forcing-through process and I have no hesitation in saying that the baton charge made with the object of clearing a way for the second tramcar was the beginning of the trouble in the square. The temper of some hundreds of the strikers was immediately fired, stones were picked up from the macadam streets.[35]

The *Daily News*' special correspondent clearly sympathised with the strikers, believing the policy of the government was 'merely one of repression' designed to break the strike.[36] However, in his immediate report of the trouble written on Friday evening he had taken a different line:

> Just before half past twelve a determined attempt was made by a section of the crowd to hold up a line of tramcars which were slowly forcing a way through the square . . .[37]

He described the first car rounding the corner and the police trying to do the same for the second:

> An ugly rush against [the police] was organised and for a moment it seemed likely that they would be broken up and isolated in the crowd. Swiftly rallying, however, they responded to an order and in an instant were belabouring their assailants with batons. There was a wild rush from this part of the square, but the police discontinued the baton charge as soon as a way was cleared for the tramcars.[38]

While the mainstream press was broadly consistent in its coverage and was corroborated by a range of witnesses, the *Strike Bulletin* on Saturday and Sunday 1 and 2 February 1919 provided a range of often mutually contradictory explanations. Some were adopted at the trial by the defence and formed what has become the foundation of the widely accepted narrative:

> Henceforth January 31, 1919, will be known in Glasgow as Bloody Friday, and, for the crime of attacking defenceless workers, the citizens will hold the authorities responsible. The police have once more been used as hirelings to bludgeon the workers.
>
> The outrage looks like a prearranged affair by the master class . . . the deputation were kept waiting for twenty minutes, and, while there, the police were ordered to draw their batons and forcibly disperse the crowd of strikers who were standing in George Square until the deputation returned.
>
> The bludgeon attack on the strikers in front of the City Chambers was deliberately ordered by the officers, **and was unprovoked** [original emphasis]**.** The attack was sheer brutality by the police to satisfy the lust of the masters for broken skulls. The masters, afraid to do their own dirty work, employ the police to do it for them.[39]

The *Strike Bulletin* does not mention the trams in the south-east corner at all. It also claimed after two motor vehicles were allowed to run into the crowd, causing injury, that the 'police attack' was the response to 'a not unreasonable request' that motor traffic be diverted, adding that the level of police violence was the result of wounded *amour propre*, when the crowd jeered at two police horses falling with their riders. Both Isaac Sim and Alexander Duncan saw the accident, but beyond it 'annoying people', they did not mention this as the cause of the riot.[40] The *Strike Bulletin* described the 25,000 strikers as doing 'nobly' against 'big odds' – that is, the 140-160 or so policemen in the Square.[41] The alleged police violence had been an attempt 'to crush the 40 hours movement by force':

> They may arrest members of the Joint Committee; they may attack a defenceless crowd; they may proclaim martial law; they may bring out troops and guns; they may try to starve us; they may sneer and lie about the strike; they may employ blacklegs; they may employ cheap alien labour; they may bully as they care; but all these and other efforts will be futile if the workers be true to one another.[42]

The *Strike Bulletin* placed great emphasis on the police violence, their alleged loss of control and the injuries to strikers and non-strikers and women. The absurdity of some of the account does little to strengthen the *Strike Bulletin*'s credibility:

> A big fur-coated profiteer, who was standing in the George Square, admiring the police knocking down defenceless women and men to the ground, was heard to remark – "Serve the b----s's right. That's the stuff to give them!" One of the Strikers, hearing him, gave the profiteer a robust tap in his 'bread basket' and toppled him over like a ninepin. We hope he likes his own medicine.[43]

Elsewhere, the *Strike Bulletin* ascribed another and different cause of the violence: 'the attempt of an Australian solider, in sympathy with the strike, to prevent a tramcar going through the crowd'.[44] In reality, all witnesses to the actions of Australian and other soldiers described them protecting tram staff from the violence of the crowd and trying to keep the trams moving, and the hostility and name-calling between soldiers and strikers is notable. Sunday's *Strike Bulletin* continued in a similarly overwrought vein:

> Apparently, if the workers do not accept what the employers give them, it is to be rammed down their throats at the point of the bayonet. The Czar's Government shot down the people who asked for votes in 1905, and the British Government represses the people in 1919 who ask for a shorter working week. . . . [The strikers] repudiate any responsibility for what occurred. If the police had not attacked the crowd in

> George Square the Demonstration would have passed off quietly, as did former Demonstrations. The attack by the police was carefully planned. Of this there can be no doubt in view of what happened. We knew all about the plot to smash the Demonstration, and will reveal it in due course.[45]

This alleged revelation never materialised, but the 'carefully planned attack' has become a 'fact' that forms part of the catechism of the Battle. Sunday's *Strike Bulletin* also appears to have contributed to the subsequent creation of the 'all the troops were English' mythology:

> Can anyone tell us if it is true that Scottish soldiers declined to take part in the attack on workers? The armed soldiers now on duty in the city are apparently strangers. What have the soldiers been brought out for? Give this a thought![46]

Other mythological elements originated here too:

> It is reported to us that all the policemen did not use their batons when ordered to attack the crowd, and it is alleged a number of them downed truncheons in sympathy with the strikers. All honour to these men, whose hearts proved stronger than Prussianism.
>
> During the George Square battle the soldier spectators, it is reported, were commandeered by the police in 'the name of the King,' taken to the City Chambers, and there supplied with full equipment in view of further action. This was stated by one of the soldiers involved to a meeting of strikers in the Gorbals.[47]

There is no prosecution or defence testimony whatsoever to support the claim of any police 'mutiny' nor of soldiers being equipped in the City Chambers. Five days later, the *Strike Bulletin* jibed: 'The policemen who cracked skulls in George Square were, it is stated, all asked to volunteer for the massacre. The same men were not so anxious to volunteer during the war'.[48] This is a calumny. By the end of

1915, 692 men, over a third of the police force, had volunteered for military service and about 500-600 men were still away in the army in January 1919.[49] In contrast, many of the strikers – skilled engineers – had spent the war at home in reserved occupations: the proportion of men enlisting from jobs in 'metals' manufacturing, which included engineering, had been 25 per cent (and the national recruitment figure for the 'treacherous' tram staff was 50 per cent).[50] The *Strike Bulletin*'s scattergun of misinformation seemed to be designed to obscure the complexities of the immediate causes of the riot, to exculpate the strike leadership and the strikers themselves, placing the blame firmly at the feet of the police, the trams, the 'masters', 'an Australian soldier', 'hooligans', or the careless drivers of two vans in front of the Chambers. There was no reflection on what part some of the strikers or their leaders might have played in starting the riot in the south-east corner.

---

1. JC36/31/07 [07/M], James McLellan, Machine Man.
2. JC36/31/07 [07/S], Rennie Ferrie.
3. JC36/31/07 [07/L], Frederick Sievwright, Sheriff Court shorthand writer.
4. JC36/31/08 [08/H], Robert Johnston, Traveller. The rest of his evidence concerns the northern part of the Square where he had been struck on the shoulder by a policeman aiming at his head as he tried to dodge out of the way of a mounted policeman. In cross-examination Johnston was asked if the crowd had been 'very infuriated' after the baton charge in the south-east corner, to which he replied 'They were infuriated'. The Lord Advocate picked up on the opinion he had been led into giving.
5. JC36/31/08 [08/C], John Forman, Iron Turner.
6. JC36/31/07 [07/T], Edith Hughes, Strike Committee.
7. JC36/31/06 [06/E], William Inglis, Railway Vehicle Builders' Society.
8. JC36/31/08 [08/P], Allison Moir, District Nurse.
9. JC36/31/05 [05/MM], E. R. Mitchell; Minutes of the Corporation of Glasgow, 31 January 1919, Parks, Open Spaces and North of River Clyde subcommittee.
10. JC36/31/05 [05/MM], E. R. Mitchell, Councillor.
11. JC36/31/05 [05/MM], Mitchell, Councillor.
12. JC36/31/05 [05/MM], Mitchell, Councillor.
13. JC36/31/05 [05/MM], Mitchell, Councillor.

14. JC36/31/06 [06/B], Stewart, Councillor.
15. JC36/31/06 [06/B], Stewart, Councillor; JC36/31/06 [06/D], John Mackenzie, Member of the Shipwrights' Society.
16. JC36/31/06 [06/C], Walter Stewart, Engineer and Chairman of the Partick Strike Committee.
17. P. M. Slowe, *Manny Shinwell: An Authorised Biography* (Pluto Press, 1993), p.98.
18. *Strike Bulletin*, 1 February 1919; JC36/31/08 [08/E], Archibald McPhie, Flour Millers' Union; JC36/31 [08F], Frank Chappell, Organising Secretary, Amalgamated Instrument Makers. It is not clear how all the witnesses who testified about the boy knew how old he was.
19. JC36/31/06 [06/D], John Mackenzie, Member of the Shipwrights' Society.
20. *Strike Bulletin,* 1 February 1919; J. Maclean, *Sack Dalrymple; Sack Stevenson. Let Labour Revenge Bloody Friday* (J. Maclean, 1919), pp.1-2, 6, 12-13; JC36/31/06 [06/D], Mackenzie, Shipwrights' Society.
21. JC36/31/06 [06/F], Archibald Wallace, Sheet Metal Worker.
22. JC36/31/07 [07/E], Archibald Stewart, Pattern Maker.
23. JC36/31/07 [07/U], John Mann, Pattern Maker.
24. JC36/31/08 [08/B], John Thom, Strike Committee.
25. JC36/31/08 [08/E], Archibald McPhie, Flour Millers' Union.
26. JC36/31/09 [09/V], Maclean, MP.
27. JC36/31/09 [09/V], Maclean, MP.
28. JC36/31/08 [08/B], Thom, Strike Committee.
29. JC36/31/08 [08/N], Peter Campbell, Municipal Employees' Association.
30. *Glasgow Herald,* 1 February 1919.
31. It is occasionally claimed that Siegfried Sassoon was the *Guardian*'s special correspondent and was in the Square, but he only arrived in the city on Monday 3 February, representing the *Nation*; J. M. Wilson, *Siegfried Sassoon: The Journey from the Trenches: A Biography (1918-1967)* (Duckworth, 2003), p.37.
32. *Manchester Guardian,* 1 February 1919.
33. *The Times,* 1 February 1919.
34. *Daily Record,* 1 February 1919.
35. *Daily News*, 3 February 1919; McLean, *Legend*, pp.132, 133.
36. We have been unable to identify the *Daily News'* special correspondent, but it may have been H. N. Brailsford, the distinguished left-wing journalist and ILP member, who had links with Glasgow.

37. *Daily News*, 1 February 1919.

38. *Daily News*, 1 February 1919. Other newspapers appear to have taken syndicated copy: *Aberdeen Press and Journal*, 1 February 1919; *Daily Mirror*, 1 February 1919; *Daily Sketch*, 1 February 1919.

39. *Strike Bulletin*, 3 February 1919, p.4.

40. JC36/31/09 [09/B], Sim; JC36/31/07 [07/N], Alexander Duncan, machinist.

41. *Strike Bulletin*, 1 February 1919.

42. *Strike Bulletin*, 1 February 1919, p.4.

43. *Strike* Bulletin, 1 February 1919.

44. *Strike Bulletin*, 1 February 1919. The *Strike Bulletin's* editor, Pat Dollan, repeated this version in his memoir in the *Sunday Mail* on 6 October 1957; AD15/19/11 [A15], Thomas Gargan, Police Constable.

45. *Strike Bulletin*, 2 February 1919.

46. *Strike Bulletin*, 2 February 1919.

47. *Strike Bulletin*, 2 February 1919.

48. *Strike Bulletin*, 5 February 1919, p.4.

49. The drain on manpower was so great that Chief Constable Stevenson issued an order in May 1915 that no further policemen were to join the armed forces, other than in exceptional circumstances; D. Grant, *Thin Blue Line: The Story of the City of Glasgow Police* (John Long, 1973), p. 63; CAB23/9/9, War Cabinet Minutes, meeting 522, 30 January 1919.

50. P. E. Dewey, 'Military Recruiting and the British Labour Force During the First World War', *The Historical Journal*, 27 (1984), Table 6.

13 31 January 1919: Trouble Spreads across the Square

There is evidence that a deliberate attempt was also made to halt the tram traffic in the north-east corner. The Sheriff and Councillor Mitchell both reported they had seen large bodies of men gathering not only in the south-east, but also the north-east corner of the Square.[1] At about midday, Tram Inspector Andrew Imrie joined a car at the south-west corner of the Square, proceeding north and east (Map 4). It took fifteen minutes to reach North Frederick Street. At the trial he recalled men in the crowd shouting, 'We are out here to prevent the cars running, and tomorrow there will be no cars running', and they refused repeated requests to get out of the way. Imrie said there had been plenty of room for the crowd to have remained clear of the rails. Having piloted this car through, he tried to get the following car through, but was held up this time at North Hanover Street by the crowd which again shouted they were intent on holding up the traffic, calling the tram crew scabs and blacklegs.[2]

Tram Inspector Allan McCaskill was at the corner of George Square and North Frederick Street around noon. He remembered eight or ten cars going east and fourteen going west held up by the crowd standing on the rails; he described their behaviour as a 'quite stubborn obstruction'. McCaskill assisted several cars through the crowd at the bottom of North Frederick Street before 'the first attack by the strikers' forced him to 'stop the cars in consequence'. When the police drove the crowd back up North Frederick Street, he was able to guide more cars through.[3] No particular effort seems to have been made by the police to clear the crowd from in front of the trams, as the tram inspectors appear to have managed to keep the traffic moving.

The Second and Third Baton Charges

There were two baton charges from the front of the City Chambers. The first of these appears to have followed on immediately from the one in the south-east corner to clear the blocked trams, which had forced the crowd northwards to the front of the Chambers. This baton charge from the front of the Chambers drove the crowd back only to the other side of the road. The second baton charge from the Buildings drove the crowd into the centre of the Square. There were probably about 30 to 50 police positioned in front of the Buildings at this stage, in addition to 20 to 30 men in the south-east corner.[4]

Many police witnesses claimed elements of the crowd had shouted 'rush them', 'rush the police', 'rush the ____ police', 'rush the Buildings', with intent to force their way inside. While police witnesses stressed the violent nature of the crowd, close up to the City Chambers, defence counsel insisted the crowd was neither close to the police nor to the Buildings; there was no intent to rush the Buildings, and the baton charge from the Buildings had been unjustified. A close reading of the evidence provides greater clarity.

Lieutenant Gray asserted the crowd had 'surged right on towards the door' of the Chambers and the police had drawn 'their batons and charged the crowd'. Sergeant Murdoch claimed, 'There was a rush made towards the entrance to the Municipal Buildings, and the police drew their batons all the way up [the line] and I rushed along with a few others up to the front entrance of the Buildings, the crowd crying "Rush the _____ police"'. Other police witnesses echo these accounts.[5]

Defence witnesses claimed there was no cause for the first charge from the front of the Chambers.[6] Viewing events from the Council Officer's room on the second floor, Rosslyn Mitchell said he had seen no reason for this charge, because the crowd's movement had been caused solely by pressure; not that the police charges had been without 'rhyme or reason', but that 'it was without cause that I saw'. He confirmed, however, he did not believe the police were 'guilty of an unprovoked attack'.[7]

John Mann, who had been driven from the south-east corner with the crowd as far as the flagpole outside the Chambers, said the crowd was not close to the Chambers.[8] In contrast, defence witness McPhie reported the roadway in front of the Chambers had been 'pretty well filled by the crowd' and the crowd had been 'up against the police in front of the buildings' and qualified police action as 'quite right to try to clear them away . . . but not to use force'.[9]

The key fact is that most witnesses reported there had been no pause between the first baton charge in the south-east corner and the second charge, the first from the Chambers, one leading to and possibly causing, the other. Thus, the crowd being pushed back from the south-east corner had in turn pushed the crowd gathered in front of the Buildings closer to the police positioned there. This is confirmed by Inspector Noble, standing near the Gladstone Statue, who saw the crowd recoiling from the first police baton charge in the corner: 'They came pretty much towards the door of the Municipal Buildings, but they were turned there by the police and put right across the Square'.[10] Chief Detective Inspector Weir and defence witness Sievwright agreed the baton charge in the south-east corner had set off the movement of the police in front of the Chambers.[11]

Police witnesses may have interpreted the movement towards the Chambers' entrance as 'a deliberate rush', because this is what they expected.[12] It seems this almost certainly unintended surge by a confused crowd prompted the baton charge to clear the front of the Buildings. Whether the baton charge was justified will continue to be debated. It is certain that many people were batoned who had no violent intent and some constables were unnecessarily violent. There is certainly evidence, in the short surviving film clip, of a policeman striking out indiscriminately.[13]

After the first baton charge from the front of the Chambers drove the crowd back only as far as the other side of the street, 'The mob thereupon surged forward again and the Police again attacked them with their battons [sic] and drove them back about 100 yards. This left half the Square clear'.[14] The Chief Constable had followed his men forward and then ordered them back to the Municipal Buildings where they formed up again. As they withdrew, witnesses for both sides reported the crowd drifting eastwards behind them.[15] As they returned towards the Buildings, they threw mud, stones and pieces of wood.[16] The *Glasgow Herald* described the crowd driven from the south-east corner and for some distance into the Square surging back and the police 'making a straight charge along the front of the Chambers'.[17] The northernmost part of the police line appears not to have charged, which led to some of the crowd being driven past them northwards up North Hanover Street and North Frederick Street. From this point the 'avalanche of bottles' started from North Frederick Street.[18]

As the crowd retreated from the baton charge, Gallacher had been left stranded on the plinth of the Gladstone Statue. Having been ordered to get down, he was finally pulled off by Sergeant Murdoch.[19] Three constables claimed Gallacher had shouted to the crowd to attack the police, although Acting Detective Constable Miller's testimony appears rehearsed and Gallacher's long cross-examination undermined his credibility.[20] Shinwell's biographer, Peter Slowe, however, prefers the police version, that Gallacher was encouraging the strikers to 'Rush them up behind!'.[21] Chief Constable Stevenson, when passing the Gladstone Statue, reported that 'a man rushed up to me. He said something in an angry and excited tone . . . put his hand on my breast here (indicating) and I thought he wanted to speak to me'. Stevenson had 'turned to see what he had got to say, and he suddenly struck me a swinging blow with his right hand'. Stevenson said he had given no provocation and was not prepared for the blow. He saw the man fall and some constables arrest him, then went on 'to look after the Police and the crowd'.[22] Gallacher admitted to striking the Chief Constable, claiming 'batons were raised all around' him.[23] The Chief Constable's account was corroborated by a number of police witnesses.[24] Defence witness James Kerlie claimed Gallacher attacked the Chief Constable only after he had been batoned, but no other witness, not even Gallacher himself, suggests this.[25] Gallacher was detained by Sergeant MacKinnon and Constable Gargan. Assistant Chief Constable Mennie saw Gallacher immediately after he was arrested; he described him as 'violent and excited' and 'outrageous'. As Gallacher was on the point of overpowering MacKinnon, Gargan said he knocked him down with his baton. Although Gargan and other police witnesses at trial denied any other policeman had hit Gallacher, defence witnesses suggested he was surrounded by up to eight policemen and they described a rain of blows.[26]

Neil Alexander* was accused of trying to rescue Gallacher from the police. Gallacher said at the trial (corroborated by Charles Gibson and Robert Chalmers) and later in his memoirs, that Alexander had thrown himself on top of him to protect him from police blows when he was already lying stunned.[27] In the police version of events, Neil Alexander did not intervene until Gallacher was being taken to the Chambers, and had thrown his arms round Gallacher's waist trying to drag him away.[28] Constable Rennie also claimed Kirkwood had cried 'Come on boys . . . Comrade Gallacher is being arrested'.[29] Significantly, a number of police witnesses said they had seen no attempt at rescue.[30] Blood was streaming down Gallacher's face as he was walked across to the Buildings.[31]

The evidence suggests strongly that Gallacher was batoned violently several times after he hit the Chief Constable and Alexander acted to shield him. Consequently, the version recounted by Gargan, Rennie and Turner appears to have been invented to exculpate themselves from a disproportionately violent attack on Gallacher and to justify their arrest of Alexander. Whatever the rights and wrongs of Gallacher's arrest, for the last century no one has believed the police account of David Kirkwood's arrest, that he had rushed forward from the Chambers and incited the crowd to attack the police and to 'rescue Comrade Gallacher'.[32]

As the police baton-charged the crowd from the front of the City Chambers, the strikers' delegation left the library, where they had been waiting to meet the Lord Provost. Delegate William Harvey described hearing 'a large commotion which seemed to be taking place outside' and the police using their batons 'between the corners of South Frederick Street right across to the Municipal Buildings' and other police exiting the Chambers' quadrangle with their batons drawn (presumably into Cochrane Street, from the quadrangle entrance beside the library windows, Map 4).

As Harvey emerged from the front of the City Chambers, Kirkwood was a few paces ahead of him with his 'hands up in front of him shouting steady men steady'. About halfway across the road in

* Neil McCulloch Alexander (1886-1952) was a riveter and was apparently still working when he died of pneumonia with complications at the age of 66. He had five children under twelve in 1919. Tried and acquitted.

front of the Chambers, 'a Sergeant came from behind the ranks drew a baton and struck him on the back of the head, and he went down'. Harvey denied very firmly that Kirkwood had attempted to incite the crowd, which was, in any case at that moment gathered some considerable distance away at the Scott Monument, in the centre of the Square (Fig 13.1, Map 4). Harvey very robustly rejected the claim that Kirkwood had brushed a constable out of his way, while saying 'To Hell with you', and 'it was after that that he came in contact with the policeman's baton', stating there had been no provocation for the batoning.[33] Sergeant Steele claimed he saw Kirkwood:

> come out of the Municipal Buildings. He ran towards the crowd with both arms above his head waving to the crowd and at the same time shouting, 'Come on men, come on men, rally round men, rush the Buildings, rush them!'[34]

Steele also claimed the crowd had again broken towards the police 'as a result of Kirkwood's shouting and gesticulating':

> I was standing quite near to him at the time. I ordered him to go away. He was very excited and angry. He said, 'To hell with you.' I had my baton in my hand and I struck him with it on the back and shoulders and he fell.[35]

Steele did not materially alter his story at trial and was corroborated by colleagues.[36] Constable Andrew Gallagher faltered under cross-examination, making and then adhering to a statement that Kirkwood had stood for two whole minutes inciting the crowd to attack, at which defence counsel was incredulous that 'nobody laid a hand on him'.[37] Sergeant Steele was pressed by defence advocate Mr Watt on Kirkwood's alleged words, 'this story of "Come rally up men", is made up simply to justify your improper conduct?'[38] Edward Devine called the police version 'a deliberate lie', which seems fair comment.[39]

A series of defence witnesses provided fairly consistent, but not obviously orchestrated, descriptions of Kirkwood's batoning and arrest.[40] Isaac Sim described how Kirkwood, just in front of him, had

13.1. *Kirkwood being batoned by Sergeant Steele between the door of the City Chambers and the Gladstone Statue. Note that there is no crowd for Kirkwood to incite, as was claimed by Steele and others. The figure immediately to the right of Kirkwood is probably Neil Maclean MP. (Reproduced by kind permission; Crown copyright. National Records of Scotland, AD15/19/11/7.)*

'brushed through between the cordon of police' and had proceeded to the middle of the street holding up his hands: 'A big policeman came rushing from behind and passed me, and knocked Mr Kirkwood an unmerciful blow on the head'. Sim denied Kirkwood had said anything to incite the crowd and believed 'the constable had committed a crime'. He ran forward and 'took his number, and immediately jotted it down in a small notebook that I had, and I gave that number to Mr Maclean later on'.[41] Neil Maclean also denied Kirkwood had shouted any words to incite the crowd and confirmed in court that a photograph from the following day's *Bulletin* represented the scene as Kirkwood was being batoned and that he, Maclean, was the figure standing on the right.[42]

In summary, the defence evidence all agreed that Kirkwood had emerged, raised his hands, shouted something like 'steady men, steady' or 'stop men', and had not in any way incited the crowd.

Shinwell was last seen by Neil Maclean MP 'in the group standing around the Lord Provost's door' on their way from the library, but Maclean did not see him in the Square. Shinwell's absence from the Square and the crowd became part of his defence: he could not be part of a riotous crowd if he had not been there. As Maclean stated, 'the Crown are still searching for anyone who can make Shinwell part of the disorderly crowd'.[43] The *Strike Bulletin* reported that Shinwell and Kirkwood had rushed out to help in restoring order, and 'the strikers covered Shinwell successfully and got him away without injury'.[44] Many years later, Shinwell claimed he had tried to 'shout to the people to walk steadily from the square to avoid further injury and bloodshed, standing on a seat to make my voice heard above the general bedlam'.[45] But since no witness at all mentioned Shinwell in the Square after the delegation left the Municipal Buildings, it seems very likely he had left immediately, as Slowe wrote: Shinwell 'left the City Chambers by the same back entrance as the Sheriff and headed for the strike committee's office' where he 'set about burning any materials or plans for the acts of sabotage the committee had discussed. Into the fire went maps and notes, names and designs'.[46] Shinwell found:

> Willie Shaw, our Secretary, destroying some papers, and [I] asked what he was doing. He said that during our discussions some of the Communist members had made fantastic suggestions about how to frighten the Government and he decided to burn anything subversive they had written.[47]

Shinwell's attempt to shift the blame onto 'Communist members' is undermined by Slowe's account:[48]

> What did Bell, Hopkins and Shinwell burn when they reached the strike committee's office? There remain only snippets in Bell's and Gallacher's memoirs, and a notebook that was used in the trial, to suggest at least acts of sabotage to disrupt transport and electricity were planned.[49]

The Sheriff's Concerns

At some point between 12.15pm and 12.30pm the Sheriff had become sufficiently concerned by events in the Square that he determined to read the proclamation of the Riot Act. After the crowd had dispersed from in front of the Chambers after the second baton charge, a large crowd began to gather again and he:

> thought, from the movement and appearance of the crowd and the fact that after the serious disorder which had occurred it had again assembled in front of the Buildings, that renewed disorder was to be apprehended unless the crowd could be induced to depart. I came accordingly to the conclusion that the time had probably come when I should read the Riot Act. Before doing so I thought I should intimate my opinion to the Lord Provost, who was then engaged at a Magistrates meeting . . . and being admitted to the room I informed the Lord Provost in presence of the Magistrates, that I thought the time had come when I should read the proclamation. I then went downstairs and went out by the main entrance to the front of the Buildings in order to make a closer observation of the crowd.[50]

The Town Clerk and Lord Provost corroborated this.[51] At trial, Bailie Stewart reported, after the Sheriff's statement at the magistrates' meeting:

> certain of the magistrates [took] a very serious view of the situation; in fact I thought they were unduly excited about the matter. One of the magistrates even went the length of suggesting that they should get machine guns to clear the Square. Bailie Wheatley and I said we thought the police were quite sufficient to deal with the situation and we thought there was no occasion for bringing in the military [reading the Riot Act did not in fact necessarily mean that the military would be called], that the police were quite strong enough to handle the crowd. We then, with the consent of the Sheriff of the County and the Lord Provost and the Chief Constable, Bailie

> Wheatley and myself, were deputed to go down and address the crowd and advise them to go away as the Sheriff had said he was prepared to read the Riot Act. We did go down and when we arrived opposite the Gladstone Statue . . . we told the crowd that if they did not disperse they were threatened with the military, and we thought it advisable that they should go.[52]

The Town Clerk believed 'there were not more than a dozen or a score heard them owing to the uproar which then prevailed. The noise was very great and quite a number of the more active members of the crowd were gesticulating and shouting and roaring'.[53]

The baton charges had pushed some of the crowd into North Frederick Street. The violence was beginning to spread beyond the Square, into the streets to the north. This is where some of the most violent events occurred.

The Crowd

Understanding the size and behaviour of the crowd is essential to explaining the origins and spread of violence, an aspect to which little attention has been paid. It is impossible now to determine precisely how many people were in the Square, how many strikers, how many onlookers, and how many 'corner boys' or hooligans. However, by combining witness statements and the reports of crowd movements, some understanding can be reached.

Any estimation of crowd size is fraught with difficulties and even people experienced in crowd management can inflate the size of a crowd by a factor of ten.[54] If the person estimating the size sees advantage in exaggerating or minimising the crowd size this will cause further problems. In an evenly-distributed crowd, a more distant part of the crowd will appear denser – the 'density perspective illusion'.[55] In 1919, arguably the police had more experience in estimating the size of crowds than anyone else, but even amongst experienced officers there was considerable variation on 31 January 1919, from a low suggested by Constable McCormick at 6,000-7,000, to Constable Ritchie's high of 70,000. Most police placed the crowd between

20,000 and 30,000.[56] Foster quotes a figure of 60,000 given in a Ministry of Munitions report dated 3 February 1919, but the source of this number is unknown.[57] The size accepted by both sides at the trial was 20,000-25,000.[58]

It is certain that the crowd varied considerably in density in different parts of the Square at different times, and that the eastern part of the Square, closer to the City Chambers, which occupied the whole of the eastern side of the Square, was more densely packed than the west. People in a crowd that starts as evenly distributed will tend to move towards a centre of attraction. A number of defence witnesses described leaving their procession's allocated place in George Square to move towards the City Chambers, and particularly into the south-east corner, where the riot began.

At the trial, descriptions of the crowd's density and the way it moved were influenced by the arguments of prosecution and defence counsel. The defence wished to establish that the crowd in the south-east corner had been on the tram tracks only because of pressure from a dense crowd behind. But the descriptions of the crowd's reaction to the first baton charge reveal that people had room to run away from the police, although it was sufficiently dense to set off a movement of people towards the door of the City Chambers. However, this sudden and violent movement appears not to have led to fall or crush injuries. The crowd also recoiled rapidly from the second and third baton charges – westward from the Chambers – without many falls or consequent crush injuries; only one witness noted tripping over the plinth of the Gladstone Statue where 'some men had fallen over there already'.[59] The only newsreel film of Friday 31 January shows the crowd not particularly dense and running freely past the front of the City Chambers.[60]

The trial evidence confirms, after the clearing of the obstructions in the south-east and north-east corners, the tram traffic ran without hindrance for the rest of the afternoon, and a series of prosecution witnesses recalled there being space between the crowd around the trams and the main body in the Square. If this was correct, the crowd did not need to spill into the surrounding streets: it could be accommodated within the Square. Nevertheless, some witnesses described crowds in the adjacent streets; it is unclear whether they were sightseers or people driven from the Square. Certainly, some were processions arriving late, after the trouble began.[61] In the south-east corner, the accused McKenzie reported having been unable to raise his arms, because the crowd was so densely packed up against the trams.[62] Police witnesses recalled being jammed against the cars, which the *Daily News* corroborated in its report the following day.[63]

Stephen Pheasant has calculated the average area occupied in a crowd by male and female individuals from different populations as 0.2 sq m, including a small amount of space round each body. Theoretically at least, five people could fit into a metre square, and 500 could fit in an area 10m by 10m (100 sq m). This high density, however, would require all individuals to occupy the same amount of space, to be evenly distributed and unmoving.[64] At this density, someone falling might find it difficult to stand again. According to Still, at higher densities, of six or seven per square metre, individuals are surrounded on all sides and are in physical contact with each other. In this scenario, the energy of a push at one side of the crowd will be transmitted through the crowd as a compression wave or shockwave, gaining momentum as it proceeds.[65] In these circumstances individuals cannot move their feet to counter the push, people fall like dominoes, have difficulty rising, and others trip over them. There were no crush or trampling injuries noted in the evidence for the Battle; although some individuals fell, witnesses mainly reported people being struck by police batons, not falling or tripping. Even at five people per square metre, movement is slow and awkward, and people have difficulty maintaining balance. In George Square, the evidence suggests the crowd was generally not so dense even when under the stress of the police baton charges. The crowd recoiled; people ran.

The area of George Square can be measured in two different ways: to the facades of the buildings fronting the Square (19,127 sq m), or to the inner edge of the perimeter road surrounding the Square (10,600 sq m). Within these areas there were hard constraints creating obstacles to movement: thirteen statues and a cabman's shelter that stood in the Square in 1919 (286 sq m). Soft constraints such as areas of grass and flowerbeds (fortunately the trip-hazard fencing had recently been removed) provided a further 3,618 sq m of soft obstacles.[66] Using a theoretical 'maximum packing' capacity of 500 people in 100 sq m, 51,500 people might be crammed into the internal space of the Square, but this crowd would be incapable of movement. However, a crowd of 30,000 would create a density of around two people per square metre in the larger area, or just over four people per square metre in the internal area.

The calculations and the anecdotal evidence suggest strongly that in every part of the Square where the police charged the crowd, the crowd was able to move away rapidly, without any of the problems normally experienced in a tightly packed crowd, as evidenced in the short piece of newsreel film. This supports the case for the lower crowd estimate of 20,000-25,000 as described by most contemporaries and accepted at the trial.

---

1. JC36/31/04 [04/S], MacKenzie, Sheriff of Lanarkshire; JC36/31/05 [05/MM], Mitchell, Councillor.
2. JC36/31/02 [02/E], Andrew Imrie, Tram Inspector.
3. AD15/19/11 [B15], Allan McCaskill, Tram Inspector.
4. AD15/19/11 [A09], Ritchie, Police Constable; AD15/19/11 [A11], F. Mccormick, Police Constable.
5. JC36/31/01 [01/C], Gray, Police Lieutenant; JC36/31/02 [02/B], Murdoch, Police Sergeant; AD15/19/11 [A08], John Steele, Police Sergeant; JC36/31/03 [03/E], Andrew Gallagher, Police Constable; AD15/19/11 [A14], Robert Davidson, Police Constable; AD15/19/11 [A15], Gargan, Police Constable.
6. JC36/31/06 [06/C], Walter Stewart, ASE.
7. JC36/31/05 [05/MM], Mitchell, Councillor.
8. JC36/31/07 [07/U], Mann, Pattern Maker.
9. JC36/31/08 [08/E], McPhie, Flour Millers' Union.
10. AD15/19/11 [A29], Louis Noble, Detective Inspector.
11. JC36/31/03 [03/D], Weir, Chief Detective Inspector; JC36/31/07 [07/L], Sievwright, Sheriff Court shorthand writer.
12. JC36/31/04 [04/K], Thomas Turner, Police Constable.
13. Pathé Films 'Striking workers in Glasgow, 1919'.
14. AD15/19/11 [A14], Robert Davidson, Police Constable.
15. AD15/19/11 [A05], Stevenson, Chief Constable; JC36/31/04 [04/H], Stevenson, Chief Constable; JC36/31/01 [01/C], Gray, Police Lieutenant.

16. JC36/31/04 [04/B], Louis Noble, Detective Inspector.

17. This phrase may have misled McLean (1972) to interpret the baton charge being across the front of the Chambers, south to north, rather than a charge into the Square (east to west) by the line of police who were standing along the frontage of the building; *Glasgow Herald*, 1 February 1919.

18. JC36/31/05 [05/MM], Mitchell, Councillor.

19. JC36/31/04 [04/B], Noble, Detective Inspector; AD15/19/11 [A06], Mennie, Asst Chief Constable.

20. AD15/19/11 [A58] and JC36/31/04 [04/E1], John Miller, Acting Detective Constable.

21. P. Slowe, *Manny Shinwell: An Authorised Biography* (Pluto Press, 1993), p.85. This line may reflect Shinwell's desire to put the blame on Gallacher.

22. AD15/19/11 [A05] and JC36/31/04 [04/H], Stevenson, Chief Constable.

23. Gallacher, W., *Revolt on the Clyde*, 5th edn (Lawrence and Wishart, 2017 [1936]) p.160.

24. AD15/19/11 [A60], Melrose, Police Constable; AD15/19/11 [A19] and JC36/31/04 [04/K], T. Turner, Police Constable.

25. JC36/31/08 [08/H], Johnston, Traveller.

26. AD15/19/11 [A06], Mennie, Asst Chief Constable; JC36/31/04 [04/N], Thomas Burke, Police Constable; AD15/19/11 [A69] and JC36/31/04 [04/G], John Mackinnon, Police Sergeant; JC36/31/04 [04/J], Gargan, Police Constable; JC36/31/04 [04/K], Turner, Police Constable.

27. Gallacher, *Revolt*, pp.160-61; JC36/31/09 [09/Q], Charles Gibson, Iron Roof Constructor; JC36/31/09 [09/R], Robert Chalmers, Boiler-maker.

28. JC36/31/04 [04/J], Gargan, Police Constable; AD15/19/11 [A14], Robert Davidson, Police Constable; JC36/31/04 [04/K], Turner, Police Constable.

29. JC36/31/04 [04/L], William Rennie, Police Constable.

30. AD15/19/11 [A69] and JC36/31/04 [04/G], Mackinnon, Police Sergeant; AD15/19/11 [A20], Gray, Police Lieutenant; AD15/19/11 [A60], Melrose, Police Constable.

31. JC36/31/04 [04/K], Turner, Police Constable.

32. AD15/19/11 [A14], Davidson, Police Constable; AD15/19/11 [A19], Turner, Police Constable.

33. JC36/31/08 [08/Q], Harvey, ASE.

34. AD15/19/11 [A08], Steele, Police Sergeant.

35. AD15/19/11 [A08], Steele, Police Sergeant.

36. AD15/19/11 [A09], Ritchie, Police Constable; AD15/19/11 [A17],

Andrew Gallagher, Police Constable; JC36/31/04 [04/B], Noble, Detective Inspector; AD15/19/11 [A33], James Wilson, Detective Sergeant.

37. JC36/31/03 [03/E], Andrew Gallagher, Police Constable.

38. JC36/31/03 [03/G], Steele, Police Sergeant.

39. JC36/31/09 [09/F], Devine, Machine Man.

40. JC36/31/09 [09/C], Kennedy, Miner; JC36/31/06 [06/C], Walter Stewart, ASE; JC36/31/08 [08/H], Johnston, Traveller; JC36/31/08 [08/Q], Harvey, ASE.

41. JC36/31/09 [09/B], Sim, Discharged Soldier.

42. JC36/31/09 [09/V], Maclean, MP.

43. JC36/31/09 [09/V], Maclean, MP.

44. *Strike Bulletin*, 1 February 1919.

45. E. Shinwell, *Conflict without Malice* (Odhams, 1955), p.63; E. Shinwell, *Lead with the Left: My First Ninety-Six Years* (Cassell, 1981), p.63.

46. The Sheriff had in fact left by the main front entrance in preparation to read the Riot Act, JC36/31/04 [04/S]; Slowe, *Shinwell*, p.85.

47. Shinwell, *Lead with the Left*, p.63.

48. *Daily News*, 3 February 1919.

49. Slowe, *Shinwell*, p.87.

50. AD15/19/11 [A01], MacKenzie, Sheriff of Lanarkshire.

51. AD15/19/11 [A04], Lindsay, Town Clerk; JC36/31/03 [03/C], Stewart, Lord Provost.

52. JC36/31/06 [06/B], Stewart, Councillor.

53. AD15/19/11 [A04], Lindsay, Town Clerk; JC36/31/06 [06/B], Stewart, Councillor.

54. G. K. Still, *Introduction to Crowd Science* (CRC Press, 2019), p.47.

55. Still, *Crowd Science*, p.50.

56. AD15/19/11 [A11], Francis McCormick, Police Constable; JC36/31/02 [02/G], William Murray, Police Inspector; JC36/31/02 [02/B], David Murdoch, Police Sergeant; AD15/19/11 [A60]; William Melrose, Police Constable; JC36/31/01 [01/C] and AD15/19/11 [A20], Lawrence Gray, Police Lieutenant; AD15/19/11 [A33], James Wilson, Detective Sergeant; JC36/31/04 [04/H], James Stevenson, Chief Constable; AD15/19/11 [A15], Thomas Gargan, Police Constable; JC36/31/03 [03/H] & AD15/19/11 [A09], James Ritchie, Police Constable; AD15/19/11 [A08], John Steele, Police Sergeant.

57. MUN 1/18 Ministry of Munitions: Munitions Council Daily Reports, Report 427-446 (no. 427 Monday 3 February 1919); National Archives,

Kew; J. Foster, 'The 1919 Forty Hours Strike', *Theory and Struggle*, 120 (2019), p.34; Foster, 'Red Clyde, Red Scotland', in I. L. Donnachie and C. A. Wheatley, *The Manufacture of Scottish History* (Polygon, 1992), p.107; J. Foster, 'Working-class mobilisation on the Clyde 1917-20', in Wrigley, C. (ed), *Challenges of Labour: Central and Western Europe* (Routledge, 1993), pp.149-75, p.170.

58. JC36/31/04 [04/H], James Verdier Stevenson, Chief Constable; AD15/19/11 [A04], Sir John Lindsay, Town Clerk; JC26/1919/85, draft charge sheet and final indictment.

59. JC36/31/07 [07/G], Hodge, Sheet Iron Worker.

60. Pathé, 'Striking Workers on the Streets of Glasgow', (1919).

61. JC36/31/07 [07/B], Herbert Highton, Iron Turner.

62. JC36/31/06 [06/D], John Mackenzie, Shipwright.

63. AD15/19/11 [A68], Alexander Sutherland, Police Inspector; *Daily News*, 1 February 1919.

64. S. Pheasant, *Bodyspace* (CRC Press, 1998), quoted in Still, *Crowd Science*, p.36.

65. Still, *Crowd Science*, p.44.

66. JC36/31/05 [05/MM], E R Mitchell, Councillor. The presence of these trip hazards on the 31st would surely have increased the number of injuries.

14 'The horrors that attend on conflict with the executive power': the Violence Spreads North

Part of the crowd had turned very ugly after it was driven into North Frederick Street during the baton charges in the Square. The *Glasgow Herald*'s account is corroborated by eye-witnesses:

> At the George Square end of the street the crowd was composed largely of young men, evidently strikers disposed to take drastic action if occasion arose. Higher up the street the crowd appeared to be made up to a considerable extent of persons who desired merely to be spectators of the demonstration. This section included groups of women and children, many of them apparently resident in the neighbourhood . . .
>
> About a score of policemen were formed into line on the clear space in front of the Chambers and advanced towards the crowd in businesslike fashion. The strikers retreated, more or less precipitately, but a rearguard, composed mostly of youths, gave the police a hot reception as they were retiring. The police drew their batons, but the fleeing rearguard never suffered them to come within striking distance, although they themselves kept steadily pelting the oncoming constables. The police paused about halfway up the street and re-formed their ranks, intending evidently to stay there as a cordon to keep the crowd at a distance from the Square. When the strikers saw the police pausing, the bolder spirits among them endeavoured to organise a counter-attack. They were quickly reinforced by others, and a very ugly rush was made, stones and bottles being thrown towards the line of uniformed men. The officers dodged the missiles, and held their ground, and deterred by their steadiness, the rush lost its momentum

> before the police were reached. The moment the crowd hesitated the police charged with drawn batons, and the strikers fled before them.[1]

The bottles used as missiles were taken from a horse-drawn delivery lorry in the charge of seventeen-year-old George Binnie who was delivering to Owen McQuade, manager of licensed premises at 46 North Frederick Street (Map 4, 'No. 46'). He pulled up about 12.15pm to deliver fourteen dozen bottles of beer and collect sixteen dozen empties. As Binnie headed across the street to make his next delivery at no. 41, 'several men who came from the mob seized hold' of his horse's head and shouted to him to stop. Binnie 'jumped down and seized hold of' the bridle, but he was grabbed and 'dragged some distance away'. Binnie returned to McQuade's shop and telephoned his employers for instructions. The crowd had surrounded his lorry, many climbing on top, pulling down boxes of bottles, a large number of which were then thrown through McQuade's windows.[2] McQuade was struck on the shoulder and cut on the face and then the situation became more dramatic:

> When the windows had been thoroughly smashed a number of the crowd got up on to the window. One of them held a revolver at me. He threatened to shoot if I did not hand out all the bottles I had in the shop. I rushed behind a partition. I really thought he would fire.[3]

McQuade was discharged from the army in 1916, after he had suffered shell-shock in the Dardanelles, where he had been 'buried in a trench'. He put on his coat bearing his silver discharged soldier's badge, collected his assistant, his brother John, and locked the door telling the crowd, 'If any of you want bottles go in and get them'.[4]

As the crowd retreated, Binnie took the opportunity to lead his horse and lorry away into North Hanover Street, via North Frederick Lane. He walked back to North Frederick Street to collect his cases, but was told to leave them or he would 'get a severe kicking'. His stock had contained 'over 1,000 bottles', of which 'every one was

14.1 *The police withdraw after a baton charge in North Frederick Street. The barricade of boxes taken from Binnie's lorry is visible (*Illustrated London News*, 8 February 1919).*

stolen'. The empty crates had been piled across the road forming a low barricade (Fig. 14.1).[5]

Witnessing the ransacking of the lorry from near the Chambers, Detective Inspector Noble ran to report events to Superintendent Williamson.[6] Seeing that the Sheriff was 'in imminent danger of being struck with bottles', Lieutenant Gray, who had himself sustained an injury to his foot, 'spoke to an inspector [Fraser] and instructed him to get a number of men to go up North Frederick Street to stop the bottle throwing'. Approximately twenty men were gathered and when they were about 25-30m in front of the barricade of crates, the crowd fled. Both Inspectors Fraser and Gray described the charge 'through practically a hail of bottles'.[7] Sergeant Murdoch reported that the crowd retreated to Cathedral Street but then returned, requiring a second charge by around twenty policemen.[8]

Constable Thomas Gargan, one of Fraser's men in North Frederick Street, saw 'practically all the windows in North Frederick Street had been broken'.[9] Constable Andrew Gallagher who had been involved in the main charge across the Square, was knocked out by a half brick to the back of the head during the charge up North Frederick Street.[10] Inspector Sutherland had been in front of the Municipal Buildings when bottles began to fly down from North Frederick Street, and he sustained a cut from a bottle fragment.[11]

At trial, the defence tried to dissociate the crowd in North Frederick Street from the demonstration, suggesting to a number of witnesses that 'the character of the crowd up at North Frederick Street was rather different from most of the crowd elsewhere . . . like a band of hooligans'.[12] Detective Inspector Noble responded by describing the crowd as 'young men . . . working chaps . . . most of them were apprentices'.[13] The Town Clerk responded, 'There is really no justification for suggesting that they were any different from the other part of the procession'.[14] Defence witness, Seafarers' Union delegate William Blamires, said they looked like a 'hooligan crowd . . . not a fair sample of the crowd' nor 'decent men' and expressed surprise at the suggestion that the people in North Frederick Street had been driven there out of the Square. During his examination of witnesses, William Gallacher suggested to Blamires that Parliamentary Road and Cathedral Square were some 'of the toughest districts in the City . . . where there are always crowds of corner boys' only four minutes from the Square.[15] All this sits rather awkwardly with D. S. Morton's and later accounts in some of the strike leaders' memoirs and some modern writers, which characterise the bottle-throwing and the charges of the crowd as noble self-defence or a justified response to the police violence, rather than the actions of opportunistic hooligans.[16]

Edith Hughes's account is once again problematic. In contrast to every other witness, she did not consider there to have been any disorder in North Frederick Street, nor broken windows there or in Cathedral Street; she had seen missiles thrown 'from both sides of a lane' but did not know by whom. She was sure 'there was absolutely no violence in any part of the Square' except that perpetrated by the police.[17]

Prosecution witness Juvenile Delinquency Board Officer Alexander McKendrick had taken shelter at the north-east corner of the Square for about twenty minutes. He described young men behind the barricade of boxes holding bottles and other missiles such as walking sticks. As with other witnesses, defence counsel pressed McKendrick on the make-up of the crowd: to the suggestion 'may I take it they were young men of 18 to 20?' McKendrick responded 'the majority were young men', but 'some of them were pretty much older than that . . . just the same sort of crowd up there as they were down below' in the Square. McKendrick described the behaviour of the crowd as 'brutal and cowardly in the extreme. Despite its great number when 10 or 12 Policemen advanced against it they immediately took to their heels and ran'.[18]

Gallacher's 1936 account of the fighting in the Square and in particular in North Frederick Street is unpleasantly triumphalist about the violence meted out by the demonstrators. He claimed the police were 'driven back in disorder at every attempt' to cross the barricade – he was, of course, in custody by this time and claimed to be repeating the words of Jock McBain.[19] Writing 60 years after the event, Harry McShane was clear that the bottle-throwers in the streets to the north of the Square, which included himself, were demonstrators driven north by the police rather than the defence's alleged 'hooligans'.[20] This accords with an account recorded 58 years after the event (the reliability of which may be questioned), which identifies the North Frederick Street crowd as strikers from the Govan shipyards.[21] Kenny MacAskill's account of the violence is, unfortunately, based to a great extent on an uncritical acceptance of McShane's memoir, including its fantasies of 'fleeing police'.[22]

The Town Clerk described the bottle-throwing:

> At this time the danger of the missiles was seriously added to by the mob on the north side of the Square starting the throwing of bottles too. One or two of the windows in the City Chambers at the north east corner of the Square at George Street were broken . . . While bottle throwing from North Frederick Street was continuing part of the police body in the George Square space charged the mob in that street and they, like the earlier part of the mob at the tramway cars thereon turned and ran.[23]

The Chief Constable said:

> The Police had to charge the crowd up North Frederick Street . . . [who] were on a higher level. They had a large quantity of missiles of a very dangerous type which they were throwing deliberately at the Police. The crowd were in numbers greatly superior to the Police. It was only a last resort on the part of the Police to draw their batons . . . The crowd ran in front of the Police when they charged up North Frederick Street. The Police were then drawn back towards the City Chambers. The crowd surged forward repeatedly on all sides and had to be put back.[24]

After protecting Margaret Buchanan, the tram driver embroiled in the violence at the south-east corner, Private Cecil Naismith observed the crowd in North Frederick Street:

> The bottles were flying like a thick shower. I saw a barracade [sic] across the street. It was composed of boxes and barrels. A body of the Police were then lined up in the Square. They went up the street and chased the crowd some distance and returned. The crowd returned and threw more bottles and stones. A second charge was made by about 8 or 9 Policemen. They drove the crowd right up North Frederick Street. I followed the Police up the Street and went into Cathedral Street . . .[25]

During the bottle-throwing in North Frederick Street, the Town Clerk noted the proclamation of the Riot Act being read:

> The Sheriff did not read the proclamation under the Riot Act at the moment he emerged from the buildings. He waited in the Square for I should say about 5 or 7 minutes before doing so. When the mob were throwing the bottles, he said to the Lord Provost and me that he intended to read it and he did.[26]

14.2. *Sheriff MacKenzie (marked with a cross) shortly before reading the proclamation of the Riot Act. Assistant Chief Constable Mennie is on the right; Chief Constable Stevenson is third from right. Friday 31 January 1919. The ground is littered with mud (*Bulletin, *1 February 1919).*

The Sheriff's party comprised the Town Clerk, John Lamb, the Lord Provost, the Chief Constable and Assistant Chief Constable Mennie. They walked towards the north-east corner of the Square towards North Frederick Street, where the Sheriff:

> saw some men, or lads, moving about a lorry which appeared to contain boxes of bottles, and which they were apparently engaged in unloading . . . I concluded that an attack with the bottles was imminent, and resolved to take the step of reading the Riot Act at that corner of the Square. I hoped that this might have the effect of inducing the disorderly elements of the crowd to disperse.
>
> I then proceeded, accompanied by the [police] guard, on to the roadway at the foot of North Frederick Street – on my way there two bottles went over my head and smashed on the

> roadway behind me – and halting there I called out that I was going to read the Riot Act.

A small crowd then 'set up a clamour, with what appeared to me to be the evident intention of drowning my voice'.[27] 'At the pitch of [his] voice', the Sheriff started reading the proclamation and had reached the word 'habitations':

> when a young man, who was standing about two yards from me, made a spring forward and snatched the document from which I was reading out of my hand, and having done so immediately dived behind some other people. As I did not know the words of the proclamation by heart, I concluded with the words 'under the pains of Law. God Save the King' . . .

As he walked towards the Municipal Buildings he turned 'and saw what I took to be a bottle flying towards me. I had not time to get out of the way and it struck me on the abdomen'.[28] The Lord Provost confirmed that bottles had struck the City Chambers.[29] The individual who snatched the Riot Act from MacKenzie's hand was not apprehended, although the man who allegedly assisted his escape was.

The Riot Act became law in 1714, early in the reign of George I, in the face of Jacobite unrest and civil disorder in the City of London. The reading of the proclamation of the Act meant any person remaining assembled an hour afterwards was breaking the law. It was not necessary to prove any individual act or intention, mere presence was enough.[30] Section 3 of the Act 'expressly indemnifies justices, constables and others should any of the rioters be killed, maimed or hurt in the process of dispersal' and 'innocent' spectators could be treated as those engaged in the riot.[31] The proclamation reads:

> Our sovereign lord the King chargeth and commandeth all persons, being assembled, immediately to disperse themselves, and peaceably to depart to their habitations or to their lawful business, upon the pains contained in the Act made in the first year of King George, for preventing tumults and riotous assemblies. God save the King.

The person reading the proclamation was adjured to approach the crowd 'as near to them as he can safely come'.[32] The Act makes specific provision for the sort of problem encountered by the Sheriff in George Square, as it requires the proclamation only to be made 'in these words, or like in effect'. By 1919, the reading of the proclamation of the Act was rare. The last certain reading of the Riot Act occurred in Birkenhead on 3 August 1919 during the police strike, although it has been claimed it was read in the Scottish town of Airdrie in 1971.[33] The Act was repealed in England and Wales in 1967 and in 1973 in Scotland.[34] A number of individuals seem, on 31 January 1919, to have believed that reading the proclamation inevitably would lead to calling out the military: this was not the case.

There is an almost complete divergence between prosecution and defence witnesses about the actions of Robert Loudon,* accused of impeding Assistant Chief Constable Mennie in apprehending the person who tore the paper from the Sheriff's hand. Mennie claimed Loudon 'caught me by the coat tails and held me back. He prevented me from pursuing the prisoner who escaped'. Mennie seized Loudon and while holding him was struck on the head and stabbed on the inner side of his right leg below the knee.[35] Loudon was arrested and taken into the City Chambers.[36] Alexander McKendrick corroborated the prosecution's version of events. McKendrick had gone to Mennie's assistance and had been hit on the nose in Loudon's struggles, causing a nosebleed.[37] Several defence witnesses, however, claimed Loudon's innocence, as it was unlikely a man with his infirmities – 'peering vision' and slight build – would have become physically involved.[38]

Prosecution and defence witnesses both confirmed that missiles were also being thrown in the Square after the second baton charge, while bottles also rained down from North Frederick Street.[39] Material thrown in the Square was collected subsequently: 'two pinion wheels; a tramcar motor handle; an iron bolt with pieces of leather attached; a walking stick; an iron bar; broken glass; stones; mud;

* Robert Loudon (*c*1884-1943) was a labourer at a timber merchant and then a dock labourer who had been rejected for military service owing to defective eyesight. Not a member of any trade union, and although not affected by the strike, remained off his work attending strike meetings. Tried and acquitted.

and pieces of iron and other missiles'.[40] Only Gallacher later disputed that any missiles had been thrown in front of the Chambers.[41]

Cathedral Street

The worst violence in the vicinity of the Square occurred in Cathedral Street, into which the crowd from North Frederick Street had been driven. Inspector MacDonald and Sergeant Caskie, both of St Rollox Division, had been on duty together in St James Road around noon when they received word of serious trouble in the Square. They reached North Frederick Street coming eastward along Cathedral Street and were spotted by a crowd of about 500 men who shouted, 'Go for them'. They were pinned against a wall for about ten minutes by the crowd throwing stones, a half-brick and bottles. Caskie saw the inspector struck on the face and all over the body, including both legs struck with a piece of iron, and on the left hand, and was hit by missiles. Relief came from Lieutenant McGowan of St Rollox Division.[42] Only Caskie gave evidence at the trial, as the 60-year-old MacDonald's health had not recovered from the beating; indeed, he never returned to duty. The violence in Cathedral Street – including the assault against MacDonald and Caskie – was later described, notably by McShane, in gloating terms which glorified it for a contemporary readership then experiencing union and police conflicts:

> Finally the police ran for it, and we ran after them. They rushed up the Cathedral Street closes and tried to go over the back walls, but the strikers got them by the legs and pulled them back; some of them got a terrible hiding. I'm sure the best fight of the riot took place in Cathedral Street.[43]

As preparations were being made for the baton charge up North Frederick Street, a request for assistance to be sent to Cathedral Street was telephoned to St Rollox police station.[44] Lieutenant McGowan, Sergeants Murdoch, Waters and Corbett and ten constables set off and found MacDonald and Caskie 'being badly pelted with stones and bottles. They had nowhere to shelter and were quite unable to cope with the crowd'. McGowan and his men charged the crowd as far as Canning Place, but the much larger crowd had 'regathered behind us'. They made a stand between John Street and Grafton Street where they were reinforced by Superintendent James Muir,* Sergeant McArthur and some constables from St Rollox. The presence of the 51-year-old superintendent, commander of St Rollox Division, carrying a baton in the front line, indicates how hard-pressed the force was at this time. Ten constables were injured.[45] At the top of North Frederick Street, the police met a mob of about 100 men who attacked them with stones, but were driven by the police down Holmhead Street. The crowd in North Frederick Street attacked the small number of policemen with bottles and stones but the police detachment drove them back to Cathedral Street, where a mob was breaking windows.[46] Constable Smart, separated from Lieutenant McGowan's group in the charge, was hit by a bottle and a colleague rushed him into the entrance of Messrs Chambers & Co's premises at 400 Cathedral Street for shelter, followed by two other constables. Thomas Graham, a clerk at Graham & Sons, saw a crowd of 'many hundreds' coming into Cathedral Street from North Frederick Street with the four isolated constables 'being maltreated all along'. Graham's premises were immediately 'bombarded with stones and bottles' – 91 panes of glass were broken. Constable Campbell Smart, the injured man, had served in France right up to the Armistice and when asked at trial if he had experienced anything worse than this in France, he replied 'it was pretty bad in Cathedral Street'.[47]

Constable Frederick Cameron saw accused James Murray, an ex-policeman, in Cathedral Street where he had been 'one of the leaders of the mob'. Murray was seen holding a short iron bar, which he subsequently threw.[48] Constable Smillie had watched Murray throwing things from the crowd for 'three quarters of an hour'.[49]

Sergeant Blackhall was in the charge up North Frederick Street and reported how 'seriously mauled' the police had been in Cathedral Street. He had seen a bottle thrown through the window of the City Chambers.[50] Constable Smith received a cut on the face in Cathedral Street before being surrounded by the crowd, tripped up, kicked in

* Superintendent James Muir (1868-1964). Born Fife. Four of his six brothers also became Glasgow policemen. Joined the Glasgow police aged 19. Reached rank of Superintendent by 1912. Superintendent of St Rollox Division in 1916. On leaving the division, a local newspaper described his courtesy, good humour and kindness. Retired 1932, after 45 years' service.

the head, body, face and legs and rendered unconscious. He woke up in a house in Cathedral Street and was subsequently off duty for ten days.[51] Constable Thomas Burke was sent to Cathedral Street with nine other men under a sergeant to relieve the St Rollox contingent. Burke's small party was surrounded and 'brutally abused' until further relief came from George Square, and he was hit twice on the face with missiles, necessitating a week-long absence from duty.[52]

After Gallacher was arrested, he had been taken to the Municipal Buildings where he was offered, and refused, a glass of whisky. His wife, who had accompanied him to the demonstration, came to speak to him. Constable Turner's evidence described Gallacher having his wounds dressed before he and Kirkwood, somewhat recovered, 'were taken up to a room and given some tea'.[53] Defence witness McBain also visited Gallacher and Kirkwood in the Chambers and both men asked McBain to go out on the balcony to speak to the crowd.[54]

After reading the Riot Act, Sheriff MacKenzie had stood among the police in front of the Buildings' entrance noting, 'There were at that time no signs of the crowd dispersing'. He saw Neil Maclean

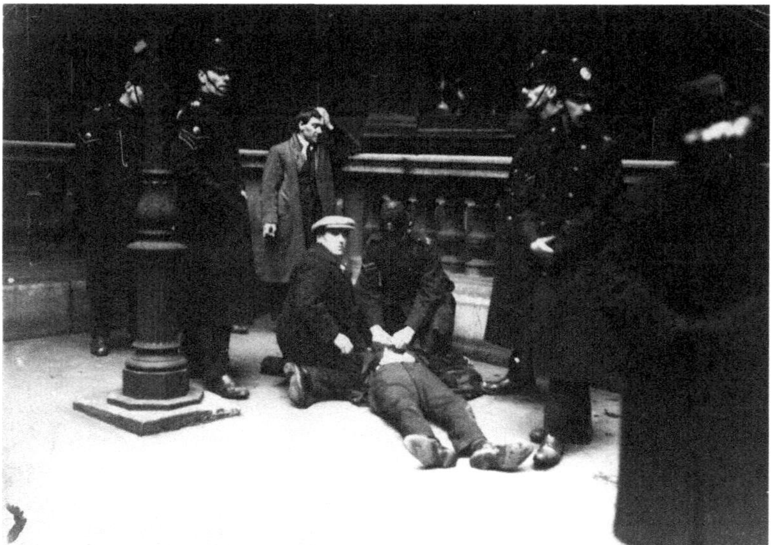

14.3. *Kirkwood being brought round in the City Chambers quadrangle* (Graphic, *8 February 1919).*

14.4. *Gallacher, bandaged, in the City Chambers quadrangle. Kirkwood is just visible, still prone, at the bottom right (*Illustrated London News, *8 February 1919).*

in conversation with the Chief Constable, and the Chief Constable then informed the Sheriff that the crowd wanted to see Kirkwood and Gallacher, 'and that he had been asked if they might be allowed to address the crowd in order to appeal to them to depart peaceably from the Square'.[55] John Foster's claim that 'Gallacher demanded to go on to the balcony' is contradicted by Gallacher's own account, that Jock McBain asked him and Kirkwood to appear on the balcony because the crowd 'wouldn't leave without word from us'.[56] The Sheriff consented because 'granting the request might end the mobbing without further trouble, risk and danger'.[57] Gallacher and Kirkwood complied with the Sheriff's request that they confine themselves to urging the crowd to disperse.

> Both appealed [from a balcony] to the crowd to depart peaceably from the Square . . . After these appeals had been made the crowd slowly dispersed, although the Square continued to be a centre of attraction to a large number of people for the rest of the afternoon.[58]

Defence witness Rosslyn Mitchell testified he could not hear Kirkwood very well, but he heard Gallacher clearly, 'Now, men, clear away from here. Don't mind us, we are all right. Our only concern is for you, and we plead that you should form up in procession and go down to Glasgow Green. For God's sake get out of here at once'.[59] The prosecution attempted to cast a sinister interpretation on Kirkwood's closing remark that 'this was not an opportune time for them but that their time would come later on'. Gallacher commented: 'It is rather a contemptible thing that a man after being batoned and in a bad condition and excited, without any time to consider what he was saying' would have his words used to convict him.[60]

Unsuccessful attempts had been made to organise the crowd to leave the Square before Gallacher and Kirkwood's balcony appearance.[61] Councillor Mitchell heard Herbert Highton's 'very loud voice' in the Square saying, 'I am not one of the Strike Committee, but I have been instructed to tell you all to form up in order and march down to Glasgow Green'.[62] Walter Stewart, chair of the Partick Strike Committee also tried to organise men to march to the Green.[63] Hopkins and Thomas Henderson each led 'a detachment of the strikers' to the Green.[64]

Inspector Sutherland recalled in precognition and at trial that the police had assisted some of the discharged soldiers calling 'upon them to form up in a processional order with a view to leaving the Square' and they successfully got them 'quietly away'.[65] Both prosecution and defence noted ex-servicemen were present in the police and amongst the demonstrators. Constable Johnson's shell-shock symptoms recurred and Owen McQuade, the off-licence manager threatened with a pistol, had felt it appropriate to mention his Gallipoli service.[66] In the century since the riot, the presence of ex-servicemen amongst the demonstrators has been given greater prominence than the military service of policemen present. Foster has claimed that 'some of the 3,000-strong Glasgow Association of Ex-Servicemen formed up in nearby North Frederick Street, moved into action and drove the police back towards the City Chambers' to the extent that police had to take refuge in the quadrangle of the Chambers.[67] Is Foster suggesting the 'hooligans' throwing bottles at the police in North Frederick Street were in fact discharged soldiers acting in concert? The claims that there was an organised group of ex-servicemen at this stage in the riot, and that they drove the police back into the quadrangle, are not independently corroborated by the accounts published in the *Strike Bulletin,* contemporary newspaper accounts or any evidence given at the trial.[68]

In his summing-up at the trial, the Lord Justice-Clerk referred to 'one of the evils of mobbing and rioting' being the potential for police violence against rioters and bystanders alike, which might lead to complaints about police behaviour.[69] A number of defence witnesses gave evidence only on two of the matters forming the main thrust of the defence: first, they saw no justification for police baton charges, especially the charges from the front of the City Chambers; second, on what they saw as unrestrained and indiscriminate violence by the police. James McLellan said the police 'conducted themselves like a lot of savages' being himself struck twice by a policeman.[70] John Hodge had also been close to the Gladstone monument when policemen, returning from a charge in North Frederick Street, turned and charged using their batons 'very severely'. He ended up in the Royal Infirmary

14.5. *A police casualty being put in an ambulance (*Illustrated London News, *8 February 1919).*

ST. GEORGE'S SQUARE, THE SCENE OF THE BATON CHARGE

14.6. *George Square in the immediate aftermath of the riot (*Graphic, *8 February 1919).*

14.7. *The immediate aftermath of the Battle; the broken flagpole outside the City Chambers, and Gladstone's statue, from which the strike leaders addressed the crowd (*Bulletin, *1 February 1919).*

on a stretcher. He said that the police 'had lost control of themselves'.[71] John Forrest was struck on the back of the neck while helping 'an old grey-haired woman' who 'had been tumbled'. He went to Kirkwood's aid and was again batoned and 'knocked out after that'. He claimed to have seen no missiles or any unruliness in the crowd, only the 'very brutal' and 'unwarranted' violence of the police.[72]

Gordon's father described to him two charges he participated in as a constable in Aberdeen in the 1930s. Police were trained to baton the shoulders and upper arms, not the head, but Gordon's father described tall, powerfully-built constables, formerly farm labourers, laying about people's heads with violent abandon. There are sufficient eye-witness accounts from the Square to be certain that some of the police struck out indiscriminately.[73]

The *Glasgow Herald* reported the aftermath of the riot and the injuries in dramatic terms:

> The Square soon acquired the appearance of a miniature battlefield. Figures prone and sitting strewed the ground. In a melee of that description there can be no respect paid to the individual and all come within the sweep of the weapon of the law. Men could be seen nursing broken heads as the results of the use of batons wielded by lusty arms, and who had gone down like ninepins in the sweep of the police charge; others, and they were both young and old, had come by injury either in the crush or through the circumstances, and the hysterical cries of women and girls who had become engulfed in it struggled and suffered in various forms made the picture a composite one of all the horrors that attend on conflict with the executive authority.

There were 'piteous scenes' of casualties arriving at the City Chambers, among them 'young girls who were both injured and terror-stricken'. The mounted police held in the quadrangle had been released into the Square and 'joined the large force of foot policeman'. A 'casualty station' on the ground floor of the City Chambers received men and women 'bearing the marks of injury or complaining of having been hurt. Bruised and bleeding figures were carried in, sometimes seemingly unconscious' who were treated by a 'rapidly requisitioned' medical team. Police and strikers alike arrived, 'and meantime a man was lying on the floor of the entrance hall evidently unconscious, and was carried through to the quadrangle for treatment'.[74]

Iain McLean referred to the 'official injury list' given in the *Glasgow Herald* on 1 February: nineteen police hurt and 34 civilians. However, this latter figure seems to relate solely to civilians treated at the Royal Infirmary. The newspaper claimed only two policemen were severely injured.[75] However, amongst the precognition papers, physician to the police force, Dr Halliday lists 41 policemen injured in George Square alone, with a further ten at Jail Square and vicinity, and three elsewhere; that is over a quarter of the policemen involved. The list included half a dozen men who had sustained serious injury. Among them was a man hit with an iron bar and a shovel and 60-year-old Inspector MacDonald, who had been 'severely mauled'. In addition, 'a large number of men suffered from general bruising and contusions caused by stones and pieces of bottle but did not consider their injuries of sufficient importance to be recorded'.[76] Despite the *Glasgow Herald*'s report, no women were included in the official list of injured.

There were no immediate fatalities as a consequence of the violence, but Constable William McGregor, aged 25, recently returned from military service, died on 1 June 1919 of septicaemia as a result of head injuries sustained at Jail Square.[77] Shinwell, via Peter Slowe, conjures up two further deaths, supposedly reported in the *Glasgow Herald* of 3 February: a maid burned to death in a fire started by looters in the suburbs, and a policeman shot in the stomach by a householder who had mistaken him for a demonstrator.[78] No such newspaper report has been found.

---

1. *Glasgow Herald*, 1 February 1919.
2. AD15/19/11 [A72], Owen McQuade, Off-Licence Manager; AD15/19/11 [A74] & JC36/31/04 [04/R], George Binnie, Lorryman.
3. AD15/19/11 [A72], McQuade, Off-Licence Manager.
4. AD15/19/11 [A72], McQuade, Off-Licence Manager.
5. AD15/19/11 [A74] and JC36/31/04 [04/R], Binnie, Lorryman.

6. JC36/31/04 [04/B], Louis Noble, Detective Inspector; JC36/31/02 [02/J], Thomas McClure, Police Sergeant.
7. JC36/31/01 [01/C], Lawrence Gray, Lieutenant; AD15/19/11 [A21], adopted by Police Sergeant David Murdoch, originally given by the late Inspector Simon Fraser.
8. JC36/31/02 [02/B], David Murdoch, Police Sergeant.
9. AD15/19/11 [A15] and JC36/31/04 [04/7], Thomas Gargan, Police Constable.
10. AD15/19/11 [A17] and JC36/31/03 [03/E], Andrew Gallagher, Police Constable.
11. AD15/19/11 [A68] and JC36/31/02 [02/Q], Alexander Sutherland, Police Inspector.
12. JC36/31/01 [01/C], Gray, Police Lieutenant.
13. JC36/31/04 [04/B], Noble, Detective Inspector.
14. JC36/31/08 [08/C], John Forman, Iron Turner.
15. JC36/31/09 [09/D], William Blamires, Seafarers' Union.
16. D. S. Morton, *The 40 Hours Strike: An Historic Survey of the First General Strike in Scotland* (Clydebank Branch SLP, 1919), p.34; J. Foster, 'Mobilising Working Class Action on Clydeside, 1919 and 1971: How the Arguments Were Won', *Colloque Internationale Discours et Dispositivs Anti-syndicaux* (Lyon, 2010), p.23.
17. JC36/31/07 [07/T], Edith Hughes, Strike Committee.
18. AD15/19/11 [A76] and JC36/31/05 [05/B], Alexander McKendrick, Juvenile Delinquency Board.
19. W. Gallacher, *Revolt on the Clyde* (Lawrence and Wishart, 2017 [1936]), pp.162-63.
20. H. McShane and J. Smith, *Harry McShane: No Mean Fighter* (Pluto Press, 1978), p.106.
21. Tape recorded by Thomas Graham (19 July 1977) NLS Reference Acc. 14114 Special Collections 3/13/2 TGA. William Gallacher Memorial Library.
22. K. MacAskill, *Glasgow 1919: The Rise of Red Clydeside* (Biteback, 2019), pp.213-14.
23. AD15/19/11 [A04], Sir John Lindsay, Town Clerk.
24. AD15/19/11 [A05], James Verdier Stevenson, Chief Constable.
25. AD15/19/11 [A111], Cecil Naismith, Private, Royal Scots.
26. AD15/19/11 [A04], Lindsay, Town Clerk.
27. AD15/19/11 [A01], Alastair Oswald MacKenzie, Sheriff of Lanarkshire;

AD15/19/11 [A04], Lindsay, Town Clerk; JC36/31/04 [04/T], Alexander Mennie, Asst Chief Constable.

28. AD15/19/11 [A01], MacKenzie, Sheriff.

29. JC36/31/03 [03/C] James Stewart, Lord Provost.

30. R. Vogler, *Reading the Riot Act: The Magistracy, the Police and the Army in Civil Disorder* (Open University Press, 1991), p.1.

31. D. Williams, *Keeping the Peace: The Police and Public Order* (Hutchison, 1967), p.31.

32. Williams, *Keeping the Peace*, p.32.

33. A-M. Kilday, *Crime in Scotland 1660-1960: The Violent North* (Routledge, 2018), pp.156-7; *The Times*, 4 August 1919; G. W. Reynolds and A. Judge, *The Night the Police Went on Strike* (Weidenfeld and Nicholson, 1968), p.163. We can find no reliable reference for the rumoured reading in Airdrie.

34. The Criminal Law Act 1967 (Schedule 3, Part III); The Statute Law (Repeals) Act 1973 (Schedule 1, Pt V). Gordon's father, uncorroborated, described an Inspector reading the proclamation of the Riot Act prior to ordering a baton charge at two riots in Aberdeen in the 1930s.

35. AD15/19/11 [A06] and JC36/31/04 [04/T], Mennie, Asst Chief Constable.

36. JC36/31/04 [04/P], Keith, Detective Inspector.

37. AD15/19/11 [A76] and JC36/31/05 [05/B], McKendrick, Juvenile Delinquency Board.

38. JC36/31/06 [06/F], Archibald Wallace, Sheet Metal Worker; JC36/31/07 [07/C], Lawrence Anderson, Machine Man; JC36/31/09 [09/F], Edward Devine, Machine Man.

39. AD15/19/11 [A60], William Melrose, Police Constable; AD15/19/11 [A59], Ross, Police Constable; JC36/31/04 [04/F], Ross, Police Constable; JC36/31/02 [02/C], Neil Gillies, Police Inspector; JC36/31/04 [04/K], Thomas Turner, Police Constable; AD15/19/11 [A20], Gray, Police Lieutenant; Slowe, *Shinwell*, p.85; AD15/19/11 [A109], Dr Halliday, Medical Report on Police Casualties; AD15/19/11 [A64], Alexander McLennan, Police Inspector; JC36/31/04 [04/E], McLennan, Police Inspector; AD15/19/11 [A111], Naismith, Private, Royal Scots; JC36/31/06 [06/D], Mackenzie, Shipwrights' Society; JC36/31/08 [08/E], McPhie, Flour Millers' Union; JC36/31/05 [05/MM], Mitchell, Councillor; JC36/31/08 [08/H], Johnston, Traveller.

40. AD15/19/11 [A28], Duncan Weir, Chief Detective Inspector; JC36/31/03 [03/D], Weir, Chief Detective Inspector; AD15/19/11 [A77], Charles Robertson, Keeper of the Municipal Buildings.

41. Gallacher, *Revolt*, p.162.
42. JC36/31/05 [05/G], John Caskie, Police Sergeant; AD15/19/11 [A78], Alexander MacDonald, Police Inspector.
43. H. McShane and J. Smith, *Harry McShane: No Mean Fighter* (Pluto Press, 1978), p.106.
44. AD15/19/11 [A33], James Wilson, Detective Sergeant.
45. AD15/19/11 [A82], Walter McGowan, Police Lieutenant.
46. JC36/31/05 [05/E], James Smillie, Police Constable.
47. AD15/19/11 [A81], Thomas Graham, Clerk; AD15/19/11 [A80], Arthur Smith, Caretaker; AD15/19/11 [A83] and JC36/31/05 [05/H], Campbell Smart, Police Constable.
48. AD15/19/11 [A38], Frederick Cameron, Police Constable.
49. JC36/31/05 [05/E], Smillie, Police Constable.
50. AD15/19/11 [A16], Henry Blackhall, Police Sergeant.
51. AD15/19/11 [A18] and JC36/31/03 [03/F], Charles Smith, Police Constable.
52. AD15/19/11 [A10] and JC36/31/04 [04/N], Thomas Burke, Police Constable.
53. JC36/31/04 [04/K], Thomas Turner, Police Constable; JC36/31/04 [04/L], William Rennie, Police Constable.
54. JC36/31/07 [07/Q], McBain, Iron Moulder.
55. AD15/19/11 [A01], MacKenzie, Sheriff.
56. Foster, J., 'The 1919 Forty Hours Strike', *Theory and Struggle,* 120 (2019), p.34; Gallacher, *Revolt*, p.163.
57. AD15/19/11 [A04], Lindsay, Town Clerk.
58. AD15/19/11 [A01], MacKenzie, Sheriff.
59. JC36/31/05 [05/MM], Mitchell, Councillor.
60. JC36/31/09 [09/V], Neil Maclean, MP.
61. JC36/31/08 [08/G], James Kerlie, Beardmore's Parkhead Forge.
62. JC36/31/05 [05/MM], Mitchell, Councillor.
63. JC36/31/06 [06/C], Walter Stewart, Amalgamated Society of Engineers.
64. JC36/31/08 [08/D], Thomas Henderson, Amalgamated Society of Carpenters and Joiners.
65. AD15/19/11 [A68] and JC36/31/02 [02/Q], Sutherland, Police Inspector.
66. AD15/19/11 [A109], Dr Halliday, Medical Report on Police Casualties; AD15/19/11 [A72] and JC36/31/04 [04/Q], McQuade, Off-Licence Manager.

67. Foster, 'Forty Hours Strike', p.34; J. Foster, 'Mobilising Working Class Action on Clydeside, 1919 and 1971: How the Arguments Were Won', *Colloque Internationale Discours et Dispositivs Anti-syndicaux* (Lyon, 2010), p.23.

68. Foster references four narratives recorded over 50 years after the Battle as indicating the presence of 'very significant numbers of ex-soldiers' in the Square, explaining 'the effectiveness with which the demonstrators fought back'. The tapes form part of the William Gallacher Memorial Library collection, which was held in the STUC archive between 1987 and 1997 and is now in the National Library of Scotland. They are now digitised. They do not, in our view, support this interpretation. J. Foster, 'Working-class mobilisation on the Clyde 1917-20', in Wrigley, C. (ed), *Challenges of Labour: Central and Western Europe* (Routledge, 1993), pp.149-75; p.170. p.174 note 32. Tapes held in National Library of Scotland, Special Collections, Acc.14114, William Gallacher Memorial Library: William Ferguson (24 July 1974) 3/13/2 WFA; Thomas Graham (19 July 1977) 3/13/2 TGA; Finlay Hart (13 June 1970) 3/13/2 FHA and FHB; Bob Saunders (February 1976) 3/13/2 BSA.

69. JC36/31/10, The Lord Justice-Clerk's charge to the jury; Weinberger, *Keeping the Peace*, pp.45-8.

70. JC36/31/07 [07/M], James McLellan, Machine Man.

71. JC36/31/07 [07/G], John Hodge, Sheet Iron Worker.

72. Queen Street dressing station appears to have been a formal Red Cross First Aid post which citizens could attend; we have been unable to find archival reference to it elsewhere; JC36/31/07 [07/H], John Forrest, Moulder.

73. A. Davies, 'Police Violence and Judicial Bias in the Age of Mass Democracy: Glasgow 1933-1935', *Social History*, 44:1 (2019), pp.58-9; Davies discussed police conflicts in working-class districts of Glasgow in the 1930s.

74. *Glasgow Herald*, 1 February 1919.

75. *Glasgow Herald*, 1 February 1919.

76. AD15/19/11 [A109], Halliday, Medical Report on Police Casualties.

77. Scottish Police Memorial Trust Roll of Honour; A. Dinsmor personal communication, October 2020.

78. P. Slowe, *Manny Shinwell: An Authorised Biography* (Pluto Press, 1993), p.87.

15 A 'scene of great disorder': the Violence Spreads South

And so, parts of the crowd were marshalled and marched off to Glasgow Green, a large public space approximately 1km south-south-east of George Square, running for 2km along the north bank of the Clyde (Map 3). The street known as Saltmarket forms the Green's western boundary, and the High Court of Justiciary and Jail Square lie on the western side of Saltmarket, opposite the end of the Green. The *Glasgow Herald*'s reporter described Glasgow Green as:

> the scene of great disorder . . . some of the crowd held up a [tram]car, smashed the windows with missiles, and roughly handled the conductor. Another car was also interfered with, the trolley rope being cut and the trolley itself twisted. At the foot of Saltmarket several shop windows were smashed . . . There was considerable confusion, with no concerted action on the part of the demonstrators.[1]

D. S. Morton claimed:

> The action of the police gave the hooligan elements in the city an opportunity to come into the fray, and thereafter followed a lot of window-smashing, looting, etc., which always follows any disorder. The strikers were entirely free from blame for this disorder, even the non-strikers admit this.[2]

This exculpatory version of events is, however, contradicted by later writers who characterise much of the violence as a legitimate response by the strikers, evidenced by the discharged soldiers' procession which was responsible for much of the violence at the Green,[3] and by the way in which the crowd continued to target the tramway system and its staff through the city. The level of violence and destruction is often scarcely mentioned. Harry McShane's account particularly reflects his personal predilection for a brand of hyper-masculinity: 'Two policemen tried to intervene at the Saltmarket; the strikers stripped them and they had to run off naked'.[4] This is uncorroborated. In reality, massively outnumbered policemen and tram crew were, if caught alone or in small numbers, stoned and badly beaten; two were left unconscious.[5] Looting by one striker is attested in an interview, albeit taped long after the events, in 1977, in which he claimed to have looted a suit and pair of shoes. The same individual also reported the mob encountering 'two innocent-looking policemen and giving those two bloody policemen hell . . . kicked them and gave them an awful belting'.[6]

The *Glasgow Herald* provided an account of events around the Green, the court building, Trongate and Saltmarket:

> Nine cars were held up near the bridge, the trolley poles bent, and the glass smashed. Fully half a dozen windows on the east front of the Justiciary Court Buildings were broken, and similar damage was done to several windows on the side of the buildings facing the river. Windows were also smashed in the police barracks in East Clyde Street, in several shops facing the river, and in a public house in the Saltmarket.[7]

When Tram Inspector Andrew Imrie reached Queen Street, he saw cars standing from Jamaica Street to Glasgow Cross, because four cars had been disabled at Glasgow Cross with their trolleys and windows broken.[8] At about 1.25pm, driving a tram by way of Saltmarket, Mary Beattie reached the Justiciary Buildings in Jail Square. She described a huge crowd of people standing on the car rails, several of whom held up their hands, compelling her to stop outside 74 Trongate. Some of the crowd mounted her tram, seized the reversing handle and removed it; pushing her out of the way, they cut the trolley rope and smashed all the windows. They 'told me in a menacing way to leave my car'; she was afraid and complied, relieved they had not attempted to assault her. She noted there was another tramcar behind her and three on the other line, and that windows had been broken in all the cars, and their trolleys had been bent.[9]

At approximately 1.25pm, John McNair, driving his tram into Trongate, saw a crowd, which he estimated at between 100 and 300 strong, emerging from Hutchison Street, about 250m west of Glasgow Cross. They held their hands up to stop the car and then surrounded it. They called McNair a 'scab and a blackleg' and a man tried to take McNair's whistle. However, a female passenger grabbed it, went upstairs and blew it to summon assistance. McNair's female conductor got the trolley back on the wires and he took his point shifter – an iron bar – out to change the points for his car. He had to wave the shifter threateningly to fend off the crowd and it was taken from him by force. Two policemen came to his assistance and he tried to get the car moving. The crowd started smashing the windows with a stick and missiles, and McNair was cut on the face. His passengers took flight. Dazed, McNair secured the car to prevent it being moved. He found an unconscious policeman lying face down inside the car, probably Constable Joseph Orr. Then McNair himself lay down, feeling 'stunned'. As he left the car, two women took him to safety in a nearby house, where he remained for about two hours before returning to duty.[10]

Constable Orr had been walking his beat when he was called to Trongate at South Albion Street about 1.25pm. He found two stationary cars with most of their windows smashed, surrounded by a crowd of 'thousands'. He forced his way through the crowd and got aboard the first car. He managed to get the passengers off before assisting the driver. Throughout, 'quite a barrage' of bricks and stones was thrown at the driver and himself, and after approximately ten minutes, Orr was 'rendered unconscious' by a thrown brick and came round in the Royal Infirmary. He was off duty for 21 days.[11] The assault on Constable Orr was witnessed by Margaret Quaill, who described the assailant as 'a man of from 25 to 30 years of age . . . of a respectable appearance'. She saw:

> a Constable in the midst of the crowd trying to escape. The crowd around him were assaulting him. I saw him assaulted from behind. I saw a man coming out of the car with a broken hand rail. It was taken off the car. He had it in his hand. He was proceeding to strike the Constable with it. I seized hold of it and took it from him.[12]

Constable Orr was carried into Albion Street by some civilians and was then taken into the Tron House for his own safety by two men and a woman.[13]

On hearing of a driver being 'badly mauled in the Trongate' with his car smashed by the strikers, Tram Inspector Erskine headed towards Trongate where he found John McNair's empty and damaged tram. The car remained driveable, so he drove it to the Whitevale depot in Rochester Street. Fifteen or sixteen trams in Trongate were held up behind a car with its windows broken, trolleys bent and ropes cut. Erskine returned to Saltmarket at 3pm and found six cars all 'more or less damaged by having the windows broken and the trolleys bent'.[14]

Two groups of police were called up from Southern Division – Police Inspectors Innes and Fordyce, Sergeants Ferguson, Sellars and Wishart and Detective Sergeant Lobhan and 30 constables – and from Eastern Division, Inspector Stewart, Sergeant Beaton and eight constables. A 'very riotous' mob took bottles from another stricken lorry to use as missiles. Innes ordered his men to draw batons and they succeeded in breaking up the crowd, before a further baton charge in Jail Square against another barrage of missiles.[15] Two constables were so badly injured by bottles they had to be taken off duty. Detective Sergeant John Lobban was in Jail Square and saw one 'struck on the back of the head with part of a bottle'.[16]

A crowd 2,000-3,000 strong emerged from Glasgow Green, led by bagpipes and 'the large red banner of a branch of a discharged soldiers' society on which 'We want justice' was inscribed in white letters.[17] While the police tried to clear a way for the trams at the north end of Albert Bridge, this crowd began to shout, jeer and throw missiles. More people crossed northwards over the Albert Bridge and Inspector Innes became alarmed by his men's position sandwiched between the two groups. There was another baton charge. The crowd moved off along the north bank of the river, and on Great Clyde Street between Stockwell Street and Jamaica Street, seized a lorry and stripped it of beer bottles which were either thrown or stolen.[18] More policemen crossed the Albert Bridge, drew their batons and charged. There was a panic in the dense crowd, 'Composed largely of curious people who in their anxiety to see' what was happening, found 'themselves in the storm centre'. The battle at the bridge lasted for about a quarter of an hour.[19]

Other constables reported injuries to themselves and others.[20] The *Glasgow Herald* described a policeman supported by two colleagues, bareheaded and scarcely able to walk, having been struck on the head. His uniform sleeve displayed a gold stripe denoting war service and wounds. The newspaper also reported an attack by rioters in Saltmarket on a motor van used by disabled schoolchildren which had all its windows smashed; fortunately there were no injuries.[21]

Some of the crowd turned south over Glasgow Bridge. Inspector Innes and Sergeant Sellars seized William McCartney in Bridge Street, south of the river while still holding a broken bottle, which was later presented as evidence. They were followed by a hostile crowd as they took him to the Southern Division police office, only about 200m away. On being searched, McCartney's pockets revealed two bottles of stout and a butcher's knife.[22] McCartney was later given a three-month sentence for mobbing and rioting. Nevertheless, defence witness John Forman, in the middle of the violent chaos, claimed he had seen 'no trouble between the crowd and police', and no damaged tram cars despite describing passing through a baton charge and a field of wrecked trams.[23]

Tram Inspector Imrie was in Paisley Road, south of the river, at about 3pm when he saw the procession that had left the Green, with its large red banner, going westwards interfering with tramcars.[24] When the procession reached 75 Paisley Road West, at about 3.10pm a jeweller's shop was looted, the owner being struck on the head as he tried to stop a mob of about 50 men looting his window. The overall loss was estimated at £1,000.[25] Special Constable Denis Stewart had seen a man 'standing taking things from [the] window and putting them in his coat pocket' and he followed him until he encountered other policemen.[26] Together, they arrested Daniel Oliver* and were immediately attacked by the crowd. Sergeant Milne had held them off with his baton while his colleagues got Oliver, resisting

* Daniel Stewart Oliver (1893-1968). Employed Singer Sewing Machine Co. as labourer. 1915-1918 supervisor in shell factory of Mavor & Colston. Employed at Beardmore until 23 December 1918. Convicted May 1916 for assaulting a constable. Died as a 'retired gardener'. Tried and acquitted of mobbing and rioting. Not tried for theft (Chapter 21).

all the way, to the police station. Oliver admitted the jewellery did not belong to him. Oliver was unemployed and had no known link to socialist politics or the strike; he was an opportunist who had taken advantage of the situation.[27]

The War Cabinet

At some point between 12.08pm, when Margaret Buchanan's tram was held up in George Square, and 3pm when the War Cabinet met, someone (most probably John Lamb of the Scottish Office) had acquainted London with the events in Glasgow either by telephone or telegram. Glasgow was discussed briefly at the War Cabinet. The Deputy Prime Minister and MP for Glasgow Central, Bonar Law, was again in the chair. Only one other War Cabinet member was present, Sir Eric Geddes. Six other ministers were in attendance: Churchill (War and Air); Auckland Geddes (Eric's brother, Reconstruction); Horne (Labour); Munro (Scotland); Clyde (Lord Advocate). Three Major-Generals attended, fewer and less senior soldiers than the day before: Romer with a role in UK domestic security; Harington (Deputy Chief of the Imperial General Staff [D-CIGS]); Childs (Director of Personal Services).[28] Sir Henry Wilson, CIGS, was *en route* to Paris, summoned by the Prime Minister to discuss the British military presence in Russia, Constantinople and Syria.[29]

The first item on the agenda was 'Industrial Unrest' and the first report concerned the situation in Belfast, where 'the workmen had formed a "Soviet" Committee'. Then Horne reported that in Glasgow:

> a crowd had met in front of the Municipal Buildings in order to receive the Government's reply to the Lord Provost's telegram. He had no details, but understood that foot and mounted police had charged the crowd in order to quell a riot and casualties had resulted.

At this point Munro, Scottish Secretary, made his infamous remark:

> in his opinion, it was more clear than ever that it was a misnomer to call the situation in Glasgow a strike – it was a Bolshevist rising.[30]

Munro continued that the numbers involved had 'limited dimensions' and 'public opinion would support the Government in quelling any disorder . . . the strike gave the appearance of breaking up at an early date'.[31] Unfortunately, only the sensationalist element of Munro's speech has been used by writers to characterise the War Cabinet's discussions about Glasgow during the strike, presenting it as more alarmed and panicky than it was. No other War Cabinet member or minister in attendance on Friday afternoon supported Munro's assessment of the situation, although General Romer then reported:

> The necessary orders had been given to the G.O.C. [General Officer Commanding] Scotland, with regard to the movement of troops. An officer had been sent to the headquarters of the Scottish Command last night [30 January] to explain the situation. The number of troops which could be put into Glasgow at short notice was about 12,000.

Deputy CIGS Harington reported '6 tanks and 100 motor lorries were going north by rail that night'. The discussion then addressed the strike leadership. The Lord Advocate noted that action would be possible under Defence of the Realm Regulations (DORA): he noted Regulation 14 allowed deportation 'if the Army Council gave the necessary instructions to a competent military authority, Regulation 42 allowed arrest for causing disaffection and Regulation 55 offered wide-ranging powers of arrest, but considered deportation was 'practically the only means of procedure if instant action were required'. Churchill said the necessary authority for implementing Regulation 14 'could be given in a very few minutes, if necessary'.[32] Weinberger's claim that the arrests of the strike leaders were 'decided on by the government' may rely on a mistaken interpretation of this discussion because all the arrests were made under Scots Criminal Law for riot and associated offences, not DORA.[33] Before moving on to discuss 'Unrest of Troops at Calais', the War Cabinet decided: 'That for the moment no further action was necessary by the Government'.[34]

Before the War Cabinet's meeting at 3pm, at about 1.30pm, news of the spreading violence had already reached the City Chambers, at which point the Sheriff had begun to consider his options.

1. *Glasgow Herald*, 1 February 1919.
2. D. S. Morton, *The 40 Hours Strike: An Historic Survey of the First General Strike in Scotland* (Clydebank Branch SLP, 1919), p.9.
3. *Glasgow Herald*, 1 February 1919.
4. H. McShane and J. Smith, *Harry McShane: No Mean Fighter* (Pluto Press, 1978), p.107.
5. JC36/31/05 [05/W] and AD15/19/11 [A85], John McNair, Tram Driver; *Glasgow Herald*, 1 February 1919; AD15/19/11 [A18] and JC36/31/03 [03/F], Charles Smith, Police Constable.
6. Tape recorded by Thomas Graham (19 July 1977) NLS Reference Acc. 14114 Special Collections 3/13/2 TGA. William Gallacher Memorial Library.
7. *Glasgow Herald*, 1 February 1919.
8. JC36/31/02 [02/E], Andrew Imrie, Tram Inspector.
9. AD15/19/11 [A90] and JC36/31/05 [05/Z], Mary Beattie, Tram Driver.
10. JC36/31/05 [05/W] and AD15/19/11 [A85], John McNair, Tram Driver; he appears to have changed points at the junction east of the Cross.
11. AD15/19/11 [A86] and JC36/31/05 [05/X], Joseph Orr, Police Constable; *Glasgow Herald*, 1 February 1919; AD15/19/11 [A109], Halliday, Medical Report on Police Casualties.
12. AD15/19/11 [A88], Margaret Quail or Connelly.
13. AD15/19/11 [A87] and JC36/31/05 [05/Y], Christopher Player, Police Constable. Tron House is a major Scottish Baronial building at the corner of Albion Street and Trongate, which in 1919 was the premises of a large shop.
14. AD15/19/11 [A27] and JC36/31/06 [06/C], James Erskine, Tram Inspector.
15. AD15/19/11 [A41] and JC36/31/05 [05/V], William Ferguson, Police Sergeant. At some point after his precognition was taken on 13 February 1919, Inspector Innes died and his precognition was assumed by Sergeant Ferguson.
16. AD15/19/11 [A46], John Lobban, Detective Sergeant.
17. *Glasgow Herald*, 1 February 1919.
18. AD15/19/11 [A41] and JC36/31/05 [05/V], Ferguson, Police Sergeant.
19. *Glasgow Herald*, 1 February 1919.
20. AD15/19/11 [B47], David Latto, Police Constable; AD15/19/11 [B49], James Tait, Police Constable; AD15/19/11 [B50], John Samuel, Police Constable.

21. *Glasgow Herald*, 1 February 1919.
22. AD15/19/11 [A41], Ferguson, Police Sergeant.
23. JC36/31/08 [08/C], John Forman, Iron Turner.
24. JC36/31/02 [02/E], Andrew Imrie, Tram Inspector.
25. AD15/19/11 [A95], Agnes Gilfillan or Macfarlane; AD15/19/11 [A93], Lawrence Hunter, Jeweller; AD15/19/11 [A94], Margaret Russell, Saleswoman.
26. AD15/19/11 [A96], Denis Stewart, Special Police Constable.
27. AD15/19/11 [A100], John Gray, Lorryman; JC36/31/05 [05/CC], Farquhar McVean, Secretary, A. G. Barr & Co. Ltd.
28. CAB23/9/10, War Cabinet Minutes, meeting 523, 31 January 1919.
29. C. E. Callwell, *Field-Marshall Sir Henry Wilson: His Life and Diaries* (Cassell, 1927), p.167; M. Gilbert, *Churchill: A Life* (Random House, 2000), p.192.
30. The incorrect use of 'Bolshevik uprising' in any quotation instead of 'Bolshevist rising' alerts the reader to an author who has not actually consulted the War Cabinet minutes but has relied on erroneous secondary sources.
31. CAB23/9/10, War Cabinet Minutes, meeting 523, 31 January 1919.
32. CAB23/9/10, War Cabinet Minutes, meeting 523, 31 January 1919.
33. B. Weinberger, *Keeping the Peace: Policing Strikes in Britain, 1906-1926* (Berg, 1991), p.157.
34. CAB23/9/10, War Cabinet Minutes, meeting 523, 31 January 1919.

16 The Sheriff Calls the Troops: Friday Afternoon

In Iain McLean's view the military deployment, particularly the tanks in the Cattle Market, gave the strike 'a romantic history which successfully concealed an otherwise ignominious failure'.[1] It has become a commonplace to assert that, to paraphrase, the government sent the troops/tanks to crush the strike/a revolution, and this has dominated not only the popular but also the academic narrative. Barbara Weinberger asserts not only 'The military were not called in by the local authority' but also had 'the Provost thought that extra police or military aid was necessary he could easily have arranged for or asked for this directly. He did neither . . .'. Weinberger may have confused the situation in England, where a mayor could call for military aid, with the arrangements in Scotland, where the equivalent, the Lord Provost, could not. Weinberger also claims the posting of troops and tanks around the city and the arrest of the strike leaders 'were decided on by the government without consultation with the local authority and not necessarily in accord with its wishes'.[2] In reality, 'military aid to the civil power' was summoned by the Sheriff and all arrests were made for ordinary criminal offences by Glasgow City Police.

In his survey of the tank and its symbolism, Patrick Wright emphasised the oppressive impact of the tank, and his version of events in Glasgow conforms to the traditional narrative: a deliberate attack by the police aimed to precipitate the military deployment; Churchill was responsible for the deployment, and so on. Although unreferenced, Wright follows Weinberger's line by omitting any mention of the calling of military aid by the Sheriff and skirting the conspiracist argument that a deliberate attack was made on the crowd to carry through government policy.[3]

Lynch also claims 'the government sent in troops and tanks to quash . . . a "Bolshevist rising"', while Jenkinson asserts the government ordered the deployment 'in a show of force designed to restore order'.[4] Fry presents a mythical version of the government's and

Churchill's roles and further includes the claims that troops had already been deployed before the riot, a force of English soldiers, with machine-guns on rooftops, and a fanciful howitzer.[5] Harvie not only claims the government sent the troops, but that they were despatched on Thursday 30 January.[6] In his school history, Kerr includes '12,000 English troops . . . brought in by the government to restore order'.[7] McGonigle and Wood, in their school text, also claim '12,000 English troops' sent by the government 'in case a revolution broke out'.[8] Kilday claims the government 'sent an estimated 10,000 English troops . . . to maintain order'.[9] Marwick not only blames the government, but asserts they anticipated events by moving troops in advance.[10]

The reality is that the Sheriff described his decision to call for military aid in both his precognition and trial evidence. At some time between 1.15pm and 1.30pm on Friday, the Sheriff had heard of the spreading violence in Trongate and towards Glasgow Green. After considering all he had experienced and heard about, he consulted the Lord Provost and the Chief Constable.

> Q. And did you tell them you had come to the conclusion that the resources of the Civil Authorities were insufficient for securing the maintenance of order in the City at that time?
>
> A. Yes, we were all agreed. We had heard other things of more disorder.
>
> Q. You had heard of disorder in the Trongate and elsewhere?
>
> A. Yes.
>
> Q. And did you in consequence make up your mind that the necessity had arisen for appealing to the Military Authorities?
>
> A. Yes.[11]

In his precognition he added: 'accordingly I requisitioned for military aid by taking a written requisition to the Officer in Command of District Headquarters in Lynedoch Place in the West End'.[12]

It is important to understand the context in which the Sheriff thought military aid was necessary. Perhaps as many as 220 policemen had become involved in the disturbances throughout the city centre during the first hour or two of the violence. Because around a third of the force was still in the armed forces, only about 569 men were on duty in the whole city (Map 1), even on a 12-hour shift. Given the scale and spread of the violence and the attrition in police numbers through injury, one may appreciate the Sheriff's apprehension as to their capacity to maintain order.

As exemplified above, a persistent feature of the mythology of the Battle, which appears in a number of academic and popular accounts, is that troops were already on the move in other parts of Scotland before the Sheriff called for them at around 1.30pm on Friday 31 January. This misrepresentation or misunderstanding has been used to justify the conspiracist version of events, first promoted by John Maclean, D. S. Morton, William Gallacher, Emanuel Shinwell, Tom Bell and others, and subsequently accepted by some historians – that the riot was deliberately fomented, to provide an excuse for a deployment of troops that they claimed had already begun before the riot started.[13] At the War Cabinet meeting on 30 January, there had been an exchange which has been used to support the claim that troops were already moving:

> Sir Eric Geddes drew attention to the fact that the President of the Board of Trade anticipated that the railways might shut down on Saturday, as the men were threatening to work only eight hours. This would inevitably disorganise all railway traffic. This might affect the movement of troops into Glasgow.
>
> Mr Churchill said that the War Office would take all the necessary steps to meet such eventuality, and would consider arrangements for placing troops in the vicinity of Glasgow.[14]

The War Cabinet minutes and all the files and newspaper accounts we have consulted provide no evidence of a pre-emptive movement ordered by Churchill or anyone else.

At least four newspapers reported what seems to have been a syndicated story that 'arrangements were being made for calling out military assistance, when the order was cancelled' owing to the temporarily calming effect of the speeches made from the City Chambers by Gallacher and Kirkwood.[15] How this contemporary story spread is unclear, because the Sheriff's requisition to the military was sent *after* Kirkwood's and Gallacher's address to the crowd, and was influenced by events beyond the environs of the Square. Was it a misunderstanding of the effects of reading the Riot Act? Some of those involved, notably Bailies Stewart and Wheatley, appear to have believed reading the Riot Act inevitably meant calling out the military.

The force taken to Glasgow comprised 10,000 men and six tanks, larger than any home deployment before or since in mainland Britain. The much greater and more prolonged violence in Liverpool in August 1919 during the police strike merited only 900 soldiers and perhaps the same number of sailors, and tanks were parked in public view in the city centre, unlike Glasgow where the tanks, when they arrived, were kept under cover. There are three practical reasons that may explain the size and strength of the deployment to Glasgow.

First, to avoid officers having to negotiate a path between inadequate and excessive use of force, 'the army tried to ensure that it would always confront a crowd in such overawing strength that the decision to open fire would never have to be taken'.[16] Second, Sir Redver Bullers noted the military had repeatedly found that magistrates requested detachments of troops should be 'distributed as widely as possible over a disturbed area' which resulted in 'dangerously small' groups who might be 'compelled to use their weapons, where a larger force would not have been reduced to this extremity'.[17] Glasgow was a large area to patrol with numerous vulnerable points. Last, the army would have prepared for the worst contingency, in the absence of certainty about what they might face in a city that had gained a radical reputation during the war. One historian has suggested they had prepared to meet, at worst, an extreme situation, such as a repeat of Dublin in 1916.[18] Direct references to events in Dublin had allegedly been made by Hopkins, one of the strike leaders, on 29 January.[19]

However, these three explanations alone are insufficient to justify the scale of the deployment and the inclusion of six tanks. Sir Henry Wilson's personal agenda for the military and his cabal of reactionary senior commanders may have been instrumental in deciding the size of the deployment.[20] As Foster explains, 'although Glasgow did not become Britain's Petrograd, its experience was nonetheless somewhat exceptional' and even if widespread revolutionary intent and possibility in Glasgow did not exist, there appears to have been sufficient belief in such a possibility.[21] By sending so many troops to Glasgow, Wilson's supporters were able to paint the city as particularly threatening, thus convincing others that his great response indicated a great and real risk of revolution. Wilson's support for and perhaps even enthusiasm for the tank arm may also have influenced the inclusion of six tanks.[22] Wilson travelled to Paris on Friday 31 January to speak to Lloyd George about troop deployments in the Middle East and in Russia. Thus, if he had been involved in the decision to send tanks, it occurred between the Cabinet meeting on Thursday afternoon and the beginning of the riot at approximately 12.10pm on Friday. Wilson seems only to have been informed of events in Glasgow on 2 February by telegram: 'Wire tonight shows Glasgow in riot, and troops beginning to occupy the streets'.[23]

To support the view that 'the government sent the tanks' it has been asserted that the Sheriff calling for military aid was a mere device to provide legal cover for a deployment the government wished to make; that is, if the Sheriff's involvement is mentioned at all. Blake describes 'the Sheriff of Glasgow' amongst those civil authorities, 'legally if only formally, responsible for directing and controlling the use of military aid [to] the civil power'.[24] There is no evidence to support any suggestion that he had responsibility in name only. First, there is no indication in the George Square trial or War Cabinet papers that the Sheriff was encouraged by the government to make a request for military aid. The Sheriff's own testimony supports the opposite conclusion. Second, the idea of a military deployment does not appear in the War Cabinet minutes until Thursday 30 January, which had been prompted by the Sheriff's enquiry about the availability of troops should he need them. Finally, the commander of troops in Great Britain, Sir William Robertson, reminded the War Cabinet on 30 January that it was the Sheriff, not the government, who had the power to send troops.[25] The minutes of the War Cabinet remained secret under the 50-year closure rule until 1969, and furthermore 'secret minutes' were at that time typed up and distributed to avoid sensitive material being seen by the unionised government printers, thus there was nothing to be gained by dissembling in that forum on the Thursday afternoon.[26]

Was Glasgow under martial law? In his response to the Lord Provost's statement to the Town Council on 6 February 1919, Bailie John Wheatley said, 'we are under military control today'. Occasionally, authors have taken this to imply that Wheatley understood martial law to have been imposed in Glasgow.[27] Martial law was, however, formally declared only once in the UK in the twentieth century, in parts of Ireland in 1921. Categorically, martial law was not imposed in Glasgow in 1919. The running of the city was not taken out of the hands of the Town Council, nor were the civil courts replaced by courts martial.[28]

Another part of the mythology of the Battle is that men of the 'local' regiment, the Highland Light Infantry (HLI), were locked into Maryhill Barracks, because it was feared that local men might side with the strikers.[29] However, the HLI was not based at Maryhill in 1919. The barracks had been occupied since December 1918 by the 4th (Reserve) Battalion of the Royal Scots Fusiliers, the county regiment of Ayrshire and the south-west of Scotland, apart from 27 men of an HLI Garrison Battalion being disbanded.[30]

Since the Childers reforms of 1881, the 1st and 2nd Battalions of each regiment formed the two 'Regular' or professional, full-time battalions of the regiment; in peacetime, one was usually based somewhere in the UK, the other somewhere in the Empire. After the Haldane Reforms in the first decade of the twentieth century, a regiment's Territorial Battalions would take subsequent battalion numbers, 4th, 5th and so on. In peacetime, recruitment and training were undertaken at the regimental depot; from there drafts of men would be sent out to reinforce the 1st and 2nd Battalions. During the First World War, an infantry regiment might have had over twenty battalions – Regular, Territorial and New Army units. A significant part of the work of inducting and training the huge number of men needed to form and reinforce so many units was undertaken by what was usually known as the 3rd (Reserve) Battalion, although some regiments at times also had a 4th or even 5th (Reserve) Battalion with the same function. The force deployed to Glasgow on the last day of January 1919 was drawn from these Reserve Battalions, described by General Robertson at the War Cabinet meeting on 30 January:

Regiment	Reserve Battalion/ Depot	Location Jan 1919	Strength Jan 1919
Royal Scots	Depot	Glencorse, near Edinburgh	4,197
	3rd (R) Bn	Mullingar (Ireland)	2227
	4th (R) Bn	***Cupar***	***2,275***
Royal Scots Fusiliers	Depot	Ayr	3066
	3rd (R) Bn	**Fort Matilda** [Greenock]	**2,195**
	4th (R) Bn	**Glasgow** [Maryhill]	**1,475**
Kings Own Scottish Borderers	Depot	Berwick-upon-Tweed	2663
	3rd (R) Bn	Curragh [Ireland]	1939
	4th (R) Bn	***Dunfermline***	***1,438***
Cameronians	Depot	Hamilton	3,417
	3rd (R) Bn	**Invergordon**	**3,067**
	4th (R) Bn	**Redford** [Edinburgh]	**1,171**
	5th (R) Bn	Bridge of Allan	2
East Surrey [Depot: Kingston-upon-Thames]	***3rd (R) Bn***	***Bridge of Allan***	***2,904***
Black Watch	Depot	Perth	2,033
	3rd (R) Bn	Curragh [Ireland]	1,390
	4th (R) Bn	**Fort George**	**1,553**
Highland Light Infantry	Depot	Hamilton	3,741
	3rd (R) Bn	**Haddington**	**3,824**
	4th (R) Bn	**Arbroath**	**1,537**
	1st (R) Garrison Bn	Glasgow [Maryhill]	27
Seaforth Highlanders	Depot	Fort George	1,589
	3rd (R) Bn	***Cromarty***	***2,187***
	4th (R) Bn	***Glencorse*** *[Midlothian]*	***651***
Gordon Highlanders	Depot	Aberdeen	2,724
	3rd (R) Bn	***Aberdeen***	***2,143***
	4th (R) Bn	***Colinton*** *[Edinburgh]*	***2,172***
Cameron Highlanders	Depot	Inverness	1,416
	3rd (R) Bn	Ballyvonare (Ireland)	1,730
Argyll & Sutherland Highlanders	Depot	Stirling	1,783
	3rd (R) Bn	Kinsale (Ireland)	1,713
	4th (R) Bn	***Dunbar***	***1,807***
	5th (R) Bn	***Galashiels***	***2,257***
Outwith Scotland			
East Surrey [Depot: Kingston on Thames]	5th (R) Bn	Tunbridge Wells	72
Durham Light Infantry [Depot: Newcastle]	***3rd (R) Bn***	***South Shields***	***3,941***
	4th (R) Bn	Seaham Harbour	1,427

> all reserve-finding units, and consisted of all sorts of men, old, young, convalescent, and men with wounds. As regards their officers, these were not very efficient.[31]

By 1919, the Reserve Battalions were based mainly in vast purpose-built hutted camps. The table opposite shows the location of the regimental depots and the Reserve Battalion camps and their strength at the end of January 1919; the number of 'effectives' in each unit would have been smaller.

At the War Cabinet meeting on 30 January, Robertson noted only one non-Scottish battalion, which was an English unit, the 3rd (Reserve) Battalion of the East Surrey regiment, then based at Bridge of Allan. Only sixteen battalions are recorded in the official returns as having been stationed in Scotland at that time. Two of them, both of the Royal Scots Fusiliers, are noted as at Glasgow (Maryhill) and Fort Matilda (Gourock). Robertson stated that twelve battalions were in the vicinity of Edinburgh. If units as far apart as Bridge of Allan, Cupar, Galashiels and Haddington are included, the monthly return suggests there were only nine, unless Robertson was thinking of east coast units more generally, which would include Aberdeen and Arbroath, which leaves three battalions in the north at Fort George, Cromarty and Invergordon. Robertson is likely to have been working from hastily collected figures, as the published January return would not have been available on 31 January. Romer's statement at the 31 January meeting that 12,000 men could be put into Glasgow at short notice presumably reflected the numbers of fit and effective men who could

Opposite: The location and strength of units in Scotland and the north of England in January 1919. Units in **bold** *were within Scotland or the north of England and available for deployment. Units in **bold italic** may have been in the Glasgow deployment. Also shown are the strengths of the 4th Bn Durham Light Infantry and the 5th Bn East Surrey regiments, which were probably not involved. The regimental depots also contained between 900 and 4,900 men, but the War Cabinet minutes were explicit in naming the Reserve Battalions as the source of the troops. The unit locations were the same in December 1918 and January 1919, apart from the 4th (Reserve) Battalion, Royal Scots Fusiliers, which moved from Kinross to Maryhill, Glasgow in December 1918. (Source: WO73/109 & WO73/110).*

be mustered from these Reserve Battalions. As Robertson noted, these units also included many convalescent or other ineffective men.

There had been ten Scottish infantry regiments since 1881. Map 5 shows the recruiting areas in 1919. The effective elements of the 3rd (Reserve) Battalions of the Royal Scots, King's Own Scottish Borderers (KOSB), Queen's Own Cameron Highlanders, the Black Watch and the Argyll and Sutherland Highlanders had been added to the garrison of Ireland after 1916.[32]

The regiments involved in the deployment to Glasgow are identifiable almost entirely from contemporary newspaper accounts, including the *New York Times*. No War Office list has been found and regimental histories are largely silent. Of the ten Scottish infantry regiments, elements of four seem *not* to have been deployed, even though they were present in Scotland: Highland Light Infantry; Royal Scots Fusiliers; Cameronians (Scottish Rifles) and Black Watch. The Black Watch 4th (Reserve) Battalion was based at Fort George, but its effectiveness in January 1919 is unknown. The other three were traditionally based in and recruited from west-central Scotland.

The choice of troops and the weeding out of Glasgow men reported from at least one Seaforth battalion that was sent to Glasgow conforms to the army's long-standing policy of 'distant locality' – only to use men originating from outside the affected area when military aid was provided.[33] As Blake explains, because of 'the fear that local troops, originating from the troubled community itself, would be more likely to sympathise with the aims of the disturbances, and the people involved in them, or at least be loath to act against them'.[34] However, the Argyll and Sutherland Highlanders, who were deployed to Glasgow in 1919, generally recruited from areas close to Glasgow, including Renfrewshire (see Fig16.3).

The soldiers in these very mixed Reserve Battalions chosen to deploy to Glasgow would first have to be selected for the duty, then issued with equipment, arms, ammunition and rations, and finally paraded and inspected. How much of this might have been achieved before lunchtime on Friday, in anticipation of being needed, is unknown. When ready, the contingents would be marched to the nearest railway stations large enough to accommodate special

16.1. *Troops marching in George Square 1 or 2 February 1919. Note the variety of headgear: flat forage caps; Tam o'Shanter bonnets; fore-and-aft caps; even a bush hat, such is the variety of units represented (*Illustrated London News*, 8 February 1919).*

military trains. The Gordon Highlanders unit was recorded as being at 'Colinton', probably the Redford Barracks complex, within 2km of the nearest suitable goods sidings, at the 'New Markets' at Inglis Green or the sidings at Slateford Junction. Glencorse Barracks had its own railway station. Meanwhile, special military trains of carriages and goods wagons would have had to be got ready and moved to platforms or sidings set aside for the army. The loading of men and equipment into the trains may reasonably be estimated to have taken an hour or two. The first troops are reported as arriving in Glasgow at Queen Street Station at around 10pm on 31 January, after a rail journey of approximately two hours from Edinburgh.[35] It seems reasonable that it took the army some eight to nine hours to go through the processes to reach Glasgow, having had eighteen hours' notice from Thursday afternoon to prepare and await further orders.

A number of those involved in the strike provided accounts of the arrival of the military in memoirs, some published many years after the event. D. S. Morton's account, written between Friday 31 January and April's trial, is alone in suggesting the government sent aeroplanes as part of the force to Glasgow.[36] One or more howitzers appear in the narrative from the 1970s onwards. Troops continued to arrive over the weekend and the tanks arrived on Monday. The most immediate account of the arrival of the army appeared in the Glasgow *Evening Times* on Saturday 1 February:

> Large forces of military reached Glasgow yesterday evening and are now stationed at various points throughout the city, including railway stations and bridges. The regiments are English and Scottish. Commencing at ten o'clock last night and continuing till an early hour this morning, a steady stream of troops was poured into the city through the medium of Queen Street Station. Men of the Seaforths, mingled with the Gordons and the East Surreys, are quartered in different parts of the city, including the railway stations. At the Central Station, to which the men marched accompanied by ammunition waggons, they were supplied with food and refreshment. Pipe bands accompanied the Highland troops.
>
> Men of the 3rd and 5th Battalions of the East Surrey Regiment are in St Enoch Station. Piles of baggage, blankets and other necessary material, standing between platforms 5 and 6, are guarded by sturdy English lads, with rifle and bayonet. They are wearing the 'soup-plate' hats which they have brought back with them from France last year, and over the greatcoats are slung canvas cases containing an extra allowance of 100 cartridges. On the paved way between platforms 2 and 3 about 100 rifles are stacked in batches of five, while machine guns of the Lewis pattern are placed at intervals along the row. Those of the men who are not at post-duty are strolling about unconcernedly, chaffing the station hands (male and female alike) buying from the cigarette kiosk and writing post-cards to friends. The railway bridge over the Clyde is guarded at both ends by a strong military detachment, and sentries are also posted at intervals along the bridge.[37]

Saturday's *Daily Record* added:

> The troops were first marched to the Central Station . . . and were then marched to quarters in different parts of the city,

> some of the contingents being headed by pipe bands. They were accompanied by heavy ammunition wagons, and the general appearance of the long columns of khaki-clad men, who belonged to the Seaforth Highlanders, the Gordons and other Highland regiments . . . [38]

Sunday's *Observer* continued:

> The military is now in full possession of the more important points of the city, such as City Chambers, the Post Office, the railway stations, river bridges, and electric power stations. The City Chambers is like an armed camp. The quadrangle is full of troops and equipment, including machine guns, as also are the corridors upstairs, where conferences between the Sheriff, the Lord Provost, and other authorities took place this morning. Soldiers' accoutrements fill the passages.[39]

Men with fixed bayonets were posted at the electricity stations, railway stations and bridges and tramway depots. The *Bulletin* and the *Daily Sketch* both published photographs of the soldiers.[40] These reveal the variety of uniform and headgear worn by the troops marching together – soft trench caps; Glengarry caps; Tam o' Shanter bonnets; even a slouch (bush) hat. This might be explained by the haste with which a very mixed body of men – older, younger, more or less experienced, returned from the trenches or never having left the base – were gathered. The photographs show men wearing either the kilt or battledress trousers.

Monday's *Glasgow Herald* and Edinburgh's *Evening News* claimed that cavalry had also been drafted into the city, but this is not corroborated elsewhere. Both newspapers noted the presence of machine-guns and large quantities of barbed wire.[41] Although the 1912 army booklet *Duties in Aid of the Civil Power* noted that machine-guns were not to be taken on such deployments, by 1919 Lewis guns were an integral part of an infantry battalion's equipment. The force in Glasgow was under the command of General Fanshawe, who had been the commander of the military forces defending the Firth of Forth since August 1918.[42]

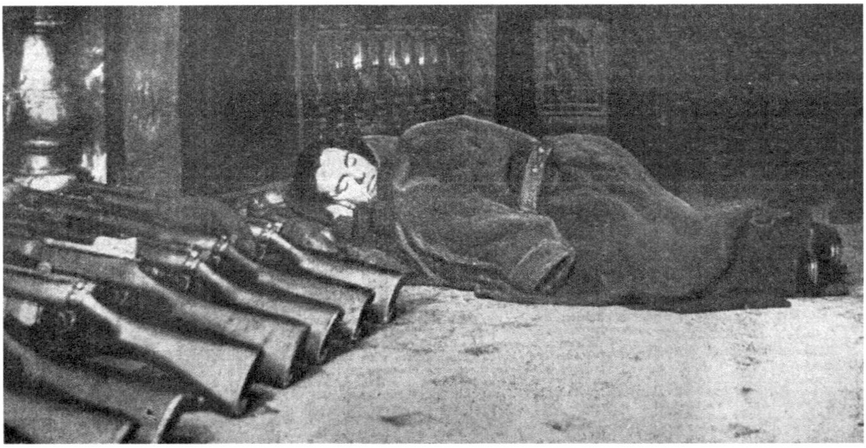

16.2. *A soldier sleeping in the City Chambers, 3 February 1919 (*Bulletin*, 4 February 1919).*

16.3. *Soldiers of the Argyll & Sutherland Highlanders guard Coplaw [Tram]Car Works (*Bulletin*, 5 February 1919).*

Some authors state that all, or the majority, of the men deployed were inexperienced or 'raw' recruits, used in preference to experienced men who might sympathise with the workers. This idea appears to have been introduced by Gallacher in his 1936 autobiography and reinforced by McShane in his 1978 memoir, in which he recalled going to Buchanan Street Station to talk to the soldiers and 'explain what the strike was for' and described 'young soldiers . . . recruits with no experience . . . very aggressive . . . [who] had no knowledge

16.4. *Mortars set up for the cameras in the quadrangle of the City Chambers, 1 or 2 February 1919 (*New York Times*, 2 March 1919).*

of the labour movement . . . those young ones would have shot us down'.[43] The idea that such men would be used in such a delicate and potentially dangerous duty, where inexperienced troops might overreact under stress, is unlikely. Whatever the number of young men deployed, it is clear that many were older, experienced men, who had served in France and were demobilising, because as the *Daily Record* stated:

> Tartans known to every Scot were here, and many of those who swung along in the noble dress of the Gael wore a [medal] ribbon on their tunic's face and showed the thread of gold [a wound stripe] on the left sleeve.[44]

The *Manchester Guardian* noted that, 'They were, many of them, soldiers just returned from France who had been hurriedly drafted here from demobilisation camps'.[45] Additionally, photographs of the soldiers show mature and middle-aged men unlikely, in 1919, to be 'raw recruits'.

In his 1955 memoir Manny Shinwell eccentrically wrote about the 'Tanks, which few civilians in Glasgow had ever seen'.[46] In reality, Glaswegians were no strangers to the presence of tanks. In January 1918's 'Tank Week', the tank 'Julian' had been paraded

16.5. *Soldiers in Scottish military headgear, some of them of mature years, resting at the City Chambers (*Bulletin*, 4 February 1919).*

16.6. *Soldiers with fixed bayonets, some wearing steel helmets, escort a supplies cart, 1 or 2 February 1919 (*Illustrated London News*, 8 February 1919).*

through the streets and had gone through its paces climbing obstacles on Glasgow Green, watched by vast crowds.[47] And in January 1919, at the request of the city authorities, a second 'Tank Week' was held, re-titled 'Victory Savings Week'. Two heavy tanks, 'Haig' and 'Beatty' and one light Whippet known as 'Julian's Baby' rolled through the streets, and on Glasgow Green the two heavy tanks once again displayed their capabilities on a specially created landscape of shell-holes and barbed wire. Finally, they were stationed outside the City Chambers in George Square, where Victory Bonds were being sold. Plausibly, some of the 'memories' of 'tanks in George Square' conflated these tank parades with the violent events in the Square barely a week later.

16.7. *Soldiers pose on one of the three Mark V* tanks stationed in the Cattle Market (*Bulletin, *3 February 1919).*

16.8. *The most frequently used image of the tanks in the Cattle Market, 3 February 1919. Three Medium C tanks are in the front rank; parts of the Mark V* tanks in the second rank can be glimpsed (*Daily Mirror, *5 February 1919).*

16.9. *Soldiers guarding a railway bridge over the Clyde, 1 or 2 February 1919 (*Illustrated London News, *8 February 1919).*

All the operational tanks in the UK in January 1919 were held at the Tank Corps depot at Bovington in Dorset, from where three Medium C tanks and three Mark V* (Mark V Star) tanks were despatched by rail on 31 January or 1 February 1919, arriving in Glasgow on Monday 3 February. The three tanks featuring in the fund-raising event in mid-January 1919 had arrived at College Goods Station, and it seems likely the six tanks despatched after the riot arrived at the same place. From there, the tanks would have proceeded by road to their temporary base at the Cattle Market. One report mentioned them travelling via the Gallowgate. By this route, they would have had to travel 1,500m, a drive of approximately fifteen minutes (Map 2, nos. 13 and 14).[48] The arrival of the vehicles was covered extensively by the press, but no photographs have emerged of their progress to the Cattle Market.

The contingent included three Medium C 'Hornet' tanks, built by William Foster & Co Ltd of Lincoln (7.87m long; 2.53m wide; 2.76m high; weight 19.8 tonnes; maximum road speed 7.9 mph). The version sent to Glasgow was armed with four Hotchkiss Mk 1 machine-guns and had a crew of four; it carried 7,200 rounds of ammunition.[49] The other three tanks were larger Mark V* tanks, visible in the background of some of the photographs taken in the Cattle Market (e.g. Fig. 16.8). Tank number 10034, visible on one image, was allocated to a 'male'-type tank (9.8m long; 4.1m wide; 2.6m high; weight 34.5 tonnes; maximum road speed 4mph). It was armed with two 6-pdr guns in the side sponsons, and 5 x 7.62mm Hotchkiss machine-guns. The 'star' variant was 1.8m longer than the normal Mark V, which aided trench crossing.[50]

In his history of the Royal Tank Regiment, Liddell-Hart included a misleading account of the use of the tanks in Glasgow: 'in January 1919 there had been a call for tanks to overawe rioters in Glasgow; six were sent and, besides their moral effect, proved useful as armoured transport for the police'.[51] No contemporary source, however, records the tanks leaving the Cattle Market throughout their sojourn in Glasgow, and at no time did circumstances in the streets after 3 February require the Glasgow Police to request the support of armoured transport. Wright alone repeats Liddell-Hart's anecdote.[52]

So, in January 1919, what was the legal and political structure that made provision for the arrival of this formidable force as 'military aid to the civil power' on the streets of Glasgow?

---

1. I. McLean, *The Legend of Red Clydeside* (John Donald, 1999), p.138.
2. B. Weinberger, *Keeping the Peace: Policing Strikes in Britain, 1906-1926* (Berg, 1991), p.157.
3. P. Wright, *Tank: The Progress of a Monstrous War Machine* (Faber, 2000), p.126-8.
4. M. Lynch, *Scotland: A New History* (Century, 1991), p.425; J. Jenkinson, *Black 1919: Riots, Racism and Resistance in Imperial Britain* (Liverpool University Press, 2009), p.42.
5. M. Fry, *Glasgow: A History of the City* (Head of Zeus, 2017), pp.321, 421.
6. C. Harvie, *No Gods and Precious Few Heroes: Twentieth-century Scotland* (Edinburgh University Press, 3rd edition, 2000), p.25.
7. J. Kerr, *Scotland and the Impact of the Great War* (Hodder Gibson, 2010), p.106.
8. J. McGonigle and C. Wood, *The Era of the Great War 1910-1928* (Hodder Gibson, 2013), p.84.
9. A-M. Kilday, *Crime in Scotland 1660-1960: The Violent North* (Routledge, 2018), p.182.

10. A. Marwick, *The Deluge: British Society and the First World War* (Macmillan, 1973), p.273.

11. JC36/31/04 [04/S], Alastair Oswald MacKenzie, Sheriff of Lanarkshire.

12. AD15/19/11 [A01], Alastair Oswald MacKenzie, Sheriff of Lanarkshire.

13. J. Maclean, *Sack Dalrymple; Sack Stevenson. Let Labour Revenge Bloody Friday* (J. Maclean, 1919), pp.1, 7; D. S. Morton, *The 40 Hours Strike: An Historic Survey of the First General Strike in Scotland* (Clydebank Branch SLP, 1919), p.9; W. Gallacher, *Revolt on the Clyde* (Lawrence and Wishart, 2017 [1936]), pp.223, 227; E. Shinwell, *I've Lived through It All* (Gollancz, 1973), p.45; T. Bell, *John Maclean: A Fighter for Freedom*, (Communist Party Scottish Committee, 1944), p.85-6; N. H. Morrison, *Official Responses to Industrial Unrest in Post-war Britain 1919-1921* (University of Swansea PhD Thesis, 1986), p.76; Weinberger, *Keeping the Peace*, pp.70-8.

14. CAB 23/9/9, War Cabinet Minutes, meeting 522, 30 January 1919, p.5.

15. [Glasgow] *Evening News*, 1 February 1919; *Aberdeen Press and Journal*, 1 February 1919; *Manchester Guardian*, 1 February 1919; *Daily News*, 1 February 1919.

16. C. Townshend, 'Military Force and Civil Authority in the United Kingdom, 1914-1921', *Journal of British Studies*, 28 (1989), p.265.

17. Townshend, 'Military Force', p.266.

18. M. Pittock, *Scottish Nationality* (Palgrave, 2001), p.103.

19. AD15/19/11 [A38], Frederick Cameron, Police Constable.

20. Wilson's possible role is discussed in the next chapter.

21. J. Foster, 'Strike Action and Working-Class Politics on Clydeside 1914–1919', *International Review of Social History*, 35 (1990), p.58.

22. W. S. Churchill (and M. Gilbert) *The World Crisis 1911-1918* (Penguin, 2007), p.760; M. Gilbert, *World in Torment 1916-1922* (Heinemann, 1975), pp.60 and 73.

23. C. E. Callwell, *Field-Marshall Sir Henry Wilson: His Life and Diaries* (Cassell, 1927), p.168.

24. J. Blake, *Civil Disorder in Britain, 1910-1939: The Roles of Civil Government and Military Authority* (DPhil, University of Sussex, 1979), p.316.

25. CAB 23/9/9, War Cabinet Minutes, meeting 522, 30 January 1919, p.3.

26. A set of the 'secret minutes' survives in Bonar Law's papers in the Parliamentary Archives. No secret minutes for 30 or 31 January are known to exist.

27. *Glasgow Herald*, 7 February 1919; AD15/19/11 Doc 02, 'At a meeting of the Town Council of the City of Glasgow held within the City

Chambers on Thursday 6th February 1919, Lord Provost J. W. Stewart presiding, the Lord Provost made a statement with regard to recent riotous proceedings in connection with the strike of Clyde Workers'; BBC London, Documentary 'Manny at 100: The Fighter', (1984).

28. *Report of the Select Committee on Employment of Military in Cases of Disturbances* (HMSO, 1908), p.11.

29. For example, see K. MacAskill, *Glasgow 1919: The Rise of Red Clydeside* (Biteback, 2019), pp.223-4. The author considers in detail the effect on HLI families in married quarters at Maryhill!

30. National Archives, Kew, WO73/109 and WO73/110; Office of the Commander in Chief and War Office: distribution of the army monthly returns, Jul-Dec 1918 and Jan-Jun 1919, respectively.

31. CAB23/9/9, War Cabinet Minutes, meeting 522, 30 January 1919.

32. WO73/110, 'General Monthly Return of the Regimental Strength of the British Army', 1919 Jan-June.

33. Blake, *Civil Disorder*, p.85.

34. Blake, *Civil Disorder*, p.85.

35. *Daily Record*, 3 February 1919, p.1; *The Observer*, 2 February 1919, p.9; *Glasgow Herald*, 3 February 1919, p.5; *Daily Mirror*, 3 February 1919, p.3.

36. Morton, *40 Hours Strike*, p.12.

37. *Evening Times,* 1 February 1919. Reference to the 5th (Reserve) Battalion of the East Surreys appears to be an error. In January 1919, they were stationed at Kingston-upon-Thames and were in the process of disbanding, being reduced to 72 men. It is possible some men of the 5th had been transferred to the 3rd and still bore the relevant insignia (WO73/110, January return).

38. *Daily Record*, 1 February 1919.

39. *The Observer*, 2 February 1919.

40. *Bulletin*, 3, 4 and 5 February; *Daily Sketch*, 3, 4 and 5 February 1919.

41. A close reading of the two papers suggests the Edinburgh *Evening News* followed the practice of generations of newspaper editors by merely lifting the copy, almost verbatim, of that morning's *Glasgow Herald.*

42. 'Lieut.-Gen. Sir E. Fanshawe [Obituary]', *The Times* (1952).

43. W. Gallacher, *Revolt on the Clyde* (Lawrence and Wishart, 2017 [1936]), pp.163-4; H. McShane and J. Smith, *Harry Mcshane: No Mean Fighter* (Pluto Press, 1978), p.107.

44. *Daily Record*, 3 February 1919.

45. *Manchester Guardian*, 3 February 1919.

46. E. Shinwell, *Conflict without Malice* (Odhams, 1955), p.64.

47. *Preston Guardian*, 26 January 1918; Glasgow raised £14.5million, more than twice that of Birmingham, the second-highest contributor to War Bonds.

48. *Evening News*, 4 February 1919.

49. K. Jeffery, 'Military Aid to the Civil Power in the United Kingdom: an Historical Perspective', in P. Rowe and C.J. Whelan (eds), *Military Intervention in Democratic Societies* (Routledge, 1985), pp.51-67, 56; C. Chant, *World Encyclopaedia of the Tank: An International History of the Armoured Fighting Machine*, 2nd edition (Sutton, 2002), pp.32-3; A. Hills, 'Medium Mark C 'Hornet': The Online Tank Museum: Tank Encyclopedia' (2017); B. T. White, *British Tanks, 1915-1945* (Ian Allan, ND).

50. D. Fletcher and H. Morshead, *Mark V Tank* (Osprey, 2011), p.36; White, *British Tanks*, p.26; Fletcher and Morshead, *Mark V Tank*, pp.16-18.

51. B. L. Hart, *The Tanks: The History of the Royal Tank Regiment and Its Predecessors - Heavy Branch Machine-Gun Corps, Tank Corps and Royal Tank Corps, 1914-1945*, (Cassell, 1959), p.205.

52. Wright, *Tank*, p.130.

Part IV
INTERLUDE

17 'A subject not unattended with obscurity': Military Aid to the Civil Power

. . . for a soldier there is no more distasteful duty than that of aiding the civil power.[1]

As Richard Haldane, Secretary of State for War, admitted, the law regarding military aid to the civil power was 'a subject not unattended with obscurity'.[2] The events in Glasgow in early 1919 fall almost midway between the beginning of the 'Great Unrest' in 1910, and the final gasp of early twentieth-century industrial action in 1926. Within a year of the Armistice in November 1918, the government had set up a framework to secure the maintenance of essential supplies and services in the face of continuing industrial stoppages. By 1920 it had 'become a permanent feature of modern British government'.[3] It is not clear how far events in Glasgow influenced the way in which this came about. In part, that opacity is due to a problematic feature of the extensive literature on the use of military aid in Britain in the twentieth century. The academic emphasis has been on the changing relationship between the Metropolitan and local police forces, and between the local magistracy and the Home Office, within the framework of the common law of England and Wales, all of which are largely irrelevant in Scotland. It is rarely acknowledged in this literature that Scotland has a separate legal system; that Scottish police did not have powers to decide whether to prosecute or not (unlike England and Wales prior to 1986); that the functions of the Home Office in Scotland had been exercised by the Scottish Office since 1885; and ultimately, that the Metropolitan Police had no role in Scottish policing.[4] Where the events in Glasgow in 1919 are included, such accounts are themselves of varying accuracy and are divorced from this legal and administrative context.

For example, John Blake undertakes an impressively detailed analysis of events in Wales in 1910 and 1911 and during the police strikes of 1918 and 1919. However, in considering events in Glasgow he relies on only one secondary source, Mowat's general history of Britain between the wars, which in turn references only Gallacher's and Kirkwood's memoirs and the *Annual Register* for 1919. Blake notes the Sheriff 'of Glasgow' read the Riot Act but does not mention his calling for the troops; he repeats Mowat's invention that the troops were 'massed on the outskirts of the city' before they marched in to 'occupy' Glasgow.[5]

Towards the end of the nineteenth century, during which there had been frequent recourse to the military to deal with unrest around industrial disputes, the idea of public order in Victorian Britain was seriously challenged by the riots in 1893 in the Yorkshire coalfields. These revealed how quickly police resources could be exhausted and the dangers posed by the police acting as mere extensions of local magnates. After the events at Featherstone in that year, when soldiers were ordered to open fire by magistrates and two miners were killed, the question arose, 'could modern governments afford to leave their national law and order and anti-strike policies in the hands of often incompetent and biased magistrates who until then had had the sole power to call for troops?'[6] The 1908 Select Committee on Employment of Military in Cases of Disturbance recorded 24 occasions on which troops had been called out in England and Wales since the later 1870s.[7] It was the over-reliance on military aid in recent decades to maintain order that led to the investigation by the Select Committee.

The Select Committee was limited to taking evidence as to 'the powers possessed by Civil Authorities in England and Ireland, the manner in which they are exercised, the constitution and regulation of the Police Forces, the functions and practices of the Home Office in relation thereto'.[8] It is not clear how Scotland was to be included, if at all, in the Select Committee's considerations. In giving evidence, the Secretary of State for War, Richard Haldane, dissented to a limited extent from the general understanding that the 'military have no discretion when they are called on' by the civil authorities – they must respond, in that he suggested that if having been called upon, an officer might find a situation where his presence was in fact unnecessary, he should have the discretion not to act.[9] This possibility was carried into the wording of the subsequent edition of the *King's Regulations*, published in 1912 and still in force in 1919. But the military *had* to respond and required no separate government permission to do so.

In the 'Great Unrest' between 1910 and 1914, in pursuit of union recognition and better working conditions, and in part inspired by syndicalist ideas, there were over 3,000 strikes.[10] Some of these included violence, rioting, and troops opening fire on civilians, and major concerns were expressed about the legal basis of the use of the military. Some of the government's actions in this period were 'widely thought to be unconstitutional or even illegal'.[11] Although there was a 'strong disinclination on the part of the Home Office and the War Office to use troops during industrial disputes until all alternative means had been exhausted', in the summer of 1911, up to 58,000 troops were deployed in 35 towns in England in a situation described by Churchill as 'without any previous experience in this country'.[12] Twenty-eight local authorities requested military aid; troops were sent without request to a further 32. Only Manchester and Blackburn objected, while some local authorities even asked for more troops; the Liverpool and Birkenhead mayors jointly telegraphed the Home Office requesting a warship and more soldiers.[13] The deployment of the military even where their presence had not been requested by the appropriate civil authorities 'meant ignoring the constitution and the law'.[14] Although generally deployed in response to industrial unrest, troops were despatched in August 1911 to protect Jews in Wales from the depredations of 'respectable miners and their wives', in the 'Tredegar Pogrom'.[15]

The deployment of troops without prior request from local authorities, contrary to the provisions in the *King's Regulations*, resulted in considerable criticism. There was a lengthy debate in the House of Commons during which the Home Secretary attracted some sharp disapproval: Churchill denied the move was in any way illegal, claiming the *King's Regulations*, which had hitherto restricted the employment of troops without local authority requisition, 'was only a regulation for the convenience of the War Office and generally of the Government'. 'The scale of the emergency . . . was the real justification of the unusual measures taken'.[16]

South Wales and Liverpool tend to dominate the history of the Great Unrest. In Scotland, Kenefick has summarised 1910 as 'a year of few strikes'; 1911, however, saw the famous Singer strike in Glasgow, strikes by textile workers in Dundee and Kirkcaldy, a major dock strike in Glasgow and even a series of strikes by schoolchildren, none of which became violent.[17] However, the Dundee carters' and dockers' strike in late 1911 involved considerable unrest and, on 19 December, during a day of particular violence, the Lord Provost (improperly, as it should have been the Sheriff) called for military aid. Three hundred men of the Black Watch entered the town that night. One hundred and ten policemen drafted in from Glasgow and Edinburgh had also arrived during the day.[18] Although the Glasgow Tram Strike in 1911 was violent, the police were sufficient to maintain order. In 1912, there were 30 separate strikes across Scotland by the end of April, in only two of which was rioting reported. In only one of these, a dock strike at Leith, was naval assistance called for, amid accusations of police provocation and brutality; six gunboats and their crews were supplied.[19]

The industrial unrest between 1914 and 1918 never reached the levels of dislocation or violence experienced before the war. Of the wave of disputes which beset Britain in the summer of 1918, the most alarming was the London police strike in August, when 10,000 of the 19,000 Metropolitan Police struck. Lloyd George remarked afterwards that the country 'was nearer to Bolshevism that day than at any time since'.[20] By 1919, however, the world had changed irrevocably. The Russian Revolution had struck terror into established monarchies, and the official reaction to strikes, both during and after the war, reflected the fear that such unrest was the precursor to political revolution.[21] This fear was fanned by influential government advisers of very reactionary inclination, notably Basil Thomson,*

* (Sir) Basil Thomson was Assistant Commissioner (Crime) of the Metropolitan Police from June 1913 and head of Special Branch. During the war he had been responsible for the surveillance of labour organisations for the Ministry of Munitions. In 1919 he was appointed Director of Intelligence at the Home Office, but an official report in 1921 accused his oganisation of producing misleading reports as well as duplicating the

head of Special Branch, and Sir Henry Wilson,* Chief of the Imperial General Staff. Such men believed labour militancy might be the harbinger of revolution, and wanted appropriate preparations to be made.[22]

General militancy in early 1919 did not encourage reliance on the military in the face of revolution, as their loyalty and reliability were questioned.[23] Already, on 6 January 1919, 3,000 soldiers had taken over Horse Guards Parade in London and had to be disarmed by a Guards regiment; there were further demonstrations in Whitehall the following day.[24] From late January 1919, commanding officers were routinely circularised to determine the mood of their men and which units could be relied upon. In Edinburgh, a deputation of 100 men of the Highland Light Infantry, Glasgow's 'local' regiment, complained to General Rome, Demobilisation Officer at Scottish Command, that they had not been demobilised.[25]

As a result of what was seen by troops and their families as a slow and unfair process of demobilisation, parts of the armed forces simmered on the brink of mutiny.[26] Demobilisation and the prosecution of the war in Russia absorbed most of Churchill's attention in the week of 27 January: the details of his fairer demobilisation scheme were discussed at the War Cabinet on Tuesday 28 January and published in the press on 30 January.[27]

Developments within a year of the deployment to Glasgow may explain what happened there. Known as 'the worst political general', an inveterate intriguer, deeply conservative and an active Irish Unionist, Sir Henry Wilson was one of an influential group of reactionary senior officers who were particularly fearful of revolution. They actively promoted the view that the army was the bulwark against the imminent threat of revolution and sought to influence their colleagues and their political masters. Despite supporting the army officers in the

work of other agencies. He was asked to resign.

* Sir Henry Wilson (1864–1922). Born Co Antrim, son of a Protestant Ulster landowner. Career regular soldier. He became youngest staff officer in the Army. Director of Military Operations 1910-14. Regarded as a rabid Ulster Unionist. Chief of the Imperial General Staff January 1918. Although very able and articulate, considered too mercurial and too obsessed with Irish affairs to inspire wholehearted trust among all his military and political colleagues.

'Curragh Incident', who made it clear they would refuse to lead their men to implement the Home Rule Bill in Ulster, Wilson had nevertheless risen to be professional head of the British Army, Chief of the Imperial General Staff.[28] The relationship between Wilson and Lloyd George deteriorated, in particular over government policy in Ireland. The Prime Minister indeed declared he could 'never get a sane discussion' with him.[29]

Wilson wished to establish a comprehensive network of military bases in which a force under a single commander would be responsible for military aid to the civil power. The responsibility for such troops had long lain with the Adjutant General, but Wilson wanted it to be transferred to the Military Operations Directorate, where he could exercise greater control. By November 1919, Wilson declared it was 'essential that a senior officer and staff should be earmarked to take over executive command of all troops in Great Britain in the event of a serious internal upheaval'. His preferred candidate was Major-General Romer, who had been 'extensively occupied in duties connected with industrial unrest'.[30] It was Romer who reported to the War Cabinet on 31 January that orders had been issued to General Officer Commanding Scotland 'with regard to the movement of troops' to Glasgow.[31] He had also been present at the War Cabinet meeting the day before.

The views of senior army officers who did not share Wilson's perspective were represented by General Macdonogh,* the Adjutant General. One of the main objections to Wilson's plans was that soldiers scattered around Britain ready to be deployed to deal with unrest were not doing their main job – training.[32] Wilson and Macdonogh were opposites. The former a dyed-in-the-wool Ulster Protestant, the latter a Catholic. The former siding with the potentially mutinous officers at the Curragh Incident; the latter willing to use the army to enforce Home Rule on Ulster.[33]

* Sir George Mark Watson Macdonogh (1865-1942) was a career regular soldier 'of considerable intellectual ability and with a penetrating analytical mind'. Director of Military Intelligence 1916 to January 1918. Adjutant-General 1918 (lieutenant-general). A Roman Catholic, which excited the prejudice of Field Marshall Haig and Sir Henry Wilson. Retired 1925, then had a distinguished career in business and public life, notably as commissioner for the Imperial War Graves Commission.

Wilson's views dominated in the early months of 1919 and in September 1919. Churchill retrospectively wrote that he had been directed by the War Cabinet early in 1919 'to prepare a complete scheme and organisation of Military Forces throughout the UK to act in aid of the Civil Power in the event of a national strike of a revolutionary character'. Morgan appears to suggest the order to Churchill to redistribute troops around the country was issued at the War Cabinet meeting of 30 January 1919, which scrutiny of the War Cabinet documents has failed to evidence, and it is not possible to determine how accurately Churchill described his remit.[34] This scheme, Churchill wrote, had 'involved the distribution of mobile troops throughout the country in a manner which renders them readily available, but which, of course, results in an expense far greater than would attend their normal peace distribution'. As a consequence of the planned reductions to army numbers, Churchill believed it 'will scarcely be possible and it will certainly not be worthwhile [sic] to maintain this exceptional distribution'.[35]

However, the redistribution of troops did take place. The War Office records for April 1919 of the locations of Reserve Battalions of the infantry regiments reveals many were moved to new stations in March. For example, the 10th (Reserve) Battalion of the Liverpool Regiment moved to Pembroke docks. The Royal Scots Fusiliers at Maryhill, Glasgow, were replaced by the Royal Scots, which was an Edinburgh regiment. Troops were concentrated near dockyards, like Chatham and Rosyth, and near industrial cities. As part of the scheme, by 18 March 1919 tanks had been moved to various points round Britain, with sections at Edinburgh, Liverpool, Cannock Chase and Catterick, and two others in reserve at Wool, one of which was earmarked for use in South Wales.[36]

Sir George Macdonogh began his fightback in October 1919:

> I am of opinion that we ought not to keep up large forces in the U.K. for the purpose of dealing with civil disturbance . . . If in any district the civil forces should prove insufficient, such troops as are available should reinforce them, but it will be a bad day for the Empire if the Government of this country has to look to the bayonets of its troops for its support.[37]

In conjunction with Churchill's assertion that the scheme was not worth continuing with, Macdonogh's minute had an immediate effect; within ten days, the Army Council had agreed to the return of all troops in Great Britain to their peacetime stations.[38] Wilson, however, continued to promote his alarmist views, warning Macdonogh:

> I hope with you that no such awful thing as a Revolution is going to take place in this country but in view of all we have been through in the last 5 years and of all that we know is going on all over our Empire and all over the world it would indeed be madness not to have the nucleus of an organisation capable of instant expansion and possessed of sufficient knowledge and authority to prepare plans.[39]

The only written regulations governing military aid which existed in 1919 were those in the *King's Regulations and Orders for the Army*, revised and published in 1912 in light of the findings of the 1908 Select Committee. The Committee determined 'the King's regulations must harmonise with the common law, they cannot in any way override it or conflict with it'.[40] This is important because it confirms that any troops despatched as 'military aid to the civil power' were bound by civil, not military, law. None of the amendments issued between 1912 and 1919 affected the relevant paragraphs:

> Duties in Aid of the Civil Power
>
> 955. When troops are called out in aid of the civil power at home, the general or other officer to whom application is made for assistance will immediately report the fact by telegraph to the War Office and to the G.O.C.-in-C. The commander of the party will report daily in writing to the War Office as well as to the O.C. [Officer Commanding] the station from which he has been detached, the progress of the service on which he is employed.
>
> 956. Except in cases of great and sudden emergency (as explained in para. 974), an officer will not order out nor take out troops for the purpose of aiding in the suppression of riot,

the maintenance of the public peace, or the execution of the law, or of assisting the civil power in case of an expected riot, without the requisition in writing, or by telegram of the civil authority.

The civil authority by whom the requisition should be made is –

[Text omitted for brevity – a list of persons having authority in the Metropolitan Police Area; English counties; English cities and boroughs]

In Scotland, the sheriff having jurisdiction in the place where the services of the troops are required.

[Omitted – a list of persons having the authority in Ireland]

In cases when a disturbance of the peace takes place in or near a station where troops are quartered, the military authority will, subject to paying due attention to the general obligations imposed by the common law, as explained in the Manual of Military Law, Chapter VIII, Appendix I, exercise his discretion as to the necessity of complying with the requisition of the civil authorities.[41]

When troops are from a distance the military authority will make all arrangements for the despatch of the troops, but will not send them until he has received authority from the War Office. On arrival at the place to which the troops were requisitioned, the O.C. the troops will, subject to the obligations of the common law as above stated, exercise his discretion as to the necessity for intervention by the troops. When troops are despatched, the civil officer who requisitioned them will be informed of their numbers, and of the time at which they may be expected to reach their destination.

The responsibility for deciding as to the strength and composition of the force detailed rests with the military authorities. If the civil officer mentions them, it will only be as a guide to aid in estimating the force required.[42]

The Scottish Secretary circulated the Sheriffs on 13 October 1909, setting out the procedures for calling for military aid in Scotland:

> When the occasion for such aid appears likely to arise, a telegram should be sent to the General Officer Commanding in Chief [of] the Scottish Command enquiring who is the officer to whom the application for aid should be sent, and the telegram should be repeated to the Secretary, War Office, London.
>
> When the GOC-in-C has designated the officer, the requisition should be sent to him direct, and he should be informed as far as possible of the general situation and the force of police available, as well as of the nature and number of those from whom trouble is apprehended.[43]

Thus, the Sheriff of Lanarkshire followed the correct procedure by writing to the local Army District commander, but it is unclear whether the Sheriff repeated that telegram to the War Office.

Troops despatched as an oppressive tool of the government, rather than as military aid called by the civil power, forms only one element of the mythology that grew up round the Battle, in the first instance to lay the foundations of the defence at the trial in April, and in the century since.

---

1. E. Ironside, *Archangel 1918-1919* (Constable, 1953), p.188.
2. Select Committee on Employment of Military in Cases of Disturbances, *Report of the Select Committee on Employment of Military in Cases of Disturbances* (HMSO, 1908), p.11.
3. K. Jeffery and P. Hennessy, *States of Emergency: British Governments and Strikebreaking since 1919* (Routledge and Kegan Paul, 1983), p.1.
4. For example, B. Weinberger, *Keeping the Peace: Policing Strikes in Britain, 1906-1926* (Berg, 1991). See S. Peak, *Troops in Strikes: Military Intervention in Industrial Disputes* (Cobden Trust, 1984); R. Vogler, *Reading the Riot Act: The Magistracy, the Police and the Army in Civil Disorder* (Open University Press, 1991).
5. J. Blake, *Civil Disorder in Britain, 1910-1939: The Roles of Civil Government and Military Authority* (DPhil, University of Sussex, 1979), chapters 3 and 4 *passim*; C. L. Mowat, *Britain between the Wars 1918-1940*

(Cambridge University Press, 1987), p.24; *The Annual Register: A Review of Public Events at Home and Abroad for the Year 1919* (Rivingtons, 1920), p.9.

6. C. Townshend, 'Military Force and Civil Authority in the United Kingdom, 1914-1921', *Journal of British Studies,* 28 (1989), p.264.
7. Select Committee, *Employment of Military*, p.v.
8. Select Committee, *Employment of Military*, p.vii. Given the *King's Regulations for the Army* in which the rules for calling out the military make also no specific mention of Wales, we have presumed the Select Committee and *Regulations* both meant to include 'Wales' as at that time legally and administratively part of England.
9. Select Committee, *Employment of Military*, p.12. Until 1920 the legal basis for providing military aid to the civil power lay in Crown Prerogative and the common law (of England and Wales) and was codified solely in the *King's Regulations*, which were published by the Army and had no separate statutory basis.
10. Y. Beliard, 'Introduction: Revisiting the Great Labour Unrest, 1911-1914', *Labour History Review,* 79(1) (2014), pp.1-2.
11. Peak, *Troops in Strikes*, p.26; Vogler, *Riot Act*, p.89. Weinberger, *Keeping the Peace*, p.37. Blake, *Civil Disorder*, pp.91-93.
12. *Hansard* 22 August 1911, col 2286, quoted in Peak, *Troops in Strikes*, p.30.
13. Weinberger, *Keeping the Peace*, p.93.
14. Peak, *Troops in Strikes*, p.30.
15. S. Webb, *1919: Britain's Year of Revolution* (Pen and Sword, 2016), p.35.
16. Weinberger, *Keeping the Peace*, p.95.
17. W. Kenefick, *Red Scotland! The Rise and Fall of the Radical Left, c. 1872 to 1932* (Edinburgh University Press, 2007), p.4.
18. [Dundee] *Courier,* 20 December 1911. [Dundee] *Evening Telegraph and Post,* 19 December 1911. The War Office in London had complained to the Scottish Office that the request for aid had come direct to them, not to Scottish Command, as was current practice. Apparently in 1909, the procedures for calling for military aid had been sent by the Scottish Office only to Sheriffs, not to the Lords Provost; WO32/8466 'Aid to Civil Power: Procedure to be followed when Troops are required to aid civil power', *Report of Select Committee,* 1908.
19. Kenefick, *Red Scotland*, p.10.
20. Weinberger, *Keeping the Peace*, p.5.
21. Jeffery and Hennessy, *States of Emergency*, p.5.

22. K. Jeffery, 'The British Army and Internal Security 1919-1939', *The Historical Journal,* 24 (1981), p.377. N. Rutherford, 'Thomson, Sir Basil Home', *Oxford Dictionary of National Biography*. Spartacus Educational https://spartacus-educational.com/SSthomson.htm.

23. Blake, *Civil Disorder*, p.152.

24. Jeffery and Hennessy, *States of Emergency*, pp.6 and 9.

25. *Belfast Newsletter*, 9 January 1919.

26. Webb, *1919*, Ch.3 *passim.*

27. CAB 23/9/8, War Cabinet Minutes, meeting 521, 28 January 1919, 3pm. M. S. Gilbert, *Winston S. Churchill: World in Torment, 1916-1922* (Heinemann, 1975), pp.181-96; *Scotsman*, 30 January 1919.

28. Townshend, 'Military Force', p.269.

29. K. Jeffery, *Field Marshal Sir Henry Wilson: A Political Soldier* (Oxford University Press, 2006), *passim* (pp.241, 242, 279-80, ebook location 4895).

30. Jeffery and Hennessy, *States of Emergency*, p.26.

31. CAB23/9/10, War Cabinet Minutes, meeting 523, 31 January 1919.

32. WO32/5611, 'Redistribution of forces to peace stations affecting aid to civil power and quartering of troops; suggestions for effecting economies'.

33. J. F. W. Beckett, 'Macdonogh, Sir George Mark Watson', *Oxford Dictionary of National Biography* (2020).

34. Morgan, *Conflict and Order*, p.26.

35. W. S. Churchill, *Churchill Documents: Disruption and Chaos, July 1919-March 1921* (Hillsdale College Press, 2008), pp.881-2.

36. WO32/18920, 'Use of Military Personnel in Aid of Civil Powers in Event of Civil Disturbances and Strikes: Great Britain, 1919'; WO73/110, 'General Monthly Return of the Regimental Strength of the British Army', 1919 Jan-Jun; Return for April 1919. It is possible the tanks in Edinburgh by March were those that had been deployed to Glasgow in February.

37. Jeffery, 'Internal Security', p.380, FN.12.

38. WO32/5611, 'Employment of Military Forces: Organisation: Redistribution of Forces to Peace Stations Affecting Aid to Civil Power and Quartering of Troops; Suggestions for Effecting Economies', 1919; Jeffery, 'Internal Security', p.381.

39. WO32/4812, 'Employment of Military Forces: Aid to Civil Power: Civil Disturbances Requiring Military Intervention; Responsibility for Operations', 1919-1920.

40. Select Committee, *Employment of Military*, *passim.* Army, Great Britain, *The King's Regulations and Orders for the Army* (Army, 1912);

WO32/8466, 'Aid to Civil Power: Procedure to Be Followed When Troops Are Required to Aid Civil Power. Report of Select Committee, 1908', 1908-1912.

41. The final sentence seems to reflect Haldane's evidence to the 1908 Select Committee.

42. The text of the 1914 edition is available at: https://hdl.handle.net/2027/hvd.32044048604474. Paragraph 974 gives authority to act without the civil power's request only to an officer on the ground in case of 'immediate and pressing danger – when violent crimes are being or are likely to be committed – which, in the opinion of the officer, demand his immediate interference.'

43. WO32/8466, 'Aid to Civil Power: Procedure to Be Followed When Troops Are Required to Aid Civil Power. Report of Select Committee, 1908', 1908-1912.

18 Aspects of the Mythology

. . . a good tale always overtakes the history it purports to tell.[1]

The Battle of George Square is arguably the most mythologised event in twentieth-century Scottish history. The main elements of the myths now appearing in a range of media and which form the basic catechism of the Battle are listed below. These myths are widely accepted 'facts' that at worst run directly contrary to contemporary evidence, or for which there is no contemporary evidence, or the invention of which can be documented. It is widely claimed that:

- the riot was deliberately provoked;
- the baton charge was unprovoked and against a peaceful crowd;
- the police were 'routed' and forced from George Square;
- the army was on the move before the riot began;
- the government/Churchill/'the English' sent the army;
- the army was sent to crush the strike;
- a revolution or 'Bolshevist rising' was under way or possible;
- the troops were raw recruits and all or mostly English;
- there were tanks in George Square during and/or after the riot;
- the crowd in George Square was 90,000 or even 100,000 strong;
- Martial Law was declared;
- the deployment was illegal;
- Scottish troops were locked in their barracks in case they joined the strikers;
- there were one or more howitzers in the Square;

- machine-gun nests were set up in George Square or on the surrounding rooftops;
- there were orders to shoot to kill and the army injured or killed people.

None of these claims is true. None is supported by contemporary evidence. Most are directly contradicted by that evidence.

Elements of this largely mythologised narrative have been used in a range of media: academic textbooks and journal articles; general histories of Scotland; popular histories of Glasgow or Red Clydeside; school textbooks; political pamphlets; magazines and newspapers; and TV documentaries. Into the twenty-first century, online outlets – educational resources, blogs and social media – have dominated the dissemination of the myths.[2]

In Chapter 12 it was noted how, in the immediate aftermath of the riot, the *Strike Bulletin* promoted a number of mutually contradictory explanations for the outbreak of violence. In the weeks between the riot and the trial two pamphlets were published which seem intended to consolidate the exculpatory accounts in the *Strike Bulletin* and the wider socialist press: describing a pre-planned attack on a peaceful crowd. Taken together, these accounts laid the foundations for the mythology, as summarised above, which was then consolidated and expanded in the writings of the strike leaders and by later writers who have followed their line.

One of the two pamphlets was written by D. S. Morton, one of the secretaries of the strike committee. He failed to mention any disruption of the tram service in the south-east corner, claiming instead a very different origin for the violence:

> The Police allowed two motors to run into the crowd, and as a result two men were injured. The strikers appealed to the police to turn all vehicular traffic by another street, quite a reasonable request when one considers the density of the mass. The answer of the police was a baton charge.[3]

In contrast with the defence line at the trial, which tried to dissociate the strikers from the violence that occurred shortly afterwards in North Frederick Street, Morton explained the bottle-throwing as self-defence by the strikers:

> The strikers having nothing but their bare fists to defend themselves with were forced to bear the brutal attack. At this juncture a lorry loaded with bottles passing down a side street was immediately commandeered by the strikers, who used them against the police in self-defence.[4]

John Maclean, although absent on a lecturing tour in England on 31 January, also wrote about events in the Square, before the trial.[5] His text veers between the tram strike in 1911 and events in 1919 and is full of accusations of conspiracy. He claimed the Lord Provost 'told the strikers' deputation to return on the Friday', which he did not, and that the Lord Provost had been 'under instructions from Bonar Law' which he was not. Maclean's invention provided 'the required provocation' for the trams being deliberately driven into the crowd.[6] Maclean blamed not only James Dalrymple, the tramways' manager, but also the tram workers, whose failure to respond to the strike call and whose 'treachery' had 'embittered the strikers'. Consequently, he claimed, it had been 'planned that cars should run through George Square on Bloody Friday'.[7]

In Shinwell's authorised biography, written long after January 1919, Slowe adheres to a 'conspiracy lite' version of events, presumably following his subject's line: the police 'knew when to act' and had a 'sign for the police to move', and the trouble was caused when a 'tram provocatively advanced on the south-east corner'. The tram driver, he claimed, 'jumped out and disappeared – no one ever found out who he [sic] was'.[8] Is Slowe suggesting a *provocateur*? Both these statements are, however, untrue: the tram was driven by a woman who gave evidence at the trial and who managed to drive her tram out of the Square.

Shinwell himself described the events in four 'entertaining but unreliable' memoirs written over 30 years. Reading them in sequence, it is clear how he developed his narrative and where he introduced elements of what would become the catechism of the modern mythology. Shinwell stuck to the 'deliberate plan' story but introduced greater and greater confusion, eventually describing the trouble with the trams *after* the bottle-throwing in North Frederick Street and moving the first meeting with the Lord Provost from Wednesday to Friday 31 January.[9]

Popular accounts relying on unreliable sources have both incorporated these sources' errors and have added mere inventions, such as a Tiananmen Square-like scene in which Manny Shinwell 'had faced down a hostile army tank in George Square'.[10] Shinwell had been in police custody for three days by the time the tanks arrived on 3 February. Another author claims the 'mainly English' troops 'were posted on rooftops in an attempt to identify the ringleaders'; in reality the mainly Scots force arrived at least ten hours too late on a dark January night to see anything of the kind.[11]

Harry McShane, later a well-known communist figure in Glasgow, was involved with the strike leadership as a young man and described events in his memoir published 60 years later.[12] He claimed the strike committee had 'warned the magistrates that the trams must be off the road while the 40-hour strike was on' and that it was the continued running of the trams through the Square 'that started the riot':

> One of the strikers pulled a rope down and cut it, and a soldier on leave struck him. The fight broke out just as the tram was turning from George Square down South Frederick Street by the post office, and the riot started. The police charged but the crowd stood.[13]

The actions of this or other soldiers as the genesis of the riot has been adopted uncritically by MacAskill, who describes a tramcar arriving with a striker and soldier already on board, who were fighting when the tram was halted, which somehow caused the riot.[14] None of this is substantiated by precognitions, trial testimony or any contemporary eyewitness. The crowd standing firm against the police is, incidentally, yet another myth, as will become clear.

Great reliance is also placed on first-hand narratives, although most were recorded decades after the events and, in important instances, are directly contradicted by contemporary eyewitness accounts.[15] One generation has passed on to another accounts which have become unassailable because of their source. For example, that there were 'English troops' and tanks in the Square on Friday 31 January or waiting just outside the Square during the riot. Oral history indeed records 'not just what people did, but what they wanted to do, what they believed they were doing, and what they thought they did'.[16] Chapter 3 explored why this material should be discounted. On social media, the events of George Square and its aftermath are now most often referenced to make a political point: anti-capitalist, anti-British, or anti-English. Increasingly, as symbol of one or more of these, Churchill is held personally responsible in his 'culture wars' persona as all-purpose bogeyman.[17]

The extent to which the mythology has poisoned the wells of history is illustrated most clearly in the Scottish education system. A school history textbook in use in Scotland between 2013 and 2018 and approved by the Scottish Qualifications Authority presented a largely mythologised version of events:

> In response, the government rushed 12,000 English troops to Glasgow in case a revolution broke out. Scottish troops were locked in their barracks at Maryhill in case they supported the strikers. There were tanks in George Square and machine gun posts in buildings around the area. Newspapers reported that 90,000 people attended this demonstration . . .[18]

The Scottish Government's lead education body, Education Scotland, contributed its own 'alternative facts' in its teaching aid *The Road to the Scottish Parliament*, which has subsequently been removed from the agency's website. The section on the Battle read:

> In an event unique in British history, Winston Churchill dispatched English troops and tanks against a large demonstration in George Square on 31st January 1919. The event became known as The Battle of George Square. Scottish troops already present in Glasgow were locked in Maryhill Barracks for fear that they might join the demonstrators and precipitate a major revolution. Thousands of English troops remained in Scotland for many months.

Nothing in these two extracts is true. The Maryhill myth is lifted straight from Gallacher; the force was mainly Scots; there were no tanks in George Square nor machine-gun posts in buildings around the Square, and all military left within three weeks; the crowd was between 20,000 and 25,000 strong at most; 90,000 people could not physically fit in the Square. There was no 'revolution' and Churchill was not to blame.

Responding to enquiries how they could have published such obviously fake history, Education Scotland not only claimed their account was 'on the whole factually correct' but invented ten further wholly imaginary armoured vehicles being sent to the city, in addition to the six tanks.[19] An online search shows individual schools prepared study and revision aids following the line established in the textbooks and the Education Scotland learning resource. Beyond that, it is difficult to know to what extent this mythologised version of history was actually taught in Scottish schools or formed the basis for examination questions. Both these texts became a *cause célèbre* in 2020 when prominent historians accused the Scottish Government of distributing 'arrant propaganda', 'dangerous nonsense' and a 'perversion of history . . . frightening as it was blatantly political and clearly designed to support the cause of Scottish independence'.[20] The mythology and especially the 'English invasion' have become part of a number of invented pieces of 'history' centred round Scotland's military, now regularly repeated as examples of grievances about what 'the English have done to us'.[21]

Frequently cited as 'evidence' in exchanges on social media, the key drivers of the mythology are modern newspaper or other journalistic accounts. For example, the *Sunday Post* in its 'Scotland's Iconic Moments' section repeated a number of myths, including the '10,000 English troops', Winston Churchill sending in the army and 'No Scottish soldiers were deployed, as the government feared some might go over to the workers' side'.[22] A particularly inaccurate article in the *Observer* is frequently referenced as proof of the traditional narrative's truthfulness, and is even referenced in Open University learning materials.[23]

Photographs and the powerful ability of the human mind to counterfactually imagine, can amplify false memories. Studies have revealed that real, doctored and embellished photographs can facilitate the creation of false memories.[24] And if a viewer is told authoritatively what an image shows, they will rarely look for themselves. Frequently, images have been used to add impact to claims about the events of George Square. However, many are sourced from different years and places, and are used either deliberately or inadvertently to misrepresent the events.

The most frequently appearing image in books, newspapers, television documentaries and on social media, is a tank surrounded by a crowd. (Fig. 18.1) This is the tank 'Julian' in a fundraising parade on 17 January 1918, which has long been used both in good faith and with intent to deceive as an image of tanks approaching George Square on 31 January 1919; the accompanying caption claims the same. However, a moment's careful examination shows this is a parade through an enthusiastic crowd. Much of the mischief was caused by the mislabelling of the image as 'January 1919' in the *Herald* photo library until 2018.[25] On 29 January 2018, the *Herald* revealed its mistake and also scotched the 'English soldiers' myth.[26]

Television documentaries covering the Battle have further complicated the 'alternative facts' issue. The BBC's 'Making of Modern Britain' and the accompanying book have played a significant role in popularising the mythology, in particular the notion 'there were tanks in George Square', for which no mention has been discovered before 1990.[27] At least twelve documentaries covering Scottish or British history or accounts of Red Clydeside between 1965 and 2017 have included the events in George Square. Around 1980, documentary producers began using archive film of events in other places and other times to 'evoke' events in Glasgow in 1919. One 1980 documentary took a still image from a newsreel of a tank parked in a street in Liverpool in August 1919, and used it in a context that strongly suggested it showed Glasgow eight months earlier (Fig.18.2).[28] This misrepresentation has been repeated in at least three subsequent programmes. Arguably, this misuse of the Liverpool tank footage may be the source for there being 'tanks on the streets' in Glasgow. One academic writer, while noting, 'there are many myths about the Red Clyde', insists 'the troops and tanks were for real; these incidents were filmed and the footage still exists': there is no such archive film.[29] On social media, someone convinced that tanks had been seen in George

18.1. *Tank 'Julian' parading along Trongate on 18 January 1918, during the 'Tank Week' War Bond sales drive. This image has frequently been misrepresented as a tank in Glasgow after the Battle of George Square a year later (*Bulletin, *18 January 1918).*

Square on 31 January 1919 stated 'I have seen archive film quite a few times. Tanks can be clearly seen as can troops. These films come from the BBC so should be easy enough to find'.[30] They are, but the footage is not of soldiers and tanks in Glasgow; it is of Liverpool and proves nothing of the sort. In reality, the Glasgow tanks were driven the short distance from College Goods Station to the Cattle Market where they remained unused.

A clip of a crowd roiling around a trapped horse-drawn waggon during the 1911 Dundee carters' strike was also used in the same documentary and has since appeared several times to accompany a voice-over about Glasgow in 1919. Further, a clip of a boisterous crowd round a tram in Queen Street, Cardiff in 1926 is also used to 'illustrate' events in Glasgow seven years earlier.[31] The most recent example of this sort of misuse of images and film footage is the 'Age of Tanks' documentary, in which misleading archive material is used to illustrate events in Glasgow accompanied by an ominous narration of 'revolution' and tanks as tools of oppression 'paraded through the streets'.[32] It claims the citizens of Glasgow were the first

18.2. *A still from Pathé film of tanks in Liverpool in August 1919.*

civilian population to be faced with tanks, a dubious honour which actually belongs to Liverpool in August 1919. The image of 'Julian's Baby' on its fundraising tour of Glasgow in mid-January 1919 (Fig. 3.1) is edited together with the Liverpool tank footage and film from another anonymous fundraising parade, which is reinforced by the sequence's voice-over to 'recreate' Glasgow on 31 January 1919.

A few films make small, uncontentious allusions to Glasgow in 1919, but the key TV documentaries contributing to the mythology are:

1965 *What about the workers?: A History of the British Trade Union Movement since 1880*, Mithras Films

Wide-ranging documentary on the progress of workers' rights. It does not misuse film clips but is probably the source reel for other less exacting producers. e.g. footage of tanks in Liverpool.[33]

1980 *The Revolutionaries: John Maclean*, BBC

Includes original filmed interviews. First documentary in which still images are presented to suggest Glasgow in 1919.

Shinwell claims 'there was no question of a riot'; eyewitness Willie Maley described Gallacher's assault on the Chief Constable, 'a real blow' and his subsequent beating by the police; McShane repeats his story of a 'humorous' incident of two policemen being stripped. A 1962 interview with Willie Gallacher is included, repeating the Maryhill Barracks part of the mythology. Includes film of 1911 Dundee Carters' Strike and General Strike in Cardiff in 1926.

1984 *Manny at 100: the Fighter*, BBC

Re-uses eyewitness material from 'The Revolutionaries'. Film of 1911 Dundee Carters' Strike and Cardiff in 1926 is used to represent Glasgow.

1997 *Stirring Times: John Maclean*, BBC Scotland

Claims riot caused by police batoning the rioters because of fears of Bolshevism. Government sent the tanks. Film from other places used to represent Glasgow, including Liverpool tank film and 1926 Cardiff tram.

2004 *Power to the People.*

Ominous music and a serious tone of voice set a scene over images which are in fact rioting in other places and times. Presents English troops mythology; suggests army was already on the move before the riot, includes misleading film of 1911 Dundee Carters' Strike and Cardiff and other scenes from the General Strike of 1926. Images from riot in Downing Street in 1920.[34]

2009 *Andrew Marr's The Making of Modern Britain*, BBC

A largely mythologised account; still image of the fundraising 'Julian' 1918 tank is used as 1919; myth about the force comprising only 'English troops' restated.

2014 *'From Scotland with Love'*, Glasgow Commonwealth Games Cultural Festival.

Claims to be made using only 'Scottish film archive' but includes footage of the tanks in Liverpool in August 1919 in its section on Red Clydeside.

2016 *Scotland: The Promised Land*, BBC Scotland, episode 1
Claimed red flag flown on Friday 31st; 1919 image of tank 'Julian's Baby' included with voiceover talking of 'tanks sent onto the streets to maintain order'.

The common feature of all these documentaries is that the role of the Sheriff in calling for military aid is omitted; 'the government sent the army' is the preferred explanation. Shinwell's, Gallacher's and McShane's memoirs, and indeed interviews, are used uncritically and unchallenged to frame the narrative. Only 'The Revolutionaries' includes a wider range of witnesses.

Only one contemporary film was shot of the events in George Square, a 'Gaumont Graphic Newsreel'.[35] It lasts 34 seconds and is filmed from a single raised position on the north side of the tram lines on the north side of the Square, just to the west of the opening of North Frederick Street. It seems that trams may occasionally have cut off the view and the camera was stopped. The first three seconds show a moderately dense crowd milling about in front of the City Chambers. The film then jumps: a tram partially occupies the right-hand frame; a very loose crowd is moving, some running vigorously, some walking quickly, north, towards the camera, towards North Frederick Street and to the right, between the tram and camera. At around 11 seconds, a lone policeman runs in the opposite direction, into the crowd running past him, striking out with a baton to left and right, the crowd parting to run past him. At 15 seconds the film jumps again. A different tram is leaving the frame and five mounted police are stationary, still in front of the Chambers' decorative lamp standards. The crowd is moving towards the camera, pursued by a handful of foot police. One or two women are visible in the crowd. A loose body of police runs westwards into the Square between the mounted men and the tram. A tram encroaches from the west and at 18 seconds the film jumps again. For two seconds a very loose crowd walks towards the camera and waves. A horsedrawn lorry stands in the foreground. From 20 seconds, a denser crowd mills around. Some walk north, waving. There is a lone sailor waving his cap to the camera. A man carries a large French horn or tuba. Up to a dozen policemen stand on the pavement north of the entrance of the Chambers. The film ends.

The Battle has appeared in fiction and has inspired (rotten) poetry, folksongs and illustrations, for example, of tanks chasing strikers. And most of all it has inspired invention and myth-making on an industrial scale.

Why have the myths become so firmly rooted? They were first accepted in working class circles because they were created by those considered more estimable and believable than any 'establishment' figure – the 'dominant narrators' discussed in Chapter 3. Further, there was no competing version in circulation after the trial in 1919. Also, those myths centring on 'deliberate attacks' begun by 'some signal given to the police' or by 'the deliberate driving of trams through the crowd', tended to reinforce the perceptions of those who saw and continue to see a 'hidden hand' in affairs, particularly in relation to the treatment of the workers. In more recent times the myths have provided support or validation for a range of beliefs, from the oppression of the workers to, more recently, the oppression of the Scots by the English. People tend not to question narratives coinciding with their beliefs. Finally, academic history, popular history, journalism and education have signally failed to provide an adequate evidence-based challenge.

Thus far, the mechanisms that have contributed to the remembering of the events and the creation, deliberate or unintentional, of the mythology have been considered. However, the historiography of the Battle, in particular the way in which historical writing has, at best, failed to challenge the mythology and at worst, contributed to its creation, must now be considered.

---

1. A. H. Radjy, review of 'A turbulent tale of ninth-century Cairo', *Times Literary Supplement*, 6250 (January, 2023), p.18.
2. For example, I. McLean, *The Legend of Red Clydeside* (John Donald, 1999); J. Foster, 'Mobilising Working Class Action on Clydeside, 1919 and 1971: How the Arguments Were Won', *Colloque Internationale Discours et Dispositivs Anti-syndicaux* (Lyon, 2010); T. Devine, *The Scottish Nation: A Modern History* (Penguin, 2012); M. Craig, *When the Clyde Ran Red: A Social History of Red Clydeside* (Mainstream, 2011); J. Kerr,

Scotland and the Impact of the Great War (Hodder Gibson, 2010); J. Cameron, *Red Flag over the Clyde: The Story of John Maclean and Red Clydeside* (Scottish Militant Labour, 1993). A preliminary consideration of the mythology of the Battle was published in 2019 and of the historiography in 2021; G. J. Barclay, '"Churchill Rolled the Tanks into the Crowd": Mythology and Reality in the Military Deployment to Glasgow in 1919', *Scottish Affairs*, 28.1 (2019); G. J. Barclay, '"The Evidence Has Always Been There": Unreliable Narrators and Archival Sources for the Battle of George Square, Glasgow, 31 January 1919', *Scottish Archives*, 25/26 (2021), pp.108-122.

3. D. S. Morton, *The 40 Hours Strike: An Historic Survey of the First General Strike in Scotland* (Clydebank Branch SLP, 1919), p.9.
4. Morton, *The 40 Hours Strike*, p.9.
5. J. Maclean, *Sack Dalrymple; Sack Stevenson. Let Labour Revenge Bloody Friday* (J. Maclean, 1919).
6. Maclean, *Sack Dalrymple*, p.1.
7. Maclean, *Sack Dalrymple*, p.2.
8. P. Slowe, *Manny Shinwell: An Authorised Biography* (Pluto Press, 1993), pp.84-85.
9. E. Shinwell, *Conflict without Malice* (Odhams, 1955); *I've Lived through It All* (Gollancz, 1973); *Lead with the Left, My First Ninety-Six Years* (Cassell, 1981); E. Shinwell and John Doxat, *Shinwell Talking: A Conversational Biography to Celebrate His Hundredth Birthday* (Quiller, 1984); K. Robbins and J. S. Rowett, *The Blackwell Biographical Dictionary of British Political Life in the Twentieth Century* (Oxford Blackwell Reference, 1990), p.372.
10. N. Naughton, *Glasgow's East End: From Bishops to Barraboys* (Mainstream, 2014), pp.91–4; an anonymous article in *Scotland on Sunday* for 4 October 2009 appears to have been the origin for this myth: 'Seamen's leader Shinwell was thrown in jail for his part in the revolt after he faced down the tanks on 31 January that year'.
11. M. Hutton, *1919 – A Land Fit for Heroes: Britain at Peace* (Amberley, 2019), p.27.
12. H. McShane and J. Smith, *Harry McShane: No Mean Fighter* (Pluto Press, 1978). Smith worked with McShane to create this political biography, working from hours of taped interviews. Smith is straightforward about her subject's failures of memory (Appendix, pp.267-75).
13. McShane and Smith, *Harry McShane*, p.106.
14. K. MacAskill, *Glasgow 1919: The Rise of Red Clydeside* (Biteback, 2019), p.204.

15. See Chapter 3 above. S. Damer, 'Review of Mclean's 'Legend of the Red Clyde [Sic]", *History Workshop*, 18 (1984), pp.199–203; J. Foster, 'Working-class mobilisation on the Clyde 1917-20', in Wrigley, C. (ed), *Challenges of Labour: Central and Western Europe* (Routledge, 1993), pp.149-75. See p.170 in particular.
16. A. Portelli, *The Death of Luigi Trastulli and Other Stories: Form and Meaning in Oral History* (State University of New York, 1991), p.50.
17. For example, T. Ali, *Churchill: His Life and Crimes* (Verso, 2022), p.166; G. J. Barclay, 'A "villain for all seasons": Churchill and Scottish Mythologies of Grievance', *Finest Hour*, 189 (2020), pp.14-18.
18. J. McGonigle and C. Wood, *The Era of the Great War 1910-1928* (Hodder Gibson, 2013), p.84.
19. Education Scotland, 'Education Scotland review into "Road to the Scottish Parliament", FOI (3 June 2021).
20. *Scotsman*, 12 December 2020.
21. Barclay, 'A villain for all seasons'.
22. *Sunday Post*, 1 October 2015.
23. R. McKie, '100 years on: the day they read the Riot Act as chaos engulfed Glasgow', *Observer*, 6 January 2019. https://www.theguardian.com/uk-news/2019/jan/06/100-years-on-the-day-they-read-the-riot-act-in-glasgow. https://www.open.edu/openlearn/society-politics-law/sociology/section-3-red-clydeside-key-elements-and-events
24. S. J. Frenda, E. D. Knowles, W. Saletan and E. F. Loftus, 'False Memories of Fabricated Political Events', *Journal of Experimental Social Psychology*, 49 (2013), pp.280-86.
25. *Herald*, 29 January 2018.
26. R. Leadbetter, 'Revealed: truth about the tank and Glasgow's "Bolshevik rising"', *Herald*, 29 January 2018.
27. BBC Documentary, 'The Making of Modern Britain' (2009); A. Marr, *The Making of Modern Britain* (Macmillan, 2009), p.231-2; S. Damer, *Glasgow: Going for a Song* (Lawrence and Wishart, 1990, p.31.
28. BBC London, 'The Revolutionaries: John Maclean', (1980).
29. Damer, *Glasgow: Going for a Song*, p.131. Enquiries at likely film repositories for early twentieth-century footage of 'troops and tanks' in Glasgow have been made and so far, no such footage has been located; we do not believe it exists.
30. Twitter, @IsleOfButeMan, 2 March 2022, 11.13pm.
31. BBC, 'The Revolutionaries'. Tram in Queen Street, Cardiff: https://www.bbc.co.uk/programmes/p01292bt, at 32 minutes, 43 seconds.

32. 'The Age of Tanks', Netflix co-production (2017), episode 1.

33. National Library of Scotland, Moving Image Archive, Ref. No. 0913 (1965). We are grateful to Rebecca Younger for undertaking the analysis of the film.

34. Downing Street riot, 1920: images of police pushing a crowd and first aiders treating an injured man. https://www.britishpathe.com/asset/48472/

35. Pathé Films, Gaumont Graphic Newsreel, 'Strikers on the Streets of Glasgow', 1919. https://www.britishpathe.com/video/asset/170243/.

19 Historiography

It often seems to me as if history is like a child's box of letters, with which we can spell any word we please. We have only to pick out such letters as we want, arrange them as we like, and say nothing about those which do not suit our purpose.[1]

With the historical reality and the mythology so widely divergent, how has the mythology come to dominate?

Evans has argued, 'Far from looking for evidence that may support his thesis, [the historian] needs to look for vulnerabilities in that thesis and to contrive means of testing them'.[2] Rolf Gruner, to the contrary, has defended the view that hypothesis testing is *not* appropriate to describe historians' methodology and in the process he inadvertently exposes some of the concerns around the construction of the historical narratives of the Battle. Gruner suggests, 'Every historian has to take an enormous number of historical facts for granted because it is impossible to check everything and to look up the evidence for every fact from which an inference is made'. The historian:

> is interested in a certain historical period and looks at the data which in the light of his knowledge and experience are relevant to it . . . he argues to himself: 'If I have interpreted correctly, then this is evidence, and sufficient evidence, for such and such a fact. It shows that it must have happened like this . . .'.

The crucial difficulty is, what is 'sufficient'? Gruner accepts a version of events may be 'falsified' or disproved 'at least in principle, by the discovery of new evidence' which is often through an '*accidental discovery* of new evidence' [our emphasis].[3]

There are three problems with Gruner's view: first, the assumption that the historian will make a reasonable decision about what to 'take for granted' when they do not have to 'look up the evidence'; second, ensuring the decision regarding 'sufficient evidence' to substantiate a 'fact' is not merely sufficient evidence to confirm a pre-existing view; and finally, that the falsification, or revision, of an account requires the 'accidental discovery' of new evidence, which would be obviated if easily accessible sources had been consulted in the first instance.

In his seminal historiography of Red Clydeside, John Foster suggested the 'Legend of Red Clydeside' had been 'invented years after the event by left-wing propagandists such as Gallacher, Tom Bell, and McShane'. The paradox is that this wider 'legend' has been subjected to intense and competing critical analysis by Iain McLean and Foster and their supporters and critics for almost 40 years.[4] But the 'legend' of the Battle, the iconic event for which the Forty Hours Strike is most widely remembered, has remained largely undisturbed, created not only by Gallacher, Bell and McShane, but also by Shinwell, John Maclean, D. S. Morton and others. Foster has also described the passage of Red Clydeside into history as 'dislocated and incoherent'.[5] Once again, the 'legend' of the Battle is different, having been created by the defence at the trial and subsequently by a handful of contemporary authors. This version continues to frame the narrative.

The frequently used but over-simple paraphrase, which might be expressed as, 'the government sent the tanks to crush a revolution/strike', ignores the complexity of events, notably the inconvenient reality that Alastair MacKenzie, the Sheriff of Lanarkshire, alone was authorised to and called for 'military aid to the civil power'. Yet the city authorities' crucial role in the military deployment has rarely been mentioned in academic and popular accounts; indeed, in one academic account it has been emphatically denied.[6]

As noted earlier, Foster's argument relies on the military deployment being an oppressive act undertaken by the government at its own hand, 'to terrorise workers into industrial serfdom', as the *Strike Bulletin* of 10 February put it, an action largely unrelated to events in George Square. Not surprisingly, therefore, he does not mention the source of the violence in the south-east corner of the Square and refers instead only to a police decision to 'clear the square', nor does he mention the Sheriff's role in calling for the military.[7]

In trawling the extensive secondary literature, popular and academic, it is possible to consider how each author has selected, used or ignored archival material in creating their narrative. Some authors seem to have consulted the trial papers, at least in part, but these amount to nearly a thousand pages of trial transcript and pre-trial statements. Before digital scanning, this would have required many days of reading in the National Records of Scotland, more than could be justified in any wider-ranging account of Red Clydeside. Therefore, it is not surprising that important aspects have been overlooked or omitted.[8]

However, analysing the academic histories, what has been selected as worth mentioning or necessary to support an author's interpretation of events, or what has been omitted, suggest the selection has been predominantly directed towards telling the story as framed by the strike leaders. Inevitably, there will be differences in the weight given to and the interpretation of evidence, but where more than one voice exists in the archive, the historian should surely listen to them all. Jobson notes how contemporary political polarisation informed by binary views of the past represents a challenge to the ideal of multi-perspectivity in historical writing. It is ironic that the criticisms levelled against the then UK government's ill-judged attempts around 2013 to re-establish a simplistic history of imperial British 'heroes' may also be directed towards some writing about the Battle, particularly a desire to identify a category of people, in this case Scottish working-class 'heroes', whose actions are by definition to be protected from the criticism that might arise from multi-perspectivity.[9]

In the popular histories, there is also a world of difference between celebrating or mythologising a heritage to create an uplifting nostalgic 'wha's like us' version of Scotland's past and writing a history in which the protagonists are individuals, with a variety of personal and political motivations and ambitions.[10] These protagonists cannot be mere ciphers representing 'the workers' or 'the establishment', heroic or villainous according to the author's taste.

There has been a surprising willingness to accept uncritically significant 'facts' provided by the protagonists of one side. For example, in his 1936 memoir William Gallacher quoted an editorial in the

Glasgow Herald published on Saturday 8 February 1919 to make his point about the fears of the establishment:

> the panic of the civic and national authorities can only be explained thus. That they actually believed a Spartacus coup was planned to start in Glasgow, and that they were prepared to suppress it at all costs.[11]

One biographer of John Maclean has on social media described this quotation as 'key to the question of revision and myth in the Battle of George Square', because it reveals the true fears and intentions of the government in the editorial columns of a violently anti-strike newspaper.[12] The same quotation has also been given prominence in a popular account of Red Clydeside, in a review article on the subject and repeated in another history of post-Great War Britain.[13] However, these words do not appear in the *Glasgow Herald* of 8 February 1919, nor on Friday 7 or Monday 10 February, nor apparently in any national newspaper published that month.[14] The quote seems to have first appeared in Gallacher's book. Was it a failure of memory or an invention? If this quotation is so significant, why has no one thought it prudent to check?

The elements of the mythology originated at different times and have been subject to further elaboration as the years have passed but the mythologising started at lunchtime on Friday 31 January. It gained momentum as the case for the defence was prepared, with Maclean and Morton's pamphlets, and then presented in court. And it was cemented in place by about fourteen other books and articles, written over a period of 60 years by eight men closely associated with the Forty Hours Strike. In chronological order:

John Maclean, socialist leader, strike supporter. Pamphlet, *Sack Dalrymple, Sack Stevenson. Let Labour Revenge Bloody Friday* (1919).

D. S. Morton, Joint Secretary, Strike Committee. Pamphlet, *The 40 hours Strike: An Historic Survey of the First General Strike in Scotland* (1919).

David Kirkwood, strike leader. *My Life of Revolt* (1935).

W. Gallacher, strike leader. *The Clyde in Wartime* (1935).

W. Gallacher, *Revolt on the Clyde* (1936).

Tom Bell, Clyde Workers' Committee, Union leader and shop steward. *Pioneering Days* (1941).

Tom Bell, *John Maclean, a Fighter for Freedom* (1944).

E. Shinwell, Chair of Strike Committee and Glasgow Trades Council. *Conflict without Malice* (1955).

P. Dollan, Editor, *Strike Bulletin*. 'Riot Act: when Glasgow faced an army of tanks and guns', *Sunday Mail* (6 October 1957).

W. Gallacher, *The Last Memoirs of William Gallacher* (1966).

E. Shinwell, *I've Lived through It All* (1973)

Harry McShane (and J. Smith), follower of Maclean. *Harry McShane: No Mean Fighter* (1978).

Harry McShane, *Glasgow 1919: The Story of the 40 Hours Strike* (1978)

E. Shinwell, *Lead with the Left: My First Ninety-six Years* (1981).

E. Shinwell (and J. Doxat), *Shinwell Talking: A Conversational Biography to Celebrate His Hundredth Birthday* (1984).

Peter Slowe, biographer, *Manny Shinwell: An Authorised Biography* (1993). Shinwell seems to have been Slowe's main source.

These works, together with the version of events presented at the trial and the *Strike Bulletin*'s accusation of a 'savage, unprovoked attack on a peaceful crowd' have been the foundations of the dominant narrative. The prosecution's account, recorded in the press coverage of the trial and the rather overheated 'Bolshevik Terrorists!' commentary in newspapers like the *Glasgow Herald*, sank from view quite quickly once the trial verdict had been delivered.[15] There was no longer a case to prove and more pressing concerns absorbed the government. The prosecution's and 'establishment's' account never contributed to a burgeoning identity: that of Red Clydeside.

Unfortunately, the sixteen publications listed above have too often been allowed to frame the narrative. The first two, apparently written before the trial by John Maclean and D. S. Morton,* were part of the effort to place the blame for the violence in the Square wholly on the police; both works allege a conspiracy. Maclean blamed the manager of the Tramways Department and the Chief Constable for deliberately fomenting the riot by driving trams into the crowd. Tom Bell repeated and elaborated upon Maclean's accusations.[16] Maclean was absent from Glasgow on 31 January 1919 and no evidence for his and Morton's accusations has ever been offered.[17]

The personal memoirs are entertaining, but Gallacher and the other memoirists were not writing history; they were attempting to establish their place *in history*, occasionally at the expense of their contemporaries. For example, Gallacher described John Maclean as 'a mentally unstable, historically marginal, Scottish socialist', and Shinwell both blamed Kirkwood for the unfortunate outcome of the meeting with the Lord Provost on 29 January, and accused his colleague Edith Hughes of being a police spy.[18] More than anything else, Gallacher's and Shinwell's memoirs attempted to shift blame for the violence, or even the failure of the strike, onto the police, the government, and in Shinwell's case onto his fellow strike leaders.

Historians and authors of more general books on Red Clydeside, and twentieth-century Scottish history and school textbooks, have accepted a great part of the version recounted in the sixteen publications, or have followed other writers who have previously relied upon them. Thus, errors and myths are repeated from one text to another, as exemplified throughout this text. Depressingly, much of the mythology could be dismissed by any author taking time to read the *Glasgow Herald*'s reportage for late January and early February 1919, rather than waiting for Gruner's 'accidental discovery'. That newspaper was indeed hostile to the strike, but its bias appeared largely in its fulminating editorials, not so much in its eyewitness journalists' reporting. Their coverage was generally corroborated

* David S. Morton (1878-1966). Born Montrose. Believed to have been a railway brakeman. Joint Secretary of the strike committee. He was advertised as giving a lecture at the Socialist Labour Party in Renfrew Street on 12 January 1919, another on 9 March 1919.

by other newspapers' journalists, including those more in sympathy with the strike, such as the *Daily News* and *Manchester Guardian*.

Shinwell, whose memoirs have been described as 'entertaining but unreliable' certainly invented things, and examples have been provided at various points in this text. His most lasting invention is the claim, in his autobiography *I've Lived Through It All*, that 'Churchill persuaded the Cabinet that troops, machine guns and tanks should be deployed in the Clydeside area'.[19] 'Churchill sent the tanks' has subsequently been repeated in a variety of forms and is the constant refrain on social media. Previously, Shinwell had claimed Westminster sent the army and in two later volumes of autobiography he blamed Lloyd George personally instead, claiming the Prime Minister had acted in revenge for his humiliation in Glasgow in 1915. Shinwell did not substantiate any of these claims.[20] Modern academic and popular authors have focused on his accusation of Churchill.[21] Shinwell also contributed lavishly to the mythology in his recorded interviews, memorably claiming angrily 'there was no riot' in George Square in a television documentary.[22]

Shinwell wrote four of the sixteen key texts and a fifth was his authorised biography. His various memoirs reveal how the story developed, even within one man's publications. In *Conflict Without Malice*, Shinwell claimed to have rushed out into the Square in the hope of calming the crowd. By the time he reached the door, the crowd had been 'driven back' by the police. Then the crowd on the north side of the Square 'came rushing back to the entrance of the building'. Shinwell claimed he was surrounded and carried by the crowd up Hanover Street, to where he mislocates the events in North Frederick Street. It was only at this very late stage in the proceedings that, in Shinwell's version, a tram was driven into the crowd in the south-east corner. He then recounted going to destroy documents at the Trades Council offices. His own account of the military deployment described 'machine gun nests built at strategic points' and Peter Slowe, Shinwell's authorised biographer, describes Shinwell and his wife approaching the machine-gunners and being warned off. Although he writes as an eyewitness, Shinwell was in prison for the whole time the soldiers were in the city.[23] One of the strangest statements in any of Shinwell's memoirs concerned the tanks, which he claimed 'few in Glasgow had ever seen'.[24] Glaswegians were not only 'familiar' with tanks, but at two points in the previous year had become quite dotty about them, in January 1918 and mid-January 1919, during 'Tank Weeks'.

In *I've Lived Through It All*, Shinwell introduced the myth that Churchill was responsible for the military deployment because 'undoubtedly Whitehall had ordered strong measures . . .'. He claimed again that tanks were 'ostentatiously parked at strategic points', whereas, once in Glasgow, they remained undercover in the Cattle Market and had departed before Shinwell was released on bail.[25] By the time he published *Lead with the Left* eight years later, Shinwell had seriously confused events. He transposed the first meeting with the Lord Provost on 29 January to 31 January, immediately prior to the outbreak of the riot. He invented a force of 'hundreds of police', which he wove into a story of premeditated violence.[26] He elaborated:

> I have no hesitation in saying that what happened in George Square that Friday, the presence of the police and the tanks in the street and soldiers on the roof tops, and the attitude of the police to those who were committing no offence, was a deliberate act on the part of Lloyd George.[27]

There were no troops or tanks in or near George Square on 31 January; soldiers did not begin to arrive until late that night.

In *Lead with the Left* Shinwell asked what at first appear to be pertinent questions. First, why did the Sheriff appear so readily? Second, why were hundreds of police available within seconds of the tramcar incident? The problem is these are rhetorical questions which allowed him to invent and place 'facts' in the reader's mind. The Sheriff did not miraculously appear in the Square. It was a considered process from his first assessment that the Riot Act should be read, to alerting the Lord Provost at the magistrates' meeting, before entering the Square, and finally deciding to read the Act. Equally 'hundreds of police' were not 'available within seconds'; only around 180-200 police became involved with events in the Square and in reserve in the quadrangle. Few more were involved at any point during the day. Shinwell's third question was disingenuous: 'why, when twelve persons including myself were arrested and accused of incitement to riot, was no evidence to that effect adduced at our trial?'[28] A great deal of evidence was presented by the Crown at the trial, and even if it were open to interpretation, the jury convicted Shinwell and Gallacher on that evidence. By the time *Shinwell Talking* was published to mark his hundredth birthday, the confusion was complete. He now claimed the crowd was 80,000 strong, repeated the questions concerning the 'hundreds of police' and the 'sudden' appearance of the Sheriff, and Lloyd George was once again accused of a 'deliberate act'.[29] Shinwell's claims about hundreds of police have, as with many aspects of the mythology, been the foundations for further development of the story. For example, Cameron's polemic of 1993 introduces 'thousands of police . . . ready to attack the strikers when ordered to'.[30]

The fabled 'howitzer' as part of the deployment is quickly dealt with. No artillery was deployed and none was mentioned until it appeared in Harry McShane's memoir in the 1970s.[31] It has unfortunately been given credibility by, for example, a subsequent appearance in a general history of Scotland.[32] The *Strike Bulletin*, which with outrage listed the military equipment taken to Glasgow, did not mention artillery. Fortunately, there is an explanation: in October 1918 a German 'trophy' howitzer had been gifted to the city and was displayed in George Square. The *Daily Record* printed an image of it festooned with small boys.[33] The 'machine gun nests' (or 'posts') originated in Shinwell's 1955 memoir and have made regular appearances in a wide range of publications since.[34] Two photographs exist of machine-gunners, posed for the press in the quadrangle of the City Chambers, in the *Daily Sketch* of 3 February and the *Daily Record* two days later, but there is no mention of 'nests' before 1955.[35]

Shinwell promoted a narrative of conspiracy, prior planning and intent, and modern writers have gone beyond the sixteen publications, in support of the conspiracy of a deliberately-fomented riot first floated by John Maclean in the immediate aftermath. Such a conspiracy might, for example, be proved if it could be shown that troops were en route to Glasgow before the riot began, which some writers have indeed claimed. For example, MacAskill quoted a newspaper article supposedly published in Edinburgh on the afternoon of 31 January to support his claim that troops were already moving through Edinburgh on Friday morning, before the Sheriff called for help around 1.30pm.[36] However, the newspaper he quoted was actually the *Daily Record*, published in Glasgow on Saturday 1 February, describing the arrival of the army in Glasgow late on Friday night.[37] Another writer transposed significant parts of the discussion at Friday's War Cabinet meeting, after the troops had been set in motion, to the meeting on Thursday 30 January, including Munro's infamous 'Bolshevist rising' remark.[38] Yet another places the ordering of the troops on 30 January, the day before the riot.[39] One academic writer has argued, 'that Glasgow could have been placed under armed occupation without prior planning and consultation is inconceivable'.[40] In reality, the British Army, the most efficiently organised army in the world at the time, could easily undertake a deployment 80km from its local HQ in peacetime conditions in nine to eighteen hours, with approximately eighteen hours advance notice. One academic historian does not provide evidence for their claim that the government engineered the military intervention in Glasgow to 'simply [provide] the necessary trigger for the anti-strike measures agreed by the cabinet . . .', while simultaneously denying the role of the local authorities in calling for military aid.[41]

Dramatic elaboration is found more at the popular end of the market, but the omission of important parts of the history is widespread. The train of events leading to the deployment of the army is surely too important to omit from any narrative. From the Sheriff's concerns after the Lord Provost's meeting with the strikers on 29 January to his subsequent contact with the government to check troops would be available if needed, followed by Thursday's War Cabinet discussion prompted by this request, to the Sheriff's growing anxiety on Friday as the violence escalated and his discussions with colleagues, to his call for 'military aid to the civil power' in the middle of the riot can all be summarised in one sentence, as here. Yet too often one reads the inaccurate explanation, 'the government sent the troops', invented in the *Strike Bulletin* and Maclean's and Morton's pamphlets in the days after the riot. Variants occur in a wide range of academic articles and books, popular histories, school textbooks and political tracts. Of the modern publications surveyed in detail for this research, fifteen explicitly state that the government sent the troops while the others leave responsibility unclear.[42] Until 2019, no-one had mentioned the Sheriff's role; and that occurrence reflected an article on the topic in the *Herald* newspaper during 2018.[43] In *Pioneering Days*, Tom Bell is the only contemporary witness to note 'in the meantime military assistance was called for' rather than 'was sent'.[44]

Few academic or popular works mention the strike leadership's alleged 'anarchic schemes' to sabotage the city's power stations, described by Middlemas. Slowe repeats them, and Tom Bell and Gallacher refer to them indirectly, suggesting their disinclination to be involved.[45] McLean offers an alternative interpretation of the plans as an assault on the City Chambers (ironically, the accusation levelled by the prosecution) or 'to lead the workers along the well-to-do streets and let them loose'; Bell referred explicitly to plans 'to blow the [Pinkston power] station up with dynamite'.[46] Although 'authoritatively denied later in the evening', was the power blackout on Friday afternoon, 31 January 1919, 'due to sabotage on the part of the strikers'?[47] It is hardly surprising that Shinwell and the others did not mention these plans in their autobiographical writings, but its omission from almost every modern academic or popular account of the events, Middlemas and Slowe excepted, raises questions about modern authors' decision-making on what to include or omit.

That so much of the framing and indeed the detail of the dominant narrative in secondary accounts of the Battle have been derived from the *Strike Bulletin* and the sixteen key sources is problematic. It is as if a history of the General Strike of 1926 had been written by Tory historians on the basis of an uncritical acceptance of the government propaganda sheet, the *British Gazette*, and Churchill's memoirs.

Gallacher contributed to the mythology of the Battle. He wrote, in a memoir, 'If we had gone [to Maryhill Barracks] we could easily have persuaded the soldiers to come out and Glasgow would have been in our hands', suggesting the Highland Light Infantry (HLI) had been locked in for fear they would join the demonstrators.[48] But the HLI was not based at Maryhill in 1919 and the Barracks had been occupied since December 1918 by the 4th (Reserve) Battalion of the

Royal Scots Fusiliers, the county regiment of Ayrshire and the south-west of Scotland.[49] Gallacher referred to this again in a television interview in 1962 and then in print in 1966, when he claimed all the troops including 'young conscripts' were 'rushed up from England' and 'startling events' would have occurred in Glasgow. The same year, he persisted, 'in the view that the workers were ready to support an uprising in Glasgow', an assertion which has been taken to show 'a complete lack of understanding of the political situation at the time'.[50] Although Gallacher's retrospective claims of revolutionary potential have been dismissed by academic writers, they continue to appear as part of the catechism of Glasgow in 1919, in both academic and popular writing.[51]

Iain McLean was the first to use the War Cabinet minutes to inform his magisterial reconsideration of Red Clydeside. Unfortunately, a misunderstanding carried over from his thesis into the subsequent book, about the location and direction of the baton charges, divorced the police charges from the unrest in the south-east corner. This led him to conclude, 'These charges can therefore only be regarded as unprovoked attacks by the police designed to intimidate or scatter the crowd . . .' giving renewed vigour to Gallacher's accusation of a 'savage and totally unexpected assault' and the alleged 'police-provoked riot'.[52] Other writers have echoed Gallacher with an 'unprovoked and doubtlessly pre-planned police riot'.[53] Another popular writer has reframed the War Cabinet minutes to place the blame on Churchill.[54] Others have suggested that much writing about Red Clydeside is second-hand or over-reliant on accounts written by the strike leaders, but since McLean's book any more critical approach to the 'Legend of Red Clydeside' has not extended anything like as far to the 'legend' of the Battle itself.[55] Foster has gone so far as to assert: 'We cannot . . . assess subsequent accounts against any real evidence of what the principal protagonists might have thought at the time because the evidence just will not be there'.[56] Will it not?

Clearly, much of what has been published about the Battle reveals how difficult it is for one person to write dispassionately about this contested event.[57] Some mistakes may have been unconscious, while others may reflect oversights or the careless handling of material. Others, however, may stray into 'motivated misrepresentation', demonstrated by the 'convergence of historiographical errors' which tend consistently to reflect a preference for one version of the past.[58]

Labour history since the 1970s has been described by Evans as an 'explicitly politically committed form of historical writing and research', written 'from the point of view of the industrial working class . . . to recover the history of workers . . . as a means of strengthening their class-consciousness and political commitment'.[59] In writing about the Battle, authors sympathetic to the struggle of working people to achieve better working conditions have perhaps been insufficiently critical in their choice and interpretation of sources, and perhaps have listened only to some of the 'voices' from the past, perhaps showing their hearts are, as Damer put it, 'in the left place'.[60] The entry on the 'Red Clyde Strike' in the *St James Encyclopedia of Labor History Worldwide* is illustrative. Based on Shinwell's, Gallacher's and Kirkwood's accounts, a handful of secondary accounts mentioned elsewhere in this text, and, to a great extent, on the heavily-mythologised version on the Glasgow Digital Library website, a number of 'facts' are accepted without demur: a crowd number of 60,000; the 'violent and unprovoked attack'; English troops sent by government to prevent a revolution, and so on.[61]

The events after the riot have suffered rather less mythologisation in the intervening century.

---

1. J. A. Froude, *Short Studies on Great Subjects: The Science of History* (Longmans Green, 1867), p.1.
2. R. Evans, *In Defence of History* (Granta, 2000), p.121, quoting Hexter, quoting Hill.
3. R. Gruner, 'Historical Facts and the Testing of Hypotheses', *American Philosophical Quarterly*, 5 (1968), pp.124 Note 2, 125, 128.
4. I. McLean, *The Legend of Red Clydeside* (John Donald 1999); J. Foster, 'Red Clyde, Red Scotland', *The Manufacture of Scottish History*, eds I. Donnachie and C. Whatley (Polygon, 1992).
5. J. Foster, 'Red Clyde, Red Scotland', p.118.
6. B. Weinberger, *Keeping the Peace: Policing Strikes in Britain, 1906-1926* (Berg, 1991), pp.155-6. For the general issue in academic, popular, school text and political writing, for example: M. Archibald, *Glasgow: The Real Mean City* (Black and White, 2013), preface; C. Bambery, *A People's History of Scotland* (Verso, 2014), p.157; J. Cameron, *Red Flag over the*

Clyde: The Story of John MacLean and Red Clydeside (Scottish Militant Labour, 1993), p.22; T. Devine, *The Scottish Nation: A Modern History* (Penguin, 2012), p.314-5; R. Finlay, *The Turbulent Century: Scotland since 1900* (Oxford University Press, 2005), p.206; M. Fry, *Glasgow: A History of the City* (Head of Zeus, 2017), p.430; A. M. Gray, *A History of Scotland: Book 5, Modern Times* (Oxford University Press, 1999), p.63; C. Harvie, *No Gods and Precious Few Heroes: Twentieth-century Scotland* (Edinburgh University Press, 3rd edn 2000), p.25; M. Hutton, *1919 – A Land Fit for Heroes* (Amberley, 2019), p.27; J. Jenkinson, *Black 1919: Riots, Racism and Resistance in imperial Britain* (Liverpool University Press, 2009), p.42; J. A. Kerr, *Scotland and the impact of the Great War 1914-1928* (Hodder Gibson, 2010), p.107; A-M. Kilday, *Crime in Scotland 1660-1960: The Violent North* (Routledge, 2019), p.182; A. Marr, *The Making of Modern Britain* (Macmillan, 2009), p.231-2; G. Mooney, 'Tanks on the streets of Glasgow to stop revolt in 1919', *Socialist Worker* 28 January 2019. This lengthy list is necessitated by a referee's assertion that the paraphrase was *not* in fact a common feature of academic, popular and other accounts. It is.

7. J. Foster, 'Strike Action and Working-Class Politics on Clydeside 1914–1919', *International Review of Social History*, 35 (1990), pp.33-70; Foster, 'Red Clyde', pp.106-124; J. Foster, 'Working-class mobilisation on the Clyde 1917-20', in Wrigley, C. (ed), *Challenges of Labour: Central and Western Europe* (Routledge, 1993), pp.149-75; J. Foster, "Mobilising Working Class Action on Clydeside, 1919 and 1971: How the Arguments Were Won', *Colloque Internationale Discours et Dispositivs Anti-syndicaux* (Lyon, 2010), p.23; J. Foster, 'The 1919 Forty Hours Strike', *Theory and Struggle*, 120 (2019), pp.30-40.
8. Files AD15/19/11 and JC36/31 at the National Records of Scotland.
9. A. Low-Beer, *The Council of Europe and School History* (Council of Europe, 1997), pp.54-5; R. Jobson, 'Teaching modern British history in a politically polarised and "post-truth" environment', *Transactions of the Royal Historical Society*, 2 (2024), pp.389-400; M. Weston, 'Michael Gove's war on professional historical expertise: conservative curriculum reform, extreme whig history and the place of imperial heroes in a modern multicultural Britain', *British Politics*, 15 (2020), pp.271-90.
10. S. Damer, 'In the Rapids of Revolution?', *Scottish Affairs*, 28 (2019), p.113.
11. W. Gallacher, *Revolt on the Clyde* (Lawrence and Wishart, 2017 [1936]), p.164.
12. Twitter, Henry Bell (@henbell), 9 May 2019.
13. K. MacAskill, *Glasgow 1919: The Rise of Red Clydeside* (Biteback, 2019), p.225; J. McNicol, 'The Radical Atmosphere of the Red Clyde',

London Review of Books, 2 January 2020; S. Fowler and D. Weinbren, *Now the War Is Over: Britain 1919-1920* (Pen and Sword Military, 2018), p.33.

14. *The Times*, *Observer*, *Glasgow Herald*, *Manchester Guardian*, *Daily News*, *Scotsman*, the *Bulletin* and others have all been checked for 8 February 1919 and surrounding dates. As explored in this text, the notion of any uprising in Glasgow was only voiced by Robert Munro at the War Cabinet Meeting.

15. Commentary on events contained in the various Clyde Shipbuilders Association Minute Books and other papers would not have been publicly circulated, and it appears have not often been investigated to provide another dimension to this history.

16. T. Bell, *John Maclean: A Fighter for Freedom* (Communist Party, 1944), p.85.

17. At the trial, defence witness John Mackenzie also asserted that the riot had been deliberately fomented; JC36/31/06 [06/D], John Mackenzie, Shipwrights' Society.

18. T. Brotherstone, 'John Maclean and the Russian Revolution: A Discussion Article', *Scottish Labour History Society Journal,* 23 (1988) p.17; P. Slowe, *Manny Shinwell: An Authorised Biography* (Pluto Press, 1993), pp. 81-2.

19. K. Robbins and J. Rowett, *The Blackwell Biographical Dictionary of British Political Life in the Twentieth Century* (Wiley, 1990), pp.372-4; E. Shinwell, *I've Lived through It All* (Gollancz, 1973), p.45.

20. E. Shinwell and J. Doxat, *Shinwell Talking: A Conversational Biography to Celebrate His Hundredth Birthday* (Quiller, 1984), pp.93-4; E. Shinwell, *Lead with the Left: My First Ninety-Six Years* (Cassell, 1981), p.63; E. Shinwell, *Conflict without Malice* (Odhams, 1955), p.64.

21. For example, B. Weinberger, *Keeping the Peace: Policing Strikes in Britain, 1906-1926* (Berg, 1991), p.158; M. Fry, *Glasgow: A History of the City* (Head of Zeus, 2017), pp.320, 429; J. Burrowes, *Great Glasgow Stories* (Mainstream, 2010), ebook ref 629.5/640.

22. BBC London, 'Manny at 100' (1984).

23. Shinwell, *Conflict*, pp.62-64.

24. Shinwell, *Conflict*, p.45.

25. Shinwell, *I've Lived through It All*, p.45.

26. Shinwell, *Lead with the Left*, pp.61-2, 65.

27. Shinwell, *Lead with the Left*, p.65.

28. Shinwell, *Lead with the Left*, p.62.

29. Shinwell and Doxat, *Shinwell Talking*, pp.90, 93.

30. J. Cameron, *Red Flag over the Clyde: The Story of John MacLean and Red Clydeside* (Scottish Militant Labour, 1993), p.21.

31. H. McShane and J. Smith, *Harry McShane: No Mean Fighter* (Pluto Press, 1978), p.107.

32. T. C. Smout, *A Century of the Scottish People: 1830-1950* (Collins, 1986), p.265.

33. MacNeill, personal communication. *Daily Record and Mail,* 21 December 1918.

34. R. K. Middlemas, *The Clydesiders: A Left-wing Struggle for Parliamentary Power* (Hutchison, 1965), p.95; R. Challinor, *The Origins of British Bolshevism* (Rowman and Littlefield, 1977), p.12; Jeffery and Hennessy, *States of Emergency*, p.10; Smout, *Century of the Scottish People*, p.265; J. Burrowes, *Great Glasgow Stories* (Mainstream, 1998), ebook ref 629.5/640; S. Wood, *Higher History: Britain and Scotland, 1850s-1979* (Hodder and Stoughton, 1999), p.58; R. Goring, *Scotland: The Autobiography, 2,000 Years of Scottish History by Those Who Saw It Happen* (Viking, 2007), p.302; J. McGonigle and C. Wood, *The Era of the Great War 1910-1928* (Hodder Gibson, 2013), p.84; K. MacAskill, *Glasgow 1919: The Rise of Red Clydeside* (Biteback, 2019), p.226; S. Damer, *Glasgow: Going for a Song* (Lawrence and Wishart, 1990), p.131; Shinwell, *Conflict,* p.62-4.

35. *Daily News*, 3 February 1919; *Daily Sketch,* 'With Lewis Gun at a Dangerous Corner, Ready for Action', 3 February 1919. The 'dangerous corner' was inside the quadrangle of the City Chambers!

36. MacAskill, *Glasgow 1919*, p.228; Barclay, 'Unreliable Narrators', p.8.

37. *Daily Record,* 1 February 1919.

38. M. Craig, *When the Clyde Ran Red: A Social History of Red Clydeside* (Mainstream, 2011), p.162 [2018 edn pp.181-82].

39. C. Harvie, *No Gods and Precious Few Heroes: Twentieth-century Scotland* (Edinburgh University Press, (3rd edn, 2000), p.25.

40. W. Kendall, *The Revolutionary Movement in Britain, 1900-21: The Origins of British Communism*, (Weidenfeld and Nicolson, 1969), p.139; also quoted in J. Leopold, 'The Forty Hours Strike,' in L. Flynn (ed), *We Shall Be All: Recent Chapters in the History of Working-class Struggle in Scotland* (Bookmarks, 1978), pp.34-44.

41. Weinberger, *Keeping the Peace*, pp.152-62.

42. For example: M. Archibald, *Glasgow: The Real Mean City* (Black and White, 2013), preface; C. Bambery, *A People's History of Scotland* (Verso, 2014), p.157; J. Cameron, *Red Flag over the Clyde: The Story of John*

MacLean and Red Clydeside (Scottish Militant Labour, 1993), p.22. T. Devine, *The Scottish Nation: A Modern History* (2012), p.314-5; R. Finlay *The Turbulent Century: Scotland since 1900* (Oxford University Press, 2005), p.206; M. Fry, *Glasgow: A History of the City* (Head of Zeus, 2017), p.430; A. M. Gray, *A History of Scotland: Book 5, Modern Times* (Oxford University Press, 1999), p.63. C. Harvie, *No Gods and Precious Few Heroes: Twentieth-century Scotland* (Edinburgh University Press, (3rd edn 2000), p.25; M. Hutton, *1919 – A Land Fit for Heroes* (Amberley, 2019) ebook; J. Jenkinson, *Black 1919: Riots, Racism and Resistance in Imperial Britain* (Liverpool University Press, 2009), p.42; J. A. Kerr, *Scotland and the Impact of the Great War 1914-1928* (Hodder Gibson, 2010), pp.107, 182; A. Marr, *The Making of Modern Britain* (Macmillan, 2009), p.231-2; B. Weinberger, *Keeping the Peace: Policing Strikes in Britain, 1906-1926* (Berg, 1991), pp.155-6.

43. MacAskill, *Glasgow 1919*, p. 214.

44. T. Bell, *Pioneering Days* (Lawrence and Wishart, 1941), p.169; G. J. Barclay, 'The Evidence Has Always Been There', p.117.

45. Middlemas, *Clydesiders*, p.92; Slowe, *Manny*, p.85; Bell, *Pioneering Days*, p.166; Gallacher, *Revolt*, p.158; McLean, *Labour Movement*, p.206.

46. Bell, *Pioneering Days*, p.166.

47. *Glasgow Herald,* 1 February 1919.

48. Gallacher, *Revolt*, pp163-4; MacAskill, *Glasgow 1919*, pp.223-24.

49. TNA WO73/109 and WO73/110. Office of the Commander in Chief and War Office: distribution of the army monthly returns. Jul-Dec 1918 and Jan-Jun 1919, respectively.

50. BBC Scotland, 'Interview with Willie Gallacher', Edmond Wright (1962); W. Gallacher, *The Last Memoirs of William Gallacher* (Lawrence and Wishart, 1966), pp.43, 120; L. J. Macfarlane, *The British Communist Party: Its Origin and Development until 1929* (MacGibbon and Kee, 1966), p.43.

51. J. Broom, *John Maclean* (Macdonald, 1973), p.20; J. Kerr, *Scotland and the Impact of the Great War* (Hodder Gibson, 2010), p.107; Kilday, *Crime in Scotland,* p.179; MacAskill, *Glasgow 1919*, pp. 223-24.

52. We have already noted, Chapter 13, that McLean erroneously placed the beginnings of the riot in the *south-west* corner of the Square instead of the *south-east*, and presumed the first baton charge was west to east along the south side of the Square, in front of the Post Office, and the second, as noted above, south to north along the front of the City Chambers; (I. McLean, *Labour Movement*, p.213).

53. Damer, *Glasgow*, p.131; Bambery, *A People's History of Scotland*, p.156; Mowat, *Britain between the Wars* p.24; Harvie, '*No Gods and Precious Few Heroes*' (Arnold, 1st edn 1981), p.22; Jenkinson, *Black 1919*, p.42; Marwick, *The Deluge*, p.273.

54. J. Burrowes, *Great Glasgow Stories* (Mainstream, 2010) ebook reference 629.5/640; see also G. J. Barclay, '"Duties in Aid of the Civil Power": the Deployment of the Army to Glasgow, 31 January to 17 February 1919', *Journal of Scottish Historical Studies*, 38.2 (2018), p.271-2.

55. S. Damer, 'And If You Know the History', pp.112-15.

56. Foster, 'Red Clyde', p.108.

57. Damer, 'And If You Know the History', pp.112-15. One anonymous referee chided us that our approach was 'not how most Glaswegians would like their history to be presented' and feared we might 'belittle' the Battle. No comment is necessary.

58. The Hon Mr Justice Gray, 'Judgement of the Libel Case between Claimant David Irving and Defendants Penguin Books Ltd and Deborah E. Lipstadt', 2000.

59. Evans, *Defence*, p.196.

60. G. J. Barclay, '"The evidence has always been there": unreliable narrators and archival sources for the Battle of George Square, Glasgow, 31 January 1919', *Scottish Archives*, 25/26 (2019-21), pp.108-122, p.121; S. Damer, 'And If You Know the History', *Scottish Affairs*, 28.1 (2019), p.114.

61. D. G. Lilleker, 'Red Clydeside Strike', in N. Schlager (ed), *St James Encyclopedia of Labor History Worldwide*, pp.170-4; Glasgow Digital Library http://gdl.cdlr.strath.ac.uk/redclyde/redclyeve14.htm

Part V
AFTERMATH

20 Evening of 31 January to Sunday 6 April 1919

Evening, Friday 31 January

The *Glasgow Herald* reported there had been an interruption to the power supply during the evening, leaving some principal streets in darkness:

> Alarming stories got abroad that the breakdown in the service was due to sabotage on the part of the strikers. The explanation, however, was that certain difficulties were experienced at the Port Dundas power station, causing a suspension of the works.[1]

It is possible that the power failure may indeed have resulted from sabotage, but the authorities may have preferred not to publicise it for fear of spreading panic among the citizens and possibly jubilation among the strikers. The newspaper continued:

> For several hours last night large crowds were constantly on the move in George Square and in the streets in that neighbourhood . . . Strong forces of police including a number of special constables, were on duty at the Municipal Buildings and other points in the Square and its vicinity.
>
> Shortly after 9 o'clock, however a distinctly disorderly section began to make its presence manifest among the crowd in George Square. Stones and bottles were thrown at the police on duty at the City Chambers and at the windows of the buildings. The police at once took measures to cope with the disturbance.[2]

Detective Inspector Noble reported that around 5.15pm a group of 200 men assembled in North Frederick Street and then proceeded along George Street into Queen Street, where they began breaking

20.1. *A soldier inspects a damaged tram (*Graphic, *8 February 1919).*

windows. Noble telephoned for reinforcements but the crowd, having stood under the railway bridge in Argyle Street, moved off into the darkness. Sunset had been at 4.48pm.[3] Inspector Gillies was on duty in the Square until midnight. He reported 'several riotous mobs congregated in the Square and about 9 pm, when the Military arrived to guard the Municipal Buildings, they were received with great abuse'.[4] Disorder, including bottle-throwing, continued in parts of the city until late in the evening.[5]

Around 10pm, five men were arrested and later charged with mobbing, rioting and looting shops in Argyle Street and Queen Street, as well as stopping two trams and assaulting two policemen. Two were strikers.[6] They were part of a riotous and 'very noisy' mob of around 500 people, shouting and brawling and carrying sticks into Queen Street. Glass was smashed and the crowd 'deliberately held up a number of tram cars'. They smashed windows in the Polytechnic Warehouse and goods were stolen from a jeweller, a stationer and a shoe shop. There was another baton charge after a man seen looting shoes from the windows of Cables's shoe shop was arrested and a crowd of 3-400 people objected. Of the five men charged, only the strikers Strange and Robert were convicted and sentenced to three months' imprisonment.[7]

Saturday 1 February

On Saturday 1 February 1919, the *Glasgow Herald*'s leading article described the 'disgraceful proceedings' in the city and placed responsibility firmly on:

> the men who from the outset flouted the law and decency, and deliberately set themselves to paralyse the orderly functionings of the community. But no small share of the responsibility rests on the shoulders of the Chief Magistrate [the Lord Provost]. When he was approached by a blustering, threatening delegation of lawless men with a demand that he should communicate with the Government, it was the duty of Lord Provost Stewart to take up resolutely and inflexibly the

20.2. *One of the smashed and looted windows of the Cable Shoe Shop, as joiners prepare to board it up (*Graphic, *8 February 1919).*

> position that it was neither the province of the strikers to submit nor his to concede a demand which involved himself in humiliation and the city in a probable emeute.[8]

The *Glasgow Herald* described events in detail, as did many other newspapers in their weekend editions. However, it is remarkable how quickly news of other events overtook the trouble in Glasgow. London-based papers moved on to the strikes in the capital and Glasgow dropped quickly out of the news. Some continued to publish photographs of the military, and the weeklies published 'round-ups' at the end of the week, but the riot was scarcely mentioned after the weekend. The Clyde employers issued their own statement blaming the malcontents among the strikers for the violence, the revolutionary element among the trade unionists who, they claimed, had used unemployment as the catalyst for their ulterior political motives, aiming at unravelling society.[9]

At 12.10am on Saturday 1 February, Chief Detective Inspector John Storrar and Detective Inspector Coulter went to Shinwell's home in Govan, where he was informed he was being charged, *inter alia*, with inciting a mob to riot. Later that day, Storrar, Coulter and Detective Constable Inkster searched Shinwell's house. Nothing incriminating was found.[10] On the same day, the police also visited the offices of the Glasgow Trades Council.[11]

On Sunday 2 February at about 2.20am, David McKenzie* was arrested, accused of smashing a tram window in the Square. Later, at 7am Constable Cameron, in company with Constable Smillie and two plainclothes officers, arrested James Murray and charged him with mobbing and rioting and also with assaulting Constable Cochran in Cathedral Street on 31 January.[12]

The first troops had arrived around 10pm on Friday night, and further trainloads of men arrived over the weekend, bringing the total number up to approximately 10,000.[13] On Monday 3 February the tanks arrived by rail, as did Siegfried Sassoon, who had been sent north by the *Nation*'s editor Henry Massingham.[14]

* David McKenzie (*c*1884- unknown). A native of Caithness. Labourer in the granary at Partick, but unemployed when arrested. Member of the Partick Branch of the ILP and regular attender at socialist meetings and seller of socialist literature. Tried and acquitted.

The *Glasgow Herald* of Friday 7 February contained the Lord Provost's statement, made the previous day to his fellow councillors. It was, in his usual style, lengthy and orotund. The Lord Provost claimed his statement was intended to reassert 'common sense and reason and mutual confidence', but in reality, it was nothing but self-exculpation. He said in the early days, although 'traffic undoubtedly was obstructed . . . there was no violence used, there was no disturbance created, and there was no overt act committed'. However, he said the situation had changed on Wednesday 29 January when he had met the deputation. He made some dubious claims to justify the meeting: if he had refused to see them it 'would undoubtedly have immediately led to threats which had been made being carried into effect'; the available police force was 'quite inadequate to control such a vast number of men already beginning to show symptoms of rowdyism'; and there was no military aid available.[15]

However, no substantive threats had been made prior to the meeting with the delegates; no witness described any great rowdyism in the Square on 29 January and the calling of the military appears to have been contemplated only *after* the perceived threats were made at the meeting with the delegation; that is after the Lord Provost had decided to meet them. The Lord Provost claimed that sending the telegram allowed him to inform the government of 'the critical position in which the city was placed, and their necessity for immediately providing a sufficient force to aid the civilian force in any emergency which might arise' and gave 'time to obtain sufficient military aid'. This distortion of the sequence of events to exaggerate his own prescience does not bear scrutiny. There is no evidence to support any contention that the Lord Provost or the Sheriff believed military aid would be needed before the meeting with the delegation. The Sheriff testified he had considered the possible need for military aid only after the Lord Provost's meeting on Wednesday with the delegation. The Lord Provost went on to praise the police to applause from the councillors. He concluded with thanks to his colleagues for their forbearance and sympathy 'throughout [his] time of trial'.[16] He sat down to loud applause.

Bailie Wheatley insisted on commenting on the statement and said, 'after having made all due allowance for provocation', he considered the police had 'acted in an unnecessarily brutal manner'. Wheatley minimised the violence in the Square, claiming 'merely because there had been a scrap between two or three policemen and two or three youths in the south-west corner [sic]' the Sheriff had proposed to use the military 'to shoot down possibly their brothers and their fathers'. He went on to assert, inaccurately, 'the whole control of the City has been taken out of the hands of the Magistrates without consultation with them'. Erroneously, he believed the city was 'under military control'.[17]

The Lord Provost responded that the Sheriff, John Lamb and the Town Clerk and himself had on Friday watched 'the rioting proceeding for a considerable time' until he had joined the magistrates' meeting. That was when, 'as Bailie Wheatley had explained, the Sheriff Principal came in and said he had satisfied himself that the time had arisen when there was no help but to read the Riot Act'. The account of the discussion after the statement shows considerable confusion about the consequences of reading the Riot Act, particularly the erroneous belief held by the Provost and Bailies Stewart and Wheatley that the Sheriff had no option but to call troops once it was read. It was to this that Bailies Stewart and Wheatley objected. To avoid it, they suggested that, 'it was ultimately agreed that we should go down and interview the crowd ourselves and prevent any rioting'. Proceedings at the meeting on 6 February ended with a vote of confidence in the Lord Provost, which was passed unanimously.[18]

In the same edition in which the Lord Provost's statement was published, the *Glasgow Herald*'s editor objected in the strongest terms to the Lord Provost's actions on 29 January by meeting the delegation and agreeing to send the telegram. The editor blustered about 'lawless men' and blackguards becoming even more verbose and pompous than the Lord Provost. However, the editor provided a good summary of the problems of providing 'military aid to the civil power':

> it may safely be said that there are few military duties more utterly repellent to both the commissioned and non-commissioned ranks than that of assisting to maintain order during the progress of a serious strike. To the private soldier it is a

hateful variation of his ordinary work, with no sort of pleasurable excitement attached to it, no extra pay, no honour or glory, and involving sometimes a good deal of real discomfort and a certain amount of risk, to say nothing of painful possibility of having to use deadly weapons against a relatively defenceless crowd. To the officer strike duty may mean sudden embroilment in a difficult situation, the mishandling of which may be followed by grave official consequences. The strikers and the public, of course, view the presence of the military from other and different standpoints – the one too often with accentuated bitterness, the other with, generally speaking, relief and confidence.[19]

The End of the Strike

Excitement about the military disappeared very quickly, even from the Glasgow newspapers. The *Glasgow Herald* two weeks later reported, 'The military who were drafted into Glasgow following strike riots which took place on Friday, January 31, have been gradually withdrawn during the past week. The last of the troops who have been guarding public buildings left the city last night' [17 February].[20] There had been no hostile or violent interaction between the army and civilians and the army had even politely moved out of its billet in St Mungo's Halls to allow a prearranged meeting of the Bakers' Union to go ahead.[21] The troops stood about, guarding vulnerable points and chatting to Glaswegians. Mass picketing was suspended by the strike committee on Monday 3 February and the strike proceeded without interference.

It became clear that the strike was not going to spread on any great scale to other areas. There was a slow drift back to work, starting with the non-engineering workers. With the cessation of mass picketing some works restarted work on 4 February. Power supplies returned to normal. On 10 February, the strike committee recommended a resumption of work for 12 February, which is what happened, on the basis of the 47-hour week already in place.[22]

Many of the other desires of trade unions were met by the Restoration of Pre-War Practices Act (No. 3) (1919), which was 'designed to ensure to the trade unions of the country the right to have restored certain trade union customs and practices which they gave up during the War in order to bring about the greatest possible production of war material'.[23] These practices included manning and closed shop agreements, restriction of overtime and the employment of women. It was not feasible to achieve full restoration, because new plant and methods of production had become a permanent feature, but the real effect of the Act was to function as a bargaining counter between men and management, for example, to allow wartime changes to remain in place in exchange for better wages and conditions.[24]

The 'Fortnightly Report on Revolutionary Organisations in the United Kingdom and Abroad' for 10 February 1919 opened with a retrospective analysis of the events in Glasgow supportive of the views of the reactionary, 'reds under the bed' camp in government and the army, such as Sir Henry Wilson and the probable author of the report, Basil Thomson. The report ascribes revolutionary intentions to Shinwell *et al* and states as fact a plan to seize the Municipal Buildings. It floats the idea of a 'Civic Guard' to keep order in the streets.[25]

The Legal Process

Those accused of incitement and/or rioting made their first court appearances between 8 and 21 February to hear the charges against them and request bail, which was initially refused. Petitions for bail heard on Saturday morning, 22 February 1919, ordered by name, the date of the bail bond, the amount of bail and the charge recorded on the bail bond, were:[26]

> Shinwell, 23 February 1919, £300, inciting to riot and forming part of a riotous mob.
>
> Kirkwood, 24 February 1919, £300, mobbing and rioting and inducing to riot.
>
> Gallacher, 23 February 1919, £300, inciting to riot, mobbing and rioting, and assault.
>
> Hopkins, 22 February 1919, £300, inciting to riot, mobbing and rioting.

Loudon, 24 February 1919, £120, mobbing and rioting and assault.

Alexander, 24 February 1919, £120, mobbing and rioting and inciting to riot.

McKenzie, 24 February 1919, £120, mobbing and rioting and assault.

Murray, 24 February 1919, £120, mobbing and rioting and assault.

Ebury, 22 February 1919, £80, inciting to riot, mobbing and rioting, and assault.

Brennan, 24 February 1919, £80, inciting to riot, mobbing and rioting, and assault

Oliver, 25 February 1919, £80, mobbing and rioting.

McCartney, 24 February 1919, £80, mobbing and rioting etc.

To be guilty of 'mobbing and rioting' in Scots Law there must be a group of people who combine with a common and illegal purpose, either by violence, by demonstration of force or numbers, by intimidation, impediment or obstruction. However, the coming together in itself is not deemed illegal.[27]

In Scots legal procedure, the prosecution precognosces its own witnesses and may also precognosce the defence witnesses.[28] From the trial transcript, it is clear some defence witnesses had tried to avoid giving precognitions to the Procurator Fiscal, notably Neil Maclean MP.[29] It is possible that the absurdly large witness list presented by the defence, containing 744 non-police witnesses, was intended in part to impede the precognoscing process by making it difficult for prosecution to select witnesses who would actually be called.[30] It was only on 7 April, the day the trial started, that the defence solicitors wrote to their witnesses to advise them they would shortly be contacted by a policeman asking for a statement of evidence, noting 'the Authorities are entitled to receive such a statement'.[31] Nevertheless, Neil Maclean MP testified he did not know he was obliged to provide a precognition if asked.[32]

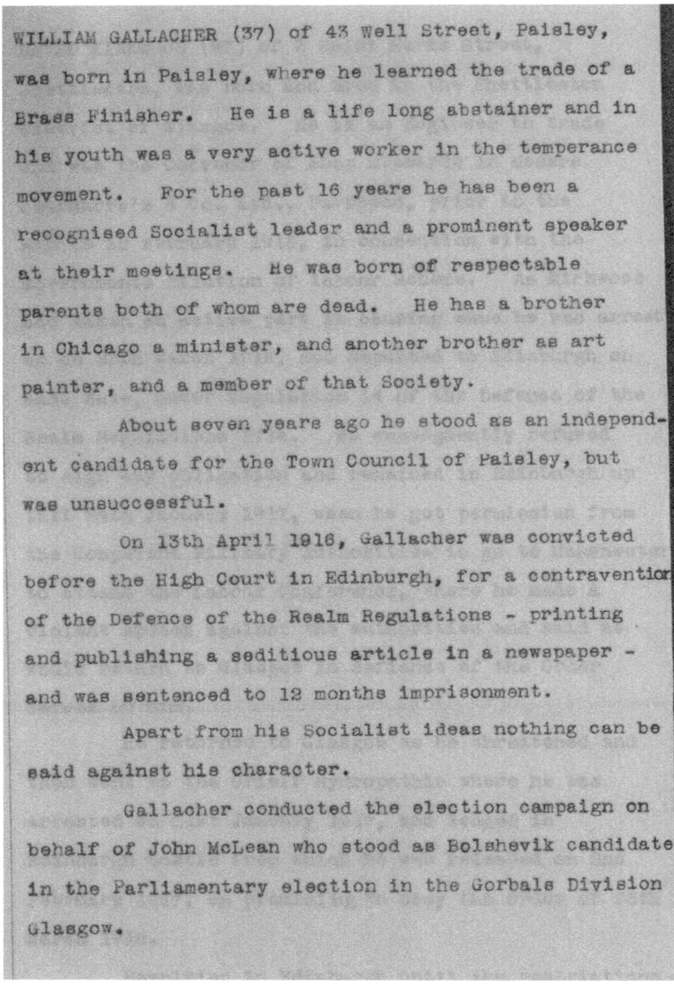

WILLIAM GALLACHER (37) of 43 Well Street, Paisley, was born in Paisley, where he learned the trade of a Brass Finisher. He is a life long abstainer and in his youth was a very active worker in the temperance movement. For the past 16 years he has been a recognised Socialist leader and a prominent speaker at their meetings. He was born of respectable parents both of whom are dead. He has a brother in Chicago a minister, and another brother as art painter, and a member of that Society.

About seven years ago he stood as an independent candidate for the Town Council of Paisley, but was unsuccessful.

On 13th April 1916, Gallacher was convicted before the High Court in Edinburgh, for a contravention of the Defence of the Realm Regulations - printing and publishing a seditious article in a newspaper - and was sentenced to 12 months imprisonment.

Apart from his Socialist ideas nothing can be said against his character.

Gallacher conducted the election campaign on behalf of John McLean who stood as Bolshevik candidate in the Parliamentary election in the Gorbals Division Glasgow.

20.3. *Biographical details on William Gallacher from police perspective gathered as evidence prior to trial. (Reproduced by kind permission; Crown copyright. National Records of Scotland, AD15/19/11.)*

At their own expense, the defence could precognosce prosecution witnesses, and Councillor Rosslyn Mitchell, who was a witness as well as the legal agent for some of the accused, attempted to obtain the prosecution's precognition statements by improper means, thus avoiding any expense. Procurator Fiscal Strathern's investigation revealed that Mitchell had telephoned the Lord Provost, Sheriff MacKenzie, the Chief Constable and Sir John Lindsay, claiming, falsely, that he had permission to see their depositions. Only Sir John was duped into handing over his precognition.[33]

The file in the National Records of Scotland containing the prosecution precognitions also includes hundreds of pages of documents relating to organising the trial, the development of the indictment, the granting of bail, the list of defence witnesses, the prosecution productions and so on. The indictment asserts that incitement to riot occurred at: George Square on 27 and 29 January; James Watt Lane, 30 January; West Street, 30 January; the Star Picture House, 30 January; and Mechan's Works on 30 January. The alleged incitement was to:

> instigate and incite large crowds of persons at said respective places to form part of a riotous mob to be assembled in George Square, Glasgow, on 31st January 1919, for the purpose of holding up the traffic in said Square and adjoining streets, of overawing and intimidating the police officers on duty there, and of forcibly taking possession of the Municipal Buildings and North British Station Hotel . . . and on 31st January 1919 a riotous mob of 20,000 or thereby evil-disposed persons, of which you [list of accused excluding Oliver and McCartney] formed part, did assemble in George Square aforesaid, and acting of common purpose, did conduct itself in a violent, riotous and tumultuous manner to the great terror and alarm of the lieges, and in breach of the public peace, and did forcibly stop tramway cars . . . and smash windows of said tramway cars and of shops and other premises situated in George Square aforesaid and in North Frederick Street and in Cathedral Street . . . and did assault Owen McQuade . . . who was then in charge of a licensed shop at 46 North Frederick Street . . . and strike him with bottles and threaten to shoot him with a revolver . . .

The indictment details the theft of bottles from George Binnie's lorry in North Frederick Street and their subsequent use as missiles; the assault on the Sheriff and snatching of the Riot Act proclamation. It then lists in detail the assaults on eleven policemen, from the Chief

Constable down, in the Square and a further six policemen in Cathedral Street. The indictment continues with events elsewhere:

> Further, said riotous mob or part thereof, consisting of you [list of accused including Oliver and McCartney], and a large number of other evil-disposed persons acting of common purpose did on said 31st January 1919 in Argyle Street, Trongate, Saltmarket Street, Jail Square, East Clyde Street, Great Clyde Street, Paisley Road West, all in Glasgow, conduct itself in a violent and riotous and tumultuous manner to the great terror and alarm of the lieges . . .

Reference was also made to the stopping and smashing of tram cars and the robbing of bottles from John Gray's lorry in Great Clyde Street. The indictment closed by detailing assaults on seven police officers and the jeweller Stewart Hunter, although the robbery from his shop was in the end removed from the indictment.[34]

A further document lists the places where incitement or key events in the riot allegedly took place, which accused were involved and the main witnesses. Another document takes each individual accused and lists their alleged words of incitement, where they were spoken and which witnesses would give evidence. In the same series as the trial transcript, a further file contains over 230 pages of papers relating to the organisation of the trial, with many earlier drafts and duplications. The file includes the special defences presented for six of the accused, outlining how they were not present at some of the places mentioned where incitement was alleged to have taken place. The papers include a letter from the Chief Constable of Edinburgh to the Clerk of Justiciary that 'adequate police arrangements [for the trial] will be made in terms of your request'.[35]

The pleading diet in front of the Sheriff in Glasgow was held on 8 March 1919 and the trial in the High Court of Justiciary in Edinburgh was originally set for 18 March 1919, suggesting the authorities were in a hurry to bring the men to trial. The accused and their agents clearly felt they had been given insufficient time to prepare their defence and the accused threatened to dismiss their solicitors, to take no part in the trial and refuse to plead.[36] At one stage, it appears the accused were finding it difficult to find senior counsel to represent them.[37] A letter from the Procurator Fiscal to the Crown Agent notes 'every Trade Union in the country and practically every branch' had been circularised by the defence to complain of 'the unusual expedition with which they have been brought to trial', and they were 'not being treated with common justice' in such an 'intricate and extensive case'. Further strike action was threatened and it was believed there might be widespread sympathy for the men. The Procurator Fiscal noted an earlier demand for a delay of two months had been reduced to two weeks.[38] A telegram dated 10 March from the Lord Advocate to the Crown Agent acceded to this request.[39] A letter from the Procurator Fiscal to the Crown Agent on 12 March records his discussions with Rosslyn Mitchell on behalf of all the agents for the accused about a trial date. It said, Mitchell 'has asked me to say how much he personally appreciates the reasonable way in which his request for a fortnight's delay has been met'. In the end a reasonably amicable settlement was reached and the trial was postponed to 7 April.[40]

The trial papers include pen portraits of the accused, prepared, it is presumed, by the police to provide the individual's background prior to appearance in court (Fig. 20.3).

On Monday morning, 7 April, the doors to the High Court of Justiciary in Edinburgh opened to swelling crowds. The people had not been deterred from attending the court despite having had to travel from Glasgow.

---

1. *Glasgow Herald*, 1 February 1919.
2. *Glasgow Herald*, 1 February 1919. This is the only mention of Special Constables actually being on duty, presumably to augment numbers after the key events.
3. AD15/19/11 [A29], Louis Noble, Detective Inspector.
4. AD15/19/11 [A36], Neil Gillies, Police Inspector.
5. AD15/19/11 [A20], Lawrence Gray, Police Lieutenant.
6. *Glasgow Herald*, 1 February 1919; AD15/19/55 & JC26/1919/33, Trial Papers Relating to Herbert Strange, Frederick Robert or Roberts, John White, William Wilson and William Hill for the Crime of Mobbing and Rioting at George Square; James Watt Lane; North Canal Bank Street; Eddington Street; Corn Street; West Street; Union Street, Glasgow and

Elsewhere in Glasgow, 1919; *Glasgow Herald,* 30 April 1919 and 1 May 1919.

7. AD15/19/55, Herbert Strange et al.
8. *Glasgow Herald,* 1 February 1919; 'emeute' French for 'insurrection'.
9. *Observer*, 2 February 1919, p.9.
10. AD15/19/11 [A99], Storrar, Chief Detective Inspector.
11. D. S. Morton, *The 40 Hours Strike: An Historic Survey of the First General Strike in Scotland* (Clydebank Branch SLP, 1919), p.13.
12. AD15/19/11 [A38], Frances Cameron, Police Constable.
13. [Edinburgh] *Evening News*, 3 February 1919; *Dundee Courier*, 3 February 1919; *Glasgow Observer*, 8 February 1919; *New York Times*, 3 February 1919.
14. Sassoon did not stay long and 'realized he was completely unqualified to produce' the article for *Nation* required of him, so he asked Independent Labour Party member, John Langdon Davies, to write it for him; J. M. Wilson, *Siegfried Sassoon: The Making of a War Poet* (Duckworth, 2013), pp.36-7.
15. *Glasgow Herald,* 7 February 1919.
16. AD15/19/11 Doc 02, 'At a meeting of the Town Council of the City of Glasgow held within the City Chambers on Thursday 6th February 1919, Lord Provost J. W. Stewart presiding, the Lord Provost made a statement with regard to recent riotous proceedings in connection with the strike of Clyde Workers'.
17. AD15/19/11 Doc 02, 'At a meeting . . .'; JC36/31/05 [05/MM], E. R. Mitchell, Councillor; JC36/31/06 [06/B], Bailie John Stewart; AD15/19/11 Doc 02, 'At a meeting . . .'.
18. AD15/19/11 Doc 02, 'At a meeting . . .'.
19. *Glasgow Herald*, 7 February 1919.
20. *Glasgow Herald,* 18 February 1919.
21. *Glasgow Herald,* 10 February 1919.
22. J. McLean, *The Legend of Red Clydeside* (John Donald, 1999), pp.126-7, 131.
23. *Hansard*, House of Commons Debates, 2 June 1919 cc1743.
24. G. R. Rubin, 'Law as a Bargaining Weapon: British Labour and the Restoration of Pre-War Practices Act 1919', *Historical Journal*, 32.4 (1989), 925-45, *passim.*
25. CAB 24/75/16. Fortnightly Report on Revolutionary Organisations in the United Kingdom and Abroad. National Archives, Kew.

26. AD15/19/11 Doc 01, 'Papers Relating to Bail of Accused'; AD15/19/11 Doc 05, 'Bail Bonds for the Accused'.

27. HM Advocate v Robertson (1842); J. H. A. MacDonald, *A Practical Treatise on the Criminal Law of Scotland*, ed R. MacGregor Mitchell (William Paterson, 1929), pp.194-6.

28. The prosecution papers have been archived for this case at the NRS, while the defence papers have not. Attempts to find defence precognitions in other repositories have failed.

29. JC36/31/09 [09/V], Neil Maclean, MP.

30. AD15/19/11 Doc 46, 'List of Witnesses for the Defence'.

31. TD2020/1/2/2/1, 'Glasgow Trades Council: Minutes, Correspondence and other papers', Glasgow Archives.

32. JC36/31/09 [09/V], Neil Maclean, MP.

33. AD15/19/55, Herbert Strange and others; Letter procurator fiscal to Crown Agent, 21 March 1919.

34. AD15/19/11 Doc 40, 'Indictment, [Version 5]'.

35. JC26/1919/85, Document 46; Letter from Chief Constable of Edinburgh.

36. AD15/19/11, Letter from Procurator Fiscal to Crown Agent, 8 March 1919.

37. AD15/19/11, Letter from Procurator Fiscal to Crown Agent, 8 March 1919.

38. AD15/19/11, Letter from Procurator Fiscal to Crown Agent, 8 March 1919.

39. AD15/19/11, Telegram from Lord Advocate to Crown Agent, 10 March 1919.

40. AD15/19/11, Letter from Procurator Fiscal to Crown Agent, 12 March 1919.

21 The Trial, 7 to 18 April 1919

The judge appointed to preside over the trial was Lord Justice-Clerk, Charles Scott Dickson, the second-most senior judge in Scotland. The trial was held in Edinburgh, which would have reduced the possibility of demonstrations outside Glasgow's High Court and would also have made it easier to appoint a jury less likely to hold partisan views, one way or the other. Over eleven days from 7 to 18 April, the evidence against twelve men charged with the offences ranging from incitement to riot to mobbing and rioting was heard.[1] In the end, four men were found guilty: two for incitement to riot and two for mobbing and rioting.

The prosecution was led by the Lord Advocate, James Avon Clyde, KC, MP, who had been present at the crucial meetings of the War Cabinet on 30 and 31 January. His position was one of the two most senior political legal appointments in Scotland.[2] Clyde was assisted by two Advocates Depute, Mr A. M. MacRobert and Mr John L. Wark. In 1919, only a qualified advocate could represent a client in the High Court of Justiciary, who was instructed by a client's

21.1. *Some of the accused in court, April 1919. According to Shinwell's caption in* Conflict without Malice*: left to right, Shinwell; Gallacher; Ebury; Brennan; Kirkwood; Hopkins; Murray (out of copyright).*

law agent or solicitor.[3] Three King's Counsel and four junior counsel were briefed for the defence. Thus the advocates defending the accused were as follows:

Mr A. H. B. Constable, KC and Mr T. Graham Robertson represented Shinwell and Hopkins;

Mr George Watt, KC and Mr D. R. Scott represented Kirkwood, Brennan and McKenzie;

Mr J. Condie Sandeman, KC and Mr C. M. Aitchison represented Ebury, Loudon, Alexander and Murray;

Mr David M. Wilson represented Oliver and McCartney;

William Gallacher represented himself.

The List of Assize for the trial in Edinburgh included 120 names of eligible jurors drawn from the city of Edinburgh, the 'Town of Leith', and the Counties of Mid-, East and West Lothian. The fifteen men balloted to serve as the jury in the riot trial were marked in pencil with a number, from '1' to '15'.[4] Juries in Scottish criminal trials were at that time divided into two categories, 'Special' and 'Common', according to a property qualification.[5] Not until the Sex Disqualification (Removal) Act received Royal Assent later in 1919, could women serve as jurors.[6] The five 'Special' jurors were a grocer, a butcher from North Berwick, a manager, a merchant and a bank agent. The ten 'Common' jurors included a book-packer, two commercial travellers, a farm manager and a tram driver. Neither the prosecution nor the defence exercised their right of peremptory challenge to any jurors.[7]

In Scots law, corroboration of all evidence is required because 'an accused person shall not be convicted on the testimony of a single witness, no matter how credible'.[8] Additionally, the examination of witnesses was based upon their precognitions, thus the judge's and jury's 'first knowledge of the case against the accused' was delivered through the original testimony of the witnesses, who had been precognosced without making 'the evidence stronger than can be fully supported in the event of a trial'.[9] Generally, the Scots Law tradition relied on asking only questions supported by the precognition statements; in practice, however, supplementary questions were inevitably asked during a counsel's examination.[10]

The defence closing statement claimed the prosecution had fielded 'only one civilian witness who was not in the employment of the Council'.[11] Their definition of 'civilian' was not established in court, but when witnesses who were not police, tram workers or employees of the Council or another public body are extracted from the list, there were nine witnesses who are identifiable as 'civilians'.

The prosecution precognosced 173 individuals whose statements were separated into two series: witnesses called to give evidence at the trial, and those not. The former list contains 111 precognitions; the latter 62 (three additional entries in the list were duplicates of three in the first series). Of the 111, 36 were given by people who were not eventually called to give evidence. Of the 111 precognitions, 79 were policemen and eight were tramway staff, with an additional man who was both a tram clerk and a Special Constable. Of the list of 62, 30 were police and twelve tram staff. There was also the Physician to the Force. The prosecution precognosced ten women and two were called to give evidence. Seventy-five witnesses were eventually summoned to give evidence for the prosecution at the trial; of these, 55 were policemen, four tram staff (plus the Special Constable who was also a tramways clerk), and six otherwise employed by the Council, leaving nine not employed by the Council.[12]

The defence submitted an initial witness list of 1,109 names, including every policeman on duty in George Square – some of whom were listed twice – and other names of people present in various places in the week of 27 January 1919. It also included the Prime Minister, David Lloyd George, the deputy Prime Minister, Andrew Bonar Law, the Scottish Secretary, Robert Munro, Sir Robert Horne, Minister of Labour, General Fanshawe, who was commander of the Forth garrison and was appointed to command the troops in Glasgow, and Winston Churchill.[13] In the end, the defence called only 58 witnesses, four of whom were women. Only five defence witnesses to events in the Square were not in some way connected with the strike.[14] On 4 March 1919, William Shaw, Secretary of the Glasgow Trades and Labour Council, had placed an advertisement in the *Evening Citizen* seeking witnesses who had been present on 27, 29 and 31 January in George Square, in James Watt Lane, West Street, or at Mechan's works on 30 January. He also arranged for a poster to be circulated: 'if you were at the Star Palace Picture House on 30 January or George Square on 27, 29 or 31 January. . .'.[15]

The evidence of the non-aligned witnesses on both sides is particularly important, notably when it contradicts the prosecution or defence lines of argument, or corroborates it in terms not replicated by the main cohorts of witnesses. The tram crew and their immediate superiors, the inspectors, felt they had been treated roughly by the strikers, subjected to physical and verbal abuse and described their ordeal in compelling detail. One of the 'civilian' defence witnesses had been batoned by the police and clearly still held a grudge. However, these witnesses were still subject to the process of precognoscing with all the possible effects of Buckley *et al*'s list of processes, described in Chapter 3, which might have affected their evidence.

Analysis of the precognitions suggests that those for prosecution witnesses provided a coherent narrative of what the witness claimed to have seen, which were recorded within 21 days of the events described, and were used at trial by the prosecution advocate to elicit an answer to a specific question seeking confirmation of an evidential detail. For example, 'Whom did you see standing on the plinth of the Gladstone Statue on 29 January?', which might elicit the answer 'I saw Shinwell, Kirkwood and Gallacher'. A more suggestive question might be, 'Did you see Shinwell, Kirkwood and Gallacher on the plinth?' to which the answer could be a straightforward 'Yes' or 'No'. Some questions allowed a witness to provide a more circumstantial and detailed reply. For example, a question posed to Rosslyn Mitchell allowed a long, uninterrupted answer. Checking the prosecution witnesses' precognitions against the trial transcripts reveals only minor differences. Of course, evidence at trial was subject to cross-examination, which often revealed problems with either prosecution or defence evidence or uncovered further details.[16]

Close scrutiny of the case papers and precognitions reveals some witnesses for both sides lied, some more obviously than others. Some may have come to believe they had seen things they could not, or felt it was justifiable to 'edit' their evidence or to swear to what they felt 'had to have happened', or to events they could not have seen, because they knew their cause was right.[17] Some witnesses on both sides colluded to present a particular version of events to support the prosecution's indictment, or the defence.

Some police witnesses were over-quick to draw direct causative effects between the speeches of strike leaders earlier in the week and the violence on Friday. Detective Sergeant James Wilson was particularly forthright in his evidence, but his obviously slanted statements became counter-productive.[18] Archibald Gillies and Edith Hughes were among defence witnesses who testified with absolute certainty to events they could not possibly have seen, because they were on the other side of the Square with the crowd intervening, were in a meeting, or had not yet arrived in the Square. These discrepancies were revealed in cross-examination.[19]

At the commencement of proceedings the indictment was read and a prolonged discussion began in open court on the 'relevancy' of parts of the indictment, seeking to exclude certain charges. The first successful exclusion was the robbery charge at Hunter's jewellers in Paisley Road, partly because a charge of personal dishonesty was not considered to be of the same seriousness as the public order charges. Mr Wilson, for Oliver and McCartney, argued for a separate trial since they were not involved with the more serious charges of incitement. This was refused. Mr Constable argued that the wording of the indictment was too loose and insufficiently explicit as to what the accusations were; for example, precision as to where events happened and how the incitement was meant to have occurred – by word of mouth or in writing.[20] Representing himself, Gallacher argued it could not be shown that the people who caused the trouble in the Square and elsewhere had been the same who had attended his speeches earlier in the week.[21] The Lord Advocate argued against the objections, concluding, 'a man who incited an assembly to meet for an illegal purpose was not entitled to turn around and say, "Oh, well, the crowd went a good deal further than I intended"'. The Lord Justice-Clerk rejected Gallacher's argument.[22]

All the accused pleaded 'not guilty' except Gallacher, who refused to plead. The Crown then led its first witness without preamble, as is the norm in Scottish proceedings. The public attendance at the trial was, after the busy first day, very variable.[23]

The Crown case was completed at 3.30pm on Friday 11 April, after which Councillor Mitchell, the first witness for the defence, was called.[24] To avoid the case extending into a third week, it was decided to sit on Saturday. None of the accused was called to give evidence, although they might have been.[25]

On the morning of Thursday 17 April, the prosecution and defence addressed the jury. Although their statements were not transcribed into the court record, the *Glasgow Herald* provided a detailed account, corroborated by other newspapers.[26] The Lord Advocate spoke for an hour and three-quarters and was followed by three senior and one junior counsel for the defence: Mr Constable, KC, representing Shinwell and Hopkins, dealt with the broader aspects of the whole case before Mr Watt, KC, Mr Sandeman, KC, and Mr D. M. Wilson summed-up for their clients. William Gallacher summed up his own defence. This occupied the rest of the day.

The Lord Advocate said the Crown had laid before the jury evidence in support of all the charges in the indictment, except the alleged incitement at the Star Picture House on 30 January, on which they were not required to reach a verdict. He explained that in investigating disorder in a great crowd, it was inevitable that no single witness could see the events as a whole. As a consequence, he said, the evidence had had to be presented 'in a great many little bits that made up a mosaic which had to be put together in order to show the drift and significance of the facts'. He warned the jury they might find 'two witnesses gave a different account of the same incident, because one might see only the beginning of it and the other might see only the end of it'.[27] As a key requirement in Scots Law, one person's part testimony could be corroborated by the facts or circumstances of another's account, so that it was 'sufficient if a complete chain of evidence is established'.[28] He emphasised the seriousness of the events and the threats to public order in George Square and the other places listed in the indictment, and set out the three elements that together constituted the crime of mobbing and rioting:

- there must be an assembly gathered together;
- the assembly acts with a common purpose 'for some illegal object';

- members of the crowd must have committed either breaches of the peace or 'such acts as terrorised the lieges'.

It is the common purpose that distinguishes the offence from a breach of the peace. A person could be guilty of the crime of mobbing and rioting in two ways, that:

- 'every disorderly act of the mob was chargeable against everyone in the mob, although there may be degrees of guilt';
- 'the instigator was just as responsible as the perpetrator'.[29]

The Lord Advocate claimed the events were 'steeped in illegality' from 27 to 31 January, starting with the hoisting of the red flag and Shinwell's remark to the crowd about taking over the Municipal Buildings. The Lord Advocate did not say it was a 'set and deliberate plan to storm the Bastille', but 'it put into the minds of the crowd the idea of disorderly occupation of the Municipal Buildings and familiarised the crowd with ideas of violence'. Gallacher had 'gone one better' by adding the hotel. The Lord Advocate noted it had been suggested these were jokes and pointed out 'the events of the week were no joke'. He noted that Wednesday's deputation had furthered the threats and criticised Neil Maclean's efforts to characterise them differently as a 'wire-drawn [i.e. a contrived] effort'. He reminded the jury that after the deputation had left, Shinwell had told the crowd in the Square that they had informed the Lord Provost that if he did not stop the trams the strikers would do it for themselves.

Regarding Ebury's speech in West Street, the Lord Advocate claimed, 'if they did not directly advise force, certainly powerfully suggested it'. He said at Mechan's Yard, Brennan had referred to the overflow meeting in the City Chambers, which 'was no joke to men whose blood was on the boil'. He said that the evidence convicted Shinwell, Kirkwood, Gallacher, Ebury and Brennan 'of a series of deliberate incitements to violence' which included 'the disorderly occupation of the City Chambers, putting the cars off the streets, and resistance to the police'. He recognised that 'much of what was done on the Friday was the action of hotheads, but hotheads made a mob'.

He recalled McKenzie had 'smashed a window of one of the cars in the Square' and Murray had been 'heard shouting, "Rush the police" and was later observed 'taking active part in the rioting in Cathedral Street'.

The Lord Advocate mentioned the defence argument that 'the riot that day was made not by the mob but by the police' who had either planned for a disturbance or 'simply went berserk'. He maintained this was absurd if they recalled the numbers involved in the Square: 140 police 'under the eye of the Chief Constable' and 25,000 other persons. He remarked that although Shinwell had 'evaporated, either through prudence on his own part or through want of the vigilance of the authorities', he bore more of 'the criminal responsibility for the action of the mob' as he 'played a leading part in the suggestions and incitements during the week to persons whose blood was on the boil'. Finally, he described events in North Frederick Street and the arrest of Loudon and Murray, before turning to the rest of the day's disorder in Trongate and Jail Square, where he believed 'every act of revolution was in progress and could be traced to the previous incitement'.[30]

Appearing for Shinwell and Hopkins, Mr Constable, KC, told the jury they could not find Shinwell guilty of incitement without first being 'satisfied that he incited this particular crowd to assemble for one or other of these specific illegal purposes'. He asked them to consider if the crowd had been 'animated by a common, preconceived, preconcerted purpose to do mischief'. He submitted the Crown's case 'had completely broken down' and there had been 'no preconcerted design to do mischief'. Therefore, if the crowd had not assembled 'with a preconceived purpose to do mischief, did it subsequently assume that character?' He concluded 'some of the baton charges were made without any excuse or provocation' and the Crown's insistence that cries of 'Rush the police' were accompanied by a 'cloud of missiles flying and a rush to attack the Municipal Buildings' was 'simply a grossly distorted and exaggerated story brought forward to excuse the acts of the police', although he admitted events in the south-east corner had provided 'a great deal to try the temper of the police'. He asked the jury to acquit Hopkins because no one had done 'more to preserve order'. Regarding Shinwell, unless the jury was satisfied the crowd had 'assembled with a preconceived arrangement and intention to do mischief', then the charge of incitement could not stand.[31]

Mr George Watt, KC, acting for Kirkwood, Brennan and McKenzie, told the jury that only 40 or 50 witnesses, out of the hundreds available, had been brought to court. He asserted that the Crown's case of a preconceived notion designed to engage in mobbing and rioting had failed. He noted that 75 witnesses had appeared for the Crown, 67 of whom were policemen or detectives or persons in the employment of the Corporation (actually 66) and there was only one civilian witness who was not in the employment of the Corporation. This is untrue. As discussed above, there were nine witnesses who were not employed by the Corporation. Watt then attacked the veracity of the police witnesses on the basis of his long experience at the Bar, that 'they exemplified the old saying that the wish was father to the thought'; in other words, they had lied. He appealed to McKenzie's youth and emphasised that he had been charged only with breaking a window on the basis of a single prosecution witness's evidence. Regarding Brennan, 'an inoffensive youth', it had been 'proved beyond the shadow of a doubt that [he] never uttered the words attributed to him by the Crown at Mechan's Works'. Regarding Kirkwood, the photograph of him being assaulted from behind showed there had been no crowd near at the time for Kirkwood to incite.[32]

Mr Sandeman, KC, for Ebury, Loudon, Alexander and Murray, said the Lord Advocate had chosen to present the case as a 'melodrama, and a wild one' at that, in which Ebury had a speaking part and the others silent parts. He averred that no 'policeman ever had any doubt about anything, and there never was any inconsistency in the evidence of policemen which one found to occur between two civilian witnesses of the same event'. He argued that the trouble had been caused 'by the hasty action of the police, and the story placed before them with such brilliance and skill by the Lord Advocate that morning was a fairy story'. There had never been any serious intention to wreck the Municipal Buildings and the Station Hotel. He argued, if the crowd had gone with intent to cause mischief, 'they would have gone armed, not with guns or revolvers, but some weapons of offence in the form of stone or brick, or missile of some kind'. The police had not invited trouble 'that morning, but they were looking for it' and events in the south-east corner 'when they were clearing the cars' had provided the opportunity. Mr Wilson, appearing for Oliver and McCartney, spoke briefly to say there was no evidence to show Oliver 'took any active part in connection with the strike, and he was not likely to associate himself with acts of violence'; McCartney had remained at work until Wednesday, which seemed to exonerate him from involvement on Friday.[33]

Finally, William Gallacher summed-up his own defence. He alone had 'made any reference to the North British Station Hotel' and he had 'learned that the authorities were going to include his remarks in the charge' while in jail; he took sole responsibility for any criminal offence attached to his reference to the hotel. He denied having spoken the 'other words alleged to have been spoken by him', and if he had anticipated trouble, 'he would not have brought his wife from Paisley to George Square' on 31 January. He maintained the crowd had had 'their backs to the police when they were batoned' although he did not make the distinction that this only described those standing listening to his speech. The police had 'concocted the story' about the trams to justify their 'brutal conduct' which had been unprovoked. He claimed to have been 'hit from eight to ten times by batons' and he had retaliated 'and would do the same again'. His appeal to the crowd to depart, he believed, had 'had a good effect, and was in accordance with his whole conduct'. He maintained that the police 'had failed to get any evidence of conspiracy' against him or the other accused. Throughout the strike 'he had acted lawfully, and was not ashamed of anything' he had said or done.[34]

By the close of the speeches the Lord Advocate had revised the charges, which he circulated in a letter to the jury: as there was no evidence of incitement against Hopkins for 27 January, that charge now applied only to Shinwell and Gallacher. On 29 January, the charge of incitement was against only Shinwell, Gallacher and Kirkwood; and for 30 January, the charges were against Shinwell at James Watt Lane, Ebury in West Street and Brennan at Mechan's Yard. Thereafter, the judge decided to adjourn for the day because there was insufficient time for him to give his charge to the jury. He joked 'the jury would get away then, or if they did not it would be their own fault'.[35]

1. The court sat on Saturday 12 April. See previous chapter.
2. The Lord Advocate remains the chief public prosecutor for Scotland and the Crown Office and the Procurators Fiscal act in his name.
3. E. R. Keedy, 'Criminal Procedure in Scotland I', *Journal of the American Institute of Criminal Law and Criminology*, vol.3 (1912), p.737.
4. AD15/19/11 Doc 28, 'List of Jurors'.
5. Jury Trials (Scotland) Act 1815, s24; E. R. Keedy, 'Criminal Procedure in Scotland I', pp.752-53.
6. Women did not appear on juries at the High Court of Justiciary until early 1921; L. Heren, *Sex and Violence in 1920s Scotland* (Bloomsbury, 2024).
7. E. R. Keedy, 'Criminal Procedure in Scotland II', *Journal of the American Institute of Criminal Law and Criminology*, vol.3, issue 6 (1913), p.837. As an indication of the status of some of the jurors, Mr Terris died two days after the case closed. His widow had no savings left after paying for his funeral and could not meet the rent. She applied to the Lord Advocate, and the Crown Office authorised a payment to her of £10 'in the exceptional circumstances'; AD15/19/11 Doc 16,
8. Keedy, 'Criminal Procedure in Scotland II', p.837.
9. Keedy, 'Criminal Procedure in Scotland II', p.836.
10. R. S. Shiels, 'The Mid-Victorian Codification of the Practice of Public Prosecution', *Scottish Historical Review,* 98 (2019), p.419.
11. *Glasgow Herald,* 18 April 1919.
12. AD15/19/11, James Cummings, Owen McQuade, George Binnie, Arthur Smith, Thomas Graham, Lawrence Stewart, Agnes Gilfillan or MacFarlane, John Gray, Farquhar McVean. Among those listed but not called was Inspector MacDonald, who had been so severely injured in Cathedral Street that he was too ill to attend and had been sent to the Highlands to convalesce on Dr Halliday's instructions; AD15/19/11, Letter from Dr Halliday to Procurator Fiscal, 2 April 1919.
13. AD15/19/11, Document 46; List of witnesses for the Defence.
14. Three further 'civilian' witnesses gave evidence only about Oliver's and McCartney's absence from the Square on the 31 January.
15. AD15/19/11, *Citizen*, 4 March 1919.
16. The style of questions posed and answers elicited in court suggest defence precognitions had actually been taken. However, a lengthy search for them with various archival bodies in Scotland has failed to discover them.
17. See discussion in Chapter 3.

18. AD15/19/11 [A33], James Wilson, Detective Sergeant.
19. JC36/31/07 [07/T], Edith Hughes, Strike Committee; JC36/31/08 [08/J], Archibald, Gillies, Engineer.
20. *Glasgow Herald,* 8 April 1919.
21. *Glasgow Herald*, 8 April 1919.
22. *Glasgow Herald*, 8 April 1919.
23. *Glasgow Herald*, 11 April 1919.
24. *Glasgow Herald*, 12 April 1919.
25. Keedy, 'Criminal Procedure in Scotland II', p.838; after the Criminal Evidence Act of 1898, the accused could be called to give evidence but was not compelled to.
26. *Glasgow Herald*, 18 April 1919.
27. *Glasgow Herald*, 18 April 1919.
28. Keedy, 'Criminal Procedure in Scotland II', p.837.
29. *Glasgow Herald*, 18 April 1919.
30. *Glasgow Herald*, 18 April 1919.
31. *Glasgow Herald*, 18 April 1919.
32. *Glasgow Herald*, 18 April 1919.
33. *Glasgow Herald*, 18 April 1919.
34. *Glasgow Herald*, 18 April 1919.
35. *Glasgow Herald*, 18 April 1919.

22 The Charge to the Jury and the Verdicts

The judge's direction to the fifteen-man jury was recorded verbatim in the transcript of the trial.[1] It is 87 pages and roughly 22,000 words long. His address covered the law, how that might affect their consideration of their verdicts on the charges of incitement, and of mobbing and rioting, particularly as so much of the prosecution and defence evidence was contradictory. Its length is partly due to his thoroughness in setting out the jury's responsibilities and rehearsing what he saw as key points of the case. In places he informed the jury directly, or hinted very strongly, that no case had been made against several of the accused. The Lord Justice-Clerk went out of his way to compliment Gallacher, whose performance in his own defence might not have been 'quite so finished as the Counsel with whom he was associated for the Defence', but he had 'played the game quite fairly'. He believed the jury had 'paid marked attention' to the evidence and concluded his introductory remarks:

> as men of commonsense and judgement, if there is any reasonable doubt whether the [Crown] case has been proved, then the Accused are entitled to get the benefit of that reasonable doubt.

The Lord Justice-Clerk first set out the relevant law concerning 'mobbing and rioting' and 'instigating and inciting'. First, there had to be 'an assemblage of men, big or little'; twelve were sufficient and in this instance they were 'dealing with an assembly of some 20,000 or 25,000 people'. Second, 'that assembly must be animated by a common purpose . . . to do something that is contrary to law'; a 'preconcerted determination' or one 'formed after a large crowd has assembled for a perfectly legitimate purpose' sufficed. Last, the result must be 'a breach of the peace to the alarm of the lieges'.[2] Regarding 'instigation' and 'incitement', this meant 'counselling a crime before it is determined upon'. The Lord Justice-Clerk quoted:

> you need not exactly tell a man in precise language the particular thing he has to do, but if your language is addressed to a man, and is likely to help him or to instigate him to go and do a crime, that is enough . . . On the other hand, though the result was not directly intended by the instigator, still if that which he counselled was not unlikely to have the consequences which did result, he is guilty.

Some of the orators' ill-judged 'performative radicalism' during the week may have crossed this line, especially when referring to the trams.

He explained that the indictment fell into three parts. First, the charges of instigation against Shinwell, Gallacher, Kirkwood, Brennan, Ebury and Hopkins. The judge reminded the jury there was 'insufficient evidence to convict Hopkins of incitement' and directed them to find him not guilty of 'incitement or instigation'. He also noted the withdrawal of the charge in relation to events at the Star Picture House on 30 January, reminding the jury the Lord Advocate had set out clearly who was accused individually of what, where and when: George Square – Shinwell, Gallacher, Kirkwood; James Watt Lane – Shinwell; West Street – Ebury; and Brennan at Mechan's.

In all cases the accused were charged with inciting crowds to attend George Square on Friday, for the purpose of performing illegal acts. The Lord Justice-Clerk counselled the jury to dismiss any charges of incitement on 27 January, because on Monday nobody had imagined there would be a meeting on Friday. This meant 'striking out the charge against Shinwell and Gallacher' for Monday and also any consideration of threats against the North British Station Hotel. The judge also determined that charges against Kirkwood and Hopkins for Monday should be struck out. He made no mention at this stage of Kirkwood's alleged incitement of the crowd from the library window on Friday. Then he turned to the red flag, which he dismissed as having 'nothing to do with this charge' but acknowledged that a red flag 'has the capacity . . . of inciting paroxysms of excitement and derision in some persons, and of exciting enthusiasms beyond bounds in others'. He considered it had been 'a trifling incident'.

He accepted the defence evidence that Wednesday's delegation to the Lord Provost had been suggested by and largely formed from the crowd. He moved on to exactly what had been said at the various places alleged, 'about which there is a great conflict of evidence' presenting examples of how the prosecution and defence accounts contradicted each other. He took a moment to consider the attacks made by the defence on the reliability of the police evidence, saying, 'it would be a very unfortunate thing if police evidence were not to be regarded as reliable evidence' and their testimony should be believed 'just as we take the evidence of other honest people, high or low, rich or poor, as being, generally speaking, honest evidence'. He asked the jury to balance any doubt in the police's honesty with their judgement of the defence evidence 'given by Trades Union people'. He noted the paucity of independent witnesses for both sides suggesting 'private and uninterested citizens' would have stayed clear of George Square on 31 January. He asked whether the words spoken by the accused on the Wednesday or Thursday had been 'calculated [or] likely to induce those who were addressed to commit a breach of the law?' Was the language used 'a direct incentive to violent proceedings on the Friday?'

In dealing with the delegation's conversation with the Lord Provost on Wednesday, the Lord Justice-Clerk relied most upon Neil Maclean's and the Town Clerk's testimonies. He seems to have concluded, whatever the delegation thought they had said, that the Lord Provost and Town Clerk *heard* and interpreted their words as threats against the tram system and against public order. At the end of a lengthy comparison between the evidence of these two witnesses, he reminded the jury this was not a primary concern because its value was retrospective. However, concerning what had been said in the Square afterwards by Shinwell and Gallacher, those words *were* important.

Forty pages into his summing-up, the Lord Justice-Clerk was reaching the end of that part of the charge concerning 'incitement'. Now that Kirkwood and Hopkins had been discounted, he stressed the seriousness of the charges brought against men in Shinwell's and Gallacher's position, that they had 'deliberately incited their fellow-workmen, their fellow Trades Unionists, to take part in a serious riot' in a city with its a 'very large population that are quite willing to take advantage of any disorder'. If the jury decided any of them were guilty, then he felt Brennan and Ebury had not taken as prominent a part in the week's events as Shinwell and Gallacher.[3]

The mobbing and rioting charge was made against all twelve accused. In relation to the supposed plan to take over the hotel, the judge reminded the jury that many demonstrators had passed by it and if the crowd had indeed been incited to take the hotel, nobody seemed to have paid any heed to that alleged incitement.

Regarding the trams, he highlighted again the conflict of evidence concerning what happened at the south-east corner and the northern side of the Square. The Crown claimed the crowd had come for an illegal purpose, but the judge reminded the jury to consider 'that there was undoubtedly a perfectly legitimate object for the crowd to gather there on Friday' which was 'to get an answer to the telegram', a purpose that 'would not bring them within miles of an infraction of the criminal law'. But the Crown averred the crowd also had an illegitimate aim to 'wilfully and deliberately' stop the traffic, yet the defence claimed there had been no deliberate 'design', only the effect of a crowd of 20,000-25,000 in the Square which had held up the tram cars. 'Every policeman who spoke about it said they were wilful and deliberate, and every Trade Unionist said it was nothing of the kind'. Again, the jury had to decide.

He reconsidered the key points made by both sides – the 'most absolute conflict of evidence' – before turning to the Town Clerk's evidence. Sir John had seen people gathering in the corner; Tram Inspector Imrie and Cummings, the commercial traveller, had described deliberate attempts to stop the traffic, the verbal abuse and physical threats. The Lord Justice-Clerk considered this evidence 'simple and strong'. He noted the defence line, 'If we had wanted to stop the tramway traffic, that place at South Frederick Street is not nearly as vulnerable as some place nearby', where a stoppage would have been more effective.

He alluded to assertions that 'you are here trying the police' whose conduct of affairs was alleged to have given 'just as much reason for putting the police in the dock as the accused'. He pointed out that the Lord Advocate was there only to present a case, not to speak in defence of the police who had no-one to speak on their behalf. He acknowledged that the police had indeed 'struck a good many people who had nothing to do with the strike' or the mob, but that was 'just one of the evils of mobbing and rioting' and if 'a baton charge takes place I am afraid it often happens that many innocent people are hit and suffer'. He regretted the idea that the police force 'which we rely on to keep order . . . would just take it into their heads because their blood is up' and they were 'anxious to show what capital police they were' in front of the Chief Constable, Lord Provost, Town Clerk, the Sheriff, to hit 'people's heads'. The thought did 'not commend itself' but again the jury had to decide. Gallacher had made a 'good jury point': would he have fomented a riot to which he took his wife? Concerning Kirkwood's alleged encouragement to the crowd to commit violence against the police, there was only one witness, Superintendent McCulloch (whose colleague had been too ill to attend court). He noted that members of the delegation, including Maclean, contradicted this, thus could Superintendent McCulloch's uncorroborated statement be taken as 'proof of what would have been a most monstrous thing [for Kirkwood] to say'? Revisiting Kirkwood's entrance into the Square and the witnesses who said he had made further cries to incite the crowd, the judge noted again the absolute contradiction between the prosecution and defence evidence: 'Well, you cannot reconcile these two stories . . . was Kirkwood acting the part of the peacemaker, or was he trying to encourage the mob in resisting the police?' The jury's eventual verdict shows who they chose to believe. And then he considered Shinwell. Even though 'Mr Shinwell – I do not use the word offensively – just disappeared' and may have taken no part in the riot, if found guilty of incitement, he would be 'just as liable as if he was personally present'.[4]

Turning to Brennan, Ebury and Hopkins, he thought 'there is very little evidence against them of having actually participated in the rioting' and considered that Hopkins 'could not be found guilty of any part of the indictment'. If the jury did not find Brennan and Ebury guilty of incitement, then he thought they 'ought to acquit them of the whole business'.

Having dealt with six of the accused, he turned to the others. Of these, matters seemed clear only in the cases of Murray, who had thrown missiles and was party to the window smashing in Cathedral Street, and McCartney, who had been seen on the back of one of the looted lorries on Jamaica Bridge, picking up a broken bottle and seen throwing bottles. It was alleged he had been an active part of the mob.

The Lord Justice-Clerk then closed his address:

> There is no question that a very grievous wrong was done in Glasgow on the 31st of January last, a most serious offence was committed, but the question you have to consider is, has it to your minds been proved by the Crown that these accused, or any of them, and if so, which of them, were guilty in whole or in part of this indictment.

During his charge to the jury, the Lord Justice-Clerk had told, advised or strongly hinted that they should dismiss the charges against five of the twelve accused: Kirkwood, Hopkins, Brennan, Ebury and Oliver.[5] He had made no recommendation in the case of the other men: McKenzie, accused of breaking the tram window, and Loudon and Alexander, accused of impeding Mennie and aiding Gallacher.

The jury returned their verdicts by a majority of 14 to 1: Shinwell and Gallacher 'guilty of incitement'; Kirkwood, Brennan, Hopkins, Ebury, McKenzie, Loudon and Alexander all not guilty. Oliver was also found not guilty, but Murray and McCartney, against whom evidence of engaging in the violence was clearest, were found 'guilty of mobbing and rioting'. The jury recommended Gallacher to the judge's leniency because of his efforts 'to induce the crowd to disperse peacefully'.[6] Then counsel made pleas in mitigation. Gallacher's final statement ended with 'I have nothing to regret, and I am prepared to face any consequences that might arise out of my actions'.[7]

The Lord Justice-Clerk said because Shinwell had already been in prison for three weeks he would 'limit the sentence to one of five months imprisonment'. Gallacher, Murray and McCartney, also in prison for the same period, were sentenced to three months each. As McLean contends, 'neither judge nor jury was in much sympathy with the Crown submission that Bloody Friday was the culmination of a violent and illegal conspiracy'.[8] MacAskill notes how even-handed and clear the judge's charge and advice to the jury had been concerning which accused should be acquitted.[9] Clearly, this had been no show trial with a predetermined verdict to railroad the strike leadership.

The following day, the *Glasgow Herald* offered a relatively (for it) subdued editorial, describing the sentences as 'a providential anti-climax' after a 'long and tedious' trial. However, with a revival of its overblown rhetoric it also bemoaned the lenient sentences in the face of 'the first steps to Bolshevism' and trusted the 'misguided men' led by Shinwell and Gallacher had realised, in the light of chaos in Central and Eastern Europe, the 'horrors of the abyss to whose edge they dragged the community'.[10]

There was widespread condemnation in labour circles of what had happened in the Square, and many meetings of protest were held, following absolutely the strike leaders' version of events, blaming the police for unjustified violence. There were also, however, widespread recriminations.[11] At the STUC meeting in May 1919, criticism was voiced over the backing of a strike disowned by union executives, and in breach of agreements already made. An Edinburgh member of the STUC Parliamentary Committee described the strike as 'the outcome of hasty and unwise action'. The chairman of Edinburgh Trades Council had said during the strike, 'in this 40 hours movement all semblance of democracy had been thrown to the winds . . . the way in which [the strike] was started was a disgrace to trades unionism'.[12]

The trial has been described briefly in a number of histories and, of course, in the memoirs of the accused. Peter Slowe's account informs us that Shinwell hoped the case against him might be 'lost in the detail', but witness 'Detective Constable [sic] Coulter . . . read out resounding and damning extracts from Shinwell's own notebook' to the court. Slowe claimed the Lord Justice-Clerk had said that the notebook 'gave a good account of Shinwell's deficiencies of character' and although it did not prove incitement to riot, Slowe concluded 'Nevertheless, a good deal of damage had been done'.[13] This is misleading, because the effect of the readings was hardly 'damning'. Detective Inspector Coulter did indeed read out extracts and defence counsel asked him to read other extracts to show the notebook contained drafts of an article. Although Slowe claims the Lord

Justice-Clerk said, 'It is quite plain it must have been written before the election' in December 1918, in fact he made no reference at all to Shinwell's notebook in his charge to the jury, nor did he refer to the 'injuries of a fifteen-year-old boy whose head had been cracked open' as Slowe claims.[14] In common with some other writers including Shinwell, Kirkwood 'remembered' that Shinwell and Gallacher were the only two found guilty, the other ten being freed.[15] After counsel for the other accused had described their shining characters, Gallacher recalled in his 1936 memoir that he had been left to face the jury as 'the villain of the piece' and also remembered himself and Shinwell as the only pair found guilty.[16]

How just were the verdicts? Two men were found guilty only of mobbing and rioting. Murray, an ex-policeman, had been seen urging the crowd to attack the police in the south-east corner of the Square, taking a leading role in the riot in Cathedral Street, holding an iron bar and throwing missiles for a considerable time. McCartney was arrested south of the river, having been seen on one of the looted beer lorries, and holding a broken bottle on Jamaica Bridge. On arrest, he was found to be armed with a butcher's knife. Their sentences are comparable to similar crimes for the period.[17]

The verdicts on Shinwell and Gallacher were seen in labour circles as unfair; Shinwell's entry in the *Dictionary of National Biography* goes so far as to claim he was 'wrongly alleged to have been involved in the disturbances'.[18] The Crown case that there had been a conspiracy certainly failed, but both men had used violently-expressed language to large and mixed crowds whose 'blood was on the boil', which appears at the very least irresponsible in the extreme, especially in relation to the constant harping about closing the tram system. As the Lord Advocate summed it up, their speeches had 'familiarised the crowd with ideas of violence'. He had explained to the jury one 'need not tell a man in precise language the particular thing he has to do, but if your language is addressed to a man, and is likely to help him or to instigate him to go and do a crime, that is enough', and the 'counsel must take effect, the advice, the prompting, the instigation must have this result, that the man to whom it is addressed takes it and goes either of his own motive, or aided and encouraged by it, and carries out his illegal design'. The jury's verdicts clearly indicated they believed Shinwell and Gallacher had indeed 'calculated' or induced 'those who were addressed to commit a breach of the law'.[19]

Iain McLean underplays the simmering hostility to the 'treacherous' tram workers that had been seen all week and the obvious frustration of the strike leadership with the continued running of the tram system, which had been expressed publicly more than once.[20] The efforts to stop the traffic in both the south-east and, less successfully, north-east corners appear to have been deliberate, as reported even by the sympathetic correspondent of the *Daily News*. Caught in the middle, the evidence of the tram workers has previously been ignored. Exhaustive reading of the precognitions and trial transcript suggests that a proportion of the crowd intended to make a demonstration by stopping the 'treacherous' tram crews for the duration of the meeting in the Square, to which the strike leaderships' performative rhetoric during the week had contributed.

---

1. JC36/31/10, 'Trial Transcript from the Trial of William McCartney, George Ebury, David McKenzie, Harry Hopkins, Robert Loudon, David Kirkwood, Emmanuel Shinwell, Neil Alexander, William Gallacher, James Murray, Joseph Brennan, Daniel Stewert Oliver for the Crime of Mobbing and Rioting at George Square, Glasgow and Other Locations. Tried at High Court, Edinburgh. Tried on 7 Apr 1919'.
2. 'Alarm of the lieges' expresses the sense not of personal fear, but, of 'alarm lest if what is going on is allowed to continue it will lead to the breaking up of social peace'; Lord Justice-Clerk Macdonald, 1889, Ferguson v Carnochan, Official Reports 16R (J) 93).
3. JC36/31/10, The Lord Justice-Clerk's charge to the jury.
4. This is the Scots Law principle of 'art and part'; J. H. A. Macdonald, *A Practical Treatise on the Criminal Law of Scotland*, ed R. MacGregor Mitchell, 4th edn (W. Green, 1929), p.3.
5. Stolen jewellery was found on Oliver, but the relatively minor offence of theft had been struck from the indictment.
6. JC36/31/10, The Lord Justice-Clerk's charge to the jury.
7. JC36/31/10, The Lord Justice-Clerk's charge to the jury.
8. I. McLean, *The Legend of Red Clydeside* (John Donald, 1999), p.129.
9. K. MacAskill, *Glasgow 1919: The Rise of Red Clydeside* (Biteback, 2019), p.244; JC36/31/10, The Lord Justice-Clerk's charge to the jury.
10. *Glasgow Herald*, 19 April 1919.

11. I. McLean, *The Labour Movement in Clydeside Politics, 1914-1922* (Dphil thesis, University of Oxford, 1972), pp.197ff.

12. Chairman, Edinburgh Trades Council, *Glasgow Herald*, 29 January 1919.

13. P. Slowe, *Manny Shinwell: An Authorised Biography* (Pluto Press, 1993), pp.96-7.

14. Slowe, *Shinwell*, pp.96-7, 98; JC36/31/10, The Lord Justice-Clerk's charge to the jury.

15. D. Kirkwood, *My Life of Revolt* (Harrap, 1935), p.174; E. Shinwell, *I've Lived through It All* (Gollancz, 1973), p.46.

16. Gallacher, *Revolt*, p.168.

17. For example, AD15/20/73, a rape case which included previous charges for breach of the peace and assault.

18. K. Morgan 'Shinwell, Emanuel, Baron Shinwell', *Oxford Dictionary of National Biography* (Oxford University Press, 1996).

19. JC36/31/10, The Lord Justice-Clerk's charge to the jury.

20. McLean, *Legend*, p.133.

23 Conclusion

The proper job of a historian is not to celebrate myths, however, but to figure out what actually happened, however much that might complicate cherished national stories.[1]

A great effort has been made here to present the evidence dispassionately, so that for the first time in over 100 years, the history of Bloody Friday can be read by a wider audience without recourse to the thousands of pages of original source material. The socialist (Louise) and the Liberal (Gordon) have argued every point where one believed the other's possible bias was visible, a process which we believe has produced a reasonably balanced account. The evidence has been allowed to lead the narrative and the analysis, as the historiography of the Battle is replete with 'analysis' that too often bears no relation to the events it purports to make sense of.

In the course of research we have been told that the desire to explore the evidence for the events and their proximate causes reflects 'no interest in interpreting the events of Bloody Friday or in discussing its meaning', and that in addressing the evidence, we have missed the point that 'the myth is the history' now.[2] But surely 'interpreting the events' based on a far from thorough investigation of the archival sources has prevented their full understanding and proper interpretation? There should be room not only to explore the power and meaning of the mythology, but also to compare the mythology with a critically evaluated version of events more securely founded on the evidence. And the deliberate creation and indeed the careful curation of such a powerful but mythologised 'usable past' against the grain of the evidence is surely worth studying in itself. However, these approaches have provoked confusion and hostility, in particular amongst those who seem unwilling to consider as valid any framing of the narrative other than as an iconic event in working-class struggle told through the eyes of the strikers and strike leaders. We have been castigated for not treating Shinwell as the most important figure in the story, when his claim to fame in January 1919 is perhaps as the least reliable of all narrators.[3]

Everyone involved in the strikes, riots and trial in 1919 had an agenda. We have argued above that some of today's historians, writers, educators, members of the public and politicians are in a similar position, whether they realise it or not – one side's story is often taken as more important and, in some cases, more believable, than the other. The story of the working-class tram drivers rarely earns a mention. Stereotypical expectations of behaviour are imposed on categories of people, notably the strikers, their 'heroic' resistance and their apparently inherently trustworthy account of what happened; contrasted with the police in their inept brutality and inherently dishonest narrative. In 1919 the strike leadership tried to shift blame onto the police and onto a supposed hooligan element in the crowd; later, when convenient, they celebrated instead the strikers' violent resistance to the police, while presenting it as a 'good fight' by a crowd of thousands facing around 200 policemen. They glossed over the extreme violence and the destructive vendetta against their fellow workers in the Tramways Department pursued throughout Friday 31 January. First-hand narratives recorded decades after the events and subject to the processes set out in Chapter 3, not surprisingly, conform to the orthodox narrative. It is ironic that oral history has seen its strength in its capacity to challenge orthodoxy; in the case of the 'Battle' it has played its part in validating the orthodoxy, established for the defence at the trial and in the writings of the strike leadership.[4] The police and prosecution counsel attempted to paint the strikers as selfish malcontents threatening the citizenry of Glasgow, with fears of revolution not far behind. There were no revolutionaries, but neither were there any tanks on the streets. There were few English troops, and, crucially, no deliberate unprovoked attack on a peaceful crowd. The defence successfully reframed the story of a violent mob as one of a peaceful crowd subjected to unprovoked violence; later commentators have painted the violence as justifiable resistance. One critic appears to suggest that the presentation of fake history and indeed crude anti-English propaganda in the education system 'can safely be ignored'.[5]

On the basis of the evidence presented at trial, we suggest the two men accused of incitement and the two accused of mobbing and rioting were justly convicted, and lucky to receive such light sentences. Shinwell's and Gallacher's rhetoric, and the speeches of others, like Thom, Ebury and Brennan, had contributed to the atmosphere in the Square; in particular the naked hostility to the tram staff, through their assertion that the trams would be off the streets on Friday. This led to the blocking of the tram traffic by some as a deliberate gesture during the demonstration. Shinwell had, after all, castigated the 'miserable attitude of the Municipal Employees' Association'; he had told his audience the 'workers on strike were not going to allow friend or foe to stand in their way in enforcing the demand for the 40 hours week'; he had told the crowd on 29 January, 'if the tramcars were not stopped "You will stop them yourselves"'.[6] Gallacher had said to the crowd at the same event, 'If the strike was not settled by the end of the week they would not hesitate to stop every tramcar, shut off every light and generally paralyse the business of the city'.[7] Unwise words to men whose 'blood was on the boil'. This was not the 'heroic resistance' preferred by many writers. The subsequent violence by elements of the crowd and the hooligans who were given licence by events was 'brutal and cowardly'; hundreds of rioters ran from baton charges by a handful of policemen, and hundreds also stoned and beat individual police and tram staff who had become isolated, but, we are told, this is 'not how most Glaswegians would like their history to be presented'.[8]

The most telling conclusion was provided by the Lord Justice-Clerk in his charge to the jury. He showed how limited the establishment had considered the threat of events in Glasgow, contrary to the subsequent mythology. By 18 April 1919, concerns about Clydeside had been replaced by more pressing matters: strikes elsewhere, housing, employment and health. The raising of the red flag had been dismissed as 'a trivial incident'.[9]

What was the impact of the military deployment? Iain McLean has suggested the strike 'would certainly have collapsed, and discredited unofficial action, without any help of the government' and the intervention of the army 'gave the strike a romantic history which successfully cancelled an otherwise ignominious failure'.[10] One

23.1. *Soldiers and police on guard at the docks (out of copyright).*

of us (Louise) feels this is too binary and 'ignominious' is overstated; a compromise may have been possible. The engineers had been offered 47 hours before the strike began; the municipal workers had already established a 48-hour working week; the workforce was not entirely behind the strike – a careful reading of the hostile *Glasgow Herald* reveals how many smaller factories and workshops either had not come out or returned to work within the first week of the strike.[11] Arguably, the strike leadership's determination to achieve a 40-hour week combined with the military deployment re-invigorated a myth which had been born earlier in the century and had grown during 1915-16. After January 1919, the leadership proved insufficiently strong to intervene locally to ameliorate the difficulties experienced in a contracting economy. Their distinct success lay in various individuals' election to Westminster.

Without the retrospective confirmation of the event's significance by the deployment, how would we remember the strike and the Battle? The violence in George Square did not develop into days of looting and rioting as occurred in Liverpool during the police strike in August; the belligerence of the mob had largely died away before the army arrived. Unlike Liverpool, there was no violent interaction between troops and civilians, nor tanks parked in the streets; no-one died in Glasgow's streets. In Belfast, control of the city had largely slipped out of the hands of the local authority and the army eventually intervened in a situation where the strike organisers had been much more successful in getting key municipal workers – power, gas and transport – out on strike. But Belfast's protest has now almost faded from memory. No 'Red Belfast' legend has emerged; there was no burgeoning identity to which to attach these events; the political and sectarian divisions in Belfast, which have had a greater impact than in Glasgow, have perhaps muddied Belfast's narrative of working-class activism.

The first government strike-breaking organisation, the Industrial Unrest Committee, was set up on 4 February 1919 in the context of the London strike situation. It was established 'to make the necessary arrangements for dealing with any situation that might arise from industrial unrest both at the present moment and in the future'.[12] Parliament was not in session in January 1919: the new session only began on 4 February, with routine business starting on 11 February.[13] By then, the strikes in London and the prospect of chaos in the capital had taken centre stage. Events in Glasgow were raised in the House of Commons only once in the immediate aftermath. On 13 February a written question by Neil Maclean MP sought to establish a public inquiry, as 'strong allegations were made that the baton charge by the police was unnecessary'. This was answered by the Secretary for Scotland that there were no grounds for such allegations, and in any case 'the men arrested in connection with the disturbances are about to undergo public trial'.[14]

Thus, events in Glasgow disappeared quickly from public and political view. The strike ended; workers resumed their trades, many on the basis of the 47-hour week in place before the strike began. The men prominent in Bloody Friday entered constitutional politics and some received knighthoods and elevation to the House of Lords. Gallacher became an apologist for Stalinism, his reputation never recovering, outside communist circles, from his eulogy for

Stalin and his acquiescence in the military suppression of the Hungarian Uprising of 1956. Shinwell's hypocrisy was breathtaking: from 1945 to 1951 he was a member of a Labour cabinet that revived the 1919-39 government strike-breaking Supply Transport Committee and, according to both Ellen and Peak, used troops at least fourteen times, not, as in Glasgow in 1919, to maintain order, but actually to strike-break.[15] Kirkwood, of the three, remained largely a man of principle.

Gallacher's release from prison and his reception at a 3,000-strong meeting at Paisley Town Hall on 3 July 1919 was described in the October 1919 issue of the USA magazine *Liberator*, which took the opportunity to promote further the mythology of an unprovoked attack, and the police reacting violently to a polite suggestion that motor traffic be diverted.[16] More recently there have been two attempts to pardon retrospectively Shinwell and Gallacher (and, oddly, David Kirkwood, who was acquitted), who were , it was claimed, doing no more than demonstrating for better working conditions, and were 'imprisoned for their role in defending the rights of workers'.[17]

In 2023 yet another academic book summarised the events of 31 January 1919. It is no surprise to find 'a pre-planned move' by the police, with no mention of any other cause for the violence; that Gallacher's attack on the Chief Constable is not mentioned as the precursor to his being 'attacked by the police'; that the mythology of the police being forced back is repeated; that there is no mention of the Sheriff's role in calling for military aid, and so on.[18] This latest account is based once again on Gallacher and the contemporary socialist press, cherry-picked quotes from one mainstream newspaper article, and one or two secondary sources. It rather makes the point that our book is overdue.

---

1. I. Buruma, 'Let Them Eat Tulip Bulbs. The Complex Aftermath of Operation Market Garden. [Review] *Times Literary Supplement* (2020), p.23.
2. S. Damer, 'In the Rapids of Revolution?', *Scottish Affairs*, 28 (2019), pp.339-48, p.341. Comment by an anonymous referee of G. J. Barclay, '*The Evidence Has Always Been There*'.
3. Comments of anonymous referees.

4. H. McShane and J. Smith, *Harry McShane: No Mean Fighter* (Pluto Press, 1978), pp.106-7; Bornat, J., 'Reminiscence and oral history: parallel universes or shared endeavour?', *Ageing and Society*, 21 (2001), pp.219-41, pp.221-2.
5. Damer, 'In the rapids', p.341.
6. *Glasgow Herald*, 30 January 1919.
7. *Glasgow Herald*, 30 January 1919.
8. AD15/19/11[A76], Alexander McKendrick, Juvenile Delinquent Board; comment from anonymous referee.
9. JC36/31/10, Lord Justice-Clerk's charge to the jury.
10. I. McLean, *The Legend of Red Clydeside* (John Donald, 1999), p.138.
11. McLean, *Legend*', p.113; Minutes of the Corporation of Glasgow November 1918-April 1919, p.569.
12. K. Jeffery and P. Hennessy, *States of Emergency: British Governments and Strikebreaking since 1919* (Routledge and Kegan Paul, 1983), pp.10-11; CAB23/9/12, War Cabinet Minutes, meeting 525, 4 February 1919.
13. *Hansard* 11 February 1919.
14. *Hansard* 13 February 1919 vol 112 c324W, 'Written Answer: House of Commons 13 February 1919: Labour Dispute, Glasgow (Police Action)'.
15. G. Ellen, 'Labour and Strike-breaking 1945-1951' *International Socialism Journal,* 2.24 (1984), pp.45-73; S. Peak, *Troops in Strikes: Military Interventions in Industrial Disputes* (Cobden Trust, 1984), p.87; R. Desmarais, 'Lloyd George and the development of the British Government's strikebreaking organisation', *Journal of Contemporary History*, 6.2 (1971), 1-15.
16. C. Eastman, 'The Workers of the Clyde', *Liberator*, October 1919, p.32.
17. J. McGuire, 'Pardon call for working class heroes . . .', *Daily Record*, 29 January 2014; J. McGuire, 'Pardon for Battle of George Square working class heroes moves closer . . .', *Daily Record*, 13 February 2014; House of Commons, Early Day Motion No. 958, 'Revolt on the Clyde', 13 January 2016.
18. T. Collins, *Raising the Red Flag: Marxism, Labourism, and the Roots of British Communism, 1884–1921* (Brill, 2023), p.135-6.

Acknowledgements

First, we must acknowledge our gratitude to Serendipity, without whose attentions neither our accidental meeting nor this book would have happened.

Over the last six years, many individuals have helped us or provided support. The late Bailie Malcolm Cunning of Glasgow City Council always had an interest in the mythologisation of the Battle. He and the then Deputy Lord Provost, Philip Braat, kindly facilitated and guided our visit to the City Chambers in 2019, where we saw places which had played an important part in the events: the Lord Provost's office, the Library, various meeting rooms, the council chamber and the quadrangle where Kirkwood and Gallacher, and later the army, were photographed.

Our thanks are also due to readers of drafts of this book. Dr Bill Knox has written on this topic himself and has offered insightful and nuanced comments. Professor Lindsay Farmer's expertise in Scots Law and his keen interest in its application to historically important trials are highly valued, as is Dr Robert Shiels's tenacious encouragement. Both Professor Farmer's and Dr Shiels's exactitude in reviewing the legal aspects of this book have been warmly appreciated. Alastair Dinsmore, Curator of the Glasgow Police Museum provided much useful information. Sam McKeand helped in exploring the place of the Battle in the school history curriculum. And Niall Murphy of Glasgow City Heritage Trust helped place the original locations of the statues in George Square. John Messner, Curator, Transport and Technology at Glasgow Life, kindly provided information on the employment patterns of Tramways Department staff after 1919. We are also grateful to friends and colleagues who commented on earlier drafts of this and/or earlier texts on the reality and mythology of the 'Battle' and who provided helpful information and insights: Paul Addison, Col (ret) W.H. Clements, John Foster, Ewan Gibbs, John Graham, Paul Latawski (RMC Sandhurst), Iain McLean, Neil McLennan and Gerry Mooney.

We are grateful to the staff of various regimental archives who undertook searches for relevant material: Royal Scots; King's Own Scottish Borderers; Royal Highlanders (Seaforths); Gordon Highlanders; Black Watch; East Surrey Regiment; Durham Light Infantry; and the Royal Tank Regiment.

Russell Leadbetter and Tina McIntyre of the *Herald* newspaper provided valuable information and leads at the early stages of our research.

Anonymous referees of various versions of this manuscript, the Pen and Sword draft and earlier articles, have contributed hugely to the development of the text.

At the National Records of Scotland in Edinburgh, our thanks go to Alison Lindsay, head of the Historical Search Room and her team. Our thanks also to Dr Irene O'Brien at the Mitchell Library and City Archives in Glasgow. We are grateful to the staff of the National Library of Scotland (including the Map Library), the National Archives at Kew, the Parliamentary Archives and Glasgow University Archives, for assistance in accessing and in some cases copying material. Claire Doohan and Jamie McIntosh of the National Library of Scotland kindly facilitated access to four tapes of reminiscences that became available late in our research, when the cataloguing and conservation of the William Gallacher Memorial Library collection was completed. Rebecca Younger kindly viewed and analysed the film *What About the Workers* at the National Library of Scotland, Moving Image Archive. The London School of Economics Library aided remote access to the Shinwell Papers during the covid pandemic. BBC archives in Glasgow and London kindly provided copies of relevant documentary programmes.

The Labour History Society kindly awarded us a grant, which has greatly assisted remote access to archives, especially when they were closed to researchers during the pandemic.

Tom Johnstone did an excellent job of copy-editing, made helpful suggestions on structure and also typeset this elegant volume.

Inevitably and excitingly, new sources may continue to emerge, and we very much welcome approaches from readers who have new material to add to this history. As ever, any errors are entirely our own.

And lastly, our families have suffered us and our cast of characters for too long. Our warmest thanks go to Gordon's son Adam Barclay BSc (Psych), MSc (Psych) who helped in transcribing documents and newspapers and who commented on the 'Memory' section; to Gordon's wife, Dr Elizabeth Goring, who kindly gave considerable help with the potted biographies of key characters. Louise's husband Eric and son Louis never expected to know so much about Glasgow's century-old labour history, its legacy and its modern relevance. They appear to be quietly grateful for the knowledge.

References

Primary Sources

Glasgow City Archives

Corporation of Glasgow, *Minutes of the Corporation of Glasgow*, 30 and 31 January 1919, 2 July 1919.

TD241, 'Clyde Shipbuilders' Association, Minute Book', 1918-19

Glasgow Police Department, *Report of the Chief Constable of the City of Glasgow* (1918).

Meteorological Office, *Daily Weather Reports 1st January 1919 to 31st March 1919* (London: Meteorological Office, 1919).

Parliamentary Archives

Bonar Law Papers

Hansard 13 February 1919 vol 112 c324W, 'Written Answer: House of Commons 13 February 1919: Labour Dispute, Glasgow (Police Action)', (1919).

House of Commons, Early Day Motion No. 958, 'Revolt on the Clyde, 13 January 2016.

National Records of Scotland

AD15/19/11, 'Precognition against Joseph Brennan, Harry Hopkins, David Kirkwood, William Gallacher, Robert Loudon, Daniel Stewert Oliver, George Ebury, Neil Alexander, James Murray, Emanuel Shinwell, David McKenzie, William McCartney for the Crime of Mobbing and Rioting at George Square, Glasgow and Other Locations', 1919. The footnotes clarify whose evidence is being referenced.

AD15/19/54, 'Precognition against Joseph Comerford, Owen Campbell, Malcolm Gardner, Thomas Hanson, Charles Hendren, Hugh Higgins, Joseph Irvine, Michael Mccue, James Mcgeachan, Frank Smith for the Crime of Mobbing and Rioting at Glasgow

Road; Whistleberry Road at Craighead Colliery, Blantyre and the Public Highway, Bothwell Parish Leading Between Bothwell Bridge and Bellshill', 1919.

AD15/19/55, 'Precognition against Herbert Strange, William Wilson, William Hill, John White, Frederick Robert for the Crime of Mobbing and Rioting at George Square; James Watt Lane; North Canal Bank Street; Eddington Street; Corn Street; West Street; Union Street, Glasgow and Elsewhere in Glasgow', 1919.

JC26/1919/33, 'Trial Papers Relating to Herbert Strange, Frederick Robert or Roberts, Jogn White, William Wilson and William Hill for the Crime of Mobbing and Rioting at George Square; James Watt Lane; North Canal Bank Street; Eddington Street; Corn Street; West Street; Union Street, Glasgow and Elsewhere in Glasgow', 1919.

JC26/1919/85, 'Trial Papers Relating to Harry Hopkins, Daniel Stewert Oliver, Neil Alexander, Joseph Brennan, George Ebury, David McKenzie, William Gallacher, David Kirkwood, Robert Loudon, Emanuel Shinwell, James Murray, William McCartney for the Crime of Mobbing and Rioting at George Square, Glasgow and Other Locations', 1919.

JC36/31/01-10, 'Trial transcript from the trial of William McCartney, George Ebury, David McKenzie, Harry Hopkins, Robert Loudon, David Kirkwood, Emanuel Shinwell, Neil Alexander, William Gallacher, James Murray, Joseph Brennan, Daniel Stewert Oliver for the crime of mobbing and rioting at George Square, Glasgow and other locations'. Tried at High Court, Edinburgh. Tried on 7 Apr 1919. Folios 1 to 10.

The National Archives, Kew

CAB23/9/8, 'War Cabinet, Minutes of Meeting 521, 28 January 1919', 1919.

CAB23/9/9, 'War Cabinet, Minutes of Meeting 522, 30 January 1919', 1919.

CAB23/9/10, 'War Cabinet, Minutes of Meeting 523, 31 January 1919', 1919.

CAB23/9/12, 'War Cabinet, Minutes of Meeting 525, 4 February 1919', 1919.

CAB24/74/13, pp.1-2; 'Report No.31' *Fortnightly Report on Revolutionary Organisations in the United Kingdom and Abroad.*

MUN 1/18, Ministry of Munitions: Munitions Council Daily Reports. Report 427-446 (no. 427 Monday 3 February 1919).

WO32/4812, 'Employment of Military Forces: Aid to Civil Power (Code 53(B)): Civil Disturbances Requiring Military Intervention; Responsibility for Operations', 1919-1920.

WO32/5611, 'Employment of Military Forces: Organisation (Code 53(C)): Redistribution of Forces to Peace Stations Affecting Aid to Civil Power and Quartering of Troops; Suggestions for Effecting Economies', 1919.

WO32/8466, 'Aid to Civil Power: Procedure to Be Followed When Troops Are Required to Aid Civil Power. Report of Select Committee, 1908', 1908-1912.

WO32/18920, 'Use of Military Personnel in Aid of Civil Powers in Event of Civil Disturbances and Strikes: Great Britain', 1919.

WO32/18921, 'Use of military personnel in aid of civil powers in event of civil disturbances and strikes: publishing of information from secret army documents', 1919.

WO73/109, 'General Monthly Return of the Regimental Strength of the British Army', 1918 Jul-Dec.

WO73/110, 'General Monthly Return of the Regimental Strength of the British Army', 1919 Jan-Jun.

Newspapers

Aberdeen Daily Journal/Aberdeen Press and Journal, 1 February 1919.

Belfast Newsletter, 9 January 1919.

Daily Mirror, 1 February 1919.

Daily News, 28 January 1919; 1 February 1919; 3 February 1919.

Daily Record and Mail, 1 February 1919; 3 February 1919; 21 December 1919; J. McGuire, 'Pardon call for working class heroes . . .', *Daily Record*, 29 January 2014; J. McGuire, 'Pardon for Battle of George Square working class heroes moves closer . . .', *Daily Record*, 13 February 2014.

Daily Sketch, 1 February 1919; 3 February 1919.

Dundee Courier, 20 December 1911; 3 February 1919.

[Edinburgh] *Evening News*, 4 February 1919; 3 February 1919.

[Dundee] *Evening Telegraph and Post*, 19 December 1911.

Forward, 1 February 1919.

[Glasgow] *Evening Times*, 29 January 1919; 1 February 1919.

[Glasgow] *Evening News*, 1 February 1919.

Glasgow Herald, 14 August 1911; 27 October 1915; 28 December 1915; 14 January1919; 15 January1919; 18 January1919; 24 January1919; 28 January1919; 29 January1919; 30 January1919; 31 January 1919; 1 February 1919; 3 February 1919; 7 February 1919; 8 February 1919; 10 February 1919; 18 February 1919; 19 February 1919; 8 April 1919; 11 April 1919; 12 April 1919; 14 April 1919; 15 April 1919; 18 April 1919; 30 April 1919; 1 May 1919. Russell Leadbetter, 'Revealed: truth about the tank and Glasgow's 'Bolshevik rising', 29 January 2018.

Glasgow Observer, 8 February 1919.

Guardian/Manchester Guardian, 28 January 1919; 30 January1919; 1 February 1919; 3 February 1919; R. McKie, '100 years on: the day they read the Riot Act as chaos engulfed Glasgow', *Observer*, 6 January 2019. https://www.theguardian.com/uk-news/2019/jan/06/100-years-on-the-day-they-read-the-riot-act-in-glasgow.

Motherwell Times, 31 February 1919.

New York Times, 14 April 1919.

Preston Guardian, 26 January 1919.

Scotsman, 28 January 1919; 30 January 1919; 30 January 1919;

19 February 1919; 2 March 1919; 18 April 1919; 12 December 2020; 4 November 2022; 12 December 2020.

Strike Bulletin [No. 1] 30 January1919; [No.3] 1 February 1919; [No.4] 2 February 1919; [No.5] 3 February 1919; [No.7] 4 February 1919; [No. 8] 5 February 1919.

The Bulletin, 28 January 1919; 30 January 1919; 1 February 1919 [also Julian 1918 and other images].

The Observer, 2 February 1919.

The Times, 1 February 1919; 'Lieut.-Gen. Sir E. Fanshawe [Obituary]', *The Times* (1952), p.10.

Tramway and Railway World, 11 May 1916.

Film and Audio

BBC, TV Documentary, 'Andrew Marr's the Making of Modern Britain', in *Episode 4: Having a Ball* (2009).

BBC London, TV Documentary, 'The Revolutionaries: John Maclean' (1980).

———, TV Documentary; 'Manny at 100: The Fighter' (1984).

BBC Scotland, TV Documentary, 'Interview with Willie Gallacher' (1962).

———, TV Documentary, 'Stirring Times: John Maclean' (1997).

———, TV Documentary, 'Power to the People' (2004).

———, TV Documentary, 'Scotland: The Promised Land', in *Episode 1* (2016).

Netflix 'The Age of Tanks', TV Documentary. Netflix co-production (2017), episode 1.

Pathé Film, 'Striking Workers on the Streets of Glasgow', (1919). https://www.britishpathe.com/

Tapes held in National Library of Scotland, Special Collections, Acc.14114, William Gallacher Memorial Library: William Ferguson (24 July 1974) 3/13/2 WFA; Thomas Graham (19 July 1977) 3/13/2 TGA; Finlay Hart (13 June 1970) 3/13/2 FHA and FHB; Bob Saunders (February 1976) 3/13/2 BSA.

Secondary Sources

Ali, T., *Churchill: His Life and Crimes* (London: Verso, 2022).

Annual Register, *The Annual Register: A Review of Public Events at Home and Abroad for the Year 1919* (London: Rivingtons, 1920).

Archibald, M., *Glasgow: The Real Mean City* (Edinburgh: Black and White, 2013)

Army Great Britain, *Duties in Aid of the Civil Power* (London: War Office, 1912). (The only known copy of this document is on National Archives file WO32/18921.)

———, *The King's Regulations and Orders for the Army* (London: Army, 1912) [1914 Reprint].

Aspinwall, B., 'Glasgow Trams and American Politics 1894-1914', *Scottish Historical Review,* 56 (1977), pp.64-84.

Bambery, C, *A People's History of Scotland* (London: Verso, 2014).

Barclay, G. J., '"Duties in Aid of the Civil Power": The Deployment of the Army to Glasgow, 31 January to 17 February 1919', *Journal of Scottish Historical Studies,* 38.2 (2018), pp.261-92.

———, '"Churchill Rolled the Tanks into the Crowd": Mythology and Reality in the Military Deployment to Glasgow in 1919', *Scottish Affairs,* 28.1 (2019), pp.32-62.

———, 'A "villain for all seasons": Churchill and Scottish Mythologies of Grievance', *Finest Hour*, 189 (2020), pp.14-18.

———, '"The Evidence Has Always Been There': Unreliable Narrators and Archival Sources for the Battle of George Square, Glasgow, 31 January 1919', *Scottish Archives,* 25/26 (2021), pp.108-22.

Beckett, J. C., *The Making of Modern Ireland 1603-1923* (London: Faber and Faber, 2008).

Beliard, Y., 'Introduction: Revisiting the Great Labour Unrest, 1911-1914', *Labour History Review,* 79(1) (2014), pp.1-17.

Bell, H., *John Maclean: Hero of Red Clydeside* (London: Pluto Press, 2018)

Bell, T., *Pioneering Days: A Workers' Library* (London: Lawrence and Wishart, 1941).

———, *John Maclean, a Fighter for Freedom [with a Portrait]* (Glasgow: Communist Party, 1944).

Blake, J., 'Civil Disorder in Britain, 1910-1939: The Roles of Civil Government and Military Authority' (PhD thesis, Sussex University, 1979).

Bornat, J., 'Reminiscence and oral history: parallel universes or shared endeavour?', *Ageing and Society*, 21 (2001), pp.219-41.

Brash, R. W., *Glasgow in the Tramway Age* (London: Longman, 1971).

Broom, J., *John Maclean* (Loanhead: Macdonald Publishers, 1973).

Brotherstone, T., 'John Maclean and the Russian Revolution: A Discussion Article', *Scottish Labour History Society Journal,* 23 (1988), pp.15-29.

Brown, A., Alin, C. and Hirst, W., 'The Role of Narratorship and Expertise in Social Remembering', *Social Psychology,* 40 (2009), pp.119-29.

Brown, A., Kouri, N. and Hirst W., 'Memory's Malleability: Its Role in Shaping Collective Memory and Social Identity', *Frontiers in Psychology,* 3 (2012), article 257.

Buckley, J. J., Brainerd, C. J., and Reyna, V. F., *The Science of False Memory* (New York: Oxford University Press USA, 2005).

Burrowes, J., *Great Glasgow Stories* (Edinburgh: Mainstream, 1998; ebook 2010).

Buruma, I., 'Let Them Eat Tulip Bulbs: The Complex Aftermath of Operation Market Garden. [Review of Book *The Hunger Winter: Fighting Famine in the Occupied Netherlands, 1944-1945* by Ingrid De Zwarte (2020) Cambridge University Press]', *Times Literary Supplement* (9 October 2020), p.23.

Callwell, C. E., *Field Marshall Sir Henry Wilson, His Life Diaries*, Vol 2 (London, Cassell, 1927).

Cameron, J. and Scottish Militant Labour, *Red Flag over the Clyde: The Story of John Maclean and Red Clydeside* (Glasgow: Scottish Militant Labour, 1993).

Challinor, R., *The Origins of British Bolshevism* (Totowa, NJ: Rowman and Littlefield, 1977).

Chant, C., *World Encyclopaedia of the Tank: An International History of the Armoured Fighting Machine*, 2nd edn (Stroud: Sutton, 2002).

Churchill, W. S., *Churchill Documents: Disruption and Chaos, July 1919-March 1921* (Hillsdale: Hillsdale College Press, 2008).

———, (and Martin Gilbert), *The World Crisis 1911-1918* (London: Penguin, 2007).

Collins, T., *Raising the Red Flag: Marxism, Labourism, and the Roots of British Communism, 1884–1921* (Leiden, Brill, 2023).

Coquelin, O., 'A Strikers' "Soviet" in Belfast'? The Great Belfast Strike of 1919', *Labour History Review*, vol.87, no.3, pp.255-75 (December 2022).

Craig, M., *When the Clyde Ran Red* (Edinburgh: Mainstream Publishing, 2011, 2nd edn 2018).

Dalrymple, J., 'Tramway Labour Problems Affected by the War', *Tramway and Railway World*, 14 October 1915, pp.281-2.

Damer, S., 'Review of Mclean's 'Legend of the Red Clyde [Sic]", *History Workshop*, 18 (1984), pp.199-203.

———, *Glasgow: Going for a Song* (London: Lawrence and Wishart, 1990).

———, 'And If You Know the History . . .', *Scottish Affairs*, 28 (2019), pp.112-15.

———, 'In the Rapids of Revolution?', *Scottish Affairs*, 28 (2019), pp.339-48.

Davies, A., 'Police Violence and Judicial Bias in the Age of Mass Democracy: Glasgow 1933-1935', *Social History*, 44:1 (2019), pp.57-85.

Desmarais, R.S., 'Lloyd George and the development of the British Government's strikebreaking organisation', *Journal of Contemporary History*, 6.2 (1971), 1-15.

Devine, T. M., *The Scottish Nation: A Modern History* (London: Penguin, 2012).

Dewey, P. E., 'Military Recruiting and the British Labour Force during the First World War', *The Historical Journal*, 27 (1984), pp.199-223.

Dollan, P., 'Riot Act: when Glasgow faced an army of tanks and guns', *Sunday Mail*, 6 October 1957.

Eastman, C., 'The Workers of the Clyde', *Liberator*, October 1919, p.28-33.

Education Scotland 1999 'The Road to the Scottish Parliament'. No longer available on the ES website but available at the time of writing (March 2024) at: https://studylib.net/doc/13067795/the-road-to-the-scottish-parliament-1296---1357-1296

Education Scotland 2021 'Education Scotland review into 'Road to the Scottish Parliament': FOI release', https://www.gov.scot/publications/foi-202100199983/ See also link to 'Annex' on linked page.

Ellen, G., 'Labour and Strike-breaking 1945-1951' *International Socialism Journal*, 2.24 (1984), pp. 45-73.

Evans, R. J., *In Defence of History*, New edn (London: Granta, 2000).

Farrell, M., 'Lessons of the Great Belfast Strike of 1919', *Workers' Liberty* (2008) https://www.workersliberty.org/story/2008-12-14/lessons-great-belfast-strike-1919.

Finlay, R., 'The Turbulent Century: Scotland since 1900' in Wormald, J. (ed), *Scotland: A History* (Oxford: Oxford University Press, 2005), pp.201-24.

Fletcher, D. and Morshead, H., *Mark V Tank* (Oxford: Osprey, 2011).

Foster, J., 'Strike Action and Working-Class Politics on Clydeside 1914-1919', *International Review of Social History*, 35 (1990), pp.33-70.

———, 'Red Clyde, Red Scotland', in *The Manufacture of Scottish History*, eds I. L. Donnachie and C. A. Whatley (Edinburgh: Polygon, 1992), pp.106-124.

———, 'Working-class mobilisation on the Clyde 1917-20', in Wrigley, C. (ed), *Challenges of Labour: Central and Western Europe* (Routledge, 1993), pp.149-75

———, 'Mobilising Working Class Action on Clydeside, 1919 and 1971: How the Arguments Were Won', *Colloque Internationale Discours et Dispositivs Anti-syndicaux* (Lyon: unpublished conference paper, 2010).

———, 'The 1919 Forty Hours Strike', *Theory and Struggle,* 120 (2019), pp.30-40.

Fowler, S. and Weinbren, D., *Now the War Is Over: Britain 1919-1920* (Yorkshire: Pen and Sword Military, 2018).

Fraser, W. H. and Morris, R. J., *People and Society in Scotland: 1830-1914* (Burlington: Tanner Ritchie, 2022).

Frenda, S. J., Knowles, E. D., Saletan, W. and Loftus, E. F., 'False Memories of Fabricated Political Events', *Journal of Experimental Social Psychology,* 49 (2013), pp.280-86.

Frenda, S. J., Nichols, R. M. and Loftus, E. F., 'Current Issues and Advances in Misinformation Research', *Current Directions in Psychological Science,* 20 (2011), pp.20-23.

Froude, J. A., *Short Studies on Great Subjects: The Science of History* (London: Longmans Green, 1867).

Fry, M., *Glasgow: A History of the City* (London: Head of Zeus, 2017).

Gallacher, W., *[Willie Gallacher's Story] The Clyde in Wartime: Sketches of a Stormy Period* (Glasgow: Collet's (Glasgow) Bookshop, 1935).

———, *The Last Memoirs of William Gallacher* (London: 1966).

———, *Revolt on the Clyde*, 5th edn (London: Lawrence and Wishart, 2017 [1936]).

Gilbert, M., *Churchill: A Life* (London: Random House, 2000).

Gilbert, M., *World in Torment 1916-1922* (Hillsdale: Hillsdale University Press, 2008).

Goldsmith, A. L., *The Development of the City of Glasgow Police c.1800–c.1939* (PhD thesis, Strathclyde University, 2002).

Goring, R., *Scotland: The Autobiography, 2,000 Years of Scottish History by Those Who Saw It Happen* (London: Viking, 2007).

Grant, D. M., *Thin Blue Line: The Story of the City of Glasgow Police* (London, John Long, 1973).

Gray, A., *A History of Scotland: Book 5, Modern Times* (Oxford: Oxford University Press, 1999).

Gray, The Hon Mr Justice, '[Judgement of the Libel Case between] Claimant David Irving and Defendants Penguin Books Ltd and Deborah E. Lipstadt' (2000).

Gruner, R., 'Historical Facts and the Testing of Hypotheses', *American Philosophical Quarterly,* 5 (1968), pp.124-29.

Hart, B. L., *The Tanks: The History of the Royal Tank Regiment and Its Predecessors – Heavy Branch Machine-Gun Corps, Tank Corps and Royal Tank Corps, 1914-1945* (London: Cassell, 1959).

Harvie, C., *No Gods and Precious Few Heroes: Scotland 1914-80*, 1st edn, (London: Arnold, 1981).

Harvie, C., *No Gods and Precious Few Heroes: Twentieth-Century Scotland*, 3rd edn, *New History of Scotland Series* (Edinburgh: Edinburgh University Press, 2000).

Heren, L., *Sex and Violence in 1920s Scotland: Incest, Rape and Lewd Practices* (London: Bloomsbury, 2024).

Heren, L. and Barclay, G. J., *Tanks on the Streets? The Battle of George Square, Glasgow 1919* (Barnsley: Pen and Sword, 2023).

Hills, A., 'Medium Mark C 'Hornet': The Online Tank Museum: Tank Encyclopedia (2017) https://tanks-encyclopedia.com/ww1/gb/Medium_Mk-C.php.

Holmes, R., *Sylvia Pankhurst: Natural Born Rebel* (London: Bloomsbury, 2020).

Hutton, M., *1919 – a Land Fit for Heroes: Britain at Peace*, *Nineteen* (Stroud: Amberley Publishing, 2019).

Ironside, E., *Archangel 1918-1919* (London: Constable, 1953).

Jackson, L. A., Davidson, N., Fleming, L., Smale, D. M. and Sparks, R., *Police and Community in Twentieth-Century Scotland* (Edinburgh: Edinburgh University Press, 2020).

Jeffery, K., 'The British Army and Internal Security 1919-1939', *The Historical Journal,* 24 (1981), pp.377-97.

———, 'Military Aid to the Civil Power in the United Kingdom: An Historical Perspective', *Military Intervention in Democratic Societies*, eds P. Rowe and C. J. Whelan (London: Routledge,1985), pp.51-67.

———, *Field Marshal Sir Henry Wilson: A Political Soldier* (Oxford: Oxford University Press, 2006).

Jeffery, K. and Hennessy, P., *States of Emergency: British Governments and Strikebreaking since 1919* (London: Routledge and Kegan Paul, 1983).

Jenkinson, J., 'Black Sailors on Red Clydeside: Rioting, Reactionary Trade Unionism and Conflicting Notions of "Britishness" following the First World War', *Twentieth Century British History*, 19, no 1 (2008), pp.29-60.

Jenkinson, J., *Black 1919: Riots, Racism and Resistance in Imperial Britain, Postcolonialism across the Disciplines* (Liverpool: Liverpool University Press, 2009).

Jobson, R., 'Teaching modern British history in a politically polarised and "post-truth" environment', *Transactions of the Royal Historical Society*, 2 (2024), pp.389-400.

Johnston, T., *The History of the Working Classes in Scotland* (Glasgow: Forward Publishing, 1922).

Keedy, E. R., 'Criminal Procedure in Scotland', *Journal of the American Institute of Criminal Law and Criminology*, 3 (1912), pp.728-53.

———, 'Criminal Procedure in Scotland II', *Journal of the American Institute of Criminal Law and Criminology*, 3 (1913), pp.834-54.

Kendall, W., *The Revolutionary Movement in Britain, 1900-21 the Origins of British Communism* (London: Weidenfeld and Nicolson, 1969).

Kenefick, W., *Red Scotland!: The Rise and Fall of the Radical Left, c. 1872 to 1932* (Edinburgh: Edinburgh University Press, 2007).

Kerr, J. A., *Scotland and the Impact of the Great War 1914-1928, New Higher History* (Paisley: Hodder Gibson, 2010).

Kilday, A. M., *Crime in Scotland 1660-1960: The Violent North*, 1st edn (London: Routledge, 2018).

Kirkwood, D., *My Life of Revolt* (London: Harrap, 1935).

Knox, W., (ed) *Scottish Labour Leaders 1918-1939: A Biographical Dictionary* (Edinburgh: Mainstream, 1984).

Leopold, J., 'The Forty Hours Strike,' *We Shall Be All: Recent Chapters in the History of Working-class Struggle in Scotland*, ed L. Flynn (Glasgow, 1978), pp.34-44.

Liddell Hart, B. H., *The Tanks: The History of the Royal Tank Regiment and Its Predecessors – Heavy Branch Machine-Gun Corps, Tank Corps and Royal Tank Corps, 1914-1945*, 2 vols (London: Cassel, 1959).

Lilleker, D. G., 'Red Clydeside Strike', in N. Schlager (ed) *St James Encyclopedia of Labor History Worldwide*, pp.170-4.

Loftus, E. F., 'Planting Misinformation in the Human Mind: A 30-Year Investigation of the Malleability of Memory', *Learning and Memory,* 12(4) (2005), pp.361-66.

Loftus, E. F. and Hoffman, H. G., 'Misinformation and Memory: The Creation of New Memories', *Journal of Experimental Psychology: General,* 118 (1989), pp.100-4.

Low-Beer, A, *The Council of Europe and School History,* (Strasbourg: Council of Europe, 1997).

Lynch, M., *Scotland: A New History* (London: Century, 1991).

MacAskill, K., *Glasgow 1919: The Rise of Red Clydeside* (London: Biteback, 2019).

Macdonald, J. H. A. and MacGregor Mitchell, R., *A Practical Treatise on the Criminal Law of Scotland*, 4th edn (Edinburgh: W. Green, 1929).

Macfarlane, L. J., *The British Communist Party: Its Origin and Development until 1929* (London: McGibbon and Kee, 1966).

Mackintosh, J. P., *The British Cabinet* (London, Stevens, 1977).

Maclean, J., *Sack Dalrymple, Sack Stevenson, Let Labour Revenge Bloody Friday* (Glasgow: J. Maclean, 1919).

Marr, A., *The Making of Modern Britain* (London: Macmillan, 2009).

Marwick, A., *The Deluge: British Society and the First World War* (London: Macmillan, 1973).

McGonigle, J. and Wood, C., *The Era of the Great War 1910-1928* (Glasgow: Hodder Gibson, 2013).

McGuire, J., 'Pardon call for working class heroes', *Daily Record*, 29 January 2014.

McGuire, J., 'Pardon for Battle of George Square working class heroes moves closer', *Daily Record*, 13 February 2014.

McLean, I., *The Labour Movement in Clydeside Politics, 1914-1922* (DPhil thesis, University of Oxford, 1972).

———, *The Legend of Red Clydeside* (Edinburgh: John Donald 1999).

McNicol, J., 'The Radical Atmosphere of the Red Clyde', *London Review of Books*, 2 January 2020. https://www.lrb.co.uk/the-paper/v42/n01/jean-mcnicol/the-atmosphere-of-the-clyde

McShane, H. and Smith, J., *Harry McShane No Mean Fighter* (London: Pluto Press, 1978).

Mercer, C. and Mercer, C. A., *Journal of the Waterloo Campaign, Kept throughout the Campaign of 1815* (Edinburgh: London, 1870).

Middlemas, K., *The Clydesiders: A Left-wing Struggle for Parliamentary Power* (London: Hutchinson, 1965).

Mooney, G., 'Tanks on the streets of Glasgow to stop revolt in 1919', *Socialist Worker*, 28 January 2019.

———, 'Why Glasgow's "Bolshevist Uprising" in 1919 wasn't quite the red threat to UK many believed', *The Conversation*, 8 February 2019, https://theconversation.com/why-glasgows-bolshevist-uprising-in-1919-wasnt-quite-the-red-threat-to-uk-many-believed-110474?utm_source=twitter&utm_medium=twitterbutton.

Morgan, J., *Conflict and Order: The Police and Labour Disputes in England and Wales, 1900-1939* (Oxford: Clarendon, 1987).

Morgan, K., 'Shinwell, Emanuel, Baron Shinwell', *Oxford Dictionary of National Biography* (Oxford: OUP, 1996).

Morris, R. J., 'Urbanisation and Scotland', *People and Society in Scotland, vol. 2, 1830-1914*, eds W. Hamish Fraser and R. J. Morris (Edinburgh: John Donald, 1990).

Morrison, N. H., *Official Responses to Industrial Unrest in Post-War Britain, 1919-1921* (PhD thesis, University of Swansea, 1986).

Morton, D. S., *The 40 Hours Strike: An Historic Survey of the First General Strike in Scotland* (Clydebank: Clydebank Branch S.L.P., 1919).

Mowat, C. L., *Britain between the Wars 1918-1940* (Cambridge: Cambridge University Press, 1987).

Naughton, N., *Glasgow's East End: From Bishops to Barraboys* (Edinburgh: Mainstream, 2014).

Oakley, C. A., *The Last Tram* (Glasgow: Glasgow Corporation, 1962).

Patterson, H., *Class Conflict and Sectarianism, the Protestant Working Class and the Belfast Labour Movement 1868-1920* (Belfast: Belfast Blackstaff, 1980).

Peak, S., *Troops in Strikes: Military Intervention in Industrial Disputes* (London: Cobden Trust, 1984).

Pheasant, S., *Bodyspace* (London: CRC Press, 1998).

Pittock, M., *Scottish Nationality, British History in Perspective* (Basingstoke: Palgrave, 2001),

Portelli, A., *The Death of Luigi Trastulli and Other Stories: Form and Meaning in Oral History* (Albany, NY: State University of New York, 1991).

Radjy, A. H., review of 'A turbulent tale of ninth-century Cairo', *Times Literary Supplement*, 6250 (January, 2023), p.18.

von Ranke, Leopold, *Geschichten Der Romanischen Und Germanischen Volker Von 1494 Bis 1514 . . . Zweite Auflage* (Leipzig, 1874).

Reynolds, G. W. and Judge, A., *The Night the Police Went on Strike* (London: Weidenfeld and Nicholson, 1968).

Robbins, K. and Rowett, J. S., *The Blackwell Biographical Dictionary of British Political Life in the Twentieth Century* (Oxford:

Oxford Blackwell Reference, 1990).

Rubin, G. R., 'Law as a bargaining weapon: British labour and the Restoration of Pre-War Practices Act 1919', *Historical Journal*, 32.4 (1989), 925-945.

Scotland Royal Commission on Housing, *Report of the Royal Commission on the Housing of the Industrial Population of Scotland, Rural and Urban* (Edinburgh, HMSO, 1917).

Select Committee on Employment of Military in Cases of Disturbances, 'Report of the Select Committee on Employment of Military in Cases of Disturbances' (London: HMSO, 1908).

Shiels, R. S., 'The Mid-Victorian Codification of the Practice of Public Prosecution', *Scottish Historical Review,* 98 (2019), pp.410-38.

Shinwell, E., *Conflict without Malice* (London: Odhams Press, 1955).

———, *I've Lived through It All* (London: Gollancz, 1973).

———, *Lead with the Left: My First Ninety-Six Years* (London: Cassell, 1981).

Shinwell, E. and Doxat, J., *Shinwell Talking: A Conversational Biography to Celebrate His Hundredth Birthday* (London: Quiller, 1984).

Slowe, P. M., *Manny Shinwell: An Authorised Biography* (London: Pluto Press, 1993).

Smith, J., 'Labour Tradition in Glasgow and Liverpool', *History Workshop* (1984), pp.32-56.

Smith, W. A. C., 'The 1911 Tramway Strike', *Scottish Transport,* 25 (1974), pp.12-15.

Smout, T. C., *A Century of the Scottish People 1830-1950* (London: Collins, 1986).

Stewart, P., McKearney, T. and Garvey, B., 'The Independent Workers Union: Class, Nation and Oppositional Labour Movements in Ireland from 1900 to the Celtic Tiger', *Labor History,* 55 (2014), pp.486-500.

Still, G. K., *Introduction to Crowd Science* (London: CRC Press, 2019).

Stone, L., 'History and Post-Modernism', *Past and Present,* 135 (1992), pp.189-94.

Thomson, D. L., *A Handbook of Glasgow Tramways*, ed Society Scottish Tramway Museum (Glasgow: Scottish Tramway Museum Society, 1962).

———, *Glasgow Tram Services* (Glossop: Venture Publications, 2009).

Townshend, C., 'Military Force and Civil Authority in the United Kingdom, 1914-1921', *Journal of British Studies*, 28 (1989), pp.262-92.

Vogler, R., *Reading the Riot Act: The Magistracy, the Police and the Army in Civil Disorder* (Milton Keynes: Open University Press, 1991).

Watson, M., 'Michael Gove's war on professional historical expertise: conservative curriculum reform, extreme whig history and the place of imperial heroes in modern multicultural Britain', *British Politics*, 15 (2020), pp.271-90.

Webb, S., *1919: Britain's Year of Revolution* (Barnsley: Pen and Sword, 2016).

Weinberger, B., *Keeping the Peace?: Policing Strikes in Britain, 1906-1926* (New York: Oxford: Berg, 1991).

White, B. T., *British Tanks, 1915-1945* (London: Ian Allan, ND).

Williams, D., *Keeping the Peace: The Police and Public Order* (London: Hutchinson, 1967).

Wilson, J. M., *Siegfried Sassoon: The Journey from the Trenches, A Biography (1918-1967)* (London: Duckworth, 2003).

Winter, J. M., 'Military Fitness and Civilian Health in Britain during the First World War', *Journal of Contemporary History*, 15 (1980), pp.211-44.

Wood, S. H., *Higher History: Britain and Scotland, 1850s-1979* (Edinburgh: Hodder Gibson, 1999).

Wright, D. B., Self, G. and Justice, C., 'Memory Conformity: Exploring Misinformation Effects When Presented by Another Person', *British Journal of Psychology*, 91.2 (2000), pp.189-202.

Wright, P., *Tank: The Progress of a Monstrous War Machine* (London: Faber, 2000).

Index